D0875682

EAST ASIAN SOCIAL SCIENCE MONOGRAPHS

A QUESTION OF CLASS

A QUESTION OF CLASS

CAPITAL, THE STATE, AND
UNEVEN DEVELOPMENT IN MALAYA

JOMO KWAME SUNDARAM

SINGAPORE
OXFORD UNIVERSITY PRESS
OXFORD NEW YORK
1986

Oxford University Press

Oxford New York Toronto
Petaling Jaya Singapore Hong Kong Tokyo
Delhi Bombay Calcutta Madras Karachi
Nairobi Dar es Salaam Cape Town
Melbourne Auckland

and associates in
Beirut Berlin Ibadan Nicosia

© Oxford University Press 1986

OXFORD is a trademark of Oxford University Press

All rights reserved. No part of this publication may be reproduced,
stored in a retrieval system, or transmitted, in any form or by any means,
electronic, mechanical, photocopying, recording or otherwise,
without the prior permission of Oxford University Press

ISBN 0 19 582552 7

HN
700.6
.Z9
S64
1986

Printed in Singapore by Koon Wah Printing Pte. Ltd.
Published by Oxford University Press Pte. Ltd.,
Unit 221, Ubi Avenue 4, Singapore 1440

Nov. 87

To my family of real friends

IN LIEU OF A PREFACE

THIS book does not pretend to be a comprehensive socio-economic history of Malaya; nor does it provide a comprehensive discussion of class formation during the colonial and post-colonial periods: its purpose is far more modest. The book is an attempt to develop a theoretically-informed analysis of selected aspects of uneven development and class relations in colonial and post-colonial Malaya. It tries to interpret class formation in Malaya by focusing on the consequences of integration of the national economy into the world market dominated by expanding capital, and of unfolding class contradictions, partly mediated by the state.

To avoid any misunderstandings over the scope or intent of this book, it is important that some of the premises and limitations of the analysis attempted are made explicit.

The Present as History

Guiding this study is the premise that it is class contention that makes history in concrete conditions beyond the complete control of any of the parties involved. This perspective maintains that classes are ultimately the determining social forces which fundamentally shape the direction and process of development in all class societies, that classes are in constant formation and necessarily exist in contradiction and conflict, and that the present is the outcome of previous social contention. Therefore, in order to understand the past and current development of the Malayan economy and society, it is necessary to examine how its class configuration has developed over time. Such an understanding of the present as history can help inform efforts seeking to transcend the very class configuration which this study attempts to explain.

Why is Colonial or Post-colonial Malaya an Appropriate Unit of Analysis?

Malaya is a territorially-defined social entity, an entity emerging from previous class contention and defined primarily by its previous common subjugation to British colonialism. The Malayan territorial entity consists of eleven States which came under direct or indirect British rule before the outbreak of World War I. The States are Johore (Johor), Kedah, Kelantan, Malacca (Melaka), Negri Sembilan, Pahang, Penang and Province Wellesley (Pulau Pinang and Seberang Perai), or simply Penang State for short, Perak, Perlis, Selangor, and Trengganu. Economically, culturally, and, at times, even administratively, the now independent city-state of Singapore (Singapura) was also very much part and parcel of Malaya, and the term 'Malaya', often refers to the island as well.

Colonial Malaya was administered under a single unified political structure for only a relatively brief period in history.[1] Yet, politically, economically, as well as culturally, a certain shared common historical heritage continues to give meaning to the notion of Malaya. However, perhaps more importantly, much recent and contemporary class and political contention continues to be perceived and related to this territorially-defined social entity. In the light of these ambiguities, Singapore has been treated as part of Malaya for much of the discussion of the colonial economy, whereas for the post-colonial period, the island is considered separately.

Returning to the question of analytical perspective in this study, contemporary 'national' economies do not exist in isolation and need to be analysed in the context of the world economy. But this does not mean that the global economy is therefore the only acceptable unit of analysis. The territory over which a state exercises or seeks to exercise political power is also a suitable unit for analysis as the state not only defines the domain for certain political relations, but also the conditions for social relations in general. As this study will show, both the colonial and post-colonial state have greatly influenced the processes of class formation in Malaya. More to the point, in so far as the state mediates class relations, the understanding of class formation cannot be abstracted from consideration of the state within the wider context of the world economy.

The Essence of the Story

This book attempts to make a historical analysis of selected aspects of uneven development and the formation of certain social classes in colonial and post-colonial Malaya. It is premised on the perspective that it is contention among classes that makes history, though in circumstances beyond the full control of any of the contending sides involved. For colonial and post-colonial Malaya, these circumstances have included not only the outcome of preceding class contention, but also the ongoing accumulation of capital. These two key features of the world economy are central to the theoretical framework proposed for this study of class formation in Malaya. Capital expansion in the world economy may be confined to circulation, but can also extend to the sphere of production. A distinction to be noted is that while circulation capital gives rise only to non-capitalist relations of production, capital in production can organize along non-capitalist as well as capitalist lines, i.e. involving the exploitation of free wage labour.

'Class' is defined primarily in terms of the social relations of production. Hence, class formation is the continuous process through which the social relations of production are reproduced. In the process of production, class relations involve the appropriation by the dominant (non-producing) class of a social surplus produced by the dominated (producing) class. Class relations are necessarily contradictory and class contradictions give rise to contention between classes. Class contention does not necessarily entail either class consciousness or class-based social organizations or movements, and may reflect underlying class interests only in a convoluted and distorted manner. Whatever its manifestations, class contention has a direct bearing on the unfolding historical process and, in particular, on the reproduction and formation of social classes.

The historical specificities of the development of Malaya determine the specific themes and issues examined in this book. To provide the historical context for this, Part I (Chapter 1) seeks to characterize the class relations existing in Malaya at the time of British colonial intervention in the Malayan hinterland as a result of the Pangkor Treaty of 1874. Identifying the class configuration of pre-colonial Malaya enables one to evaluate the nature and significance of the transformations engendered by colonialism. Peasants were subject to several forms of exploitation—such as corvée labour, and commercial as well as other taxes—while the fruits of labour by slaves and peons or debt-bondsmen belonged to the ruling class, who also comprised the state. British colonialism transformed these pre-capitalist relations of production, and integrated the pre-colonial Malay ruling class into the colonial administrative apparatus.

Part II studies the transformation of the Malay peasantry following British intervention. Three aspects of this transformation constitute the chapter themes. In so far as capital did not directly intervene to reorganize peasant production, it was capital in the sphere of circulation which was of greatest significance for the peasantry. In Chapter 2, peasants are shown to be subject to exploitation by commercial and usury capital. Next, the role of the colonial state in mediating relations between capital and the peasantry is examined. How the interests of capital were expressed in colonial policies affecting the peasantry is the main focus of Chapter 3. The implications for the peasantry of the new significance of land in the colonial economy is explored in Chapter 4, with particular attention on the differentiation of the peasantry by ownership of and access to land, their primary means of production. Such social divisions among the peasantry are viewed as the outcome of social transformations in the wake of colonialism. .

The changing forms and consequences of capital accumulation in the colonial economy provide the main theme for Part III. British intervention in Malaya is reviewed in Chapter 5 in the context of global accumulation centred in the industrializing West and the resulting colonial empires. This chapter also attempts an overview of the development and structure of commercial capital in the Malayan economy. In their examination of the changing relations between capital and labour in the tin and rubber industries, the next two chapters see the emergence of free wage labour as the outcome of class contention and in relation to the changing needs of capital accumulation.

Part IV focuses on different fractions of the capitalist class in post-colonial economic development. Chapter 8, primarily based on a discussion of the expansion of Chinese capital in the colonial economy, critically examines the often suggested distinction between the *comprador* and *national* fractions of local capital, using the criteria of relations to foreign capital and participation in international commodity circuits. The chapter following discusses industrialization in Malaya, primarily in the post-colonial era. The role of the state in creating conditions for the expansion of industrial capital and the very nature of industrialization in post-colonial Malaysia are highlighted. Chapter 10 traces the origins and recent ascendance of the statist capitalists,[2] noting that, since the 1970s, this governing class has successfully consolidated its political position and extended state power to facilitate capital accumulation on its own behalf. Finally, in Chapter 11, some theoretical issues and other implications of the preceding analysis are addressed.

Some Limitations of the Approach and Analysis

The endeavour—perhaps unsuccessful—in this book is to develop a mutually informed relationship between the theoretical premises and the subject matter of the analysis, with each influencing the other. Thus, while it is true that the theoretical approach influenced the initial selection of specific concerns for discussion, that framework itself was developed in attempting to come to grips with the processes and conditions shaping the Malayan economy, i.e. the choice of what to look at was determined by the approach, which in turn emerged from the attempts to understand the dynamics underlying class formation in Malaya. An exposition and discussion outlining the perspective adopted in this study, as well as the central concepts of class, capital, and state, are presented in Appendix 1 of this book.

Within the broad range of developments involving class formation in Malaya, the choice of particular aspects for study was subject to various criteria, including the nature and availability of accessible secondary sources. The very fact that historiography and scholarship on Malaya have not been class-neutral, inevitably had important implications for this study. Not only is relatively more attention given to the interests of the dominant classes in the existing literature, but the dominant class perspective tends to be reflected in most analyses as well. However, the focus of this study was also restricted even when readily available information was not a constraint, as this book only sets out to examine specific class relations during certain periods considered especially significant. Hence, the selection process involved should reflect theoretically-informed considerations of what is more relevant for understanding uneven development in Malaya.

However, it would not be honest to pretend that all such decisions regarding inclusion in and exclusion from the analysis attempted have been theoretically motivated. In so far as other factors have also played some part, it would be important to recognize the implications of these for the resulting focus of analysis, particularly for what has been excluded as a consequence. For instance, the class relations of fisherfolk and some peasant groups (e.g. coconut smallholders) have largely been ignored, as have the relations of production of other prominent rural social groups—such as 'new villagers'[3] or settlers in recent land development schemes[4]—and the urban petty bourgeoisie (Poulantzas, 1973a, 1975)—both 'old' (e.g. petty commodity producers and vendors) as well as 'new' (e.g. professionals, technicians, managers, and supervisors)—are almost completely ignored, except in relation to the statist petty bourgeoisie.

Temporally, too, the book does not attempt a complete periodization;

discussion tends to focus on those periods during which developments of greatest relevance (to the book's main arguments) occurred; therefore certain choices were made as to which constituted crucial formative periods. For instance, the discussion and treatment of the formation of the working class concentrates mainly on the emergence of free wage labour in both tin and rubber production during the inter-war period.

The considerable limitations in the scope of this book serve as a reminder that this book—together with several others already in existence—can at most offer some, perhaps only tentative, points of reference in the historical analysis of the Malayan economy. Eventually, this effort will probably be regarded as erroneous, perhaps even irrelevant; after all, the trajectory of progress in human knowledge has hardly been linear and incremental but, rather, dialectical, necessarily involving the constructive criticism of previous knowledge. The emergence of more profound theoretically-informed analysis undoubtedly develops best with the advance of practice-informed theory.[5] Hence, the limitations of this book are an invitation to fill the gaps and rectify the errors that exist (including those perpetuated or even promoted here) in the knowledge and consciousness of the conditions and problems of uneven development and class contention in Malaya.

Petaling Jaya　　　　　　　　　　　　　　　　JOMO KWAME SUNDARAM
1984

1. The administrative history of Malaya is long and complex. It suffices to say here that Malaya did not constitute a single unit for administrative purposes until the Japanese Occupation during World War II. Before that, the port settlements of Penang, Malacca, and Singapore had constituted the Straits Settlements (SS) from the middle of the nineteenth century. In 1895, the Federated Malay States (FMS) structure brought together the mineral-rich States of Perak, Selangor, Negri Sembilan, and Pahang which previously had been subject to indirect British control from or after 1874. The remaining States, usually collectively referred to as the Unfederated Malay States (UMS), formally came under indirect British control in the early part of the twentieth century, just before the outbreak of World War I.

After World War II, Malaya and Singapore came under the British Military Administration (BMA). In 1946, the British proposed the Malayan Union, arousing much opposition from the local population. In 1948, the Federation of Malaya (Persekutuan Tanah Melayu or PTM), excluding Singapore, was established under colonial auspices; this territory obtained formal independence from British rule in 1957. In 1963, Malaysia was formed, comprising the eleven states of Malaya as well as Singapore, Sabah (formerly British North Borneo), and Sarawak (see Wheelwright, 1974b). The latter two States had also been part of the British Empire. They are located on the northwestern part of the island of Kalimantan or Borneo, most of which is now part of Indonesia with the other exception of the former British colony of Brunei.] In 1965, Singapore seceded from Malaysia. After the formation of Malaysia, Malaya came to be officially referred to as *West Malaysia*. In the early 1970s, this term was officially dropped in favour of the name *Peninsular Malaysia*, allegedly after the secession of Bangladesh (formerly East Pakistan) from West Pakistan.

2. This term—used interchangeably in this book with the term 'bureaucrat capitalist'—refers to that fraction of the bourgeoisie which uses its influence and control over the state for the purpose of capital accumulation.

3. The predominantly Chinese 'new villagers' are those resident in government-organized settlements established as one prong of the counter-insurgency measures during the period known as the Emergency (1948-60).

4. The mainly Malay settlers on government-established land development schemes—such as those organized by the Federal Land Development Authority (Felda)—are subject to new relations of production not discussed in this book. See S. Husin Ali (1976).

5. An appreciation of the dialectics of class formation and class contention can better inform self-conscious and organized social practice seeking to transcend the very class order this work has sought to analyse.

ACKNOWLEDGEMENTS

This book is really the collective product of efforts by many different people, of whom I can mention only a few.

My intellectual and other debts to the various academic institutions I have been associated with cannot go unrecorded. The Yale scholarship which enabled me to major in Economics and begin graduate study in the subject at that university also exposed me to Yale's Economic Growth Center, where I had my first research experience in development economics. Other scholarships enabled me to extend my formal training in Economics and Development Studies at Harvard, where I also benefited considerably from teaching in the Economics Department, the Social Studies programme and the Institute of Politics. Although I have yet to take courses in either Public Administration or Sociology, my association with flexible programmes in Harvard's Kennedy School of Government and the Department of Sociology enabled me to pursue my own intellectual interests with minimal interference. My other teaching stints at Universiti Sains Malaysia, Universiti Kebangsaan Malaysia and Yale College, as well as other generous financial support enabled me to meet various economic obligations while completing graduate studies.

I am very grateful for the financial support from different sources which enabled me to research, write, present and revise the thesis upon which this book is based. In my contact with the different institutions involved, several people were especially helpful and encouraging, going beyond the normal call of duty. To these friends, I wish to express my appreciation.

Orlando Patterson, Theda Skocpol, Judy Strauch, Bill Lazonick, Jim Scott, and Don Snodgrass helped at various stages of thesis preparation. I am very appreciative of their efforts and encouragement, without which the thesis might never have seen the light of day. Other friends also participated at many points along the way in preparing the thesis. I am grateful for their interest and support, and I especially wish to thank Najwa Makhoul, David Stark and Paul Sweezy.

I have learnt much from my many friends, to whom I wish to express my profound appreciation. I greatly benefited from contact with my teachers, fellow students, and others. I have also learnt a great deal from my teaching experiences, colleagues and students.

Last, and most of all, I wish to thank the many unnamed compatriots who have contributed—in various ways—to this effort. This book truly represents a collective enterprise in which I can, at most, claim credit as coordinator, writer, and editor. In the course of production, this book gained immensely from the research, typing, proofreading, criticism, suggestions and editorial assistance of many individuals. Discussions with many individuals have been crucial to the development of this work. I wish to draw special attention to the contributions of many *ordinary* people, such as my mother, who have the clarity of vision to cut through some of the *social science* mystification and jargon which have interfered with the readability, intelligibility, and lucidity of this writing.

As author, however, I bear sole responsibility for what follows, especially in light of the many useful suggestions and criticism which I have not incorporated. Friends involved with the publication of this book—especially Vani—have been most helpful, patient, and encouraging despite my inexcusable malingering. In spite of considerable inertia on my part, which discouraged me from picking up something I would have preferred to leave behind, such encouragement obliged me to see through the final publicaton of this book so many years after completing my thesis in 1977. The other delaying factor, of course, has been the inevitable change in one's views with the passage of time and accumulation of experience. Hence, though I suspect I would no longer be so brash as to attempt an opus of such scope as my youthful—and naive—enthusiasm enabled me to in 1976-7, continuing interest in the arguments presented here inspired the final burst of effort required to see this book into print.

In conclusion, I would like to thank, in advance, those who will take the trouble to read this work, and especially those who will be generous enough to share with me their comments and suggestions, particularly those of a critical nature.

> *Hutang emas dapat dibayar,*
> *Hutang budi dibawa mati.*

> [*A debt of gold can be repaid,*
> *A favour is cherished forever.*]

CONTENTS

APPENDICES

TABLES

FIGURES

ABBREVIATIONS

API	Angkatan Pemuda Insaf (Conscious Youth Movement)
BN	Barisan Nasional (National Front)
BPMB	Bank Pertanian Malaysia Berhad (Malaysian Agriculture Bank Limited)
CPI	Consumer Price Index
DAP	Democratic Action Party
DID	Drainage and Irrigation Department
EIWU	Electrical Industry Workers' Union
FAMA	Federal Agricultural Marketing Authority
FELCRA	Federal Land Consolidation and Rehabilitation Authority
FELDA	Federal Land Development Authority
FIDA	Federal Industrial Development Authority
FIMA	Food Industries of Malaysia
FMS	Federated Malay States
GDP	Gross Domestic Product
IBRD	International Bank for Reconstruction and Development (World Bank)
IMP	Independence of Malaya Party
IRRI	International Rice Research Institute
LPN	Lembaga Padi dan Beras Negara (National Rice Authority)
MARA	Majlis Amanah Rakyat (Council of Trust for the People)
MARDEC	Malaysian Rubber Development Corporation
MCA	Malaysian (formerly Malayan) Chinese Association
MCCI	Malay Chamber of Commerce and Industry
MIC	Malaysian (formerly Malayan) Indian Congress
MIDA	Malaysian Industrial Development Authority
MIDFL	Malaysian Industrial Development and Finance Limited
MIEL	Malaysian Industrial Estates Limited
NEP	New Economic Policy
NUPW	National Union of Plantation Workers
OPEC	Out-of-pocket expenditure
PAS	Partai Islam Se Malaya (Pan-Malayan Islamic Party)
PEKEMAS	Partai Keadilan Masyarakat (Social Justice Party)
PERNAS	Perbadanan Nasional (National Corporation)
PETRONAS	Perbadanan Petroleum Nasional (National Petroleum Corporation)
PKM	Partai Komunis Malaya (Communist Party of Malaya)
PKMM	Partai Kebangsaan Melayu Malaya (Malay Nationalist Party)
PN	Partai Negara (State Party)

PNB	Permodalan Nasional Berhad (National Investment Limited)
PPP	People's Progressive Party
PUTERA	Pusat Tenaga Rakyat (Centre for Popular Forces)
RIDA	Rural and Industrial Development Authority
RISDA	Rubber Industry Smallholders Development Authority
RRI	Rubber Research Institute
RSS	Ribbed smoked sheets
SCBA	Straits Chinese British Association
SCCC	Straits Chinese Chamber of Commerce
SEDC	State Economic Development Corporation
SF	Socialist Front
UDA	Urban Development Authority
UMNO	United Malays National Organization
UMS	Unfederated Malay States
USS	Unsmoked sheets

MALAYA

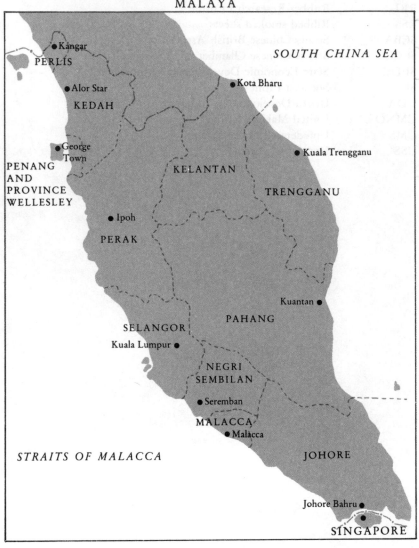

Part I

to imitate the honoured Kings of the past,
in former times, in order to consolidate
the increase of the world.

I

CLASS RELATIONS IN
PRE-COLONIAL MALAYA

WHERE and how does one begin a historical analysis of class formation in Malaya, focusing on aspects of this process in the colonial and post-colonial periods? Unbelievably, some ostensible analyses of social and economic development are written as if history began only in the colonial era. The fact of the matter is that class society existed in Malaya well before the colonial era. Therefore, to establish the socio-economic context in which the forces associated with colonialism made an impact, this introductory chapter attempts to characterize the class nature of pre-colonial society. This will distinguish changes identified with colonialism from those elements derived from pre-colonial society. The elements of continuity as well as change may thus be better identified.

Problems in Characterizing Pre-colonial Malaya

Available secondary sources do not permit a comprehensive historical overview of class relations in pre-colonial Malaya to be presented here. Yet, it must be stressed that the present effort has not exhausted the abundant material of this nature available. However, given that the central task of this book is to interpret selected aspects of class formation in the colonial and post-colonial periods, this has not been necessary. Within the limitations of the sources used, the more modest aim of this chapter is to provide a static view of Malay class relations at the time of British colonial intervention. To provide an outline of pre-colonial Malaya, this chapter reviews the social and political organization of pre-colonial Malay society identified with various types of agricultural practice and social relations of production, and evaluates the evidence on slavery, debt-bondage, corvee labour, land rent, and commercial tribute.

Given the paucity and biases of available historical evidence on Malaya in pre-colonial times, any attempt to characterize the class nature of pre-colonial Malaya on the basis of secondary sources must necessarily be highly circumspect and modest. Despite the recent increase in interest in the character of pre-colonial Malay society, most available studies appear to focus on genealogies (especially of ruling families), the political organization of the state apparatus (particularly its formal and ceremonial aspects), succession disputes, and the like. These stand as examples of how the writing of Malayan history tends to be dominated by a status quo perspective, little concerned with the foundations and interests underlying the phenomena described. The exceptions, unfortunately, are still few.

Historical records on pre-colonial Malay society were kept almost entirely by members and servants of the indigenous ruling class, or those serving the interests of one of the several alien powers present in the region. The views of early colonial administrators also need to be closely scrutinized; in many instances, the views of these officials consciously or unconsciously eulogize the virtues of British rule in contrast with the real and imaginary evils of pre-colonial rule. Similarly, members of the pre-colonial Malay ruling class who collaborated with the British are usually praised—often to justify colonial intervention (ostensibly on their behalf), as well as their retention in the service of the colonial power.

The more readily available primary sources on the nature of Malay society immediately prior to 'British intervention' are the accounts by early colonial officials which reflect the prejudices, predilections, and vested interests of their authors. This is well illustrated in the debate between Maxwell and Swettenham over the nature of the pre-colonial Malay land-tenure system (see Lim Teck Ghee, 1976; and David Wong, 1975), each arguing from a position supporting his own choice of land legislation for the colonized western Malay States of Perak and Selangor. The existence of such diametrically opposed characterizations of pre-colonial Malay society renders much else that has been written, suspect. Since the comments which follow rely largely on such sources of information, they must be considered tentative, and subject to subsequent revision as contrary evidence comes to light.

The twentieth-century Malayan nation is a product of British colonialism. Prior to the colonial impact, the area had accommodated many different societies. These societies had much in common. However, their heterogeneity should not be ignored. One important aspect of this variety is the difference in the histories of their class and state structures, which is of particular interest here. The uneven progress of colonialism in Malaya also meant that foreign-controlled parts of the peninsula could not but have affected their yet uncolonized neighbours, and vice-versa. For example, the earlier colonization of the Straits Settlements must have influenced the socio-economic formations of the then yet uncolonized Malayan hinterland.

Thus far, no mention has been made of the pre-colonial empires which, at one point or other, embraced parts of the Malayan peninsula. The pre-Muslim empires, such as Majapahit and Sri Vijaya, the contacts with China, India, the Arab world and other South-East Asian societies, must all have left their marks on the peninsula. The establishment of the Malacca Empire in the fifteenth century is generally considered a watershed in pre-colonial Malay history. At its height, the Malacca Muslim sultanate controlled a large area around the Straits, including virtually the entire peninsula (see Wheatley, 1961: 309). Some of the dynasties which have since ruled some of the other Malay States still trace their origins to the Malacca ruling family. Similarly, much of Malay law and custom, especially that involving the ruling class and the formal structure of the state, originated in fifteenth-century Malacca. While the influence of the Malacca experience on subsequent Muslim Malay society is undeniable, the real significance of its impact remains a moot issue.[1] This disparity between the formal and the substantive, the apparent and the real, poses obvious problems for an analysis of class relations in pre-colonial Malaya.

In the light of all these reservations, it may seem foolhardy to even attempt the following exercise, which is bound to be patchy and sketchy. It is nevertheless essential: it would be impossible to comprehend or evaluate the changes brought about by market integration and colonial domination without recognition of the class character of pre-colonial Malaya. As will become evident, appreciation of such historical antecedents is especially important for analysis of the peasant sector.

Malay Agricultural Settlement and the Pre-colonial Malay Negeri

Pre-colonial Malay society was organized primarily around agrarian production. Two main kinds of cultivation were practised. Shifting cultivation (*huma* or *ladang*) involved periodic jungle clearing for one or a few seasons of cultivation, after which the land would be abandoned to revert to secondary jungle. On the other hand, sedentary agriculture then mainly centred on wet-padi cultivation (*sawah* or *bendang*) by permanently settled communities. Much of the lengthy history of permanent peasant settlement—in the Kedah and Kelantan rice plains, for example—was based on *sawah* cultivation (Zahara Hj. Mahmud, 1970). Consequently, it is in such areas of long-standing permanent cultivation that the pressures of population growth have since been most acutely felt (Kessler, 1974).

The basic organizational unit of production tended to be the family, although regular and irregular cooperative activities were often organized on a wider, sometimes village (*kampung*), basis for specific purposes or communal tasks. Land clearance and infrastructural construction, for instance, tended to be communally organized, sometimes in the form of corvée labour (*kerah*) demanded by the ruling class. Village ties, often overlapping with kinship relationships, were thus strengthened by communal organization and shared responsibility for various productive and other activities. Social differentiation within pre-colonial Malay village society did not usually amount to class relations. Rather, village unity was perceived as the norm and supported by shared interests and a common lot, particularly since the ruling class did not usually reside in ordinary villages.

The waterways—both riverine and maritime—and various land routes through the dense equatorial jungle served as the primary means of inter-village communication and transport in pre-colonial times. It is therefore not surprising that the territorial boundaries of several Malay *negeri* (or countries, and referred to as 'States' since colonial times) tended to correspond geographically to those of river basins. Ease of travel and communications provided by the course of a river and its tributaries also facilitated the assertion of political control, backed by military power. Therefore, the ruler of the Malay *negeri*—holding the title of *sultan* in Islamic times—usually chose to site himself and his entourage strategically, often at the river mouth or at an important river confluence (*kuala*). Subject to the sultan, at least nominally, were the territorial chiefs who were known by various titles in different *negeri*, e.g. *raja*, *dato*.

(For those seeking an English analogy, this stratum (*bangsawan, pembesar*) has often been termed an aristocracy.) The formal political hierarchies varied in the various Malay *negeri*, and at the village level, the local chiefs (*penghulu, ketua kampung*) were to be found (see Husin Ali, 1975).

The concept of the state in South-East Asia is often thought to have its origins in Hindu influence in the region. In the Malay *negeri*, the formal structure of political authority is generally considered to have been modelled after the fifteenth-century Islamic Malaccan sultanate. This appears plausible; Malacca's conquest of virtually the whole peninsula would have allowed it to introduce new formal structures of state authority, as well as contribute to the diffusion of Islam. Of course, the state structure developed in Malacca could not possibly be fully reproduced in the other *negeri* where actual practices were also influenced by the prevailing local circumstances. A political structure erected on the basis of a maritime trading empire could not simply be transposed onto primarily agrarian riverine societies. Therefore, the actual impact of Malacca may have been confined to only the formal political structures, particularly their ritualistic and juridical aspects. These were often superimposed on societies organized on different bases and with class structures different from Malacca's. Hence, for example, even when formal designations were adopted, they came to acquire different meanings in their new context.[2]

In Malacca, as in some other Malay *negeri* subsequently, the sultan formally dominated a hierarchy of lesser chiefs and other personnel who constituted the structure of political authority. But in reality, in some *negeri*, 'the Sultan had so little real power of government he had no need of an elaborate machine of central government' (Gullick, 1958: 49). In the riverine *negeri* where shifting cultivation was the norm, the ruling class typically obtained a surplus[3] by taxing riverine commerce. This usually involved the scattered location of chiefs at strategic points on a river's course, thus ensuring the decentralization of the state structure in such *negeri*. In these circumstances, the titular head of state, the Sultan, was in less of a position to exercise effective authority. Thus, while political and economic power remained in the hands of the ruling class as a whole, it was not concentrated in the hands of the sultan.[4]

In some *negeri* where the state provided some economic infrastructure in the form of an irrigation system and thus exercised more control over a permanently settled population, power tended to be more effectively centralized, usually in the person of the Sultan—in relations comparable to a nascent form of the Asiatic mode of production. Sharom Ahmat (1970: 1) has argued that 'a different economic structure in the case of Kedah, compared to the other west coast Malay states, results [*sic*] in a different political situation'. He explained the nineteenth-century decentralization of political power in the west coast Malay *negeri* of Selangor and Perak by the economic and political impact of expansion of tin production and export for a world market. This encouraged intra-ruling class rivalry for territorial control in order to extract lucrative tributes from miners.[5]

From the evidence on pre-colonial Malay society used for this study, it has been possible to identify the existence of several types of economic relations existing in various combinations. Sometimes, different production relations coexisted in similar technological conditions. It is also true, however, that some major differences in the social relations of production were associated with differing technological conditions. For instance, societies based on sedentary cultivation differed from those based on shifting cultivation.

With the possible exception of some of the aboriginal tribes[6] (*orang asli*)—who are outside the scope of the present discussion—the evidence is overwhelming that the Malay societies in Malaya prior to European colonialism were clearly class societies. The characterization of *orang asli* societies also remains a moot issue, especially given their heterogeneity, though the predominant relations of production for at least some *orang asli* resemble the lineage mode of production.[7]

Slavery and Debt-bondage

Slavery existed in much of pre-colonial Malaya (see Aminuddin Baki, 1966; Gullick, 1958; Jang Aisjah Muttalib, 1972; Mahmud bin Mat, 1954; Maxwell, 1890; Sharom Ahmat, 1968). There was an important juridical distinction between slaves (*hamba abdi*) and debt-bondsmen or peons (*hamba berhutang* or *orang berhutang*): slaves could be acquired in a number of ways,[8] though local Malay interpretation of Islamic law (*syariah*) allowed only non-Muslims to be enslaved.

The Malay ruling class created the socio-economic conditions for debt-bondage, most importantly, by confiscating excess production, thus preventing their subjects from accumulating any substantial savings. Such practices naturally discouraged increased productivity and technological innovation. Usually devoid of savings, peasants were very vulnerable to becoming indebted to members of the ruling class, particularly in unanticipated adverse conditions.[9] There were different categories of debt-slaves.[10]

While possessing a nominal right to freedom, debt-bondsmen—who by virtue of being Muslims could not be formally enslaved—could not easily exercise this right. Thus, their condition was virtually tantamount to enslavement.[11] In practice, the right of redemption for debt-slaves was little more than nominal. Debtors' work for their creditors did not usually count towards lessening their debts.[12] A debtor could hardly ever expect to repay large loans in these circumstances,[13] especially considering the high interest rates involved.

What role did slaves and debt-bondsmen play in pre-colonial Malay society? They were put to work in at least three types of activities. First, they rendered services to and for their masters:[14] powerful members of the ruling class included debt-bondsmen in their personal entourages to enhance their political status (military and prestige); some others performed household and domestic services; while girls were 'kept as the means of satisfying the sexual appetites of the young, unmarried men who formed the chief's armed following' (Gullick, 1958: 103) and also to look after the young.[15] Secondly, debt-bondsmen participated in productive activities for their masters;[16] besides agricultural activities, Gullick (1958: 102) has also mentioned their use in tin-mining.

Thirdly, some slaves and debtors were also used to earn an income for their owners by working for others.[17]

Certain types of debt-bondsmen 'besides working full time for their creditor could also be transferred to another master if he could raise the money. In this sense, this category of debt-bondsmen could be considered as capital investment' (Sharom Ahmat, 1968). Slaves and debt-bondsmen were treated as commodities. A colonial official remarked that debt-bondage was 'a favourite form of security' (Low, as quoted in Gullick, 1958: 101)–phrased differently, slavery and debt-bondage were the preferred modes of labour control utilized by capital in pre-colonial Malay society.

How extensive were slavery and debt-bondage? The available evidence suggests that they were widely practised and constituted significant forms of exploitation by the Malay ruling class, at least in the immediate pre-colonial era.[18] Few censuses were taken in Malaya prior to the colonial era; hence, evidence on the extent of slavery and debt-bondage then is less than precise. But available evidence after British hegemony was established is suggestive. The extent of these practices in the pre-colonial period was presumably far greater than these figures (after British intervention) indicate because of British policy on this matter. By the late nineteenth century, the prevailing colonial view[19] favoured free wage labour over slavery which was felt to discourage high productivity and initiative. As British control spread in the Malay States, the institutions of slavery and debt-bondage were weakened and eventually abolished,[20] but not before British actions against slavery and debt-bondage were moderated after initially encountering fierce resistance from the Malay ruling class.[21]

In the absence of other more reliable indicators on the extent of slavery and debt-bondage, various statistics from the early colonial period are offered. An 1879 census quoted by Gullick (1958: 105) recorded about a sixteenth of the population of Perak as either slaves or debt-bondsmen.[22] For Pahang in 1889, there were estimated to be about 200 slaves and 2,000 debt-bondsmen; Pahang's total population was estimated at 35,000 in 1888, though a census in 1891 gave a figure of 57,462 (Jang Aisjah Muttalib, 1972). A 1909 report had 994 registered debt-bondsmen in Kedah, with the capital district alone accounting for 980.[23] Also, an estimated 200–300 other bondsmen indebted to members of the royal family had not been registered (Sharom Ahmat, 1968). Nevertheless, Sharom Ahmat asserts that the 'number of debt-bondsmen in Kedah was not large enough to make them an important source of labour'. He attributes the 'insignificance of debt-bondage in Kedah' to the comparatively strong and unchallenged position of the Sultan in relation to the district chiefs in that *negeri* in contrast with nineteenth-century Perak and Selangor, and to the availability of corvée labour for the ruling class.[24]

How were slaves and debt-bondsmen treated by their masters? Opinions vary. According to some, bondage was not too intolerable since bondsmen seldom chose to free themselves.[25] Others retort that leaving debt-bondage would leave the freed bondsmen without an alternative means of sustenance.[26] Assessing the nature of relations between the ruling class and the slaves and bondsmen, Gullick (1958: 101), a colonial official turned anthropologist, claimed: 'On balance, it seems fair to conclude that the ruling class treated their bondsmen and slaves fairly.' Swettenham (1948: 141), an ex-colonial official turned businessman, in a moment of insight, clarified the existence of such conflicting opinions: 'There was the practice of debt-slavery, a custom loathed by those who had to bear the burden of this iniquitous bondage, but upheld as a cherished privilege by the class which was benefited.'

Corvée Labour

Corvée labour (*hasil kerah* or simply *kerah*) appears to have been an 'obligation' (undoubtedly coerced) of the *rakyat* (people or subjects, comprising primarily of individual peasant producers) to the ruling class.[27] As noted above, Sharom Ahmat has suggested that it may have functioned to some extent as an alternative to slavery and debt-bondage in meeting the direct labour requirements of the ruling class; however, the existence of corvée labour and slavery were certainly not exclusive of each other. All members of the *rakyat* were subject to the corvée labour obligation; in fact, Maxwell has suggested that the *kerah* obligation was incidental to the right of land utilization.[28] However, this assertion about juridical reciprocity (i.e. of the *kerah* obligation in exchange for the right to land use), even as part of the ruling ideology of the times, cannot be verified. Maxwell himself knows of no written evidence to this effect. Might his interpretation be motivated by his general effort to force the feudal notion of 'eminent domain' on to the nature of pre-colonial Malay society?

It appears that the ruling class, some of its servants, and a few other privileged persons were exempted from *kerah*.[29] 'The kerah, or forced levy of men for labour, is effected through the headmen of villages or districts' (Maxwell, 1884: 110). Those who disobeyed were fined, while others who could, paid for exemption—to the economic advantage of the *kerah* labour organizer. The arbitrary nature of *kerah* exactions disrupted other activities of those subjected to it; agricultural production was constantly vulnerable to the actual as well as potential disruption by arbitrary *kerah* exactions.[30] It is no wonder that peasant attitudes to *kerah* were far from enthusiastic.

Kerah was therefore probably based upon direct control of people, not necessarily mediated by control over land. Thus, if the *rakyat* were hard pressed enough to emigrate,[31] the ruler lost the source of his surplus (i.e. the peasant producers). Even worse, emigrants could end up in the domain of nearby rivals. In the more densely populated wet-padi growing areas, however, the feasibility of emigration was diminished by the limited availability of alternative land and pre-empted by the greater amount of labour generally needed and embodied in irrigated land. A heightened sense of oppression in these circumstances was natural. (In the relatively more densely populated wet-padi areas of Vietnam and Java, where these conditions were even more pronounced, the degree of exploitation was apparently even higher.)

It has therefore been advanced that this option of emigration, or loss through a 'transfer of allegiance', served as a deterrent to excessive oppression and exploitation. As a general rule, this was probably the case. But when and where the ruling class as a whole was relatively cohesive, the significance of this option would have diminished. Assuming that this class would then act to advance its collective, rather than individual, interests, the peasantry would be in little position to use intra-ruling-class rivalries to its own advantage. (It may be telling, for example, that the most dramatic recorded evidence of peasant flight from ostensible Malay ruling-class oppression was to the British colony of Penang, and not to the domain of a rival chief or sultans, though this could, of course, be attributable to the pro-colonial predisposition of the narrator.) The significance of this option acting as a check on oppression was hence determined by specific circumstances in a heterogeneous and changing society. If this was the case, the existence of such an option presumably also checked other forms of exploitation and oppression affecting the peasants, slaves, and debt-bondsmen.

Maxwell (1884: 111), a colonial official of the day, advocated colonial recognition of the Malay ruling class's right to *kerah* exactions and proposed that 'the surrender of such a right is a perfectly legitimate consideration for demanding an enhanced land revenue or other equivalent'. Before abolishing *kerah*, the British colonial authorities were certainly not against using such pre-capitalist modes of labour control for their own ends and needs.[32] The subsequent objections to *kerah* concerned the disruptive and counter-productive consequences of its arbitrary exaction as well as its historical application in the exclusive interest of the Malay ruling class. Apart from its more obvious consequences for productivity, and besides objecting to its prime beneficiaries, the basic principle of corvée labour was never a cause of colonial concern.[33]

Evidence available confirms a certain arbitrariness and lack of systematization in the exaction of *kerah*.[34] Was it then primarily used for irregular and unusual tasks, with the more regular work assigned to slaves and debt-bondsmen? Even so, its irregular nature does not mean that it was rarely exacted. While the available evidence is inconclusive on this point, *kerah* exactions varied with the relative strengths of the ruling and subject classes, and by implication, the other options available to both, as well as the particular purpose of specific exactions. For example, it might have been easier to mobilize *kerah* for public works construction—ostensibly in the general interest—rather than for some project purely for the ruler's own personal pleasure.

Land Rent

A debate over the nature of Malay land tenure—particularly over the Sultan's claim to eminent domain as the basis for rent exaction—first began in the last century and was revived recently. The first debate involved the rival colonial officials, Maxwell and Swettenham. More recently, work by David Wong (1975) is critical of Maxwell's position in this debate, while Lim Teck Ghee (1976) is more sympathetic to Maxwell. This debate is relevant here for its implications for the nature of class relations in pre-colonial Malay society.

For the more juridically-minded social historians, an important issue is whether corvée labour and exaction of the tenth (on agricultural produce) were related to land tenurial relations. If so, then pre-colonial Malay society involved feudal relations of production where the landed class extracted the producers' surplus in the form of a feudal rent; i.e. if corvee labour and exaction of the tenth are related to land tenure, they may be regarded as species of feudal rent. Such reasoning, of course, comes up against the controversy over how feudal relations should be defined. If more restrictively, it can lead to the exclusion of most societal experiences, except for certain European ones, from the feudal category (see Anderson, 1974; Hilton, 1976). A broad loose definition clearly favours Maxwell's characterization of pre-colonial Malay society as feudal. Maxwell largely overlooked tribute extracted from trade and viewed pre-colonial Malay society as having been one dominated by feudal relations, with slavery and debt-bondage co-existing.

David Wong opposes Maxwell's use of certain juridical categories, implying certain social relations, to make the case for a feudal characterization of pre-colonial Malay society. He specifically disputes Maxwell's interpretation of exaction of the tenth–and therefore, by extension, of corvée labour as well–as part of a feudal land rent incidental to land use.

What was the nature of social relations involving agricultural land?[35] The abundance of cultivable land in most of pre-colonial Malaya and the intro-duction of irrigated padi cultivation in some areas allowed different tenurial systems to emerge. Where shifting cultivation was the general practice, the cultivator's right to the land being worked on was recognized socially. When the land was no longer being worked and the fruits of the cultivator's labour had been exhausted, this right lapsed. The land then reverted to its original status until it was cultivated once again. In these circumstances, then, the proprietary right to a particular area was directly premised on use of that land, an arrangement suitable for shifting agriculture.[36]

However, David Wong also points to various kinds of Malay land dealings, 'well developed at the time of British intervention'.[37] Land dealings presume certain transferable rights to land which, in turn, suggest the nature of the social relations prevailing. Since land was neither scarce nor widely traded as a commodity, the labour required to clear, prepare and cultivate land created the basis for a market in land in pre-colonial times. Hence, the sale price of land can be interpreted as the price of the labour required to render the land productive. This was probably also the basis for charges (rents) imposed for 'letting' out such land, though rental arrangements pre-suppose that the *proprietary right* to land is not limited to the *proprietor's* own use of the land. Similarly, the use of land as loan collateral also suggests the emerging status of land as a commodity in the late pre-colonial period. There is more evidence of such land dealings in permanently-settled areas practising sedentary agriculture. This suggests that at least two different land tenure systems adapted to different agricultural practices were present in pre-colonial Malaya.[38]

In marked contrast to this view of social relations involving land, Maxwell interpreted the pre-colonial Malay land system by using certain (controversial) categories and by invoking the notion of *eminent domain*.[39] The application of certain juridical categories and distinctions, such as *proprietary*, *alludial* and *usufructuary* rights, and the assertion of the ruler's *eminent domain* over the land in his *realm*, appear somewhat inappropriate, especially in the light of certain other statements also made by Maxwell;[40] the ambiguity in legal interpretation admitted by these statements raises serious doubts about Maxwell's other assertions.

David Wong insists that Maxwell mistook socially determined limitations on land use as legal limitations on peasant rights to land.[41] The peasant's limited right to land was conditioned by and appropriate to the prevailing agricultural technology and other socio-economic arrangements. In other words, the ecological and technological limitations on land use should be seen as the basis for Malay social and legal definitions relating to land tenure. However, by itself, this does not deny the existence of the juridical structures suggested by Maxwell. Conceivably, those legal categories emerged from, and were conditioned by, the socio-economic and ecological circumstances. However, Wong's view that 'the attribution of superior ownership in land to a Malay ruler was, indeed, a total fiction' (David Wong, 1975: 18) is not easily accepted; there is evidence[42]—though admittedly limited—which points to the contrary. While such legal claims by the ruling class—as embodied in the ideology of the state—may have had little practical significance in some circumstances, in other situations they provided the juridical, and hence ideological basis and legitimation, for surplus appropriation in the form of rent or other forms of tribute.

Maxwell suggested that the principle of rent exaction was introduced to the peninsula through Hindu influence and consequently incorporated into Malay custom (*adat*), but then went on to argue that customary Malay tenure was also based on Islamic principles (Lim Teck Ghee, 1976: 30). Could this reference to Islam for legitimation of exaction of the tenth suggest that the ruling class (state's) claim to the tenth had its origins in the Muslim religious tithe, and not in the pre-Islamic (Hindu) era, as claimed by Maxwell? Certainly, it would have been in the interest of the Malay rulers to exercise such a religiously sanctioned claim to tithe collection.

In this debate, there are two apparently controversial issues at the juridical level. First: did the Sultan really enjoy eminent domain? And relatedly: was the claim to the tenth derived from this claim? From the evidence of then existing practices, the Sultan's superior right to land was legally embodied in several instances, including seventeenth-century Kedah.[43] Predictably, the laws proclaimed by a ruler generally contain a legal claim to legitimize and enhance his own position. If, as Maxwell claimed, this was generally the case throughout the Malay *negeri*, it should come as no great surprise. A ruler's claim to a tenth of the produce could well have been legitimized in terms of his allegedly superior claim over all land in his realm. Again, such reasoning would, of course, constitute ideological reinforcement as well as a device for social control. It could be misleading, however, to understand a social relationship—in this case involving the exploitation of one class by another—solely in terms of the juridical veneer given to it by the exploiting class. Whether based on a claim to superior ownership or on religious obligation, whether or not legally legitimized, the underlying realities do not change. In the latter circumstance, there would simply be no ideological velvet glove for the mailed fist of exploitation.

Evidence on exaction of the tenth appears rather weak, even by Maxwell's own admission;[44] Swettenham, his rival, denied the existence of any evidence of payment of the tenth, as well as of any other recognized system of land tenure.[45] Instead, it has been suggested that exaction of a portion of the peasant cultivator's product was often quite arbitrary and not usually subject to any regularized system or procedure.[46] However, in certain situations where the land tenurial system was more highly developed and where property rights to land had been established, regularized patterns of rent exaction—by the state as well as by private land-owners—emerged.[47] These arrangements generally developed with the emergence of sedentary agriculture. Where shifting cultivation was still the norm, usually in relatively land-abundant circumstances, such proprietary rights were generally unknown[48] and rent exaction rarely occurred.

The principle of a poll-tax existed in at least some pre-colonial Malay *negeri*. Obviously, a capitation tax would have been easier to collect than a proportion of the harvest, which would have required a far more sophisticated collection machinery. Although the evidence on poll-taxes is scattered, it does suggest that—as with collection of the tenth—there was apparently a gap between doctrine and practice, and little uniformity in the incidence of this particular tax[49] between districts, let alone *negeri*. Nor was regularity of collection suggested by the doctrine; this, however, conforms with evidence on exaction of the tenth. In any case, whether or not the ruler's claims to *eminent domain* and hence to the tenth were embodied in law, the fact of the matter is that the exaction of the tenth was not practised throughout pre-colonial Malaya.

Whether the ruler's juridical claim to the tenth was actually exercised at all is also doubtful. Maxwell's sole example—that of Krian[50]—has been shown to be a possible (complicated) exception, where the tenth exaction may possibly have been a surrogate for some other form of surplus appropriation.[51] Of course, this does not mean that there was no direct appropriation of a portion of the cultivators' produce by the ruling class. This certainly did occur in many places, and was often arbitrary, involving the threatened or actual use of force, i.e. it essentially involved the direct use of coercion, without much recourse to ideological (legal) legitimation. It is, of course, possible that such exactions may have been regularized in certain instances, but there is little unambiguous evidence of this as yet. The case of fifteenth-century Malacca was perhaps exceptional, not only because of its atypical economy and state structure, but also because conditions then apparently gave rise to a land system which included the right to rent exaction by private land-owners.[52]

Why, then, for the rest of the peninsula, was the doctrine of the ruler's right to exact the tenth, if and where it existed, not translated into a regular system of exploitation? Referring to Perak, Emily Sadka has suggested that: 'The sparse population, the low level of productivity, and the importance of mining in the economy explains the general absence of land rent and taxes on subsistence agriculture ...' (Sadka, 1968: 385). She might have added that overland transport difficulties, the existence of a riverine communications system, and the nature of the development of commerce in pre-colonial times favoured other systems of exploitation, such as taxation of riverine commerce. Also, when the sultan's authority was weak (e.g. because of poor military support), the district chiefs had relatively more autonomy for independent action. Then, even if the sultan desired to exact the tenth, he may not have been able to supervise its actual appropriation at the district level. The exactions could then have varied from the tenth specified by law, and gone to line the pockets of strong territorial chiefs instead.

Regardless of the actual real situation existing prior to colonial intervention, '*the presumption of a Malay ruler's paramount ownership in land was certainly turned into a fait accompli with the establishment of colonial government under the Residential System in the Malay States*' (David Wong, 1975: 20, emphasis added). In the Malay States brought under direct British rule after 1874, Wong suggests 'that British influence had in the meantime contributed to new development in their land systems', citing examples from Kedah,[53] Pahang and Kelantan. One might also consider the significance of the influence of Siam and other neighbours, as well as the consequences of further integration of the region into the world economy. Presumably, the western Malay States had also been similarly subject to external influences, particularly from the British-controlled Straits Settlements. This of course implies that much of the evidence drawn upon thus far for the characterization of pre-colonial Malay society, may actually be of new social conditions, already transformed in response to increasing integration into the world economy and the British presence in the region.

Commercial Tribute

Pre-colonial societies are commonly characterized as subsistence economies.[54] What is actually meant by this? Does this mean that the basic unit of production, i.e. the peasant family, produced all or most of its own needs? Presumably not. Is it supposed to imply that the basic co-residential unit—the village—was self-sufficient? If the basic organizational unit of production was the family, this would imply that certain exchanges would have taken place between families within the village. A third and far-fetched interpretation is that Malay society as a whole, i.e. a Malay *negeri* or the entire Malay archipelago (Nusantara), met its own needs internally.

Khoo Kay Kim suggests that the period of European mercantilism—marked in Malaya by the establishment of the Straits Settlements—saw an increase in trade in the region, particularly between the Malay *negeri* and these new regional commercial centres.[55] This would mean that earlier trade was probably primarily riverine and coastal in nature, conducted largely within the bounds of the existing Malay *negeri*. But, evidence abounds to suggest that even before the period of the Malacca Sultanate of the fifteenth century, trade in at least some goods crossed these frontiers from earlier times (e.g. see Wheatley, 1961). It is very likely that the range of commodities exchanged also increased under the subsequent impact of European (Portuguese and Dutch) mercantilism.

In his study of pre-colonial Malay society prior to the British take-over, Gullick emphasizes that both the Malay village and the Malay *negeri* were far from self-sufficient and were in fact engaged in fairly developed trade, even involving money.[56] Judging from the nature of the traded commodities,[57] such commerce could not have been recent in origin. Except for goods such as opium, which cannot be termed a necessity, consumption of other items—of which many were food items—was likely to have been long-standing. Since many of these products were not produced in the villages, presumably they were obtained through trade.[58] The pattern of village settlement, typically in close proximity to rivers, could indicate that rivers served as important means of communication and trade from the time of settlement. Goods emanating from the Malayan hinterland then were mainly jungle, mining and agricultural products.[59]

The existence of considerable exchange should not, however, be interpreted to mean that all production was primarily for exchange; much of peasant production satisfied consumption needs. An excess was produced to be exchanged for other desired commodities obtainable only through trade. In other words, commodity production was not yet generalized; though commodities were being produced and exchanged for necessities, this aspect did not fundamentally determine production. Why was this so? In addition to the nascent and undeveloped nature of markets it appears plausible that, while there were strong trends for trade expansion,[60] the rapid development of commerce was stifled by the heavy and arbitrary taxation imposed on trade by the Malay ruling class.

Taxation of and control over trade constituted very important forms of surplus appropriation for the pre-colonial Malay ruling class. At least in the period immediately prior to Western penetration, it was the single most important source of income for this class in Perak, if not also in the other Malay *negeri* as well.[61]

Two sources of income were derived from trade. First, as mentioned above, the ruling class exacted a tribute from trade conducted by others. It appears common for the sultan and various chiefs to tax the import and export of goods passing through their respective domains. Fees were also obtained from merchants for the right to trade in certain commodities. Alternatively, or even supplementarily, passing crafts, rather than goods, were taxed. Such taxes by the ruling class were regarded as legitimate commercial exactions, but were secured through coercion. In theory, the right to exact such taxes by force was supposed to be formally granted by the relevant sultan; in practice, the sultan did not necessarily exercise effective control over the tax-collecting chiefs.[62]

Exactions of tax were necessarily and invariably backed by a coercive force, actual as well as potential. To tax effectively, it was common for the ruling elements concerned to secure choice locations, such as river mouths and confluences, to erect fortifications, such as stockades, from which to demand such commercial tribute. Likewise, those who controlled seaports taxed imports and exports, and also imposed harbour taxes on passing ships.

Often, the ruler did not even directly organize taxation but instead farmed out this privilege in return for a fee. According to Sharom Ahmat (1970: 9), 'the revenue farm system was the whole basis from which the state received its revenue'.[63] Wan Ibrahim (1961) has detailed the methods of state revenue collection during the reign of Kedah's Sultan Abdullah (1762-99).[64] At least for Kedah,[65] tribute exacted from trade constituted the largest source of revenue for the royal family. If, as was later the case in the nineteenth century (and there is little reason to believe otherwise), the Kedah ruling class was relatively centralized under the sultan's hegemony in the late eighteenth century, this could have been the primary income source for the Kedah ruling class as a whole. This would mean that the extent of trade within Kedah at the time (i.e. prior to the establishment of the British port at Penang in 1786) was considerable, and also, that by the monetary standards of the time, it yielded a substantial tribute for Kedah's ruling class.[66] The *kangchu* system in Johore was also a tax-farming set-up, but with an ethnic twist. In this case, the contributors of tribute in pre-colonial nineteenth-century Johore were none other than the Chinese who had been encouraged to settle in the *negeri* by the Malay ruler at the time, the Temenggong (Trocki, 1975).

While the ruling classes of the riverine-based Malay *negeri* amassed considerable wealth from commercial tribute, this was of quite a different order in comparison with that of the maritime-based empires. At an earlier stage in its history, the Johore-Riau Empire of the eighteenth century obtained much of its revenue from taxing vessels passing through its waters; this involved exacting tolls, taxes, and customs duties on vessels traversing the Riau Sea. The often arbitrary and irregular character of these exactions and the challenge of a competing authority it posed to the colonial powers of the region drove contemporary colonialists to denounce it as piracy. It is likely that most of the earlier great trade-based empires of the region were similarly organized, and the Johore-Riau Empire simply represented the last example of this tradition.[67]

Unlike the riverine-based Malay *negeri*, the maritime-based *negeri* of Johore-Riau and Malacca both rose to an empire status. Fifteenth-century Malacca, of course, represents the epitome of trading empires in Malaya, if not in all of South-East Asia. 'The importance of trade to the prosperity of Malacca cannot be overestimated' (Zainal Abidin, 1970: 25). An important element in Malacca's favour was its strategic geographic position at 'the end of monsoons and the beginning of others' and in relation to the emerging China trade. By controlling the neighbouring coastal regions politically, the Malacca Empire exercised effective control over the maritime waterways and traffic of the region. On this basis, Malacca developed its command over long-distance and mercantilist trade centred in the region, involving spices and other goods.[68] The primary source of surplus in Malacca was trade.[69] However, by the mid-nineteenth century, maritime-based trading empires were no longer significant in South-East Asia, having been largely destroyed by mercantilist as well as subsequent European contact. Therefore, by the mid-nineteenth century, the historical specificities of such societies had little contemporary significance for class structures.

The other trade-related source of income was from direct participation in commerce; however, the evidence on this is scanty, which suggests that it was not a common activity of the Malay ruling class.[70] It may be argued that such commercial involvement often meant little more than lending a person's name, and therefore the prestige and privileges derived from that person's position, to a commercial enterprise actually run by others. Jang Aisjah Muttalib (1972: 41-3) asserts that economic activity, including riverine commerce, was controlled by the ruling class in Pahang. The 'aristocratic class' also conducted trade, though only as a secondary activity. In contrast, the common people participated marginally in commerce and traded insignificant amounts. Although trade was supposedly conducted in the name of the 'aristocratic class', it was actually conducted by their entourage, including a few freemen, though the majority were slaves.

Except for the irregular participation of the ruling class, commerce was largely left to foreign (*dagang, asing*) traders, primarily Arabs and Chinese. Their widespread participation was subject to the ruling class's monopoly of trading rights, and hence tribute exactions. Much of such activity—e.g. involving opium, tobacco, and salt—was tied to concessions granted by the sultan. Arab traders used their socio-religious status to gain better access to economic concessions and facilities, which in turn gave them an economic edge over their Chinese competitors. Nonetheless, the presence of the Malay aristocracy and the Arab merchants did not prevent Chinese businessmen from creating economic opportunities for themselves.

Jang Aisjah Muttalib's discussion evidently covers a period after foreign merchants had made substantial inroads into the commercial life of Pahang. This is reflected in the ethnic identity of the traders as well as in the nature of transacted merchandise. Nevertheless riverine commerce probably predated the coming of alien merchants. While the local Malay ruling class could quite easily control trade in items produced within a Malay *negeri*, outsiders had a relative advantage with goods from elsewhere. Hence, prior to the participation of the Arabs and Chinese in these commercial activities, it is probable that such trade was handled by those with commercial connections beyond the boundaries of the Malay *negeri*, people who could have been either 'local' or 'alien'. ('Aliens' at that time would include traders from neighbouring Malay *negeri*, especially the trading empires, as well as non-Malays.)

Direct income from commerce within the riverine *negeri* can be viewed as commercial profit; this was usually of a mercantilist (monopoly) nature because of the control the Malay ruling class generally tried to exercise over riverine trade. There is no question of 'long-distance trade'[71] (Amin, 1976) arising here. However, the case of fifteenth-century Malacca was probably different. Some of Malacca's profit from participation in commerce was probably from long-distance trade, since goods from alien societies—whose actual production costs were not generally known or even mutually known to the trading partners involved—were exchanged at this great trading port of the fifteenth century. Other great trading centres gained considerably from long-distance trade, and it is most likely that Malacca, too, obtained a good share of surplus in this way.

While it is obvious that trade in certain items, e.g. tin, increased considerably with the establishment of the Straits Settlements and increased Western industrial demand for tin and other products of the region, it is likely that considerable trade in consumption items for local use existed from earlier times. The expansion of trade during the nineteenth century in items such as tin probably stimulated increased trade all round, while increased contacts with the world market, centred on the industrializing West, encouraged commodity production and exchange. The overall increase in trade and the new profitable opportunities it offered became a source of much contention within the Malay ruling class, especially in the tin-rich *negeri*. This probably contributed to the decline of the sultan's authority in relation to district chiefs, as members of the ruling class fought among themselves over the increasing tribute from the growing trade. With the increase in commerce, especially external trade, direct participation by the Malay ruling class probably declined, giving way to the better connected alien businessmen based in the Straits Settlements. It is therefore possible that, at the time of British intervention in the Malay *negeri*, direct Malay ruling class participation in trade was almost negligible, which accounts for the availability of only a few records to this effect. Malay ruling class income from trade was by this time primarily derived from tribute; whether it had been otherwise before is unclear and has yet to be determined conclusively.

Pre-colonial Malay Social Classes

While it is not possible to make any useful generalizations which transcend time and place, available evidence from recent centuries suggests that surplus extraction from trade was probably the most important income source for the pre-colonial Malay ruling class in most, if not all, pre-colonial Malay *negeri*. Generally, slavery (including peonage) and corvée labour involved use-value rather than exchange-value production and did not yield large incomes in monetary terms. What appears to be beyond doubt—at least for those *negeri* and for the periods for which evidence is available—is that tribute exacted from trade constituted a very important source of monetary income for the Malay ruling class. Tribute exacted directly from peasant production—whether or not legitimized in terms of the ruler's eminent domain—was not generally important, although it may have been significant in certain exceptional situations.

The historical evidence suggests that there were at least two primary modes of surplus appropriation (i.e. exploitation) in pre-colonial Malay society, i.e. the tribute-paying mode and the slave mode. Tribute-paying was manifest in at least three specific types of surplus extraction which affected virtually the entire peasantry—tribute on trade, corvée labour, and several variations of direct tribute from production. Religious injunctions against the enslavement of fellow Muslims contributed to the existence of two forms of the slave mode, i.e. slavery of non-Muslims and peonage or debt-bondage of Muslims.

Wealth accumulated by the pre-colonial Malay ruling class could be invested as capital. Usury capital was not only highly profitable in itself but also operated in conjunction with the institution of debt-bondage. However, usurious capital cannot be said to have been a necessary pre-condition for debt-bondage except in formal terms, since there is evidence that the existence of debts was often fabricated to force people into bondage and that some debt-slaves had actually been abducted. That debt-bondage constituted a form of capital investment was nevertheless clear enough.[72]

Wealth was sometimes also invested in trading activities. Indigenous commercial capital, though probably of greater significance in earlier periods, was apparently quite negligible in most of the peninsula by the nineteenth century. Instead, commercial capitalist activities were primarily conducted by alien merchants, many of whom were based in the Straits Settlements. Thus, capital in pre-colonial Malaya was mainly confined to the 'capitalistic' sector (Rodinson, 1973: 7), i.e. to the sphere of circulation.

As indicated earlier, peasant investment in production was discouraged by the circumstances they faced. Production in excess of consumption needs ran the risk of expropriation by the ruling class. Further, the often arbitrary demands for corvée labour discouraged 'surplus' planting (beyond requirements) because of the possibility that the crop might not be adequately tended if the farmer was summoned away; excess production over consumption requirements was primarily to be traded for other consumption items. With such disincentives to producing a substantial excess for saving and capital accumulation, it is not surprising that the peasant's lot was precarious; as pointed out earlier, this often led to indebtedness and debt-bondage. These circumstances also discouraged peasant innovation and technical progress. Hence, capital investment in peasant production did not increase significantly, except when initiated by, and hence in the interests of, the ruling class (e.g. the irrigation canals of Kedah).

The tin boom of the mid-nineteenth century opened up new opportunities for the Malay ruling class to invest in mining, though such involvement in mining enterprises tended increasingly to be in collaboration with Chinese capitalists.[73] Such 'joint-venture' arrangements were desired by the latter as they served to protect and guarantee the viability of the enterprise. Such participation by the Malay ruling class, however, was not really tantamount to the formation of a Malay capitalist class; rather, the chief's income from such arrangements constituted a sort of rent or reward for collaboration. However, there appear to have been certain other activities undertaken by the pre-colonial Malay ruling class which may be considered productive capitalist ventures, though these were generally few and far between.[74]

The use of alien labour by the Malay ruling class[75] reflects the virtual absence of an indigenous Malay proletariat, the reasons for which are to be found in the structure of Malay society at the time. Peasants generally had ready access to land in pre-colonial Malay society; the limits to acquisition were determined primarily by one's ability to cultivate since rights to land were generally only for cultivation. There was no strong systematic tendency towards the creation of a class of 'free' people *without* access to means of production, particularly land. Those Malays who were impoverished, e.g. because of credit difficulties, tended to end up in debt-bondage. Since those who became impoverished were subject to virtual enslavement in debt-bondage, no class of impoverished Malays available to sell their ability to work for a wage emerged on a significant scale in pre-colonial Malay society. The Malay ruling class utilized their slaves and debt-bondsmen on the one hand, and corvée labour on the other to meet their labour requirements. In the absence of a Malay proletariat, the Malay ruling class and alien capitalists had to find a working class elsewhere, unless it was prepared to face the potentially explosive consequences of forcing the rapid creation of a Malay proletariat. Instead, the less disruptive alternative of importing workers from abroad was preferred.

Capital in pre-colonial Malay society was apparently predominant in usurious activities. Its significance in commerce may also have been substantial prior to dominance by alien merchants in the nineteenth century, though this is unclear. The investment of capital in production, e.g. in agriculture and mining, in pre-colonial Malay society also cannot be discounted, though definitive evidence is scanty; however, even the few enterprises which existed were not generally characterized by the use of free wage labour. Capitalist relations of production as such were hence virtually non-existent in pre-colonial Malay society though capital circulated and participated in usurious and, to a lesser extent, in commercial and even in some productive activities. The primary obstacle to the emergence of capitalist relations of production, despite the existence of capital, was the absence of a class of free wage labour, which the internal dynamics of pre-colonial Malay society had not produced.

It is possible to assess the sentiments of the subject class towards the ruling class from the proverbs and idioms of the day, many of which have long histories. Unfortunately, those that were encouraged, preserved, and recorded by the ruling class and its servants have most likely been those in support of the status quo.[76] Still, some which have survived seem to reflect popular resentment against certain members of the ruling class or against that class as a whole.[77] The existence of such sentiments is not surprising in light of other evidence on class relations in pre-colonial Malaya.[78] Considered together with the advanced development of class and status distinctions in custom, ritual, and language, they suggest the long-standing existence of class relations in pre-colonial Malay society.

The class nature of pre-colonial Malay society probably contributed to the relative ease of British conquest of the Malay *negeri*. The British, for example, took full advantage of intra-ruling class weaknesses and disputes—such as succession struggles—to advance their own interests. Thus, the British were even invited to intervene by sections of the Malay ruling class who hoped to secure advantages over their rivals. Many of those who initially led opposition to the British were from those sections of the ruling class who were immediately disadvantaged by colonial intervention. After the assassination of J. W. W. Birch, the first British Resident of Perak, in 1875, the British quickly learnt their lesson. After severely, but quickly, punishing all those involved in the resistance movement, the colonialists bought off other potential ruling class dissidents with generous pensions, by providing other compensation[79] and privileges as well as by co-opting members of the pre-colonial Malay ruling class into the lower echelons of the new colonial state apparatus. The anti-colonial movement led by sections of the pre-colonial Malay ruling class probably failed partly because the latter's own oppressive and exploitative relationship to the *rakyat* limited their ability to successfully mobilize widespread popular resistance.[80] Further, as will be shown in Part II of this book, the immediate impact of colonial rule on the peasantry was not widely disruptive; for example, peasants were not dispossessed by the colonial state of land already under their cultivation; nor did the colonialists attempt to create a proletariat from among the ranks of the peasantry by other means. Thus, British colonial policy pre-empted widespread peasant-based resistance to colonial intervention.

This survey of evidence on pre-colonial Malay societies indicates that, whatever their heterogeneity, they were all clearly non-capitalist in character. In none of them did capitalist relations of production exist, let alone dominate, although capital existed, especially in usurious activities. The evidence does not, however, allow one to assess which source contributed most to the surplus appropriated by the ruling class, and this presumably varied with time and circumstances.

The distinction made between contributions to the surplus by slaves and debt-bondsmen on the one hand, and various forms of tribute on the other, is important. The former's contribution, not assessable in monetary terms, is particularly difficult to evaluate. The extent of slavery and debt-bondage also varied with place and time.

Of the various forms of tributes, those exacted in the form of land rent appear to have been significant only in certain circumstances, usually where demographic and other social, ecological, and technological conditions enabled the ruling class to effectively control access to land, e.g. in the older per-manently settled wet-padi growing plains of North Malaya.

The contribution of corvée labour was apparently uneven but widespread throughout the Malay *negeri*, and hence difficult to assess. First, as with slavery and peonage, there is no monetary criterion to measure the significance of production of use-values. Second, its incidence varied a great deal, and is particularly difficult to evaluate because of its irregular and unsystematic nature.

Tribute from trade-related activities was important for both the riverine- and maritime-based Malay *negeri*. This was particularly true for the period immediately prior to the colonial take-over, for which the best evidence is available; by this time, external commercial influences had probably stimulated a significant increase in commodity exchanges in the Malay *negeri*. This implies that the contribution to the surplus from this source was smaller previously, meaning that the ruling class was either relatively smaller or poorer in earlier times, or that other sources of income were more important then. Although it cannot be rigorously demonstrated, the impression one gets from available evidence is that tribute from trade was the primary source of income for the ruling class prior to colonial intervention in the nineteenth century.

If one leaves aside relative contributions to the surplus for a moment, and considers the social relations of production,[81] it is clear that slavery was not generalized but rather marginal—though significantly so—in many of the pre-colonial Malay *negeri*. The exploitation of the general populace then was primarily through the various forms of tribute exaction. In the case of the maritime trading empires, most notably Malacca, the sources of such tribute presumably were largely external in origin.

Summary

To reconstruct the nature and development of class relations in Malay society, and the resultant class configurations at the time of British intervention, requires, of course, a perspective going beyond the collation of the scattered,

usually static glimpses of pre-colonial Malay society just presented. Furthermore, class formation is a process also sustained by socio-political roles and
relations as well as ideological aspirations. Clearly, then, an understanding of
pre-colonial Malay socio-economic formations is incomplete without a more
thorough appraisal of the cultures, ideologies, and political structures of the
negeri. However, the available material for the former is inadequate—documentation for the period prior to the fifteenth century is meagre, and evidence
on the evolution of the Malay *negeri* for the period after the emergence of the
Malacca Empire is quite uneven. Nonetheless, establishing the factors and
processes that shaped pre-colonial Malay social organization along certain lines
would significantly clarify the antecedents of recurrent features of contemporary class formation and political consciousness.

That task is beyond the scope of the present endeavour. The more modest
purpose of this section was to attempt to specify class relations prevailing in
pre-colonial Malay society immediately prior to colonial intervention. Using
that as a point of reference, the transformations induced by integration into the
world economy under colonial auspices can now be distinguished. This task is
taken up in the following chapters.

Pre-colonial Malay society was certainly not characterized by capitalist
relations of production, usually understood to involve the exploitation of free
wage labour. However, capital was present in pre-colonial Malay society,
especially in its usurious form. Commercial capital, which grew with the
increase in trade, was largely, though not entirely, dominated by immigrants
and colonialists by the mid-nineteenth century. However, capital in productive
activities was relatively uncommon then.

The class structure of pre-colonial Malay society naturally varied with time
and circumstances. In the mid-nineteenth century, the indigenous population
could be classed into three main categories. The peasantry formed the bulk of
the population and was subject to corvée labour and other forms of exploitation. From the evidence, commercial tribute on traded commodities appears to
have been especially important, whereas the actual significance of land rent is
controversial. The other exploited category consisted of slaves and debt-
bondsmen, who generally surrendered the entire fruits of their labour to their
masters, usually receiving only the means for subsistence. In the mid-nineteenth
century, they were a small but important proportion of the local population.

Exploiting both these groups—i.e. the peasantry on the one hand, and slaves
and debt-bondsmen on the other—was the ruling class, which was internally
differentiated in various ways in different places and at various times. This
ruling class remained essentially pre-capitalist, obtaining its surplus via pre-
capitalist modes of exploitation. It hardly ever transformed its accumulated
wealth into social capital, even in the sphere of circulation, let alone establish
capitalist relations of production.

The class relations of pre-colonial Malay society would, undoubtedly, have
influenced the direction and momentum of the changes associated with
colonialism. In a sense, therefore, they serve in this study as one end of a
continuum in which subsequent transformations, particularly among the Malay
peasantry, have led to contemporary class relations.

1. For an elaboration of the Malaccan and other formal systems of political authority, see Gullick (1958); Reid and Castles (1975); Wolters (1970); and Wilkinson (1971). It is possible that a similar process operated in Malacca as in other South-East Asian kingdoms in the sense that a new form—the sultanate in this case—was used by a local ruler to dignify his claim to rule and to organize his rule both symbolically and administratively.

2. For example, the titled position of *Laksamana* (Admiral) was formally incorporated into the courts of a number of other Malay sultans, but many of these admirals never went to sea.

3. Class relations and the state presume the existence of a social surplus (henceforth referred to simply as 'a surplus'). The existence of a social surplus obviously presupposes an excess over basic and essential consumption requirements. Thus, many 'primitive' classless societies did not produce any significant excess in this sense. Consequently, low development of the forces of production may not allow the production of an excess, which is a precondition for the existence of a surplus as defined by the class relations of exploitation. Barring the exceptional situation of famine, most human societies have at least been capable of producing an excess over minimal biological subsistence requirements. Otherwise, they would simply not survive as they cannot even biologically reproduce themselves. While the actual existence of an excess takes a concrete form, the pattern of time allocation between production and other activities may also reflect the existence of a potential surplus.

The preceding should not be taken to imply that there is a strict and determinate correspondence between the forces and relations of production. Rather, certain relations of production may exist within a range of technological parameters.

4. 'The collection of taxes, whether on the tin produced by Chinese miners or on the trade goods destined for Malay and Chinese consumers alike, was correlated with the distribution of political power. In theory the Sultan and other holders of royal offices, such as the Raja Muda, were entitled to collect certain taxes throughout the State. But it was not feasible for them to maintain tax collectors in every district who could neither be supervised nor supported at a distance from the capital. It was inevitable that each district chief should collect all the taxes paid in his district. He was supposed to remit to the Sultan the proceeds of the royal dues. In practice it appears that the Sultan rarely received all that was due to him from outlying districts. He was forced to rely on what he could collect at the royal capital which typically lay at the mouth of the main river highway into the State.

'The inability of the Sultans to obtain more than a small proportion of the total revenues of the States, especially of the taxes on tin which became so important during the nineteenth century, was the main factor which caused a dispersal of power from the central government of the State to the districts. . . . The holders of ministerial offices in the Sultan's government had scattered to become district chiefs in order to obtain their share of the revenues' (Gullick, 1958: 127).

5. 'The district chiefs whose domains were fortunately endowed with this metal, became the all powerful political figures in the state. One consequence of this was the constant intrigues, and manoeuvering for power among the chiefs not only among themselves, but also between chiefs and Sultans. The end result was political instability and general chaos in these states' (Sharom Ahmat, 1970: 1).

6. While there is undoubtedly much variety among the *orang asli*, observers tend to characterize their productive practices (hunting, and gathering or agriculture) as being relatively less 'advanced' than those of the Malays.

7. A lineage is a group of persons who are in fact or fiction descended from a single male or female ancestor in either the male or the female line. At each different level the lineage can be divided into segments embracing persons descended from one or the other descendant of the founder. In a lineage-based or segmentary society, local groups—villages, districts, etc.—are constituted on the basis of membership in a lineage. The lineage or segment is the kernel of the local group, and the relationship between local groups is both antagonistic and complementary; there is no central political authority (Terray, 1972: 96; see also Rey, 1975).

8. '1. enslaved war captives (*hamba tawanan*)

  2. non-Muslims captured forcibly; e.g. aboriginal and other non-Muslim inhabitants in the region kidnapped and sold by slave-traders (*hamba diranggak*)

  3. imported African slaves; most were purchased by Malays who went to Mecca for pilgrimage; others were imported by Arab traders (*hamba habshi*). It also appears that African slaves were brought by European colonizers.

    4. criminals, usually of capital offences, who could not pay the fines imposed or faced the prospect of execution, surrendered their selves [*sic*] to the rulers as slaves (*hamba hulur*)

    5. those in economic distress who offered themselves in return for food and shelter (*hamba serah*)

    6. spouses and children of slaves (*keluarga hamba* or *anak hamba*)' (Aminuddin Baki, 1966, as quoted in Sharom Ahmat, 1968).

    9. 'Thus when a *rayat* (or subject) is in want of money he goes to his Raja or chief to lend it [to] him, because he alone can do so. Either money or goods are then lent, and at a certain time stipulated for payment. If at the expiry of that time the money is not paid, it is usual to wait some time longer, say two or three or even six months. Should payment not then be made, the debtor, if a single man, is taken into the creditor's house; he becomes one of his followers and is bound to execute any order and do any work the *Raja* as creditor may demand, until the debt is paid, however long a time that may be. During this time the *Raja* usually provides the debtor with food and clothing, but if the creditor gives him money, that money is added to the debt. Often, however, the *Raja* gives nothing and the debtor has to find food and clothing as he can' (Swettenham, as quoted in Gullick, 1958: 99).

    10. '1. the normal type of debt-bondsmen described above (*orang berhutang*)

    2. one who becomes a debt-slave by marrying the Sultan's or a chief's slaves (*anak mas*)

    3. wives and children of debt-slaves (*hamba waris*)

    4. persons given away by their masters to another as payment for debt incurred by the master (*hamba bayar*)' (Sharom Ahmat, 1968).

    11. 'While there was no difference in the nature of work which the two classes of slaves were made to do for their masters, the debt-slaves were less degrading in the eyes of society than the ordinary slaves because the former were supposed to be able to redeem themselves by paying off their debts, whereas the latter could not under any circumstances regain their freedom except by some act of grace on the part of their master. Such act was, however, very rarely conceded. Slavery was, in fact, a long recognised institution in the State' (Mahmud bin Mat, 1954: 9).

'In areas where debt-bondsmen were useful both economically and politically, chiefs tended to increase the number of such followers through a variety of means. Sometimes, a chief could invent a debt where one did not exist or he could impose a fine on an offence never committed. In this way the victim became a debt-bondsmen [*sic*], the *pesaka* or property of the chief. Another method used to prevent the decrease of debt-bondsmen was to refuse accepting payment for freedom when it was offered.... Likewise, while in theory a debtor could request to be transferred to a different master of [*sic*] he could find one, this could very easily be rejected' (Sharom Ahmat, 1968).

    12. 'Sometimes the master fed and clothed them, but more often they had to supply themselves with all necessaries, notwithstanding that their labour was forfeited to the master's service' (Maxwell, 1890: 249-50).

    13. 'Money was ... very scarce and local produce fetched very small prices. Local trade was done in many cases by a system of barter. This made it difficult for the debt slaves to raise enough cash to redeem their freedom' (Mahmud bin Mat, 1954: 9).

    14. '... as no one had a hired servant or ever paid wages, it followed that all menial work was done by debt slaves and by a very few real slaves ...' (Swettenham, 1948: 142).

    15. 'Two or three young slave girls attended on him at play, at meal time and at bed time.... Later on at the age of nine or ten years the writer had, after school hours, to bear his share of the household drudgery while the elder members of the family had to bear the full burden of the labour on the farm which formerly was done by the slaves' (Mahmud bin Mat, 1954: 10).

    16. 'They were put to agricultural work to produce food for the sustenance of their creditor and his household. They thus contributed to providing the surplus with which to maintain a section of the community in a non-productive military and political role' (Gullick, 1958: 102).

    17. For example, a woman testified: '... at nights we are to prostitute ourselves giving half of this earning to the Raja and half to supply ourselves with clothing and provisions for the Sultan's house and other slaves' (quoted in Gullick, 1958: 103). Gullick comments that such prostitution 'was clearly of common occurrence except among the women reserved as concubines of the creditor'.

    18. 'In the area where the writer's ancestors lived, almost every important family of the higher middle class had its quota of slaves varying in number according to the means of the family' (Mahmud bin Mat, 1954: 8).

'The system of detaining persons in servitude as long as a debt for which they are liable is not discharged is very generally spread among the Malay races of the Archipelago' (Maxwell, 1890: 250).

19. '... the principal evil of the debt-bondage system in Kedah is not that it entails any harsh treatment of the debtor but that it deprives him of all inducement to work, for it is not in human nature to work hard when hard work brings no reward' (quoted in Sharom Ahmat, 1968).

20. 'Shortly after the establishment of the British administration in the State, the order went forth declaring slavery illegal and requiring all owners of slaves to set them free.... The enforcement of the Government's order was not easy in those days when the machinery of Government was still very rudimentary and many of the people through whom the order was expected to be enforced—the local chiefs and headmen—were themselves interested in seeing to its enforcement being delayed indefinitely. The Government offered no inducement of any kind such as payment of compensation or the settlement of the debts in the case of debt slaves. Therefore, the practice of slavery lingered on, especially in the rural areas.... The slaves knowing that their erstwhile masters no longer had absolute control over them began to make themselves scarce and often evaded the call to any work for their master by giving excuses which in the past would not have been accepted as valid' (Mahmud bin Mat, 1954: 9-10).

21. '... after the revolt of 1875 known as the Perak War there was a more cautious and objective attitude to the subject since mishandling of the "debt-bondage" question had been one of the causes of the revolt' (Gullick, 1958: 99).

22.

Status	Male	Female
Free	24,188	23,171
Slaves	775	895
Debt-bondsmen	728	652

23. The heavy concentration of debt-bondsmen in the capital district may reflect the relatively centralized character of the state in Kedah and the consequent residential concentration of the ruling class in the capital area. Kedah State's relatively stable and centralized nature may in turn be related to its provision and control of irrigation facilities to a permanently settled, padi-growing peasantry.

24. '... the only use to which debt-bondsmen were put in Kedah was economic and this to a large extent was not particularly significant because compulsory labour was so readily available' (Sharom Ahmat, 1968).

25. 'In Kedah, however, very little is heard regarding the abuse of the system or the ill-treatment of people in bondage.... One aspect of debt-bondage which tends to be forgotten is that these people themselves often preferred to stay as they were' (Sharom Ahmat, 1968).

26. 'At the same time the slaves did not find it quite convenient to leave the premises of their masters altogether. Their living quarters were built around or near their master's house on their master's land. They had no land of their own.... Remunerative employment was not available anywhere' (Mahmud bin Mat, 1954: 10).

Other less favourable views of slavery and debt-bondage also exist. A colonial official had this to say:

'I will not harrow the reader by tales of infamies committed under the cloak of this system; they can be imagined if it is understood that the creditor did what he liked with his debt slaves, and when they found life intolerable and ran away, if caught they were killed and no one objected, because every one of any position had debt slaves of their own' (Swettenham, 1948: 196).

A victim, forced into prostitution, testified:

'If we fail to get money by prostitution we are punished with thick rattans, and sometimes with canes on our heads and back. We are prevented from marrying anyone who wishes to offer us in [sic] marriage' (quoted in Gullick, 1958: 103).

Existing laws and customs posed no constraints for the ruling class:

'... the national customs, when favourable to the debtor, have been openly disregarded, and every kind of oppression has been practised' (Maxwell, 1890: 250).

27. '... whenever the Sultan, or any Raja or chief of sufficient authority, wanted labour for any public or private work—such as the clearing of a river, the building of a mosque or house, the manning of boats for a journey—for then all the men within reach were summoned, through the

village head-men, to come and under-take this forced labour, for which no payment was ever made, and though the labourers were supposed to be fed as long as the work lasted, that was not always done' (Swettenham, 1948: 142-3).

'... there is no written definition of the nature and extent of the services which a Raja or Chief or superior proprietor can exact from the cultivator. In a Malay State, the exaction of personal service from the ra'iyat is limited only by the powers of endurance of the latter. The superior authority is obliged, from self interest, to stop short of the point at which oppression will compel the cultivator to abandon his land and emigrate' (Maxwell, 1884: 108).

'There was no restriction on the type of work which a chief might thus commission.... There was no restriction on the duration of these services or on the season of the year at which they might be required.... In practice however there were definite limitations. If men were called away at the harvest season it was a hardship which was particularly resented. In such a case, or if food was not regularly provided, the labour force would melt away before the work was completed' (Gullick, 1958: 108).

28. 'Forced service in a Malay State, too, is not merely the result of the application of the law of the stronger; it is well understood to be an incident of the lot of the cultivator of land, he acquiesces in it as one of the conditions on which he holds his fields, and he usually submits quietly to the orders of his superiors until they reach the pitch of oppression at which he decides that emigration is preferable to slavery' (Maxwell, 1884: 110).

29. 'Musicians of the royal band, elephant mahouts, magicians, etc. of the royal household in Kedah were exempt from the general obligation to do manual labour (kerah) when required.... The kerah system was an occasion for making distinctions of status. No aristocrat was required to turn out to do such work. Among the commoner class certain categories of higher status than the rest were exempt. The most detailed code of these exemption rules comes from Kedah. Those exempted were any Raja (aristocrat), Syed (descendant of the Prophet), any other person "of good birth", a Haji (returned pilgrim to Mecca), lebai (Muslim divine), pegawai (government official), penghulu (village headman), mosque official, servant of the Sultan's household or any other person individually exempted' (Gullick, 1958: 108-9).

30. 'The consequent uncertainty as to the amount of time he might have available for his own fields, had the effect of discouraging a peasant from being ambitious, for if he planted too much he might not be able to cope with the work at all' (Sharom Ahmat, 1970: 2).

31. 'No incident of native rule has contributed so much to swell the Malay population of Penang and Province Wellesley as [kerah].... The cultivator who has to leave his house and his fields at this bidding, has to find his own tools and food, which may involve the carrying of a heavy load to the place of work, and a good deal of expense or privation.

'Forced labour is naturally hated by Malays and is evaded as much as possible.... In Perak, the establishment of British influence has led to a general "strike" on the part of the peasantry against the system to which they formerly submitted peacefully' (Maxwell, 1884).

32. '... after its cession to the British Government, there was no difficulty in turning out nearly a thousand men in 1874, to commence clearing a line through the forest for a proposed road' (Maxwell, 1884: 110).

33. 'Certain months are allowed the many to plant and reap their paddy and this when stored is sacred, and cannot be taken from their possessions with this exception; all the rest of their time, exertions or acquirements may be taken by the King or his Officers, if so inclined ...' (Scott, as quoted in Bonney, 1971).

34. The observation by a British official on corvée labour in pre-colonial Kedah contained in the previous note (33) counts as one of the few pieces of evidence that the kerah system was not exercised arbitrarily. However, Kedah may have been an exceptional situation, given its highly centralized political authority and its relative order in contrast with say Perak and Selangor in the nineteenth century (Sharom Ahmat, 1970: 1).

35. For more elaborate discussions of the nature of the pre-colonial Malay land systems, see Maxwell (1884), David Wong (1975), and Lim Teck Ghee (1976).

36. 'At the time when land was abundant, anybody could, as a simple matter of fact, clear forest land for cultivation and occupation.... The basic principle was that if a person abandoned his land leaving it to become tanah mati ("dead land"), any other person could then take up such "dead land" by making use of it. It may be observed that these rules, which seemed to be providing for the

"extinguishment" of a cultivator's right in relation to land, were rather practical rules concerning the reverter of abandoned land to "forest" land, once again free to be cleared and used by someone else' (David Wong, 1975: 10).

37. '(a) Out-and-out transfer. It may, in a way, be said to be a transfer of cleared or cultivated land by sale. However, the dealing was not quite a sale of the land but one of a take-over by way of recouping the original cultivator for his labour in clearing the land as well as for any crops he had cultivated or house erected thereon.... (b) "Letting" (*sewa*). This was an arrangement whereby a cultivator allowed another person to cultivate his land for a return of a share in the produce crops or for a rent in kind or in money. (c) "security transactions" (generally called *gadai*).... Presumably, "security dealings were relatively a late development in a peasant community" ' (David Wong, 1975: 11-12).

38. 'The customary rules relating to the abandonment of land and their simple customary dealings seemed to be more concerned with actual use of land and the produce crops. Land *simpliciter* was involved as a medium rather than as an object. This is not to deny that some form of "private ownership" of land (in the wide general sense) was already in the process of evolution in an advanced agricultural settlement such as that of the Malay' (David Wong, 1975: 12).

39. '... a proprietary right is created by the clearing of the land *followed by continuous occupation*.... His right to land is absolute *as long as occupation continues, or as long as the land bears signs of appropriation* ... the doctrine that the right to the soil was in the Raja ... was not incompatible with the rights of the owners of the proprietary right, for he did not claim an allodial right to the soil, but merely the right to appropriate and keep for himself as much land as he had the power (*usaha*) to clear and keep in cultivation ... he did not claim more than a usufruct continuous as long as he chose it to be so, and terminable on abandonment' (Maxwell, 1884: 77-8, 90-1, original emphasis).

40. 'The right of the Raja to dispose of waste land *cannot have been seriously exerted* in Malay States in respect of forest land. The old Malay custom which permitted the free selection and appropriation of forest land for the purposes of cultivation was not interfered with.... That the soil of a Malay State is vested in the Raja is a doctrine not now to be questioned, though it may have *originated in confusion of thought*, the exercise of the rights to collect the tenth and to dispose of abandoned land *being assumed to imply* the existence of a superior right of property in the soil, to which the rights of proprietorship were subordinate.... The Raja's absolute property in the soil, is but a barren right, and as he undoubtedly has, *independently of it*, the right of levying tenths and taxes and of forfeiting lands for non-payment, Malay law does not trouble itself much with speculation about it. Tenant right is the cardinal doctrine of the Malay cultivator, and, as long as that is fully recognised, *it does not matter to him who or what functionary or power may, in theory, be clothed with the original and supreme right to the soil*' (Maxwell, 1884: 90-2, emphasis added).

41. 'Clearly, total ownership of land was inconceivable to the Malay cultivators themselves. The limitations of their "rights" in respect of land were in fact no more than the limitations of the uses of land in the conditions of their social and economic life. Although what a cultivator actually did on his land may be reflected in his relationship with other members of his community in terms of his right to use the land, it is an apparent "unreality" to transform the historical limitations of land uses known to them into limitations of their rights. Perhaps what is more fictitious in such a western interpretation is not so much its commitment to the concept of absolute total ownership of land as the attribution of such total ownership to the ruler under a native political system ...' (David Wong, 1975: 17).

42. For instance, section 16 of the 1667 Kedah Laws of the Dato Seri Paduka Tuan reads: 'Land without boundary marks is counted dead and belongs to the Raja' (Winstedt, 1928). This legal tenet clearly indicates the ruler's right to eminent domain. Also, the appendices of Maxwell's 1884 article contain various suggestive extracts from indigenous Malay land codes, though they are far from conclusive in themselves. Various colonial observers before Maxwell also attested to the existence of the ruler's claim to the tenth:

'Fullerton in 1928, was explicit that the Malay lands were liable to the exaction of the tenth of the produce. Newbold confirmed that the population in the Peninsula was subject to the imposition of a tenth of the produce wherever it happened to settle. Maxwell's father... had written that although it was well-known by the old Malay law that the sovereign was the owner of the soil, every man had the right to clear and occupy all forest and waste land subject to the payment to the ruler of one tenth of the produce of the land; he had concluded that the rights thus acquired were not prescriptive but customary. More recently, Sir Frederick Weld, in 1880, had said that "the Malay custom, which always appear to have been recognised as a basis for our procedure admitted the right of the cultivator to occupy the land permanently so long as he paid to Government tenths of the produce and continued to cultivate it" ' (Lim Teck Ghee, 1976: 31).

43. It can of course be argued that Kedah was exceptional in so far as it was subject to Siamese influence.

44. Maxwell, advocate of the doctrine of the Sultan's eminent domain and of his related right to collection of the tenth, admitted: 'The only purely Malay province in which I have personally seen the tenth of the grain collected by a native Government is the Krian province in Perak' (Maxwell, 1884: 97–8).

45. In 1890, Swettenham maintained:

'... there was not in the pre-Residential period any system of payment by tenths, or, indeed, any recognised system of native tenure of any kind. The people occupied and cultivated such lands as they chose, and paid nothing for them, but the authorities, Sultan, State Officer, local headman, or anak Raja, whoever had the power or might, dispossessed the occupants at pleasure, or helped themselves to any produce that they thought worth having whenever they felt able and inclined' (Swettenham, as quoted in David Wong, 1975: 18).

Three years later, in 1893, Swettenham provided yet another picture:

'The Malay cultivator was not the owner of the land he occupied, that he was a tenant at will ... that the Malays possessed no proprietary rights over the land, that no land can be said to have descended to them from their forefather, and that, while the rulers never admitted any claim to the land on the part of the people, these last never advanced any such claim, but frankly stated, as they do now, that the land belonged to the Ka-raja-an' (Swettenham, quoted in Lim Teck Ghee, 1976: 28).

One cannot but suspect that the characterizations these colonial officials made of pre-colonial Malay society were adjusted to fit the specific political positions they were advancing at particular times.

46. Sharom Ahmat (1970: 2) also mentions that 'there was always the fear that a large harvest might merely mean that the successful cultivator had to part with the excess on the demand of some chief, petty or otherwise'. Sharom is writing on Kedah, a *negeri* where agricultural settlement was of a relatively more settled and permanent character and where one would expect land rent exactions to be comparatively more regularized.

47. Fifteenth-century Malacca provides an example, according to Newbold (1971: 255). There, land was privately owned and landlords exacted a rent of a third of the produce. Evidence of what appears to be private ownership of land may be imputed from some of the laws regarding land dealings, to which mention was made earlier. Also, an examination of the Kedah Laws (Winstedt, 1928) indicates the existence of private land-ownership.

48. Quoting Marsden's *Sumatra*, Newbold suggests that, outside Malacca, 'Land is so abundant in proportion to the population that they scarcely consider it as a subject of right, any more than the elements of air and water, excepting in so far as in speculation the prince lays claim on the whole' (Newbold, 1971: 224–5).

49. In Pahang, it was called the *hasil banchi*, whereby every male Malay and Chinese was required to pay $1.33 each upon demand (Jang Aisjah Muttalib, 1972: 49). The reference to the Chinese presence may suggest that this practice began after the Chinese were in Pahang. If it was of recent origin, it may have arisen under the influence of changing conditions in the region, and may well not have been an old Malay practice. In Perak, Wilkinson (1971: 136, 138) writes that the *Bendahara*, the premier-chief of Perak, was entitled 'to collect a capitation-tax of 50 cents from every household. This revenue was known as the *beman kalur*.' The *Sadika Raja*, one of the eight Perak chiefs, enjoyed among other things, 'a capitation-tax of 70 *gantangs* of rice from every household'. Writing of the same *negeri* for the same period, Emily Sadka says that:

'The poll tax was not commonly levied, though there are references to a poll tax of fifty cents on every male in Perak, levied by the Bendahara, a poll tax of $2 on every married man in this district, levied by the Maharaja Lela, and a tax of $2.25 levied by the Sultan on every household in Krian, which was the royal district' (Sadka, 1968: 385).

50. See note 44.

51. Of course, this may also be looked at inversely. Then, the practices elsewhere would all become exceptional with Krian being the sole exemplar of the norm.

52. See note 47.

53. '... Kedah ... saw in 1883 the promulgation of two proclamations by its Sultan which purported, *inter alia*, to impose land-tax (hasil tanah) on all land-holdings, to require the obtaining of a permit for clearing forest land, and to provide for the issue of documents of title for occupied land.... All these were clearly indicative of a process of transformation of a Malay ruler's political authority into his superior ownership of land in the new conditions of the nineteenth century Malay peninsula under direct or indirect colonial influences' (David Wong, 1975: 20).

54. Evidence to evaluate these various interpretations for the case of pre-colonial Malaya is ambiguous and hard to come by. An added difficulty is that much of the available documentation was made by travellers and traders, people who accompanied the development of commercial relations. Further, the evidence is most readily available for the period by which time long-distance trade and then European mercantilism had already changed economic relations irreversibly.

It is difficult to assess the assertion that the pre-colonial Malay economy was a 'natural economy' without reference to a time period. If the period referred to is that for which evidence is most readily available, i.e. after the establishment of the Malacca sultanate, then the assertion, in all its interpretations, must be rejected. However, this does not mean that the assertion, or at least one of its interpretations, may not hold true for an earlier time. Available evidence at this point, however, does not permit comment on the matter.

55. '... speaking of the Malay States *as a whole* and bearing in mind that the volume of economic exchange between these states and outside territories increased sharply only with the foundation of the Straits Settlements, it is reasonable to speculate that the widespread establishment of a monetary economy took place in the early 19th century' (Khoo Kay Kim in Zainal Abidin, 1970: 52).

56. 'The Malay economy was by no means a closed and self-sufficient system. The export of tin provided the means of buying cloth, foodstuffs and other necessaries from abroad. As a consequence of this foreign trade the Malay economy was based on a monetary system of exchange. There is, for example, no common Malay word for "barter". It is not suggested that all economic exchanges were by payment in money. Wealth was more often accumulated in tin ingots than in coin. There had at one time been an indigenous system of tin coinage (before the nineteenth century) but at the period with which this study is concerned almost everything which had an exchange value was expressed in terms of dollars. It was this habit of valuation in monetary terms which was significant' (Gullick, 1958: 20).

57. 'The Malay peasant economy was by no means self-sufficient. Rice was imported in some deficiency areas: salt, dried fish, opium, oil, coconuts and textiles were all staple trade commodities...' (Gullick, 1958: 126).

58. 'But although the Malays were so involved in rice cultivation, their activity was not organized on a commercial basis. On the contrary, most rice planters worked within a rather tightly knit subsistence framework. To supplement their diet, they engaged in a little fishing, the raising of poultry and the planting of various fruit trees in their *dusun* (orchard). But there were still certain other basic necessities which the peasants required but did not produce, such as cloth, salt, tobacco. In order to obtain these, the Malays collected jungle produce like bamboo, dammar and rattans; and some were engaged in a very rudimentary form of tin mining; the commodities thus obtained were then exchanged for what they needed' (Sharom Ahmat, 1970: 2).

59. Some specialized craft production existed in the stockades where the ruling class lived, but this was rarely to be found in the villages. The *rakyat* generally made the agricultural and metal products required for their own use (Jang Aisjah Muttalib, 1972: 51). The system of tribute exacted by empires, such as Siam and Malacca, usually required some offerings in the form of refined craft-work. It also appears, however, that there was little trade in these items. Possibly, exceptionally distinguished crafts may have been acquired by ruling classes from other *negeri*. Commodity production of crafts was not well developed. Craft development primarily served ruling class interests and was hence correspondingly limited by it.

60. This was probably stimulated first by long-distance trade, then by European mercantilism and, subsequently, by relatively cheap manufactured exports from the industrializing West.

61. 'Both Sultan and chiefs derived their main revenues from custom taxes and taxes on production for export ... there were taxes on produce for export, often and most commonly levied as export duty. There was no levy on production for subsistence, except in Krian in Upper Perak.... The Sultan derived revenue mainly from the customs duties on the Perak river, and a share of the duties on the rivers of Larut. Custom duties were imposed on all imported articles; the

most important of these being opium, tobacco, textiles, rice, oil and salt. Export taxes were levied on tin, gutta and other wood gums, atap, rattans and hides ... the main income of chiefs was probably derived from taxes on tin, gutta and other export produce obtained in their districts. The Mentri, the Maharaja Lela, the Panglima Kinta, the Panglima Bukit Gantang, the Dato' Sagor and the Sri Adika Raja derived tribute in this way; *the tribute was paid in consideration of their political position and did not constitute private rent or profit from business undertakings* (Sadka, 1968: 385-6, emphasis added).

Wilkinson has detailed the sources of revenue of the sultan, the 'four great dignitaries' and the 'eight chiefs' of Perak. This indicates that the majority of the ruling class derived considerable income from exacting tribute on trade and related matters. The arrangement appears to resemble a situation where politically-based rights are distributed amongst the ruling class as individual means of income.

'The Ruler ... derived his principal revenues from the duty (*chukai Kuala Perak*) levied on all produce entering or leaving the State by the mouth of the Perak river. The duty probably varied from time to time,... in 1874 this source of revenue had been let for $12,000 a year.... The Bendahara ... derived his revenues mainly from a toll station (*batang Kuala Kinta*) that levied duties on all produce entering or leaving the Kinta River.... The Temenggong ... derived his revenue from a monopoly of the sale of salt and ataps.... The Maharaja Lela ... derived revenue ... from certain customs dues drawn from the Sungei Dedap.... The Laksamana ... levied tolls on the river Batang Padang and received a small share of the tolls on the Perak river itself.... The Dato' Bandar ... acted as a sort of harbour master, customs officer, protector of immigrants and superintendent of trade' (Wilkinson, 1971: 133-8).

62. For example, whereas the Sultan of Kedah appeared to be in control of matters, the situation in mid-nineteenth century Perak was far less centralized: see note 4 above.

63. This was clearly the case in late nineteenth-century Kedah, when Chinese businessmen, mainly from Penang, held many of the revenue farms. However, the collection of such revenues was not recent in origin, and at least pre-dated the British colonization of Penang in 1786.

64. The Sultan exclusively controlled the trade in elephants, salt, tobacco, cotton, opium, tin, beeswax, iron, and gunpowder, deriving an income of $81,500 from these alone. Taxes on imports and exports yielded a further $31,000; other items, including rents, contributed another $24,000. The subsequent establishment of the British port at Penang severely cut into the Sultan's income from trade by about a third. (See also Newbold, 1971: 20.)

65. While Kedah may have been exceptional, there is little apparent reason to believe that this was so, unless the practice is to be attributed solely to Siamese influence.

66. Of the nine items monopolized by the Sultan, elephants, opium, and tin alone accounted for about 70 per cent of this revenue. Elephants were exported to India, and this practice probably had a long history since the first Hindu colony on the peninsula had been established in Kedah many centuries before. Ties between India and Kedah were certainly not recent in origin. Opium was imported by the Sultan for sale to Siam, Pattani, Kelantan, and Trengganu, as well as for local consumption, presumably for consumption by the primarily Malay local population. (However, it is difficult to date the origins of this practice.) Tin from Kedah and neighbouring areas was sold by the Sultan to foreign traders, Asian as well as European. The use of tin by Asian cultures certainly pre-dated European use, but again it is difficult to assess when tin exports became financially significant. As Kedah appeared to be a trade centre in relation to some of its neighbours—at least at the time under consideration here—its ruling class may have consequently enjoyed a relatively higher income. For it to have played this role, external trade must also have existed for the neighbouring *negeri* (Wan Ibrahim, 1961).

67. 'The phenomenon of piracy is indicative of the peculiar nature of the ancient Johore kingdom. It was essentially a maritime state. The major political and economic concerns of the Sultan were the sea peoples of the Riau-Lingga Archipelago and the international trade route which passed through the Straits of Malacca. This state centered on a trading entrepot.... The Riau entrepot of 1874 was but the last in a succession of similar "urban" centers whose history stretches back to Srivijaya in the seventh century ... Malay trading empires were rarely based on riverine states. Power in this context was always sea power' (Trocki, 1975: 3).

68. 'Malacca's supremacy over the Strait was ensured when Iskandar Shah fitted out a fleet of

patrol boats, manned by Celates, to force vessels to call at Malacca. As in the days of *Sri Vijaya*, the Straits became again a private sea. . . . Whereas the other ports on both the Sumatran and Peninsular coasts existed for the export of the products of their hinterlands, Malacca was, by reason of history and geography, an entrepot, dependent for its prosperity on the volume of trade passing through the Strait. . . . But to enforce her monopoly, she needed to implement–and facilitate–control of the sea by extension of her authority over the neighbouring coasts, and during the fifteenth century this task was accomplished by a succession of able rulers. The life-blood of Malacca was commerce. During the fourteenth century the Strait was the crucial sector of the world's major trade-route which had one terminus in Venice–or even further westwards–and the other in the Molucca Islands. . . . This, as later the Portuguese were to realize, was the only point throughout the 8,000 miles of the trade-route at which the monopoly of the spice distribution could be established. . . . The fundamental basis of Malaccan trade was an exchange of the staple products of the Archipelago for the staple manufactures of India' (Wheatley, 1961: 308-13).

69. This included port dues, export and import taxes (6 per cent of the cargo of foreign traders, 3 per cent for local merchants), storage and other charges. 'One of the main sources of income for the ruler seems to have come from the taxes paid by the foreign traders that came to trade in Malacca. He also obtained wealth from his conquests and tributes for the vassal states. There is also a possibility that the rulers themselves indirectly participated in trade' (Zainal Abidin, 1970: 18).

70. Here we cite one of the rare indications of the ruling class's actual involvement in commercial operations.
'In addition to the not inconsiderable quantity of cloves and nutmegs brought to Malacca by traders of the Archipelago, every year eight ships sailed from that port directly to the Moluccas where they bartered coarse Cambay cloth and the tails of white Bengal cattle for a total of five or six thousand bahars of cloves' [1 *bahar* = 375 lb. approximately] (Wheatley, 1961: 315).
There is no clear indication of the ownership and organization of this particular commercial enterprise involving the annual dispatching of eight ships from Malacca. Nevertheless, it seems safe to guess that it belonged to the Malacca sultanate.

71. This would arise if there was lack of knowledge on the part of the eventual buyers of the actual costs of production involved. Then the long-distance traders would alone be aware of the differences between costs of production (or actual purchasing price for them) and selling prices. They would then be in a position to extract a substantial portion of the surplus because of this exclusive knowledge. Hence, an important pre-condition for success in this practice was their monopoly of knowledge on the prices involved. This could be achieved through a monopoly on trade as a whole.

72. 'Debt-bondsmen . . . were indeed an investment which could be realised by sale. They were thus of economic value as capital' (Gullick, 1958: 101).

73. '. . . aristocrats had other minor sources of income besides their tax revenues. They had the profits of trading and tin mining on a small scale. . . . Such resources as a chief could spare for economic development were usually employed in financing tin mining, which offered the prospect of the largest and most rapid returns. . . . It was very often not their own money, however, which they risked on these ventures. The financiers, European and Chinese, of the Straits Settlements were apparently reluctant to supply food and stores on credit to the Chinese headmen of a small mine. He might default or cheat them. Still more he might be robbed by the local Malay chief. They therefore preferred to go into partnership with the chief so that he would have an interest in supervising the mine and ensuring that it was allowed to succeed' (Gullick, 1958: 128-30).

74. For example, Wan Mat Saman, the chief minister (*Menteri Besar*) of Kedah, organized the construction of a 22 mile-long drainage and irrigation canal in 1885. When the canal was completed, he made a fortune selling and renting the irrigated agricultural land adjoining the canal. Interestingly, Wan Mat Saman employed Chinese coolies for the task of canal construction (Sharom Ahmat, 1970: 5).

75. See note 74.

76. For example, 'Children may be allowed to die, but not custom' (*Biar mati anak, jangan mati adat*).

77. 'The bean which forgets its pod' (*Macam kacang lupakan kulit*) refers to one who forgets his or her (family or class) origins. 'The cucumber and the thorny fruit' (*Macam timun dengan durian*) refers

to an unequal relationship (of power), such as the relationship between the subject class and the ruling class. The inequality of such relations has also been compared to that between goat and tiger (*Macam kambing dengan rimau*).

The ruler who visits the villagers is compared to the rampaging incursion of an elephant (*Gajah masuk kampung*); the hardships occasioned by the ruling class are also compared to the destructive presence of the hornbill (*Enggang lalu, ranting patah*). The suffering brought about by struggles within the ruling class is compared to that of fighting elephants (*Gajah sama gajah berjuang, pelanduk mati di tengah*). The impoverished conditions in which the subject class live has been likened to day-to-day survival (*Kais pagi, makan pagi; kais petang, makan petang*).

78. The conduct of the ruling class has been vividly described by Abdullah who worked closely with some of the early nineteenth-century British colonialists.

'It is no light tyranny that was exercised by the Malay rulers, apart from a few who were good. Women and children who caught their fancy they have abducted by force as though they were taking chickens, with no sort of fear of Allah or regard for His creatures. They have often murdered men whose offences in no way merited death, just as they would kill an ant. They have plundered the property of other men, killing the owners or dragging them off into captivity. If they owe money they refuse to pay it. They are very fond of gambling, cock-fighting, opium-eating and keeping a host of slaves.... They send the royal spear to a house demanding the owner's goods with threats, and they take away his womenfolk by force. There are many other disgraceful practices apart from these, which I feel too ashamed to mention in this book. Besides, they despise the servants of Allah, human beings like themselves, and look upon them as dogs. When they pass by on the road, they order everyone to stay by the roadside, in the mud and the filth. They keep young girls by the score, sometimes more than a hundred, as concubines in the palace.... It is obvious that the things I have mentioned are simply means of gratifying the ruler's lusts. They are neither right nor in accordance with the laws of Islam, nor are they approved or condoned by public opinion. They are done just to suit the ruler's own pleasure. Sometimes he has ten or twenty children. One or two of them may be good but the rest behave like devils.... When they grow up however wicked the things their father did they themselves may be three times worse. As for the poor people who are the victims of this oppression, this injustice, this tyranny, they are in no position to make any complaints, save only to Allah.... Was there not a time when half the world was under Malay dominion and rule?... Why have their lands been despoiled by Allah ere now, and passed into foreign bondage. Is it not because of extreme injustice and tyranny that Allah has weakened them and enslaved them under alien rule?' (Abdullah, 1970: 269-71).

79. For releasing slaves and surrendering 'rights' to taxation.

80. See Allen (1968); Mohamed Amin (1977). It is crucial to distinguish between the various tendencies of early Malay resistance to colonialism. Put rather simply, there were 'conservative' tendencies seeking to protest or retrieve old class privileges as well as more 'progressive' tendencies opposing the new oppressive order introduced by colonialism. Both kinds of tendencies might coexist in the same movement. Historical evidence suggests that the latter type became increasingly significant and this appears to be reflected by changes in the social origins of the leadership, in the social base of the movements, as well as the movements' issues, demands, and goals.

81. One practical problem of the 'mode of production and social formation' approach emerges here. How do we evaluate which is the dominant 'mode of production' in a 'social formation'? By the predominant form of surplus appropriated by the ruling class, as is maintained by Amin (1976: 18)? Or by the most generally prevalent social relations of production, i.e. those involving the largest proportion of the population? Both these criteria raise problems. One example should illustrate this. In some 'Third World' countries today, the primary source of surplus is not from the wage labour force nor are most of the working population wage workers. Yet these countries are characterized as capitalist. This is presumably because integration into the world economic system dominated by capitalism has radically transformed pre-capitalist societies. While this has rarely resulted in the immediate generalization of wage labour, and may have in fact actually created new non-capitalist relations of production, a capitalist economy is, according to this view, dominated by capital and therefore by the dynamic of its accumulation.

Part II

Do not clear the land around you
It is already someone else's property.

Usman Awang, 'A Letter from a Peasant',
October 1967

THE TRANSFORMATION OF
THE MALAY PEASANTRY
UNDER COLONIALISM

PART I (Chapter 1) outlined the class relations characteristic of pre-colonial Malay society prior to the inception of British colonial rule. The circumstances leading to British rule in Malaya, and some aspects of the parallel expansion of capital, will be discussed later in Chapter 5 (in Part III). This part offers a historical analysis of the transformation of the Malay peasantry following the imposition of British rule, focusing primarily on the indigenous peasant population settled in the peninsula before British intervention, i.e. as opposed to immigrant peasant settlers, whether from the neighbouring (now Indonesian) islands or from China, or other rural non-agricultural family-unit producers, such as fishermen (see Firth, 1966). The following analysis in Chapters 2–4 deals with developments in three areas significant for the transformation of the peasantry: circulation capital, the colonial state, and land–the peasants' primary means of production.

Chapter 2 evaluates the impact of circulation capital which encouraged greater peasant production for exchange, increased their reliance on purchased commodities for both production and consumption and thus stimulated the growth of commercial and usury capital in the peasant sector of the economy. Clearly, the expansion of both types of circulation capital was related to the accelerated growth of commodity relations involving the peasantry after colonial intervention. In treating the notion–common in many studies of peasant poverty in Malaya–that the ubiquitous middleman is the main exploiter of the peasantry, it is argued that the middleman represents the conspicuous tip of the iceberg of commercial capital exploiting peasants.

Because of the hierarchical structure of commercial capital as a whole, and of usury capital, an unequal distribution of profit shares accrues to particular capitals at different levels of this structure (see also Chapter 5). The development of commodity exchange also entailed the growth of merchant and usury capital in the peasant economy. The colonial government's desire to preserve a politically stable Malay yeoman peasantry caused it to provide–among other things–some institutional credit to check the immiserizing effects of privately supplied credit. But these efforts were paltry, probably because of the colonial state's overwhelming commitment to the interests of British capital. Other government attempts to preserve the yeoman peasantry, particularly the various Malay Reservation laws, all combined with the Islamic prohibition on usury to give rise to a distinctly Malay credit system which instead accelerated the forces of differentiation among the Malay peasantry.

In general, colonial policies subordinated peasant interests to those of capital, especially British capital, with profound implications for peasant agricultural development. Chapter 3 examines the complex relations involving capital, the state and the peasantry for much of the colonial period, particularly in colonial policy and practice affecting padi and rubber cultivation, which involved the substantial majority of the peasantry. After demonstrating that both colonial intervention in padi production and subsequent rice policies consistently served the interests of capital, the significance of the Malay Reservation legislation for peasant land-ownership is assessed. The second half of Chapter 3 looks at rubber-growing peasants in relation to plantation rubber interests and the colonial state. The significance of the class interests underlying the 1922 Stevenson Restriction Scheme and the 1934 International Rubber Regulation Scheme, together with the class implications of colonial policy on new planting and replanting of rubber, are explored.

Chapter 4 examines the social relations of the peasantry in relation to land. Since land is the primary means of production for the peasant agriculturalist, differential ownership of and access to land have resulted in corresponding differentiation among the peasantry. Such developments, together with capital expansion under colonialism, have had grave outcomes, particularly concentration in land-ownership and, consequently, the spread of tenancy. These did not, however, lead to capitalist relations of production in peasant agriculture until relatively recently, e.g. with the advent of the Green Revolution in padi farming. The differentiation among the peasantry since colonial rule cannot be directly attributed to pre-colonial class configurations; as yet this had not evolved into clearly definable social classes which may be distinguished by the criterion of ownership of land—the main means of production. The resulting non-capitalist class relations which characterize the peasantry are interpreted as a result of the specificities of British colonial intervention in Malaya. The process of peasant differentiation and impoverishment are linked to changes in relations involving land. More specifically, the development of joint ownership and subdivision of land are contrasted to the opposite trend of concentration of land-ownership. While peasant differentiation has generally not approximated a stark class demarcation between 'pure' landlords (those who do not operate any of their own land but rent it all to others) and 'pure' tenants (those who rent all the land they work), peasant strata may be differentiated according to tenurial status—though the significance of such stratification is now complicated by the new technological, and hence social, relations brought by the Green Revolution. Rent exaction, the form of surplus appropriation corresponding to these social relations of production, and its changing forms and extent are discussed, and the significance of tenurial relations for an analysis of peasant class differentiation is evaluated. Finally, the state's interest in preserving a yeoman peasantry is discussed in light of the development of tenancy.

CIRCULATION CAPITAL AND THE PEASANTRY

Commodity Production and Commercial Capital

... every person was in turn a farmer, fisherman,
labourer, or a collector of produce.
(Ooi, 1959: 165)

THIS is how some authors have described the peasant condition before (external) market forces, capital, and colonialism penetrated peasant society. A trifle
romantic, the quotation does nevertheless capture the primarily subsistence
orientation of peasant production before the development of commodity production was accelerated by increasing integration into the Western-centred
world economy. The peasant, as pointed out earlier, did not produce much in
excess of family and farm needs for fear of expropriation by the ruling class.[1]

It has not yet been possible to date the beginnings of intensified commodity
exchanges in the peasant economy. It appears from the pattern of Malay
settlement that riverine commerce, at least, was a feature of the peninsular
Malay peasant economy from the outset. Most likely, the emergence of trading
empires in the vicinity—such as at Malacca—followed later by European
(Portuguese and Dutch) mercantilism, contributed to an increase in commerce
involving the peasantry. The Industrial Revolution led to the entry of cheap
manufactured imports into the peasant economy, which further stimulated
production for exchange. Many *traditional* crops were produced in increasingly greater quantities, in excess of consumption requirements, for exchange
with imported goods. Thus, peasant production became increasingly subject
to a rationality dictated by a market, rather than subsistence orientation.

Colonial annexation of the Straits trading ports further stimulated commercial exchanges in the Malayan hinterland. The Industrial Revolution in Europe,
marked by a tremendous expansion of production and export of manufactures,
sought markets internationally; for example, Britain's overseas interests lay
not only in securing raw materials for industry, but also in developing markets
for its exports. At that time, Malaya, with its tin and other primary products to
offer, fitted well into the emerging global trade pattern. The development of
the British-controlled Straits Settlements was accompanied by significant
expansion of coastal and riverine trade in the hinterland. While tin production
controlled by the Malay ruling class accounted for some of this expansion, the
increase in peasant production for exchange—including jungle produce—was
not unimportant. As noted, the considerable expansion of such trade increased
the amount collected in tributes exacted by the Malay ruling class.

Expanded trade also brought in its trail the expansion of commercial capital which, typically, preceded other forms of capital penetration into the Malayan hinterland.[2] While large-scale international trade was dominated by British enterprises based in the Straits Settlements, local and even regional trade tended to be conducted by non-Europeans. Ethnically Chinese, Arab, Indian or from within the archipelago, these merchants were greater in number, but economically less powerful. Many were subordinate to British merchant capitalists, supplying them with the products of the region and receiving imports to be sold in the hinterland. This was the norm for goods emanating from, or destined for, the West (see Chapter 5). The peasant, as producer or consumer, almost never came into direct contact with the Straits British merchants, but only with the non-European (often Chinese) traders at the lower end of the hierarchy of commerce.

In contrast to the arbitrary exactions by the ruling class, which threatened excess production in pre-colonial times, the more predictable and stable order imposed under colonial rule was more conducive to production for the market. Hence, the establishment of colonial rule, especially in the peninsular hinterland, contributed in a decisive manner to encouraging peasant commodity production.[3] Perhaps most importantly, it established the conditions for cash-crop cultivation, primarily for export to foreign markets. Colonial administrators, intending cash-crop cultivation to be in capitalist hands, were upset by the spontaneous but nevertheless rational response of peasants to the new economic opportunities.[4] Market-oriented peasant production was, of course, not without problems. While the peasantry stood to enjoy considerably higher incomes from export-oriented cash-cropping, it was also exposed to the vicissitudes of a capitalist-dominated world market beyond its control. In the context of a world rather than a local market, the nexus between local supply and price was lost—a poor crop in a region may fetch a low price and return if producers elsewhere have good crops, i.e. the compensating movement of volume and price in a closed local market disappears (J. C. Scott, 1976).

The limited commerce in the Malay peasant economy prior to the increase in commodity exchanges in the nineteenth century had given rise to certain trading arrangements.[5] The increase in market-oriented production with the advent and spread of cash-cropping increasingly brought peasant produce into the growing commercial circuits. Despite the development of trade relations, market participation by peasant producers was largely limited to contact with the first-level purchasers of their produce.

Growing trade increased investment in commerce. Unlike the peasant who produces for exchange in order to purchase his consumption and other needs, the interests of capital in the commercial circuits lie in capital accumulation. Very simply, capital is invested to purchase commodities to be resold at a profit. The fundamental difference between the commodity producer on the one hand and commercial capital on the other has been symbolized in the following manner, where C represents commodities, M the money form of capital invested, and M' the increased monetary return to the capitalist from buying and then selling commodities at a profit:

commodity producer (peasant)	:	$C-M-C$
capitalist (merchant)	:	$M-C-M'$

Commercial Capital and Profits

Capital involved in trade, i.e. 'commercial capital' or 'merchant capital', needs to be analysed in specific circumstances—in this case, in the context of the peasant economy. In practice, strictly commercial activities are indistinguishable—except at the analytical level—from other functions essential to the realization of value as a commodity. For example, Khoo Kay Jin (1978), Tan Tat Wai (1977), Lim Sow Ching (1968: 2), and Wharton (1962: 30) identify various functions performed by dealers of smallholder rubber, especially by first-level buyers, which include collection (assembling), weighing and grading, smoking, storage, packing, and transport. Given current technological requirements, it is undeniable that many of these functions are essential to rubber production for industrial use; efforts involved towards this end would therefore be considered *productive labour*.[6] Nevertheless, commercial capital's claim to a share of the surplus value, i.e. commercial profits or the marketing margin, is based on more than the *productive* functions it purports to perform.

It is more often asserted or assumed, rather than demonstrated, that commercial capital realizes extraordinarily large profits from monopolistic/ monopsonistic involvement in the peasant economy[7] (Wharton, 1962). What are the reasons for this?[8] Some are based on the nature of the separation of the peasant producer from the consumer—geographically, socially, economically, etc.—in most market economies. The peasant's allegedly short *time horizon*, usually necessitated by poverty, is crucial here. Limited peasant storage facilities, as well as a typically chronic need for cash, also compel the peasant to sell his produce at low prices.[9] It therefore seems that the peasants' lack of processing and storage facilities necessitates the immediate disposal of crops requiring these. Often isolated from more developed communications facilities, the relatively small amounts and perhaps the seasonal nature of peasant production necessitate peasant reliance on others for transport and other essential facilities. This is, of course, in contrast with the larger capitalist enterprises which take advantage of bulk transportation and for which the basic transport infrastructure of the country was built to serve (Voon, 1971). Also, where the marketing agent also supplies rural credit, the indebted peasant seller is especially vulnerable to accepting low prices—like having to sell at harvest time when prices tend to be lowest[10] (Waide, 1967; Wharton, 1962). Approaching the issue in terms of alleged middleman monopoly and monopsony, Wharton (1962: 27) suggests that for monopsony gains to be made, 'certain power factors, singly or in combination, *must be strong enough*'; however, he is not concerned with demonstrating this assertion.[11]

Lim Sow Ching's (1968: 6-8) empirical analysis of smallholder rubber marketing in Peninsular Malaysia challenges many of the prevailing assertions that middleman marketing margins are the main cause of low smallholder incomes. On the contrary, the extension of credit, even when interest-free, did not seem to guarantee that the rubber was sold to the creditor; neither was there evidence that indebtedness compelled the borrowing smallholder to sell to his creditor, as often alleged. Equally surprising, Lim found that where loans had been provided, marketing margins were below average. However, he recognized that services, such as cash loans or smoking and processing facilities, 'are provided with the aim of attracting smallholders to do business'. He also found that grocers tended to enjoy higher marketing margins. Since first-level dealers often were also grocers, and the volume of business or the size of the market was often small, the higher margins appear to have been related to the smaller turnovers handled (see Figure 2.1).

Lim Sow Ching (1968: 3-4) maintained that marketing margins are not as high as usually asserted, being around 5 per cent for ribbed smoked sheet (RSS) and 15 per cent for unsmoked sheet (USS); margins tended to be lower for good quality sheets, as opposed to low quality RSS and USS. Yet, three-quarters of all smallholder production was sold to first-level dealers as USS. Moreover, it is likely that the tendency to sell USS declines with increasing smallholding size. Hence, peasant rather than petty capitalist smallholdings, sell mostly USS. Also, larger capitalist smallholdings tend to be better able to prepare good quality RSS. Lim's analysis suggests that USS, produced mainly by smaller peasant holdings, tended to be subject to greater marketing margins than RSS (emanating mostly from larger smallholdings) especially better quality RSS which is mainly from subdivided estates or petty capitalist smallholdings.

FIGURE 2.1

The Rubber Market Hierarchy

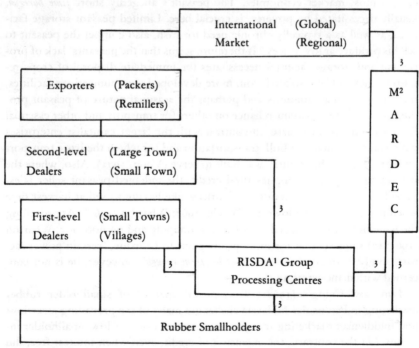

Source: Adapted from Khoo Kay Jin (1978: 10, Figure 1).
[1]RISDA: Rubber Industry Smallholders Development Authority (established 1973).
[2]MARDEC: Malaysian Rubber Development Corporation (established 1972).
[3]The new links in the marketing chain involving RISDA group processing centres and MARDEC are recent developments growing out of increasing state intervention especially since 1970.

food for local consumption, as far as possible cash-crop cultivation for export was intended to be a capitalist preserve. The measures taken by the colonial government in pursuit of this basic policy were many, and varied to fit the circumstances, time, and place. Though there was much rhetorical encouragement of both plantation and peasant agriculture, colonial policies and practices clearly discriminated against peasant interests in favour of plantation interests. In land alienation matters, plantations had greater access to better land–in terms of soil quality, terrain, drainage, accessibility, and so on. Similarly, taxation of agricultural land was generally kept low to encourage agricultural settlement, but heavier taxes were imposed on peasant agriculture compared to plantation agriculture (Lim Teck Ghee, 1976: 129). Despite the lack of government incentives and infrastructural support, peasant agriculture did develop, primarily as 'the result of a spontaneous response to the growing demand for food products from the increasing population rather than through conscious government economic planning' (Lim Teck Ghee, 1976: 134).

Peasant padi production was promoted by the colonial government for a number of reasons. In contrast to shifting cultivation, wet padi cultivation offered the prospect of permanently settled peasant farmers who would present minimal resistance or interference to plantation land expansion. Also, a peasantry catering for local consumption needs would not threaten the export-oriented plantation sector. Above all, peasant padi production was an asset to the colonial order in so far as it would reduce rice purchases from abroad, and thus reduce the foreign exchange outflows required for these.

Frustration with peasant reluctance to comply with colonial designs led the authorities to accuse the peasantry of being indolent, ignorant, stubborn, irrational, and the like. However, more objective students of the peasant condition have since found their behaviour to have been quite rational. Although per acre padi yields in Malaya were the highest in South and South-East Asia, average yields in equatorial latitudes (between 0 and 10 degrees) were lower than yields obtainable in both tropical (between 10 and 20 degrees) and sub-tropical (between 20 and 30 degrees) climates (Lim Chong-Yah, 1967: 147, 148). The fact that even low-yielding countries, such as Burma and Siam, were in a position to produce enough for export at lower prices also discouraged peasants in Malaya from padi cultivation. The higher incomes possible from other economic activities–either the cultivation of different crops or from wage labour employment–also served to dissuade peasants from padi production.[2] Even before the rubber boom, the peasant preference for cash-crop cultivation had evoked government efforts to restrict it.[3] Growing numbers of Malay peasants also turned to market gardening and growing crops other than padi for the local as well as export market. The drift away from padi production, which had preceded the advent of rubber and attained dramatic dimensions at the peak of the rubber boom in the 1910s, is clear testimony to the rationality of peasant responses to attractive economic alternatives. The demand for labour in the rapidly growing capitalist sector had 'increased wages to such a level that padi cultivation especially, with its meagre and uncertain remuneration, could attract only a few new adherents (Lim Teck Ghee, 1976: 134).[4] The following conclusion makes the point clearly:

In fact, as padi cultivation has been a very low-paying occupation, it is not unreasonable to say that where padi cultivation has been practised in Malaya, more often than not, it has been a reflection of the lack of better economic opportunities in such places, not necessarily a proof that such places have had more comparative advantages in padi growing than elsewhere (Lim Chong-Yah, 1967: 162).

Given the nature of administrative efforts in dealing with the peasantry, in retrospect, it may seem ironical that the British expressed as much frustration as they did with the failure of this peasant sector to develop.[5] Frustrated by the poor response of local Malays to efforts from the last quarter of the nineteenth century to promote padi production among them, the colonial administration began to encourage immigrant agricultural settlers, particularly people from other parts of the archipelago, who were believed to be favourably predisposed to tropical subsistence agriculture. The conditions under British rule were relatively attractive compared to those prevailing in the neighbouring islands under Dutch administration—especially the liberal conditions for land acquisition and low rates of taxation in the peninsula. This led to considerable peasant immigration and the designation of large areas for padi cultivation. However, colonial designs were to be frustrated again. In Perak, by 1889, only 7,500 acres out of a total of 36,455 acres of land alienated for padi farming were actually under cultivation (Lim Teck Ghee, 1976: 55). Like the local peasantry, immigrant settlers also found cash-cropping more attractive, inadvertently threatening plantation interests (Lim Teck Ghee, 1971: 24). On the other hand, non-Malay immigrants, who were discouraged from permanent settlement by the colonial rulers, were understandably reluctant to commit themselves to a peasant life. The wealthier non-Malay immigrants found it more profitable to engage in other occupations, while the poorer ones were generally discouraged from going into peasant agriculture; instead, they were expected to gain employment in the rapidly growing capitalist sector.

Contrary to British beliefs and pronouncements, the activities and attitudes of peasants were remarkably well adapted to the changing conditions they encountered.[6] Peasant responses to different economic opportunities demonstrate that they were not irrational in their behaviour. Nevertheless, however, peasant behaviour did not necessarily conform to British preferences, which generally reflected capital's interests. That peasants did not live up to the expectations of the colonial rulers is no reason for concluding that they were stupid or irrational. Having different interests, peasants and colonial officials usually operated on the basis of these different interests, and hence with different views of what constituted rational behaviour.

The importance of water control for the promotion of padi cultivation was recognized by government officials very early in the colonial era. However, government efforts to improve this did not begin till a quarter of a century after 1874 because of official reluctance to spend funds for the development of the peasant sector. Apparently what was foremost in colonial considerations was the feasibility of recouping the financial outlay involved in such projects. Only after the failure of the Krian padi cultivation project in northern Perak was the colonial administration stirred to commit funds to irrigate padi land there. Approved in 1899, the Krian irrigation scheme was completed in 1906, 'almost two decades after the recognition of its value and practicability' (Lim Teck Ghee, 1976: 59). The Krian scheme did not even involve solid government financial support for padi production. In sharp contrast to the colonial practice of generous infrastructural provisions to capitalist enterprises in mining and agriculture, the new irrigation scheme was hardly generous to the peasantry.[7] Typically, the colonial concern that 'profitable returns were a prior consideration in any work contemplated' (Lim Teck Ghee, 1976: 61) resulted in the exaction of an increased tax in the Krian scheme area. Nor did the scheme, covering about half the total padi area in the Federated Malay States then (Goldman, 1975: 256), mark the dawn of a new era of government drainage and irrigation construction to promote padi cultivation. Instead, another twenty-six years lapsed before the establishment of the Drainage and Irrigation Department (DID) in 1932 started a new round of such infrastructural provision by the colonial administration.

Rapid alienation of land to capitalist interests for mining and agricultural purposes during the last quarter of the nineteenth century was part of British strategy for promoting the development of the Malayan peninsula. The rubber boom from the beginning of the twentieth century resulted in a new wave of land alienation. Although cultivated peasant land was sometimes affected, e.g. in the case of mineral-rich land, most land purchases involved virgin land. The alienation of the choicest agricultural land in the country to capitalist interests—not necessarily for cultivation but often for speculative purposes or as reserves for possible future use—limited the land available to the peasantry which was growing, due not only to natural increase, but also to the immigration of agricultural settlers.

Malay Reservations Legislation and Padi Land

Lim Teck Ghee (1971: 145-59) has discussed the history of the Malay Reservations Enactment of 1913 and has argued that some of the major assumptions underlying this piece of colonial legislation were erroneous. Instead of defining the peasantry's land problem in relation to the administration's rapid alienation of land to capitalist interests, colonial legislators blamed the shortage on the sale of traditional peasant land to non-Malays. The chief villains in this British fiction were the small *chettiar* money-lenders, certainly not the large planting businesses. The magnitude of sales of traditional Malay peasant land to non-Malays was highly exaggerated as a substantial proportion of sales of Malay land to non-Malays involved non-traditional lands, 'which Malays had little regard for'. In fact, it was the practice of some Malays to organize groups to clear jungle land for cultivation, after which the land would be divided on some pre-arranged terms, of which some could be rented to tenant cultivators or sold to capitalist planters. Other non-Malay acquisitions were also made by usurious and speculating capitalists from loans as well as forfeited and purchased land property. While not ignoring these, it is necessary to point out that the colonial government's characterization of the cause of the peasant land problem *completely* absolved the big mining and agricultural capitalists from responsibility, and instead scapegoated small money-lenders and shopkeepers. Nonetheless, despite such glaring omissions in its formulation, the Enactments stemmed the possible eventual take-over of peasant land by usurious non-Malay capitalists (Lim Teck Ghee, 1971: 158).

The Malay Reservations Enactment passed in late 1913 included several major sections (see Lim Teck Ghee, 1971: 154). Official colonial Residents were empowered to declare any land within their State, reservation land, which could not be sold, leased, or otherwise disposed of to non-Malays. Limitations on the disposal of reservation lands were also imposed on the owners and land dealings contrary to the Enactment were declared null and void in the eyes of the law. Though similar legislation was later passed for the Unfederated Malay States, the application of the Reservations legislation varied among the various States. While the initial progress in the Reservations legislation was statistically impressive, 'most of the reservations were unoccupied land in the upland regions of the state where not only were there few conflicting interests to be considered but also the absence of a Malay population to take advantage of them' (Lim Teck Ghee, 1971: 154). Besides the fact that not all reservation land was suitable for settlement, in many places reservations only covered land already alienated, with no provisions for subsequent population increases and corresponding land needs.

The colonial authorities made the Malay peasantry pay a heavy price for reservation by imposing crop cultivation conditions.[8] Many peasants violated these cultivation restrictions or applied for non-reservation land, until finally, the colonial administration was forced to concede some amendments to the cultivation restrictions (Lim Teck Ghee, 1971: 159). The implementation of the reservations policy also resulted in the falling of land prices by as much as 50 per cent, so that Malay peasant land-owners often petitioned for their property to be excluded from reservation land[9] (Lim Teck Ghee, 1971: 206). Since reservation land was no longer good security for credit from non-Malays as shown in the last chapter, the participation by wealthier Malays in usurious activities was encouraged considerably since they alone were able to accept Malay peasant land as collateral for loans. With this advantage, Malay creditors could charge higher interest rates and impose stiffer conditions on loans, compared to non-Malay creditors. Consequently, wealthier Malays were able to purchase the devalued.reservation land at lower prices than on the open market. While curtailing non-Malay land acquisition, reservation policy facilitated accumulation of Malay peasant land by wealthier Malays. Generally, reservation policy did not directly affect non-Malay landholdings; in fact, indirectly, the 'procedures insured that non-Malay capitalist interests were safeguarded'[10] (Lim Teck Ghee, 1976: 205). All too often the Malay Reservations Enactment is cited as an example of British paternalism toward the Malays, but rather than 'protect Malays against themselves' (quoted in Lim Teck Ghee, 1971: 154), the reservation policy actually reinforced and accelerated the process of class differentiation among rural Malays. The Malay Reservations Enactment hence contributed to the social stratification of the Malay community and to some concentration of land-ownership among wealthier rural Malays.[11]

The Evolution of Colonial Rice Policy

The years from 1913 to 1931 have been identified as the period of the 'Great Malayan Rice Shortage' (Lim Teck Ghee, 1971: 118-44). In this context, the Malay Reservations Enactment of 1913 can be viewed as the first of various legislative and other colonial efforts to deal with the rice supply problem (Kratoska, 1975b); as the problem worsened towards the end of the decade, such efforts were intensified. In 1921, the Rice Lands Enactment was introduced; its primary effect appears to have been to prevent the expansion of peasant rubber cultivation into established padi areas, though it does not appear to have actually increased land under padi cultivation at all (Lim Teck Ghee, 1971: 128). After the impressive, but ineffectual, Food Control Enactment of 1917, the Food Production Enactment of the following year required estates to share some responsibility for food-crop production. This too failed miserably despite considerable government support—'the results especially of padi cultivation were disappointing' (Lim Teck Ghee, 1971: 144)—and was repealed within three years. Land was also specially set aside for food-crop cultivation, with special emphasis given to padi production.

The main thrust of government efforts at promoting padi cultivation was essentially negative, i.e. through cultivation restrictions; more positive measures, such as infrastructural development to boost padi production, were virtually unknown. The Indian harvest failure of 1918 diverted Burmese exports from the Malayan market, resulting in the diminution and increasing cost of rice supplies. With serious anxiety setting in over the rice problem, the colonial administration introduced rice controls in mid-1919, which lasted until February 1921. Faced with mounting frustration among the rice-consuming masses, the government was compelled to subsidize the price of rice, selling below cost.[12] In fact, this was a subsidy to employers, who would otherwise have had to increase wages or lose their workers. The estimated cost of the subsidy programme for the Federated Malay States, Straits Settlements, and Johore amounted to about 39 million dollars. Local padi production was given a boost by the rice price increase; new padi cultivators were attracted and old ones drawn back into the fold. The colonial administration—encouraged and elated by what initially appeared to be a successful campaign—was soon faced with the same old problem. When cheap rice imports resumed in 1922, a steady shrinkage of padi area to pre-1918 levels began, and with it, a decline in local rice production. The continued lack of government investments in rice production ensured that productivity in padi cultivation remained unchanged.

In the early 1920s, the declining rubber price moved the colonial administration to place severe constraints on peasant rubber production. Ostensibly to boost padi production and to raise the market price of rubber, the Stevenson Restriction Scheme from 1922 to 1928 served to prop up the rubber plantation sector, and most certainly constituted a serious attack on peasant rubber production. While the 'Restriction forced many Malay smallholders into rice production' (Goldman, 1974: 27), this phenomenon was largely temporary.

From 1920 to 1925, local rice production satisfied 38 per cent of total consumption on the average, but for the remainder of the decade declined to 28 per cent (Goldman, 1974: 29). As the price of rubber rose relative to that of rice, padi output declined correspondingly.

The failure of government efforts to promote padi cultivation cannot be whitewashed as administrative ignorance; various reports by government departments indicate clear recognition of some of the problems faced by rice producers.[13] However, in sharp contrast to its enthusiastic support for British investments, colonial efforts to promote peasant padi cultivation were generally weak, badly organized, understaffed, and poorly financed. The failure to provide effective support for padi production, coupled with the relative attraction of other agricultural activities, especially rubber and coconut, contributed to the declining interest in padi after 1922 despite the restriction policy.

While rice consumption continued to increase over the 1920s (by 31 per cent between 1920-4 and 1925-9) rice production did not expand significantly. Although no clear trend in rice production in the Federated Malay States can be discerned, production in the Unfederated Malay States actually declined slightly (Goldman, 1974: 29-30). Forced to respond to a continuing crisis situation, the colonial authorities established the Rice Cultivation Committee during the Depression in 1930. Lim Teck Ghee has also argued that the Committee Report's recommendations in 1931 to promote padi cultivation in Malaya were based on three erroneous and self-serving premises: first, that it was better for peasants to cultivate food crops, rather than cash crops, because this would minimize vulnerability to the vicissitudes of the world market; second, that rice exports by other countries would decline in the future; and third, that the Malayan environment was suited to padi cultivation. It was stated earlier that equatorial yields per acre tend to be lower than those obtainable in tropical and sub-tropical latitudes. The anticipated decline in rice exports was disproved by subsequent developments, and, as will be shown, even when the nadir of world rubber prices was reached, rubber still offered higher yearly incomes per acre compared to padi.

The Committee Report's major recommendation for promoting rice production was the establishment of drainage and irrigation facilities. To this end, the Drainage and Irrigation Department was set up, with jurisdiction only in the Federated Malay States and the Straits Settlements. The DID played a key role in consolidating existing padi production.[14] The new schemes introduced also resulted in a shift in padi production centres in the Federated Malay States, from traditional Malay river valley settlements to the coastal plains peopled mainly by immigrant Malays. By 1939, the DID had provided some degree of water control to 68 per cent of the padi area in the Federated Malay States and the Straits Settlements (Goldman, 1974: 258). These efforts had little effect in increasing padi production; instead, the DID's main contribution was to take over the farmers' own efforts at constructing and maintaining basic irrigation facilities.[15] But even though yields increased with the provision of drainage and irrigation, this was offset by constant or declining acreages elsewhere in the Federated Malay States (Goldman, 1974: 32). The moderate increase in padi production during the 1930s is primarily attributable to the substantial expansion of padi acreage in Kedah and Kelantan, two states outside DID jurisdiction then.

In 1933, a duty on imported rice was imposed in the Federated Malay States to obtain revenue for funding efforts to promote padi production, mainly through extension of drainage and irrigation facilities. Earlier attempts to introduce the duty had met with resistance 'on the ground that it would increase the cost of living and result in undesirable social repercussions' (Lim Teck Ghee, 1971: 223). Coming on top of the effects of the Depression, the tax was an added source of financial hardship for the masses, who spent an estimated 'one-third of their income on the purchase of rice' (Lim Teck Ghee, 1971: 233). Thus, the colonial administration provided price support to encourage padi production and funded padi development schemes at the expense of the non-padi growing consumer.

At the end of World War II, Malaya was brought under a single central administration for the first time under British rule. The northern States had long been the major rice-producers in the peninsula. However, in the pre-war administrative set-up, they did not come under the jurisdiction of the DID because they were not part of the Straits Settlements and the Federated Malay States. Instead, Perak and Selangor, which were less suited ecologically to wet padi cultivation, had received most drainage and irrigation facilities in the pre-war years. Pre-war production levels in British Malaya never exceeded the 1932 high of 42 per cent, averaging 34 per cent of total national consumption between 1926 and 1940. This percentage has risen steadily in the post-war years, with significant increases after 1950 (Lim Chong-Yah, 1967: 145; Goldman, 1975: 269).[16]

Colonial concern with padi production led to the formation of a Rice Production Committee in the early 1950s 'to consider ways and means whereby the acreage planted under padi in the Federation and the yield per acre can be materially increased within the next three years' (quoted in Goldman, 1975: 261). Among its numerous recommendations, the Committee's 1953 Report emphasized double-cropping as a way to increase padi production—though, significantly, it did not urge an expansion of drainage and irrigation facilities. However, in the Committee's subsequent Final Report in 1956, drainage and irrigation facilities were viewed as crucial for efforts to promote double-cropping. The rice price support policy which had emerged before the war received guarded reaffirmation in the 1956 Report. The origins of post-colonial padi production policy were thus already defined before 1957, the year of independence.[17]

Peasant Rubber Production and the Colonial State

To the peasantry, the expansion of rubber planting by capitalist interests in Malaya was not without significance.[18] So significant was peasant entry into rubber production at the end of the first decade of the century that it soon became the single most widely cultivated crop for the Malayan peasantry. Today, at least 400,000 families—and possibly over 600,000 (Risda, 1983)—are considered to be in the rubber smallholding sector, compared to about 300,000 padi farmers. It would be difficult to explain this remarkable shift into rubber cultivation as anything but a rational peasant response to new opportunities emerging from their integration into the world market. The fate of peasant rubber cultivation, especially during the colonial period, is equally mystifying, unless the conflicting interests involved in natural rubber production in Malaya are considered.[19]

The colonial administration's official criteria for distinguishing between smallholding and plantation cultivation is not very useful analytically (George Lee, 1973). All rubber holdings of less than 100 acres were categorized as smallholdings while those over 100 acres qualified as plantations. The smallholding category therefore lumped together peasant family holdings and those of small employers, although this involved different relations of production. Although relations of production are not determined solely by acreage under cultivation, peasant holdings (not employing wage labour) generally do not exceed the maximum size manageable solely with family labour—i.e. probably about 25 acres. According to statistics from the immediate post-war period, there were 345,000 smallholdings below 25 acres in size and over 7,000 smallholdings above 25 acres; a total of 101 million acres and 285,000 acres respectively (Benham, 1961: 287).

Why did the colonial authorities use the 100-acre cut-off in its categorization? While this intriguing question needs further investigation, the effect of this distinction was to subject all cultivation in the smallholding category to the various kinds of discrimination which have marked the history of rubber cultivation in Malaya. In terms of class contention, it would be useful to point out that capitalist smallholdings were generally owned by non-Europeans who tended to have less political influence compared to their larger more powerful counterparts. Although marred by the lack of a more analytical distinction between peasant and capitalist smallholdings, the literature on the development of the smallholding sector of the rubber industry is nonetheless useful. (And in so far as the distinction corresponds to that upon which the government developed its policies and researchers have conducted their studies, it will have to be used in the discussion that follows.)

Significant peasant participation in rubber cultivation began from 1909, four years after rubber first became a plantation crop on a large scale in Malaya (Lim Teck Ghee, 1971: 88). In retrospect, it is easy to see why peasants took to rubber in the circumstances prevailing then.[20] Although rubber incomes were very vulnerable to the price fluctuations of the world market, the cash returns were consistently more attractive than those from padi and other crops.[21] For a given cultivated area, a peasant could purchase more rice by producing and selling rubber than by growing padi himself. Better prospects from rubber prevailed even when rubber market prices reached their lowest in 1932.[22] This point has been made by various authors (e.g. Lim Chong-Yah, 1967: 339, Appendix 6.1), and is clearly illustrated by Table 3.1. The data from 1922 to 1930 compare cash returns from padi and rubber production for the Krian district in Perak.[23] A further difference in favour of rubber was that the cost of padi cultivation 'varied between $6–$14, while that of rubber was estimated at $3–$6' (Lim Teck

TABLE 3.1

Comparison of Cash Returns from Rubber Growing and Padi Cultivation in Krian (1922-1939) and Malaya (1929-1933)[1]

Year	Average Yield of Padi/Acre (gantang)	Price/Gantang (cents)	Gross Proceeds from Padi ($/acre)	Average Yield of Rubber[2] (lb./mature acre)	Price/lb. (cents)	Gross Proceeds from Rubber ($/acre)	Difference in Favour of Rubber[3] ($)
1922	260	13	33.80	400	25	90.00	56.20
1923	270	13	35.10	200	47	94.00	58.90
1924	260	13	33.80	200	43	86.00	52.20
1925	310	13	40.30	200	109	218.00	177.70
1926	260	13	33.80	200	75	150.00	116.20
1927	190	13	24.70	200	59	118.00	93.30
1928	230	13	29.90	200	33	66.00	36.10
1929	160 [202]	14	20.40 [28]	485	32 [30.5]	155.20 [150]	134.80 [122]
1930	200 [180]	13	26.00 [23]	460	16 [16.8]	73.60 [77]	47.60 [54]
1931	260 [248]	8	20.80 [20]	445	8 [8.0]	35.60 [36]	14.80 [16]
1932	270 [272]	7.5	20.25 [20]	385	6 [6.0]	23.10 [23]	2.85 [3]
1933	290 [260]	6.7	19.43 [17]	465	7 [8.7]	32.55 [40]	13.12 [23]
1934	280	6	16.80	330	17	56.10	36.50
1935	390	8	31.20	240	17	40.80	13.50
1936	350	8	28.00	230	24	55.20	30.70
1937	360	8	28.80	330	28	92.40	67.20
1938	310	9	27.90	200	21	42.00	21.30
1939	320	9	28.80	200	28	56.00	33.60

Sources: Lim Teck Ghee (1971: 298); Bauer (1961a: 191, Table 10; 196, Table 11).

[1]The data presented here are mainly taken from Lim Teck Ghee's work which uses padi yields in Krian for comparative purposes. Figures in parentheses were provided by Bauer based on national estimates. There are several discrepancies and inconsistencies embodied in their data which are reproduced here without comment.

[2]Rubber yields for 1922-8, the duration of the Stevenson Scheme, have been estimated at half that of plantations. Yields for 1929-39 (except for 1938 where a rough estimate was used) were obtained from Bauer (1961c).

[3]The difference in favour of rubber is greater if net proceeds are taken into account as the cost of rice production varied between $6 and $14, while that of rubber was estimated to be lower at $3-$6.

Ghee, 1971: 298). Compared to the available alternatives, especially padi, rubber cultivation had other attractions as well.[24] In this context, the rationality behind peasant preference for rubber, which has persisted despite various government propaganda efforts, is hardly bewildering.

The drift of peasants into rubber cultivation was also guided by practical and technological considerations. Rubber trees did not require substantial capital investment nor did they require a vigilant or taxing commitment of labour. In the context of a rapidly monetizing economy, the growth of peasant rubber cultivation is not surprising (Wharton, 1963; George Lee, 1973). However, in the prevailing conditions, peasant participation in rubber cultivation was a problematic undertaking.[25] There had been a time lag of about four to five years between the time the rubber estates began expanding on a large scale, and the time rubber cultivation really caught on with the peasantry. Peasants previously involved in coffee production had had bitter experiences when coffee prices had plunged and were therefore somewhat wary of cash-cropping. Also, time—i.e. loss of income—and a cash outlay were needed since rubber trees are ready for tapping only after about five years. Those already involved in cultivating other crops also needed time and resources to switch. The increase in peasant employment on estates, as well as the disruptive impact of increased land transactions, stimulated by the rubber boom must have also slowed down peasant adoption of rubber. But the most important disincentive of all was probably the attitude and policies of the colonial state.

The colonial administration's discouragement of peasant rubber cultivation operated on two main fronts: a land alienation policy biased in favour of capitalist plantation rubber cultivation and against peasants; and a similar bias in government provision of facilities for plantation interests at the expense of the peasant sector.

In the early days of colonial rule, government policy sought to encourage sedentary agriculture and to eliminate shifting cultivation, promoting both capitalist as well as peasant agriculture, with a bias for the former. As this policy bore fruit, however, administrative encouragement of peasant agriculture diminished except in so far as it was seen to serve prevailing current colonial interests, e.g. as with rice policy. Land considered superior or more desirable— for reasons of soil quality, access to transportation, etc., 'which might be usefully preserved for scientific planting'—was not alienated to peasants, but reserved for capitalist interests. Among capitalists, British interests were obviously favoured over others (Lim Teck Ghee, 1971: 111, 112; Voon, 1976). Administrative discrimination in land matters showed its claws in various other manifestations as well. For instance, as peasants took to rubber planting, the colonial government began to strictly enforce cultivation conditions on land—usually meaning that rubber was disallowed.[26] To further discourage peasant rubber cultivation, the colonial government imposed a discriminatory tax system by which rubber land was liable to a higher rate than land which bore the 'no rubber' condition.

The colonial government's provision of infrastructural and other facilities—as with the earlier development of public works in favour of tin-mining interests—was biased in favour of the big rubber estates: roads, drainage systems, and other public works were constructed; research efforts and other government measures to promote rubber cultivation were similarly in line with the interests of capital; credit facilities (which could have played an important role in the development of peasant rubber cultivation) were organized by the colonial government to serve capitalist interests;[27] and large sums were made available for estate development while peasant credit needs were ignored.[28]

The 1922 Stevenson Restriction Scheme

The role of the colonial state in favouring plantation capitalists over rubber-cultivating peasants was a recurrent manifestation of dominant class interests, especially prior to the Japanese Occupation. In a general sense, the Stevenson Restriction Scheme was yet another such manifestation; more particularly, it exemplified the class conflict inherent in Malayan rubber production, and the role of the colonial state in determining the direction of class contention.

It is interesting to note that two of the more authoritative studies of Malayan agricultural development stop at the Stevenson Restriction Scheme of 1922 (Jackson, 1967; Drabble, 1973). Fortunately, however, the work of Lim Teck Ghee (1974, 1977) offers useful insights into the longer-term implications of the scheme for the peasantry, clearly identifying the contending interests at stake, in examining how the scheme was mooted and operated, and demonstrating how the restriction policy served the interests of estate owners at the expense of the peasantry.

Soon after the end of World War I, there was a certain euphoria in the world rubber market as prices soared. In 1919, Malayan rubber production rose to 204,000 tons and until 1922, it consistently accounted for over half of world natural rubber production. However, apprehension spread as rubber prices plunged steadily after 1920; estate interests panicked, urging restrictions on rubber production as an immediate solution to the depressing price situation. Estate-owning capitalists had good reason to be alarmed by these circumstances; compared to peasant farmers, their reliance on an immigrant wage labour force and a relatively higher proportion of fixed production costs rendered plantation cultivation far less flexible in coping with unstable price conditions. The euphoria of the earlier years of the rubber boom had led to rash and excessive investments which subsequently required government protection, e.g. through a restriction policy. In contrast, peasant rubber holdings were relatively more flexible in organizational terms since they relied on family labour, involved minimal fixed investments, and often included the cultivation of other crops as well. Though not unaffected by price vicissitudes, peasants were better able to take the rubber slump in their stride.

Several factors, generated by class contention at the global level, influenced the Stevenson Committee's report: British investors perceived an imminent take-over of the rubber industry by the Americans; it was feared that the sterling area's balance-of-payments position would be threatened by a decline in rubber's contribution. Hence, British investors in the rubber industry—numbering over a quarter of a million—were naturally upset over rubber market conditions and successfully pressed for colonial state intervention on their behalf.

It comes as no surprise then, as Swettenham—a former colonial official who subsequently became deeply involved in the rubber industry—noted, 'if it had not been for the Rubber Growers Association there would have been no restriction' (quoted in Lim Teck Ghee, 1974: 107). The Stevenson Committee was appointed by the British Colonial Office to examine the condition of the rubber industry and market. Ignoring the Dutch refusal to participate (which ran contrary to a previously taken stance), the Stevenson Committee recommended the unilateral adoption of restriction by Malaya and Ceylon, Britain's two most important rubber-producing colonies. The restriction scheme, effected in November 1922, was finally terminated six years later in October 1928.

The basic principle of the restriction scheme was to limit rubber output in response to and in anticipation of rubber price trends. The actual operations of the Scheme reveal its class bias: to perpetuate the dominance of capitalist estate interests. Rubber holdings with production records (i.e. mainly estates) had quotas allocated on the basis of their production performance during a common base year. Those without records—and this meant the majority of peasant cultivators—received allocations on the basis of a Duncan scale.[29] The resulting discrimination against the peasantry caused considerable hardship and discontent, culminating in 'what could have been the first peasant rebellion in modern Malaya' (Lim Teck Ghee, 1974: 111). To avert this, a hastily appointed committee admitted that peasants had got a 'raw deal' under the restriction scheme.[30] Peasant allocations were revised upwards, seemingly brought on par with the quotas for the estates. Though this was illusory, it served to defuse the peasant threat.

A government-conducted agricultural survey used by this committee—set up in response to peasant dissatisfaction with the restriction scheme's initial allocations—'found that yields from smallholdings sampled varied between a low of 733 pounds to a high of 1,200 pounds per acre per annum' (Lim Teck Ghee, 1974: 112). Average annual yields per acre found by other studies for peasant holdings varied between 599 lb. and 1,200 lb. The higher yields from peasant holdings were neither extraordinary nor inexplicable; peasant land tended to be more tree-dense—in other words, planted more intensively. Optimum planting densities for rubber production differed between smallholdings and estates (Bauer, 1946b). Furthermore, tapping on peasant holdings tended to be more frequent, usually daily.

Despite the higher peasant yields, it was the estate sector that was favoured by the restriction scheme.[31] A veneer of legitimacy for the outright promotion of plantation interests under the Stevenson Restriction Scheme was created by under-assessment of peasant production and over-assessment of estate production.[32] Lim Teck Ghee (1974: 114-15) has demonstrated the under-assessment by comparing rubber acreages in the plantation and peasant sectors, and contrasting these with their production allocations—since average smallholder production per unit area then was at least 50 per cent above the estate sector, the quantitative significance of under-assessment for the peasantry acquires tremendous proportions. After the termination of the restriction scheme towards the end of 1928, rubber exports in 1929 amounted to 261,352 tons, registering an increase of more than 86,000 tons or about 50 per cent over the previous year. Since the estates were already producing at full capacity by the time the restriction scheme came to an end, peasant production must have accounted for most of the increase. This only confirms the lengths to which the discriminatory obstacles to peasant production were carried.[33]

The class bias against peasant interests in the operation of the Scheme extended to matters other than production quotas, perhaps the most important of which was the colonial government's land alienation policy. Between 1926 and 1930, only about 55,000 acres of land were granted to peasant applicants; in the same period, estates were granted 173,927 acres. Meanwhile, a 1921 census of rubber areas in the Federated Malay States revealed that only 761,234 acres or about 69 per cent of a total of 1,096,326 acres of estate land alienated for rubber had been planted; the corresponding figures for the smallholding sector was 405,794 acres or about 89 per cent. Hence, restrictions on land alienation ensured that peasants had less unplanted land available in reserve. Furthermore, conniving with the interests benefiting from the Scheme, the colonial administration called on members of local planter associations to conduct the field inspections for the assessment of quotas for rubber smallholders. Considering their vested interests in the matter, the partiality of these assessors is self-evident. The peasants were left with the largely empty 'right of appeal' to the *mukim* (sub-district) Smallholder Inspection Committee whose membership was dominated by colonial officials and estate representatives.

The Stevenson Restriction Scheme did succeed in raising the rubber price, though unilateral British actions towards this end resulted in a significant increase in the Netherlands East Indies' share of world rubber production. Producing only 102,000 tons—or about a quarter of world production—in 1922, when Malaya was producing 212,000 of a world total of 403,000 tons, the Dutch colony had increased production to the Malayan level by 1927, when both colonies produced 232,000 tons each out of a world total of 610,000 tons. While the rubber-cultivating peasantry shared the benefits of price increases attributable to the restriction policy, they were also the ones who bore the main, if not entire, brunt of restriction.

The 1934 International Rubber Regulation Scheme

Succeeding government policies, discriminating against the rubber-growing peasantry, continued after 1928, with no letting up in administrative propaganda to discourage peasants from rubber cultivation. Nevertheless, there was an upswing in smallholding rubber production after the termination of the Stevenson Restriction Scheme. Even during the Great Depression, normal tapping among rubber smallholders generally continued despite the low prices, and rarely did peasants abandon their rubber land. There is considerable evidence of the 'exceptional flexibility of peasant rubber producers', although as Table 3.2 shows, rubber prices were among the most volatile in the world market (Lim Teck Ghee, 1971: 227; Bauer, 1948a).

TABLE 3.2

Variations in Raw Material Prices

	Average Annual Variation, 1921–38 (%)	Lowest Price in 1921–38 as Percentage of Highest Price
Wool	24	25
Copper	26	27
Tin	28	31
Cotton	31	17
Rubber	47	3
Wheat	30	29

Source: Bauer (1961a: 186, Table 1).

The general impression created about smallholdings (whether or not actually believed by the government and the plantation propagandists involved) was that they were poorly kept, the source of disease, and subject to short-sighted tapping methods which would eventually ensure their own ruin. Only after decades of successful peasant agricultural practice did the Rubber Research Institute (RRI) revise its own position; on root diseases, for instance, the RRI admitted 'that clean weeding [then practised primarily on estates, but rarely on smallholdings] contributed to rather than controlled the spread of the major root disease, *Fomes Lignosus*' (McHale, 1965). Other common allegations—e.g. about smallholdings being the source of disease—have also been invalidated by findings of government commissions.

On the other hand, administrative efforts to support peasant agriculture were few, and mostly to promote padi cultivation by peasants. Drainage and irrigation services for peasant holdings were virtually non-existent; agricultural extension services for rubber-growing peasants were severely under-staffed. Roads and other communications were built to serve estates and mines; any benefits to peasants were mainly incidental, rather than by design. In a controversial report,[34] Bauer (1948b) accused the RRI of serving estate interests and working against the interests of smallholders. A 1930 survey by the RRI—available in 1932, but released only in 1934—presented evidence refuting many of the prevailing myths which had been the basis for existing policies[35] (Lim Teck Ghee, 1971: 228). It found, for example, that peasants were not tapping ruthlessly so that bark replacement could not keep up with bark consumption, as had been alleged; other contents of the report were equally sobering about peasant production.

However, publication of the report did not affect the prevailing policies detrimental to smallholder rubber cultivation and thus served estate interests. Though stemming from a different context, the 1934 International Rubber Regulation Scheme continued the Stevenson Scheme's attack on the rubber-growing peasantry. Unlike the earlier Scheme, the 1934 arrangement was not a unilateral one involving only the British Empire, but also included the Netherlands East Indies, thus covering almost all natural rubber production in the world at the time. This and other differences do not detract from the class bias involved in both schemes to raise the world market price for natural rubber.

Being producers of the same commodity, the smallholders also benefited from the price rise sought by estate owners, but most certainly, the schemes were not formulated or executed with their welfare in mind. The undeclared objective of the schemes, probably too politically unpalatable to be openly stated, was the advancement of plantation interests in the face of unstable world prices and the competitive local smallholding sector.[36]

As with the Stevenson Scheme, various aspects of the operation of the 1934 regulation served to under-assess smallholding production. The benefits of restriction were once again very unevenly divided to the advantage of plantations against smallholdings (Bauer, 1948a, 1961c, 1961d). Since the effect of the 1934 regulation on the smallholding sector was very much a repeat of the 1922 Stevenson Restriction Scheme, it needs only brief review.

One may begin noting that the International Rubber Regulation Scheme began in May 1934, two years after the nadir in rubber prices in 1932, by which time rubber prices were on their way up after the Great Depression.[37] Bauer's (1948a) book has detailed how the organization, guide-lines and structure of the 1934 scheme consistently under-assessed the productive capacity of rubber smallholdings: 'The losses inflicted on smallholders through underassessment exceeded 10 million pounds sterling under the International Rubber Regulation Scheme and 30 million pounds sterling under the Stevenson Restriction Scheme' (Bauer, 1948b: 88). The success of these schemes in favouring estate interests against the peasantry in the assessment of production quotas is clear from Tables 3.3 and 3.4. Bauer argued that smallholders should have received at least 45 per cent of the total Malayan quota instead of the 38 per cent which they were allocated.

TABLE 3.3

Annual Output of Rubber per Mature Acre of Malayan
Estates and Smallholdings, 1930–1940
(lb. to the nearest 5 lb.)

Year	Estates	Smallholdings	Output of Smallholdings as Percentage of Output of Estates
1930	380	460	118 (121)[1]
1931	375	445	119
1932	365	385	106 (105)[1]
1933	355	465	131
1934	(Regulation introduced during the year)		
1935	295	240	81
1936	275	230	84
1937	375	330	88
1938	290	200	69
1939	290	200	69
1940	410	370	90

Source: Bauer (1948a: 97, Table 3).
[1]The percentages in brackets are those derived from calculations using Bauer's figures, which differ from his own percentages.

TABLE 3.4

Peninsular Malaysia: Rubber Estate and Smallholding Acreage and Production, 1922-1982

Year	Planted Acreage ('000 acres)			Production ('000 tons)			Estates	
	Estate	Smallholding	Total	Estate	Smallholding	Total	Percentage of Total Acreage	Percentage of Total Production
1922	1,410	918	2,328			212.4	61	n.a.
1923	1,432	939	2,371			183.8	60	n.a.
1924	1,455	952	2,407			152.3	60	n.a.
1925	1,480	975	2,455			210.0	60	n.a.
1926	1,523	992	2,600			286.0	59	n.a.
1927	1,624	976	2,710			242.0	60	n.a.
1928	1,696	1,014	2,944			299.0	58	n.a.
1929	1,820	1,124	2,971	245	212	457.0	61	54
1930	1,876	1,173	3,049	237	215	452.0	62	52
1931	1,934	1,218	3,152	239.4	195.5	434.9	61	55
1932	1,939	1,276	3,215	240.1	177.0	417.1	60	58
1933	1,947	1,261	3,208	241.0	218.8	459.8	61	52
1934	2,010	1,272	3,282	262.4	217.0	479.4	61	55
1935	2,016	1,163	3,179	242.3	134.5	376.8	63	64
1936	2,015	1,205	3,220	232.6	130.9	363.9	63	64
1937	2,021	1,268	3,289	313.9	187.9	501.1	61	63
1938	2,026	1,254	3,280	245.7	113.8	359.5	62	68
1939	2,100	1,326	3,426	244.4	115.7	360.1	61	68
1940	2,113	1,351	3,464	333.6	213.6	547.2	61	61
1946	1,896	1,500	3,396	173.5	229.7	403.2	56	43

1947	1,934	1,500	3,434	359.9	285.3	645.2	56	56
1948	1,953	1,500	3,453	402.9	294.1	697.0	57	58
1949	1,970	1,500	3,470	400.0	270.3	670.3	57	60
1950	1,964	1,500	3,464	375.9	316.7	692.6	57	54
1951	1,964	1,500	3,464	328.0	275.9	603.9	57	54
1952	1,997	1,500	3,497	341.1	241.5	582.6	57	59
1953	2,030	1,500	3,530	341.1	231.7	572.8	58	60
1954	2,018	1,500	3,518	344.9	240.2	585.1	57	59
1955	2,015	1,500	3,515	351.8	285.3	637.1	57	55
1956	2,008	1,500	3,508	350.8	273.4	624.2	57	56
1957	2,011	1,500	3,511	367.9	268.0	635.9	57	58
1958	1,981	1,500	3,481	389.4	271.5	660.9	57	59
1959	1,942	1,500	3,442	407.2	288.3	695.5	56	59
1960	1,934.5	1,892.0	3,826.5	413.2	292.8	706.0	51	59
1961	1,937.4	1,968.0	3,905.4	428.5	306.1	734.6	50	58
1962	1,926.5	2,064.0	3,990.5	438.3	311.2	749.5	48	58
1963	1,919.4	2,145.0	4,064.4	458.3	328.4	786.7	47	58
1964	1,893.2	2,411.0	4,304.2	476.8	314.4	791.2	44	60
1965	1,859.0	2,525.0	4,384.0	490.9	347.6	838.5	42	59
1966	1,813.3	2,571.0	4,384.3	513.9	386.4	900.3	41	57
1967	1,746.4	2,602.6	4,349.0	525.8	397.5	923.3	40	57
1968	1,675.8	2,608.0	4,283.8	563.0	471.7	1,034.7	39	54
1969	1,638.8	2,636.7	4,275.5	593.4	587.1	1,180.5	38	50
1970	1,597.6	2,662.0	4,259.0	611.2	585.3	1,196.5	38	51
1971	1,560.7	2,684.0	4,244.7	651.1	599.3	1,250.4	37	52
1972	1,508.0	2,698.3	4,206.3	648.9	589.4	1,238.3	36	52
1973	1,456.5	2,729.3	4,185.8	663.0	779.0	1,442.0	35	46

(continued)

TABLE 3.4 (continued)

Year	Planted Acreage ('000 acres)			Production ('000 tons)			Estates	
	Estate	Smallholding	Total	Estate	Smallholding	Total	Percentage of Total Acreage	Percentage of Total Production
1974	1,418.9	2,761.7	4,180.6	649.1	788.3	1,437.4	34	45
1975	1,392.0	2,796.3	4,188.3	571.6	830.6	1,376.2	33	42
1976	1,367.3	2,794.1	4,161.4	641.4	870.6	1,512.0	33	42
1977	1,331.7	2,830.2	4,161.9	617.7	869.9	1,487.6	32	42
1978	1,292.9	2,905.3	4,198.2	608.2	874.0	1,482.2	31	41
1979	1,255.6	2,953.2	4,208.8	597.7	875.9	1,473.6	30	41
1980	1,214.8	2,979.4	4,194.2	577.5	863.3	1,440.8	29	40
1981	1,183.7	3,006.3	4,190.0	565.2	868.4	1,433.6	28	39
1982	1,169.3	3,006.3	4,202.6	567.6	887.9	1,455.5	28	39
1983	1,146.6	3,060.2	4,206.8	551.3	946.3	1,497.6	27	37

Sources: 1906–40: Lim Chong-Yah (1967: 328–9, Appendix 4.3); 1946–83: Department Statistics, Rubber Statistics Handbook (various years).

Notes: 1. Figures for 1922–40 include Singapore.

2. There are several discrepancies and inconsistencies in the data for 1926–9 which are reproduced here without comment.

3. Data for 1941–5 were not available.

4. No accurate figures of smallholding acreages are available for post-war years. The figure quoted, 1½ million acres, is an estimate only.

5. Estimates of smallholding acreage for 1960–4 are obtained from RRI Publication, A Revised Forecast of Malayan Rubber Production 1963–70 by Ir. E. C. Paardekooper.

6. Figures for 1982–3 are preliminary and subject to revision.

New Planting, Replanting, and Class Interests

Bauer[38] (1948a, 1948b, 1961e) has contended—and even his critics, e.g. Benham (1961: 290), have yet to disagree fundamentally—that another aspect of colonial policy[39] even more disastrous for the rubber-growing peasantry comprised the planting provisions of the colonial government. Government curbs on new planting were not limited to the 1934 scheme period, but dated from the days of the Stevenson Scheme and continued long thereafter.[40] While new planting was not legally prohibited for very long, it was effectively limited by the government's land alienation policy. The limitations on land use for rubber cultivation were therefore not due to a natural scarcity of resources, but to policies of the colonial state.[41]

With new planting effectively curbed, replanting was encouraged by the colonial government. This was promoted by means of fiscal policy, supported by government pressure and propaganda. Replanting costs were tax-deductible and partly 'subsidized' by a government-organized replanting cess (Bauer, 1961e: 302). But these 'subsidies' during colonial times were rarely enough for the poorly financed peasant even to contemplate replanting. The difficulties faced by the peasant rubber cultivator in replanting are considerable (George Lee, 1973: 452). First, the labour requirements involved in cutting, clearing, planting, fencing, soil conservation, and lalang (*Imperata cylindrica*) clearing are formidable, especially for the latter two activities if previously neglected. Secondly, the loss of income for at least five years before the trees are mature enough for tapping is, for the peasant smallholder who does not have much by way of savings or alternative sources of income, an important disincentive to replanting. Thirdly, the economies of scale involved in replanting especially discourage peasants who have small rubber holdings since it is not feasible to replant only part of a small farm at a time. There are also technical difficulties associated with small-scale replanting, such as shading and root competition from neighbouring trees.

The legislation restricting new rubber planting was repealed in 1947, and it was another five years before the colonial government began an 'ambitious' replanting programme for both smallholdings and estates in 1952 (Lim Chong-Yah, 1967: 335, Appendix 4.9). This came about because of at least three factors (George Lee, 1973: 453). First: it became obvious that, without replanting, the continued survival of the rubber growing peasantry was threatened. Second: the replacement of low-cost smallholder production by more expensive estate production would raise prices for consumers—especially for rubber users in the industrial West. Third: the nationalist sentiments fanned by World War II made it unwise for the British colonial administration to continue to disregard peasant interests at the height of waging a counter-insurgency campaign.

The supremacy of colonial interests was successively undermined in the post-war period by various developments—the challenge posed by synthetic rubber production, the pressure mounted by metropolitan industrial capitalist interests for lower rubber prices, the low rubber market prices before the Korean War boom, the threat to colonial authority raised by post-war nationalism, the increasing political assertiveness of the Malayan peasantry,

and the imminent demise of the colonial order—all of which seriously served
to erode business confidence in British Malaya. These post-war circumstances
contributed to a trend towards the subdivision of the largely European-owned
rubber plantations, resulting primarily in the organization of smaller locally
owned capitalist estates (see Aziz, 1963; Mamajiwala, 1963). Between 1947 and
1962, for instance, the planted acreage under smallholdings rose by 481,000
acres (see Table 3.4), with newly planted smallholding acreage accounting for
267,000 acres (Lim Chong-Yah, 1967: 335, Appendix 4.9), suggesting that the
remaining 214,000 acres had previously been estate land. The subdivision of
estates did not, however, result in any substantial expansion of small peasant
holdings.[42] However, smallholding acreage expanded, especially after 1955,
when new rubber planting began to get into full swing as government-
sponsored land development schemes began to increase the area under rubber
smallholdings.

The Post-colonial State and Rubber Smallholders

The post-colonial state's continued bias in favour of the interests of big capital
and against the peasantry is dramatically illustrated by the nature and operation
of the research and replanting cesses exacted against all rubber exported.
Rubber research activities were historically determined primarily by estate
interests (Bauer, 1948; Lim Teck Ghee, 1971; Barlow, 1978), though an interest
in smallholder concerns has been growing since the 1950s as a result of the
insurgency's attempts to root itself among the peasantry. Nonetheless, the
plantation sector is generally better placed and organized than the smallholders
to innovate and improve production and processing techniques or otherwise
gain from government-organized research activity.

The development of higher-yielding clones should, of course, benefit all
those who replant. However, unlike the plantation sector which has not only
replanted completely, but has also extensively undertaken second and even
third replantings, until the end of 1977, only 536 156 or 46.3 per cent of the
1 158 451 hectares of rubber smallholding land, or 66.9 per cent, i.e. about two-
thirds, of the 801 710 hectares that were eligible, involving 258,758 rubber
smallholders, had been replanted. Of those replanted by late 1977, only 27,623
or 10.7 per cent had replanted more than once (Gibbons et al., 1983: Tables 4.1
and 4.2). Furthermore, there have been numerous allegations of malpractices
in the replanting of smallholdings undertaken under the auspices of the relevant government authorities, whereas replanting in the plantation sector is
conducted by the respective estate managements themselves.

As far as the replanting cess is concerned, it is clear that since the older estates
have all replanted at least once, their contributions to the replanting cess have at
least been refunded, and they do not subsidize the smallholder sector which has
been only half replanted. The 536 156 hectares of rubber smallholding land that
had been replanted by the end of 1977 belonged to 258,758 or 52.8 per cent of
the estimated 490,460 rubber smallholders. In other words: 231,702 or 47.2 per
cent of all rubber smallholders had not replanted 622 295 hectares or 53.4 per
cent of all rubber smallholding land. Of this, 356 741 hectares were not yet due

for replanting, including the 125 546 hectares of FELDA land and the 18 780 hectares of FELCRA land operated by 21,301 FELDA settlers and 1,189 FELCRA scheme participants respectively. Hence, 265 554 hectares or 33.1 per cent of unreplanted rubber smallholding land was considered eligible for replanting by 1977. The official estimate was that more than 30 per cent of rubber smallholders had yet to replant by that year (Treasury, 1978).

Those smallholders whose overaged trees had yet to be replanted have therefore not benefited from the replanting cess despite their contributions since its inception in 1952, during the height of the Emergency and in the aftermath of the Korean War boom. Rubber smallholders have, in fact, been paying export duties and cess equivalent to a tax rate of about 30 per cent (Augustine Tan, 1965; Khoo Kay Jin, 1978); put differently, this is equivalent to the income tax rate currently payable by those in the $60,000 per annum income bracket.

The official estimate of the poverty rate among rubber smallholders for 1977—according to the *Mid-term Review of the Third Malaysia Plan*—was 198,000 or 48 per cent out of 412,600, apparently based on a poverty line of $252.36 per month in 1977 for an average family size of 5.4 (Malaysia, 1978). Another officially commissioned study—assuming the poverty line to be lower, at $225.00 per month—estimated that around 238,000 or about 48 per cent of 490,460 rubber smallholders were below the poverty line in the same year (Gibbons *et al.*, 1983). The official poverty rate for rubber smallholders, which had declined to 41.3 per cent by 1980 (Malaysia, 1981) primarily due to favourable rubber prices on the world market, rose again to 61.1 per cent in 1983 because of the fall in rubber prices in the early 1980s.

Despite government encouragement to promote substantial replanting in the smallholding sector, many poorer peasants cannot afford to bear the temporary costs of replanting[43] to attain higher productivity and incomes over the long run. In reality, replanting is most 'practicable for the smallholder who owns several lots, or who has an alternative source of income'[44] (Fisk, 1961: 22).

During 1971-7, replanting by those with a smallholding size of less than half a hectare has been disproportionately less than the proportion for all rubber smallholders, while those with smallholdings of at least 4 hectares are over-represented. More specifically, those with less than half a hectare are 20.7 per cent below the mean whereas those with at least 4 hectares are over-represented by 17.0 per cent (Gibbons *et al.*, 1983: Table 2.7). This finding suggests that the official replanting scheme not only favours the estate sector as against the smallholding sector, but is also biased in favour of larger smallholdings at the expense of smaller ones.

It has been demonstrated that the replanting cess is far from being the fund for subsidizing smallholder replanting it is often made out to be. Khoo Kay Jin (1978: 39-41) has shown that the average smallholder—even if consistently producing hypothetically low yields—receives less than his total contribution (plus interest) in the form of the so-called replanting subsidy; upward increases in the subsidy rate have apparently only kept pace with increases in yield at most. Hence, it has been advanced that the cess is far higher than is necessary to sustain replanting over an average 30-year planting cycle (Barlow, 1978). In other words, the smallholders are not beneficiaries, but rather contributors to a subsidy scheme in favour of the state and the estate sector. What purports to be a peasant-oriented replanting subsidy scheme is patently flawed, with a clear class bias—unless equity can be construed from the fact that the effective rate of taxation to which smallholder rubber producers are subject is comparable to that borne by those in the highest income-tax brackets.

The high costs of replanting, as well as the expenditure incurred by land development schemes with rubber smallholdings, have meant that heavier financing of smallholder rubber production has been required. This renders the sector less flexible than in the past, when the flexibility of smallholder rubber production—especially peasant production—was an important asset in comparison with the more highly capitalized estate sector.[45] This undoubtedly has an important bearing on the fate of rubber-growing peasants in time to come.

Summary

The main proposition that the colonial state consistently responded in the interests of capital—especially British capital—against the interests of the peasantry reflects the role of the state both as product as well as determinant of class contention. While this certainly did not mean that the peasantry was neglected, government policies toward the peasantry generally mirrored the interests of capital.

The difference in colonial policy towards the padi-growing peasantry and the rubber-growing peasantry largely reflected the different interests of capital with respect to peasant cultivation of these two crops. One of the two major prongs of colonial agricultural policy was the encouragement of increased peasant food production for consumption by the growing labour force engaged in the capitalist sector, thereby minimizing the loss of foreign exchange in payment for rice imports. Though the pro-peasant rhetoric of the British administration was strong, efforts to develop peasant food-crop cultivation were weak and poorly financed. Consequent peasant reluctance to accord with colonial designs was a source of great frustration.

Colonial legislation providing for land reservations for exclusively Malay ownership was accompanied by considerable rhetoric identifying non-Malay money-lenders and middlemen as the causes of peasant impoverishment while the administration's own encouragement of capitalist interests, e.g. in land alienation matters, was conveniently ignored. This legislation, in combination with other trends in the peasant economy, encouraged the rise of a Malay land-owning class at the expense of other Malays who were being impoverished.

The second main prong of British agricultural policy aimed to preserve export-oriented cash-crop cultivation for capitalist interests. Nevertheless, since rubber cultivation was consistently more remunerative than padi production, peasants opted to switch to rubber. Strongly backed by plantation interests, the colonial state hindered and frustrated this rationally motivated trend in a variety of ways, like prohibiting rubber cultivation on certain land.

The design and implementation of the 1922 Stevenson Restriction Scheme and the 1934 International Rubber Regulation Scheme also discriminated against peasants. Additionally, state policies regarding new planting and replanting of rubber trees not only favoured the interests of capital over the peasantry, but also wealthier peasants owning more land over poorer ones owning less.

1. Changing land-labour ratio, different rent rates, market prices, acreage yields, and per capita yields are among the factors which affect farmers' sales on the market.

2. '... the multitude of lucrative occupations in the new economic order and the flexibility of the traditional economy now enabled the Malay to reduce his level of padi cultivation and to interspace it with other occupations with more profitable results' (Lim Teck Ghee, 1976: 135).

3. For example, Goldman (1974: 16) noted that the Perak Irrigation Areas Enactment, 'the first major piece of rice land protection legislation, ... was aimed primarily at sugar cultivation in the Krian area'. Later, 'further legislation was passed to further isolate [sic] rice land from competing crops'.

4. Between 1833 and 1893, for example, the increase in wage levels kept pace with the rise in price of imported rice (Lim Teck Ghee, 1976: 139).

5. Colonial officials characterized the Malay peasants as being 'exceedingly indolent, contented and unambitious' (quoted in Lim Teck Ghee, 1976: 70).

6. See Lim Teck Ghee (1976, 1977); Bauer (1948); and George Lee (1973).

7. 'The padi cultivators of Krian were dealt another blow by the official policy that the cost of any irrigation scheme would not be shouldered by the Government alone. It was explained that "the natives are more appreciative of what is done for them by Government when they have to pay for it"' (Lim Teck Ghee, 1976: 59-60).

8. 'It had been hoped by the officials running the scheme that such a move would make the lands less attractive and discourage their sale to non-Malays. At the same time, one of the objectives behind the early moves towards a reservation policy had been the protection of the traditional padi-kampong land and from this, it must have appeared natural to insist on traditional forms of cultivation on newly alienated reservation land' (Lim Teck Ghee, 1971: 158).

9. 'A striking feature of the early reservation policy was the conspicuous lack of participation by the Malay community, the group most affected by the policy, in the making of reservations. The main force behind a reservation proposal was the District Officer...' (Lim Teck Ghee, 1971: 205).

10. Lim Teck Ghee observed that, as far as the effect on non-Malays was concerned, reservation policy:
'... did not impinge on the interests of the capitalist non-Malay elite groups who were in a position to influence policy and who had, in any case, already acquired very large areas of land. But it directly affected the growing numbers of non-Malays who were making the country their home and sought land on which to settle and earn a livelihood. In some areas, non-Malay land applicants were rejected by officers although there were no Malay applicants for the land, and reservations were wilfully created to deny them of it.... In 1928, for example, in the midst of a lot of brow beating about the protection of Malay land interests from the onslaught of Chinese intruders, the government reserved 75,000 acres of land for the Western oil palm industry. This reservation was made in all states, despite the earlier official protestations that there was very little spare land available in the west coast states, and even though oil palm had not yet been proven a successful viable economic crop' (Lim Teck Ghee, 1971: 209-10).

11. This can be seen in the case of a Malay reservation established between 1919 and 1921 which was studied forty years later by Fisk:
'Under these circumstances it must be concluded that the application of the Malay Reservations Enactment to this reservation, while preserving Malay ownership of much of the area, has not been effective as a means of promoting a sturdy, independent and relatively prosperous Malay peasantry living from the operation of its own land. On the contrary, disruptive social and economic factors are tending to produce a small number of Malay landlords renting their land ... and an

increasing body of impoverished landless Malays living within the reservation' (Fisk, 1961: 22).

12. 'The loss was less for charitable reasons than for the fact that the colonial administration felt sufficiently threatened by the spectre of hungry mobs looting rice stores and other violent consequences arising from the breakdown of rice supply, to voluntarily loosen the purse-strings to assist the population. The subsidies however, did not absorb all the increase in the rice price, and the substantial margin between the normal price and the government's selling price was borne by the masses' (Lim Teck Ghee, 1971: 131).

13. For example, the 1923 Annual Report of the Federated Malay States Department of Agriculture believed the establishment of government rice mills, the promotion of cooperative societies, and the provision of drainage and irrigation works to be necessary for the encouragement of padi cultivation (Lim Teck Ghee, 1971: 187).

14. 'It was the provision of drainage and irrigation works which was primarily responsible for the stabilization of padi area and production in the Federated Malay States throughout this period, and which prevented the decline in cultivation found in the early 20s when higher prices returned to the market for export products' (Lim Teck Ghee, 1971: 216).

15. '... if these D.I.D. figures are worked out, it will be found, contrary to expectation, that in many States, yields per acre in Government irrigated areas are lower than the corresponding yields per acre in non-irrigated areas in the same States. Yields per acre in many areas throughout the country have increased a great deal, although Government irrigation facilities have not been extended to these parts ... it seems that Government irrigation facilities have, by and large, served only a replacement function. As the 1952 Rice Production Committee observed, in the past, "... the people themselves constructed small dams and irrigation canals or ditches, which were repaired with local materials", and these functions have merely been taken over by the Government....

'Most of the D.I.D. padi land new schemes have been essentially inducements designed to attract people to the cultivation of padi, a very low-paying occupation ...' (Lim Chong-Yah, 1967: 165).

16. While there are serious discrepancies between the figures offered by these two authors, there is nevertheless no doubt about the trend towards increased national self-sufficiency in the post-war era. Although the data may be misleading for the late 1940s, when international rice control was exercised, the trend is clear from the 1950s onwards.

17. Reviewing contemporary rice policy in historical perspective, Richard Goldman has observed:
'The origins of the modern Malaysian rice policy are not to be found in Kedah drainage canal construction, but rather in the attitudes prevalent and actions taken in those western Malay States, which, between 1874-88, came under British administration' (Goldman, 1974: 8).

18. For one thing, the rubber estates required a labour force. Although most estate labour requirements were met by immigration, the new opportunities also attracted many peasants. Job options offered by expansion of estate rubber cultivation were relatively more attractive compared to the earlier opportunities arising from the expansion of capitalist enterprise in mining, agriculture, and urban commerce. Besides coming at a time when peasants were beginning to be impoverished under the colonial impact, the nature of estate labour requirements allowed many peasants to engage in plantation work on a part-time basis without uprooting themselves completely from their peasant environment. The employment of this cheap and convenient supply of labour, which did not at the same time totally transform the peasantry, easily won the approval of the colonial state and the capitalist plantation owners.

Colonial land legislation and other economic changes transformed land into a commodity which could be traded in the market. However, the continued availability of state land for private alienation minimized land transactions. Except where and when capitalist miners sought access to mineral deposits, peasant land was not in particularly great demand. However, with the rubber boom at the turn of the century, land transactions increased tremendously. Land was purchased for cultivation as well as speculative purposes. While some of these sales involved immigrants who had obtained land with the intention of subsequent sale (usually after clearing it), others involved settled local peasants who sold their land planted with padi and other *kampung* (village) crops (Lim Teck Ghee, 1971: 86). The legislation to establish Malay reservations, referred to earlier, was partly in response to these developments.

19. Historical accounts and other discussions of the development of the rubber industry as a

whole have tended not to give much attention to the peasant sector. The exception of this, of course, is the important work of Bauer (1948a, 1948b). Lim Teck Ghee's (1977) excellent book on the development of peasant agriculture in the Federated Malay States prior to the Japanese Occupation focuses primarily on the experience in rubber and padi. George Lee's (1973) short article on rubber cultivation as an instance of peasant commodity production has put the issue into useful analytical perspective.

20. These included the following (McHale, 1965; George Lee, 1973):

(a) Environmental conditions in Malaya were well suited to rubber cultivation. Besides the climatic conditions, the rolling foothills, not suitable for wet padi cultivation, were ideal for rubber cultivation.

(b) The abundance of land still not under cultivation. Where virgin or secondary jungle existed, no agricultural crops had to be immediately given up for rubber to be planted. Before restrictions were imposed by the colonial state, land was obtainable at very low rents and with no conditions imposed, to encourage agricultural settlement.

(c) For the peasantry, trees could be grown by reliance on the peasant family's own efforts in land clearing, planting and maintenance. Before the trees were ready for tapping, labour requirements were flexible and low, allowing time for other pursuits.

(d) Seeds and seedlings were available at low cost, especially after 1910. The main cash requirements were for the cheap instruments for tapping and latex processing, needed only after tapping begins between five and seven years after planting. Production needs were therefore low.

(e) Once the rubber trees are ready for tapping, they become a source of regular income. Unlike other crops, rubber production is not seasonal and therefore it constitutes a reliable source of income.

21. 'For example, average gross earning per acre from rubber with average yields of 450 pounds an acre in 1925 would have been over 20 times those from rice and 16 times those from coconuts. The labour inputs would also be less, even if one included a proportionate share of the six or seven unproductive years before rubber began to yield' (McHale, 1965).

22. 'On the assumptions of the Tables, Malay smallholders not too far from the principal rubber markets could, even in 1932, obtain more rice indirectly (i.e. by purchasing it with the proceeds of rubber growing) than by producing it direct, a somewhat unexpected state of affairs in the worst year of the acutest rubber slump of all time.... The figures are rough averages, and conditions would be valid for most of western and southern Malaya where smallholders were particularly dependent on rubber' (Bauer, 1961a: 196).

23. It should be noted that the Krian project completed in 1906 was the site of the first, and, for over three decades, the only, irrigation scheme for padi cultivation developed under colonial auspices. The higher yields possible there thus tend to represent more favourable padi yields than was generally the case.

24. 'Reference to prices and proceeds actually understates the advantages of rubber over rice. The former, indeed in spite of its violent price fluctuations, appears particularly well suited to the needs of the Asiatic smallholder. It is non-seasonal and thus the problem of maintaining the cultivator and his family until the harvest, a prime cause of the notorious indebtedness of the smallholder, does not arise. Again, the various items of expenditure in rice cultivation, such as the purchase of manures, of a plough, or of a draught animal, are all likely to send the smallholders to the money-lender-cum-shopkeeper. The weather risks, negligible in rubber production, are considerable in padi growing. Moreover, even during the spring of 1932, rubber was always easily saleable, and the ubiquitous Chinese dealers seemed to have been sufficiently numerous in all rubber-growing districts to ensure a fairly lively competition among buyers. This was by no means generally true for *padi* culture. Instead of toiling in the mud of a wet *padi* field sometimes for days on end, the rubber growing Malay native never had to work more than three or four hours a day, and could take off a day or even a week whenever he felt like it; rubber tapping is generally believed to be the least exacting form of work in tropical agriculture' (Bauer, 1961: 196-7).

25. 'The early history of peasant rubber cultivation is a struggle against great odds' (Lim Teck Ghee, 1971: 89).

26. The rationale for this, according to a colonial official quoted by Lim Teck Ghee (1971: 91), was most interesting. According to him, peasant rubber lands were most vulnerable to sale, presumably because of the higher incomes obtainable from such land. Therefore, to protect the

peasant from such vulnerability, the British effectively lowered the market price of peasant land by imposing the 'no-rubber' condition.

27. 'Credit provision was another area in which the administration's benevolent treatment of the plantation industry constrasted with its uncompromising attitude towards peasants' (Lim Teck Ghee, 1971: 89).

28. As Lim Teck Ghee (1971) has effectively argued, the administration's rationale for this discrimination, i.e. that peasants made poor credit risks while the plantations were sound credit-wise, was hardly grounded in the facts of the matter.

29. The Duncan scale's allowance for unrecorded rubber production was relatively very low, allowing for an annual maximum of 320 lb. per acre for fully mature trees of eight years and older.

30. Commenting on these developments, Lim Teck Ghee (1974: 112) notes that 'it was not the principle of justice that finally persuaded the local and imperial governments to make the partial concession, but the threat of further violence and subsequent political repercussions'.

31. 'An analysis of production returns of 537 estates in the Federated Malay States in 1923 at a time when plantations were producing at full capacity found that in 426 cases the average output was 375 pounds. Yet the original maximum standard production allowance permitted to this sector was 400 pounds. This allowance was raised to 500 pounds on 1st August 1925 and the maximum limit was removed in May 1926. The removal of the maxima was to make it possible for a plantation to obtain an assessment of any amount which it could prove capable of producing, but few plantations could avail themselves of this as they were already producing at peak capacity. Some indication can also be given of the extent of over assessment of the plantation sector. The September 1921 census had found that plantations over 100 acres comprised 63.57 per cent of the total rubber area in bearing. In the first three years of restriction, plantations, although having much lower planting densities and recording much lower yields per unit area than the other sectors of the industry, were allotted 66.25, 67.38 and 66.81 per cent of the total standard quota. There were other flaws [sic] in the operation of restriction which favoured planters ...' (Lim Teck Ghee, 1974: 116).

32. '... it is generally acknowledged now that, throughout the entire period of restriction, smallholders as a body received less than one half the average assessment of plantations, although the evidence gathered by the government at the beginning of the scheme showed that the average smallholding yield per acre was substantially higher than that on plantations' (Lim Teck Ghee, 1974: 114).

33. 'Almost all of this increase came from the peasant sector and gave smallholdings an average output of 480 pounds per mature acres [sic] as against the average of about 200 pounds allotted to it during restriction.... One authority has estimated that the smallholding sector suffered an under-assessment of 180 pounds per mature acre during the currency of the Stevenson scheme. Using this conservative estimate, it is possible to gauge the extent of financial loss suffered by peasant rubber producers. The average [sic] mature area of smallholdings in the Federated Malay States was approximately 350,000 acres, and if the average rubber export value is estimated at 49 cents per pound, the under-assessment cost the peasants $173 million' (Lim Teck Ghee, 1974: 115-16).

34. *Report on a Visit to the Rubber Growing Smallholdings of Malaya, July-September 1946* (Bauer, 1948).

35. 'The reluctance to publicise this was understandable in view of the government's own contribution to the myths held of peasant rubber production, but one might have reasonably expected that this "new" knowledge would dispel these myths once and for all as well as the invidious comparisons made between peasant and estate rubber production' (Lim Teck Ghee, 1971: 229).

36. 'An objective reading of the literature of the industry during the period from 1930-1933 leaves little doubt that the governments of Great Britain and the Netherlands were primarily—and understandably—concerned with the well-being of plantation agriculture in their colonies; and the International Rubber Regulation Agreement, which came into effect in 1934 largely on the basis of an agreement between the two major colonial governments in the Southeast Asian rubber pro-ducing areas, manifested this concern. The agreement achieved market stabilization of a sort, but largely at the expense of the smallholders. The simple fact of the matter was the inability of the plantations at the time to compete with native smallholder production on a production cost basis' (McHale, 1965).

37. '[The scheme] was thus introduced after the depression had largely passed, and its purpose had become the quasi-permanent maintenance of the high cost producers and not the assistance of the industry during acute depression' (Bauer, 1961d).

38. The discussion thus far may lead the reader to see Bauer as a champion of peasant interests against those of the capitalist estates. Yet he is the same man who opposes land reform as 'discouraging the division of labour between those efficient in managing and improving land, and those more efficient as cultivators' (Bauer and Yamey, quoted in T. B. Wilson, 1958: 93). In his book, Bauer (1948a), with anti-monopoly, pro-market instincts, argued that, without restriction of output, a greater output would have been available at lower prices: 'when full weight is given to the importance of smallholdings, ideas of the supply price of natural rubber need drastic downward revision'. A constant theme in Bauer's work has been that smallholders are 'more efficient producers' than estates. A lower supply price of rubber, obtainable 'by encouragement of the efficient low cost producers', would certainly have been preferred by rubber-using industrialists. 'For metropolitan manufacturing capitalists the peasants existed as a class of producers of a primary product necessary as one of the materials of labour in the accumulation of capital. The expansion of peasant output would lead to a reduction in costs of the imported commodity' (George Lee, 1973: 448).

There is yet another consideration in Bauer's thinking. A yeoman peasantry would certainly promise greater stability for the system than a landless proletariat. In his controversial Report from his 1946 visit, Bauer (1948b: 87) argued that the 'present policy ... is directly fostering the growth of extremist political movements'.

'The ban on the alienation of land for rubber denies access to this source of income for tens of thousands of people, Malays, Chinese, and Indians, many of whom are landless, and who are anxious to open up land for rubber cultivation; one need not be an agricultural sentimentalist to suggest that such an extension of individual ownership would be conducive to political and social stability, as well as to economic development' (Bauer, 1961e: 307).

39. Responding to Bauer's critical exposure of the class-biased British policy in favour of estate interests, some writers have sought to absolve the colonial state's responsibility in these matters. However, no one has yet denied the under-assessment of the peasants under the schemes, though some have sought to belittle its significance. Yet despite information available from government reports, some observers insist that the under-assessment of smallholder producers was 'from ignorance and not from intention' (e.g. Benham, 1961: 292). Silcock (1961: 275), for example, claimed that the reason behind government discrimination against smallholders was the desire of colonial officials 'to see the Malay peasant self-sufficient in food production'. This contention ignores the multi-racial composition of rubber smallholders. In Bauer's words:

'This argument neglects the Chinese and Indian smallholders who between them own probably rather more than one-half of the Malayan smallholding acreage. In fact, neither the planting provisions nor the under-assessment of the smallholders conduced to greater self-sufficiency in food. The Chinese and Indian owners were in practice barred from wet padi cultivation' (Bauer, 1961d: 282).

40. Writing in 1957, the year the British relinquished direct colonial rule over Malaya, Bauer noted:

'New planting of rubber has been officially banned or severely restricted in Malaya since the early 1920s. From 1922 to 1928 ... new planting was not formally prohibited but it was discouraged, and little land was alienated for rubber planting. From 1928 to 1930, alienation of land for rubber planting was not banned officially, but it was restricted, partly by high alienation premiums, and partly by administrative discouragement of alienation to smallholders. In 1934, the International Rubber Regulation Scheme was introduced. Under this scheme new planting was prohibited (with insignificant exceptions in 1939 and 1940 which did not substantially affect the Malayan smallholders). The prohibition of new planting was not repealed in Malaya until 1947, and since then practically no land has been made available for rubber planting. In short, very little land has been made available for planting since 1922, and for a large part of the period new planting was completely prohibited.

'Most of these restrictions applied to Malaya only, and they were thus unilateral restrictions on the extension of capacity.... These restrictive policies ... have been a major factor in the decline of the Malayan industry relative to its competitors. Since the mid-1920s, the acreage under rubber in Malaya has increased by about two-fifths, while in Indonesia it has at least trebled' (Bauer, 1961: 303).

41. 'The fact that three-quarters of Malaya is unplanted while many people are anxious to plant shows that the relative decline cannot be ascribed to shortage of land but has been the result largely of restrictive official policies' (Bauer, 1961e: 304).

42. See Lim Chong-Yah (1967: 329, 335, Appendices 4.3 and 4.9).

43. 'However, replanting is fraught with an almost insuperable difficulty for the smallholder who owns little land, for in the replanting process old trees have to be eradicated before new trees can be planted and, further, the new trees take seven years to mature. It therefore involves foregoing the income from the land for seven to eight years. Where the smallholders' only asset and source of income is his land, there is a natural tendency for him to postpone replanting, and accept the consequences, so long as he can derive some income, however small, from the old trees' (Fisk, 1961: 20).

44. 'It is even more significant that 81% of the owners who had commenced replanting operations owned more than one lot, and could depend upon the income from other land until the new trees mature. The remaining 19% had other adequate sources of income and were not dependent on the land for their living. The replanting owners were, in fact, relatively well off; they were actively engaged in the process of land aggregation, and to them the replanted land was an investment and not a means of livelihood' (Fisk, 1961: 20).

45. '... the most significant transformation that is taking place in the Malayan smallholder sector of the rubber industry is the dramatic increase in the capital intensity of production.... If such capitalization is to amortize on an individual smallholder firm basis, it is clear that a growing number of smallholder operations face a far more difficult road to economic survival than the typical estate in Malaya' (McHale, 1965).

4
LAND AND THE PEASANTRY

Colonial Land Policy

THE bases of land rights prior to colonial intervention were described in Chapter 1 as resting primarily on the condition that it was worked. Consequently, there was little accumulation of real property for purposes other than cultivation. Since land was not rendered scarce by the prevailing system, most farmers could cultivate as much land as they needed or were able to manage. However, ownership under colonial land legislation—in all its variations—bore no relation to the pre-colonial premises based on use.

Two aspects of colonial land policy worked in tandem to fundamentally transform land tenure conditions involving the peasantry. First, the new land laws introduced by the British juridically defined a new relationship between peasant and land, and hence to the rest of society. Secondly, colonial land alienation policy controlled the availability of land for peasant cultivation, and also required cultivators to farm under conditions defined by the colonial state. Land policy was also to have its effect on land prices and on the use of land as collateral for obtaining credit.

There were many differences between the land legislation introduced in the Straits Settlements and that adopted in the Malay States of the hinterland. Significant variations also existed among the peninsular Malay States, especially between the Federated Malay States (FMS) and the other States collectively referred to as the Unfederated Malay States (UMS).[1] Lack of uniformity also extends to matters of land administration. The Torrens system of land registration—developed in the British settler colony of Australia to facilitate capitalist expansion in land matters—was adopted in the Malay States; British land law, with its strong feudal heritage, was considered less suitable. Unlike the 'less efficacious system of registering deeds' adopted in the Straits Settlements—which had been colonized earlier—the Torrens system established an 'indisputable right of ownership to registered land' through the issue of title certificates. Nevertheless, several crucial elements are common to the land laws of Malaya.[2] Though subsequent post-colonial land codes have managed some degree of standardization, the British legal legacy is very much alive.

Under the colonial land laws, ownership involved obtaining legal rights to land properly alienated by the authorities. 'The practical goals of the land code were to establish a favourable climate for outside investment in land, and to bring Malay smallholdings under Government control' (Kratoska, 1975b: 135). As capitalist interests and immigrant peasants from neighbouring islands, attracted by the conditions established under colonial rule, began to acquire land, the balance available for cultivation diminished in quantity as well as quality. Colonial rule had fundamentally transformed the conditions of land alienation, and therefore of access to land.[3] Once virtually freely available, land was rendered scarce by a combination of legal, economic, and environmental conditions, making acquisition of cultivable land by purchase increasingly necessary. *In the new conditions accompanying colonial rule, land, the primary means of production in Malay peasant society, was systematically brought under state or private control, and transformed into a commodity which could be accumulated as a form of investment.* The growing commercialization and monetization of the economy hastened this process, encouraging land transactions and investment in land property.[4]

The imposition of colonial land laws signified the end of the line for shifting cultivation which was practised by most Malays in the peninsula outside the long-standing permanent Malay agricultural settlements established on artificially irrigated rice plains, especially in northern Malaya. The pre-colonial Malay land systems were compatible with prevailing agricultural practices; for example, (temporary) usufructuary rights while working the land were consistent with the needs of shifting cultivation. British-imposed land legislation, designed to serve the interests of capital, was incompatible with this long-standing practice which did not require permanent rights to land-ownership.

That was not all; colonial land legislation was only one of many blows delivered at shifting cultivation. Colonial rule also brought about a rapid expansion of mining or agricultural land alienated to capitalist interests, diminishing the land available for shifting cultivation. The new land laws meant that cultivation of land without permission from the owners constituted a violation of property rights. Whatever the validity of the pre-colonial Malay ruler's claim to eminent domain over land was, under colonial rule this became a reality with an added significance (David Wong, 1975). Land now ultimately belonged to the state, with some alienated to private interests. *Without legally recognized rights to land use, shifting cultivation—the livelihood of most Malay peasants—became illegal.* Despite this, however, shifting cultivation practices among Malays took some time to disappear. Legislation prohibiting shifting cultivation by Malays was enacted and introduced in Selangor in 1886 and in Perak a decade later (Lim Teck Ghee, 1976: 67); 'no effort [was] spared to secure a *settled* population of agriculturalists' (Swettenham, 1948: 261; emphasis added). While administrative and legislative forces put an end to an agricultural technique well adapted to the economic and demographic environment of the Malay peasantry, little effort was made to create conditions for a viable alternative: it was the peasants who had to adapt to the new conditions created by the British.

Lim Teck Ghee (1976) has suggested that, whatever their differences on legislative and administrative details, the land policies advocated by early colonial officials were unanimously 'liberal' in order to attract immigrants to engage in sedentary agriculture. In contrast to the previous emphasis on trade for the Straits Settlements, the envisaged motor of economic growth in the

Malayan hinterland was to be agricultural expansion. The policies succeeded, and there was a considerable inflow of settlers almost from the outset.

Legislation and other aspects of colonial rule, geared to promote this general policy, were especially in favour of the larger British concerns. For example, agricultural land exceeding 100 acres in size was exempted from reassessment in the 1890 Selangor land code formulated by Maxwell (Lim Teck Ghee, 1976: 19). This liberal colonial land policy was also reflected in the revenue system, e.g. in the form of low quit rent rates. Large capitalist interests, especially British mining and plantation interests, were assured by colonial administrators of easy and cheap access to land, which was often accumulated speculatively, in excess of their anticipated capacity for utilization. Better land—for instance in terms of mineral potential, soil quality, terrain or access to communications—tended to be allocated to capitalist interests, especially to the more powerful and influential ones. The British devised a 'system of dual agricultural land taxation, a light one on the affluent European planter and a heavy one on the native cultivator' (Lim Teck Ghee, 1976: 129). There were other discriminatory aspects of colonial agricultural policy and practice;[5] discrimination against the peasantry in favour of capitalist interests was not confined to land matters.[6]

Land-ownership and Peasant Differentiation

Contemporary landlord-tenant relations in Malay peasant agriculture are sometimes said to have originated from allegedly 'feudal' pre-colonial relations; according to this view, land tenancy today has its origins in 'feudalism'.[7] This perspective on class relations with regard to land is not grounded in the facts of the Malayan case. An attempt will be made to show that the contemporary process of differentiation in relation to land actually developed from conditions created by the peasantry's integration under colonial auspices into the world capitalist system.

Emphasis on the colonial origins of contemporary peasant class structure does not, of course, deny pre-colonial influences. The successful establishment of colonial hegemony was partly achieved through the cooptation of important sections of the pre-colonial ruling class. The various British concessions to secure and sponsor this alliance included the generous distribution of land property to members of this class. Most of this land is still under peasant agriculture; the rest has either become residential land or been integrated into capitalist enterprises, such as mines and plantations. The significance of these land concessions has yet to be thoroughly surveyed, let alone analysed, though suggestive glimpses are available. In Mukim Gunung, Kelantan, for example, 271.6 acres or 32 per cent of the 848.4 acres of agricultural land there was owned by the Sultan of Kelantan, with a further 37.8 acres owned by other members of the Kelantan royal family (Mohd. Noor, 1974: 41–7).

Besides large land concessions to members of the pre-colonial ruling class and their heirs, other factors contributed to the unequal distribution of land resources among the peasantry at the beginning of the colonial epoch. It was a colonial practice to encourage land development by providing those with money and or influence with undeveloped land to be worked, rent-free for some years, by agricultural settlers (T. B. Wilson, 1958: 13). After such land had been developed, rents would be introduced. Another procedure was to allow settlers to open and develop land in exchange for land portions for themselves. Husin Ali (1964) found that some of the wealthier early settlers of Kampung Bagan used bonded or indentured labourers (*orang tebusan*) from elsewhere in the Malay archipelago to develop agricultural land. Decades later, in the early 1960s, these earlier arrangements were still reflected in the tendency for descendants of the earlier settlers to be landlords, and for descendants of the indentured labourers to be tenants.

Generally, ownership of large tracts of agricultural land lends itself to the establishment of plantations employing wage labour. However, where agricultural production tends to be organized on the basis of the family unit, as has generally been the case for padi cultivation until fairly recently, such large pieces of land may instead be subdivided for operational purposes. Nevertheless, in so far as the subdivided parcels are contiguous and remain under common registered ownership, such large land areas are still represented in cadastral maps as lots, the legal units for payment of quit rent. Evidence from such maps suggests that only a small proportion of padi land is owned in large lot titles[8] (Goethals and Smith, 1965: 24; Lim Teck Ghee et al., 1974: 35). Of course this does not preclude the existence of large owners with holdings consisting of several lots of small size, but there is little evidence of this phenomenon.

Demographic pressures on socially, rather than ecologically, limited land resources have resulted in an increasing subdivision of holdings which may lead to the eventual displacement of impoverished owners in favour of wealthier ones. However, the concentration of land-ownership is not the converse of subdivision; nor is subdivision alone a sufficient condition for the impoverishment or total dispossession (in terms of land owned) of small land-owning peasants (Barnard, 1970: 34). The very importance of land as a means of production to peasant agriculturalists motivates the impoverished peasant to hold on to his property as long as it can continue to yield some income. Even when sale or forfeiture (on account of an unredeemable mortgage) becomes necessary, land tends to be reluctantly given up in bits and pieces. Hence, accumulation of land property in a situation of limited availability of land necessarily involves someone else's dispossession.

Thus, ironically, the non-substitutability of land in agriculture simultaneously emphasizes and limits the significance of land-ownership distribution patterns in understanding wealth and income distribution in peasant society. In present technological conditions, land still remains the most important means of production in agriculture,[9] though with the spread of tenancy for commercial farming, ownership—while still important—has declined in relative significance. Despite the recent relative increase in the significance of peasant agricultural means of production besides land, the peasant's relationship to land-ownership is still commonly taken as the primary criterion for identifying strata among the peasantry (Kessler, 1974; Husin Ali, 1972, 1975). (Though not without problems and limitations, this criterion will also be employed in this discussion. In the following discussion of differentiation among the Malay peasantry, the socio-demographic (rather than eco-demographic) conditions contributing to population pressure on land, to subdivision and to joint ownership of property, are discussed in relation to some of the evidence of these matters.) Generally, there has been an important trend towards some concentration of land-ownership and operation on the one hand, and growing impoverishment and dispossession on the other. The weaker tendency towards concentration is the result of a complex process, and cannot merely be attributed to 'original' inequalities in land alienation at the outset of agricultural settlement; this is perhaps most obvious on the early government-organized agricultural and development schemes where the original settlers started off with equal-sized lots (Swift, 1967: 243; Selvadurai, 1972a: 26).

One consequence of the phenomenon of 'land concentration' has been the frequently cited fragmentation of farms, involving the agglomeration of non-contiguous lots under common ownership. Another possible effect of the concentration of land-ownership is tenancy, though this is not a necessary consequence. In the past, concentration of land-ownership, especially in padi areas, has resulted in the exploitation of tenants (including share-croppers), rather than wage labour. Tenancy, and its corollary, landlordism, are the main criteria employed in the following discussion to analyse the process of class differentiation among the peasantry since the advent of colonial rule. However, it should be recognized that concentration of land-ownership or even large-scale farming on rented land can also lead to the reorganization of production involving the exploitation of wage labour; in fact, recent technological changes in padi production point towards this. This has involved the transformation of the relations of production, and hence those of exploitation, possibly involving the further extension of wage labour or capitalist relations of production into peasant society.

Joint Ownership and Land Subdivision

It is the vogue to attribute peasant poverty to population growth,[10] supporting such assertions with superficial evidence. For example, in 1970, as shown in Table 4.1, the average padi farm size of 3.1 acres (Selvadurai, 1972a) was far below the official optimum two-cultivator peasant family farm size (Lai and Ani, 1971); the situation was similar for peasant rubber holdings (Barlow and Chan, 1968), as seen in Table 4.2. Besides the 'uneconomic size' of most peasant farms, there is added evidence of considerable landlessness among the peasant population. At the present rate of rural population growth of about 2.8 per cent per annum, the number of landless families in the country is expected to increase by about 10,000 each year, according to a 1974 estimate by the then Deputy Director-General of the Federal Land Development Authority. Citing the 1970 national census, he also stated that about 342,000 Malay families in rural areas either had no land or possessed plots of inadequate size (New Straits Times, 22 June 1974).

However, careful critical examination of factors underlying the ostensibly demographic pressure on land shifts responsibility for peasant land hunger away from the population growth rate to the legal and economic aspects of the

TABLE 4.1

Size of Padi Farms, 1970 (acres)

	Average Area	Distribution of Farms by Size (%)							
		≤0.9	1-	2-	3-	4-	5-	7.5-	10-
Perlis	4.1	3	11	19	16	13	25	8	5
Kedah	4.0	8	19	19	12	10	20	6	6
Penang	2.5	9	31	23	13	11	11	2	0
Perak	2.6	14	26	19	12	9	15	4	1
Selangor	3.6	3	14	5	40	13	18	5	2
Negri Sembilan	1.1	38	36	19	4	3	0	0	0
Malacca	2.1	21	32	24	7	6	7	2	1
Johore	1.5	5	60	27	3	3.	2	0	0
Pahang	1.7	16	38	26	11	5	3	1	0
Trengganu	2.3	14	23	29	11	10	10	3	0
Kelantan	2.3	8	26	32	16	10	7	1	0
Peninsular Malaysia	3.1	10	23	21	14	10	15	4	3

Source: Selvadurai (1972a: 26).

land situation in Malaya—as suggested in the previous chapter. Land scarcity as a social condition, rather than the outcome of exclusively ecological and demographic factors,[11] accordingly, requires a shift in attention to the conditions of peasant agricultural production—specifically, to the availability of land. Over two-thirds of the peninsula remains agriculturally undeveloped (Ho, 1970: 92). The Malaysian government has estimated that 15.9 million acres or almost half of the peninsula's land area is 'suitable for agriculture'. Of this, only 6.1 million 'suitable' acres plus another million acres of 'unsuitable' land were under agricultural use in 1969, leaving 9.8 million more 'suitable' acres available (Malaysia, 1971: Table 9.3).

It is relevant to note that the related phenomenon of rural squatters as a manifestation of land hunger in Peninsular Malaysia has yet to be accorded serious and systematic study.[12] The occasional media reportage on illegal cultivators tends to deal only with crisis situations or give publicity to government solutions to specific problems, reflecting only the tip of the iceberg. T. B. Wilson (1956: 93) has estimated that it takes a single settler about four years, without assistance, to prepare 6 acres of jungle for wet padi cultivation. Although preparing a rubber holding would take less time, it takes another 4–5 years before the trees are productive. Hence, crops which yield returns within shorter time-spans are usually preferred by squatters. Given these circumstances and the insecurity of illegal cultivation, it is remarkable that rural squatters have not been deterred altogether. The existence of such illegal cultivators is testimony not only to peasant land hunger, but also to the availability of arable land, and, more specifically, to the economic and legal, rather than ecological and demographic, limits which currently constrain peasant land usage.

The distributive effects of the Islamic inheritance system have frequently been blamed for the current condition of Malay peasant landholdings, which are often subject to joint- or co-ownership, subdivision, and fragmentation. The distributive effects of customary Malay (*adat*) inheritance systems are considered to be somewhat similar, though they are cited less often.[13] The distributive consequences of these systems of inheritance are, of course, different from other systems, such as primogeniture, which upholds the right of the first-born male to exclusive inheritance, and does not therefore have similarly divisive effects through the inheritance process. It is clear that primogeniture, for example, in contrast to Islamic and *adat* inheritance systems, disadvantages those who would have a right to at least some property under the latter systems. In this sense, primogeniture is relatively more inegalitarian in principle and consequence.

Although the practice of Islamic and *adat* inheritance systems among the Malay peasantry obviously predates colonialism, the extent of joint ownership, subdivision, and fragmentation of peasant landholdings does not seem to have been significant in pre-colonial times. Rather, it appears that these features became significant only with the development of colonial land legislation and policy, particularly the constraints on land alienation for peasant cultivation. Only the imposition of colonial legal restrictions on increasing cultivated land to accommodate population increases caused peasant population growth to have such effects. Therefore, it is not the inheritance systems, but the conditions created under colonialism and persisting thereafter, which bear primary responsibility for the subdivisive effects of demographic increase on landholdings.

Subdivision—by which a lot is divided into smaller contiguous parts or fractions—is related to, but analytically distinct from, fragmentation—where the parcels comprising a particular farm are physically scattered and therefore not contiguous[14] (Aziz, 1958: 23). The physical subdivision of a lot into several parcels does not by itself result in fragmentation, in so far as a farmer may still cultivate contiguous parcels. A lot owned by several people need not necessarily be physically subdivided among the owners. If this is done such that the erstwhile co-owners receive individual parcels, joint ownership ceases in favour of individually-owned subdivided parcels.

Changes in land-ownership can be classified into three kinds: static (or neutral), divisive, and concentrative. Static or neutral transactions do not affect the number of owners or the form of land-ownership. Division involves either joint- or co-ownership by those among whom the property is divided, or the physical subdivison of the land into several parcels. Concentration involves a reduction in the number of owners of a certain piece of land, e.g. through co-owners selling out to a sole proprietor. Transactions involving land are not infrequent.[15] In Saiong Mukim, for example, division always affected a larger percentage of lots than concentration—'the net result has been an increase in the number of lots that have lapsed into joint-ownership at a rate averaging about 10 per cent of all lots per decade' (Ho, 1968: 91, 93). Static changes outnumbered changes involving division and concentration, while division affected nearly twice as many lots as concentration.[16] In Krian, 45 per cent of land transactions had a divisive effect and only 1 per cent were concentrative

TABLE 4.2

Distribution of Rubber Smallholders by Area of All Land Owned, 1977
(area in ha)

Land Area Owned	Bumiputra				Chinese			
	No.	Per Cent	Area	Per Cent	No.	Per Cent	Area	Per Cent
0.01–0.49	25,794	7.1 (94.9)	8 530	1.2 (94.9)	985	0.9 (3.6)	326	0.1
0.50–0.99	69,967	19.1 (92.2)	52 697	7.2 (92.0)	4,762	4.2 (6.3)	3 734	0.9 (6.5)
1.00–1.49	73,938	20.2 (83.3)	90 688	12.4 (83.1)	13,221	11.5 (14.9)	16 346	4.1 (15.0)
1.50–1.99	47,348	13.0 (75.2)	80 840	11.1 (74.9)	14,215	12.4 (22.6)	24 662	6.1 (22.9)
2.00–2.99	83,839	22.8 (69.5)	201 482	27.6 (70.2)	33,818	29.4 (28.1)	78 826	19.7 (27.4)
3.00–3.99	33,259	9.1 (63.0)	122 904	15.5 (62.8)	18,621	16.2 (35.2)	64 682	16.1 (35.8)
4.00–9.9	29,902	8.2 (53.1)	155 851	21.3 (51.3)	25,098	21.9 (44.6)	141 042	35.2 (46.4)
9.9–19.9	1,331	0.4 (28.7)	16 461	2.2 (27.2)	3,102	2.7 (68.0)	41 775	10.4 (69.1)
> 20.0–40.0	392	0.1 (27.1)	11 280	1.5 (26.3)	948	0.8 (67.1)	29 629	7.4 (68.9)
Total	365,750	100.0 (74.6)	730 733	100.0 (63.1)	114,768	100.0 (23.4)	401 022	100.0 (34.6)
Average land area owned		2.35				2.57		
Median land area owned		2.03				2.75		
Standard Deviation		2.36				2.40		

Source: Gibbons (1983: Tables 2.23, 2.24).

Note: A total of 10.4 per cent of the smallholders had no information on all land

while 54 per cent were neutral. The study also found the divisive effect to be highest for death distribution suits: 68 per cent were of a divisive nature, 25 per cent were neutral, and 7 per cent were concentrative. Outright sales were found to be least divisive: 61 per cent were neutral, 20 per cent were concentrative, and only 19 per cent were divisive (T. B. Wilson, 1955: 71–7).

The extent of subdivision of land-ownership in Tanjong Piandang, Krian, between 1900 and 1954, over the course of approximately two to three generations, was studied (T. B. Wilson, 1954: 125–35). Originally all lots were 7 acres in size. Over the period studied, the number of lots on the same land area increased by only about 15 per cent, a rate far lower than the increase in population size over generations. However, it has been estimated that, in some parts of the peninsula, the number of plots increased by approximately 70 per cent per generation (Ho, 1967: 40). But the rate of actual physical subdivision was less than the extent of division of ownership—in 1903, there were on average 106 co-owners to every 100 registered lots, but by 1954 this had increased to 238 co-owners per 100 lots. These trends suggest that division in

TABLE 4.2 (*continued*)

Indian				Others				Total			
No.	*Per Cent*	*Area*	*Per Cent*	*No.*	*Per Cent*	*Area*	*Per Cent*	*No.*	*Per Cent*	*Area*	*Per Cent*
254	4.4	77	0.5	161	3.9	51	0.5	27,194	5.5	8 984	0.8
	(0.9)		(0.9)		(0.6)		(0.6)		(100.0)		(100.0)
520	9.0	399	2.3	619	15.0	454	4.7	75,868	15.5	57 284	5.0
	(0.7)		(0.7)		(0.8)		(8.8)		(100.0)		(100.0)
826	14.2	1 016	5.9	835	20.2	1 041	10.9	88,820	18.1	109 091	9.4
	(0.9)		(0.9)		(0.9)		(1.0)		(100.0)		(100.0)
743	12.8	1 268	7.4	647	15.6	1 090	11.4	62,953	12.8	107 860	9.3
	(1.2)		(1.2)		(1.0)		(1.1)				(100.0)
1,795	30.9	4 228	24.7	1,073	25.9	2 606	27.2	120,525	24.6	287 142	24.8
	(1.5)		(1.5)		(0.9)		(0.9)		(100.0)		(100.0)
637	11.0	2 182	12.8	323	7.8	1 103	11.5	52,839	10.8	180 871	15.6
	(1.2)		(1.2)		(0.6)		(0.6)		(100.0)		(100.0)
853	14.7	4 520	26.4	434	10.5	2 369	24.8	56,287	11.5	303 782	26.2
	(1.5)				(0.8)		(0.8)		(100.0)		(100.0)
118	2.0	1 717	10.0	32	0.8	505	5.3	4,563	0.9	60 458	5.2
	(2.6)		(2.9)		(0.7)		(0.8)		(100.0)		(100.0)
60	1.0	1 718	10.0	12	0.3	452	3.7	1,410	0.3	42 979	3.7
	(4.3)		(4.0)		(0.9)		(0.8)		(100.0)		(100.0)
,806	100.0	17 125	100.0	4,136	100.0	9 571	100.0	490,460	100.0	1 158 451	100.0
	(1.2)		(34.6)		(0.8)		(8.8)		(100.0)		(100.0)
	2.98				2.38				2.65		
	2.39				2.41				2.04		
	1.35				1.2				1.34		

owned. They were distributed in proportion to the distribution of those for whom there was such information.

ownership tends to result in joint ownership more than the actual physical subdivision of landholdings.[17]

Ho (1968: 96, Table 8) has shown that the proportion of sole owners to all owners in Saiong Mukim declined from 50 per cent in 1910 (after rubber cultivation had become popular among peasants) to 19 per cent in 1960. In rubber alone, this ratio declined during the same half-century from 100 per cent in 1910 to 41 per cent in 1960 (see Table 4.3).

While the land-owning population in Ho's sample increased about 15 times between 1900 and 1960, the number of joint owners increased twentyfold. The acreage under sole ownership declined from 910 acres to 815 acres, while land under co-ownership grew from 575 acres to 1,050 acres. The percentage of sole ownership of padi holdings in Krian, Perak, declined from 97 per cent at first registration to 71 per cent in 1954. The average of 1.05 registered co-owners per holding had increased to 1.72 by 1954. Correspondingly, the average share per owner declined from 4.93 acres to 2.74 acres each (T. B. Wilson, 1958: 88, Table 78; 89, Table 79). However, the actual development of co-ownership is more

TABLE 4.3

Percentage of Sole Owners to All Owners, Saiong Mukim

Year	Padi	Kampong	Rubber	Mixed	Gardens	Fruits	Averages
1900	48 (62)	35 (45)	0 (0)	13 (20)	100 (100)	57 (73)	38 (49)
1910	50 (61)	44 (73)	100 (100)	40 (65)	87 (95)	56 (75)	50 (69)
1920	40 (56)	43 (64)	64 (80)	33 (53)	57 (76)	30 (52)	46 (66)
1930	33 (51)	29 (56)	61 (77)	22 (46)	52 (69)	40 (55)	37 (61)
1940	26 (40)	21 (46)	56 (75)	22 (46)	36 (58)	34 (57)	30 (55)
1950	22 (35)	18 (41)	49 (67)	18 (41)	28 (59)	37 (58)	25 (49)
1960	15 (28)	12 (33)	41 (63)	12 (30)	27 (52)	25 (58)	19 (44)

Source: Ho (1968: 96, Tables 8 and 9).
Note: Figures in brackets refer to percentages of areas involved.

advanced than suggested by these statistics since the number of actual joint owners is greater than the number of registered co-owners.[18] It was also found that the percentage of actual sole owners was 67 per cent; thus, the average number of joint owners per holding in 1954 was 1.81, with each having 2.61 acres on average (T. B. Wilson, 1958: 89, Table 80). Earlier in Krian, it was also found that the average time lapse between the death of a land-owner and the date of the petition of a distribution suit was over 8 years, implying that the extent of joint ownership is more advanced than the registered evidence may indicate (T. B. Wilson, 1955: 83).

In Saiong Mukim, 'transactions affected more than half the universe of smaller lots, and rose to over 90 percent of the largest' (Ho, 1968: 93–5). Division of ownership affected smaller lots least of all because their size rendered the process uneconomic and therefore unattractive. Also, the process

TABLE 4.4

Percentage of Padi Lots Affected by Division in Ownership,
by Size of Lots and Decades, Saiong Mukim

Decade Ending	Lot Size (acres)							
	Under 1	Under 2	Under 3	Under 4	Under 5	Under 6	Over 6	
1900	0	0	5	0	0	0	0	
1910	16	15	24	20	57[1]	20	25	50%
1920	25	33	47	54	50	50	60	100%
1930	32	51	79	79	113	117	140	200%
1940	55	58	95	79	125	167	200	
1950	63	78	116	107	163	267	280	
1960	62	86	122	120	175	267	300	

Source: Ho (1968: 95, Table 7).
[1]The apparent discrepancy suggested by this figure suggests an error in the original publication of the table.

TABLE 4.5

Ownership and Average Holdings of Padi Lots, Temerloh, Pahang

Number of Owners	Number of Lots	Percentage of Lots	Total Acreage	Average Size of Lot (acres)
1 owner only	423	61.0	757.5	1.79
2 owners only	141	20.3	331.2	2.35
3 owners only	51	7.4	162.4	3.18
4 owners only	34	4.9[1]	139.6	4.11
5 owners or more	44	6.3	155.9	3.54
Total	693	99.9[2]	1,546.7	2.23

Source: Ho (1967: Table 13).
[1]This percentage in the original table has been corrected.
[2]Percentages do not add up to 100.0 because of rounding.

of division of ownership not only affected smaller lots least, but tended to begin with larger lots and then spread to smaller ones, as shown in Table 4.4. In other words, the proportion of sole owners to all owners tends to be inversely related to the size of holdings; also, the more numerous the co-owners, the greater the likely size of the holding, as Table 4.5 shows for four *mukim* in Temerloh,

TABLE 4.6

Distribution of Original and Physically Subdivided Holdings
within Each Size Group, Krian, Perak

Acres	Number of Original Holdings	Number of Holdings which have been Subdivided	Number of Subdivided Holdings as Percentage of the Number of Original Holdings
Below $\frac{1}{2}$	40	—	—
$\frac{1}{2}$–1	140	—	—
1–1$\frac{1}{2}$	320	20	6
1$\frac{1}{2}$–2	240	—	—
2–3	1,180	100	8
3–4	1,900	100	5
4–5	4,740	100	2
5–6	4,020	600	5
6–7	1,080	160	15
7–8	600	140	23
8–9	340	100	29
9–10	180	60	33
10–14	508	140	27
15–19	146	100	68
20–49	24	—	—
50–99	3	—	—
954	1	—	—
Total	15,462	1,240	8

Source: T. B. Wilson (1958: 87, Table 77).

Pahang. The likelihood of subdivision apparently increases with the size of the original holding,[19] as reflected in Table 4.6.

Joint ownership as well as subdivision tend to have advanced furthest in longer-settled areas (Ho, 1970: 89), and to be relatively higher for subsistence and local market-oriented crop areas, such as padi, compared to cash crops such as rubber (see Table 4.1). According to the 1960 Agricultural Census, for all States, except Negri Sembilan[20] and Malacca, only a quarter to a third of all padi farms were under sole ownership; on the other hand, in most States, 'some three-quarters of the rubber farms are under single ownership, the proportion falling to two-thirds in Kelantan and to half or a little less, in Kedah and Perlis' (Hill, 1967). In Saiong Mukim, while the trend towards joint ownership was associated with every crop, it appeared to have developed most for padi and *kampung* (village residential) lots. By 1960, all padi lots above 2 acres in size were jointly owned, and of the remainder a great majority were held by two or more persons (Ho, 1968: 96).

A total of 91,009 or 18.6 per cent of all rubber smallholdings in 1977 were reported to have more than one owner, and there were estimated to be at least 247,904 such co-owners, according to RISDA's 1977 census (Gibbons, 1983). Hence, there were estimated to be 647,355 owners of rubber smallholdings in all. The census also estimated 131,988 share-croppers and wage labourers out of 532,369 operators of rubber smallholdings.

Various references have already been made to the declining acreage of a co-ownership share[21] (see Table 4.7). In Tanjong Piandang Mukim, Krian, only 2 per cent of land-ownership shares in 1900 were for less than 2 acres; by 1954 this had risen to 53 per cent. Over the same period, on the other hand, 41 per cent of the shares were for lots larger than 7 acres in 1900, dropping to 4 per cent in

TABLE 4.7

Comparison of Percentage Distribution by Size of the Same Area of
Padi Land, Tanjong Piandang, Krian, 1900 and 1954

Share Size Group	Percentage of Co-ownership Shares, 1900	Percentage of Co-ownership Shares, 1954
Less than 1 acre		24
1–2 acres	2	29
2–3 acres	7	15
3–4 acres	14	10
4–5 acres	23	13
5–6 acres	9	2
6–7 acres	4	3
7–8 acres	11	–
8–9 acres	9	–
9–10 acres	9	1
10–15 acres	7	3
More than 15 acres	5	–
Total	100	100

Source: T. B. Wilson (1954).

1954 (T. B. Wilson, 1954: 125-35). Division of land-ownership is therefore manifest in both the increase of joint- or co-ownership as well as in the physical subdivision of landholdings. Both these tendencies tend to encourage the sale of affected land, leading to the concentration of land-ownership.[22]

Fisk (1964: 1-3) has discussed some of the main problems raised by co-ownership. Joint ownership is often preferred to subdivision because of problems identified with ownership of small holdings. It may also be chosen because of the difficulties and expenses involved in the process of effecting physical subdivision, or the desire of the co-owners to keep the farm holding intact for other reasons. It has been mentioned that the process of co-ownership developing through operation of Islamic rules of inheritance has led to shares of small and awkward sizes.[23] Joint ownership discourages investment and other measures to increase productivity, especially over the long term, while encouraging tenancy as an interim solution to the problems of allocating land use among the co-owners themselves.[24]

Discussing some effects of subdivision on peasant production, Ungku Aziz (1958: 24) has pointed out that the reduction of farm size as a result of subdivision makes it less feasible to employ certain more productive techniques; certain techniques and equipment which can yield higher outputs are more difficult or expensive to employ on smaller holdings, i.e. without certain economies of scale. Certain common farming problems—e.g. different operation schedules of neighbouring farms and negligence of neighbours—are exacerbated when there are more smaller-sized farms due to subdivision. Subdivision also tends to lead to farm fragmentation.[25]

To overcome the problem of inadequate land, especially on small subdivided lots, peasant farmers increase farm sizes by various means, consolidating property rights through renouncement, gifts, exchange, and sale. Generally, however, tenancy is the most important means of enlarging farm size. The consequence of these various actions is the consolidation of various small parcels of land into farms of more viable size. As a result of such practices, T. B. Wilson (1958: 83, 92, Table 83) found that the average number of farmers on each holding in Krian in 1954 was 15 per cent less than the average number of co-owners. A majority of the consolidated holdings comprised contiguous parcels of land, though many consolidated farms, especially those involved in padi production, consisted of non-contiguous parcels. Other factors besides physical subdivision have also contributed to the phenomenon of farm fragmentation.[26]

The 1960 Agricultural Census[27] showed that 'for padi farmers, 56 per cent of them operated a single parcel, 25 per cent worked on two parcels, 11 per cent on three parcels, 4 per cent on four parcels and the remaining 4 per cent worked on 5 to 9 parcels' (Selvadurai, 1972a: 28). In Locality DII of the Muda irrigation scheme, 60 per cent of the farms consisted of more than one parcel, with an average of 3.1 parcels per farm (Lim Teck Ghee et al., 1974: 45, 46, Table 12). Elsewhere, the proportion of fragmented peasant holdings was 29 per cent in Saiong Mukim, 16 per cent in Temerloh District, and 57 per cent in Batu Hampar Mukim (Ho, 1970: 87, Table 2). Twenty-six of 40 Kedah padi farms surveyed by Barnard consisted of only one parcel, 10 of two parcels, 3 of three parcels, and 1 of four parcels; she concluded that while the dispersal of holdings was 'not excessive', fragmentation did cause inconvenience and interfered with farming activity.[28]

The dispersal of parcels incurs greater time, effort and cost in transporting the farmer, his equipment, farm animals, other farming material and, of course, his produce. Travelling time can thus affect production on fragmented rubber smallholdings as productivity in rubber tapping is affected by the time at which incisions are made and latex begins to flow. Parcelling also inhibits the introduction and utilization of new farm infrastructure, techniques, and inputs because of the greater organizational and other difficulties involved (e.g. see Ooi, 1959: 204, 205). However, operating a fragmented farm may have certain advantages for multi-cropping and spreading risk.

Concentration of Land-ownership[29]

Ignoring government alienation of new agricultural land for the moment, the accumulation of land property by some—which necessarily involves dispossessing others—or the process of concentration of land-ownership represents, in so far as land is the primary means of production in peasant agriculture, the main, though not the only, form of capital accumulation in the peasant sector.

Land sales by peasants may be necessitated or motivated by prevailing circumstances, or the desire to transform the nature of one's assets. Husin Ali (1975: 82) maintains that small land assets, low incomes, and the seasonal nature of many agricultural pursuits tend to force peasants into a spiral of chronic indebtedness, sometimes culminating in land sale or forfeiture of property offered as collateral for credit. In such circumstances, extraordinary expenditures often precipitate the actual sale of land since the impoverished, and often indebted, peasant usually has no other recourse. A superficial focus on the extraordinary spending that culminates in land sale ignores the socio-economic context in which the peasant lives, and leads to the erroneous view that peasants lose their land solely because of such expenditure.[30] It is common for such spending to be characterized as irrational and, hence, for peasant impoverishment to be attributed to peasant irrationality.

Husin Ali (1972: 106) has identified three categories of people who accumulate land. The first, a minority who are able to purchase land with their savings. Even a tenant producing an excellent padi yield cannot ever expect to achieve full ownership of the land he works, unless he inherits or otherwise obtains sufficient wealth to do so (Goethals and Smith, 1965: 33, 87-9). Consequently, very few tenants become land-owning peasants, i.e. achieve upward mobility within peasant society. The second, again a minority, are those who have extra resources and relatively high incomes from inheriting or owning a large amount of land. In the village Kuchiba and Tsubouchi (1967: 471) studied, the inheritance of only a small fraction of the 40 per cent who had inherited or could inherit land, offered sufficiently high incomes for their owners to purchase more land in turn.[31] This suggests that land inheritance alone is usually insufficient for the further accumulation of land property. The third category comprises those in business or government service who enjoy relatively high incomes. In these cases, accumulation involves the transfer of ownership of peasant land to people who do not farm. Some in this category may reside within the peasant community, while others who do not, often have links with the village community. Since much peasant land is covered by the Malay Reservations legislation, the market in such land involves Malay buyers and sellers transacting at depressed land prices.[32] More recently, rent increases have lagged behind land price increases which have been fuelled by purchases for speculation and construction development.

Evidence of the concentration of peasant land-ownership is not available on a national scale. This has been attributed to the difficulty of assessing concentration of land-ownership by simply looking at cadastral maps. It has been noted that the extent of large land-ownership which is readily identifiable from padi-land titles for big cadastral lots is not great. Land-owners with a lot of land, whose holdings consist of several small lots, cannot be detected in this manner. However, the extent of such ownership, if properly registered, can be found in the declared estates of deceased land-owners. T. B. Wilson (1958: 64-7) examined a 10 per cent sample of Krian land-owners who died in the post-war years up to 1954. The total property of the 102 deceased spread over 427 titles, averaging about 18 acres each (see Table 4.8). However, the land owned was very unevenly distributed;[33] for example, the three largest land-owners alone accounted for 56 per cent while the poorest 71 per cent of land-owners owned only 17 per cent of the land.

While the process of concentration has probably developed most in padi-growing areas, Husin Ali[34] has shown that it has also affected peasants cultivating other crops.[35] This can be seen from Table 4.9 where the extent of concentration of land-ownership in five different villages is compared. Kangkong in Kedah is mainly padi growing, with some seasonal fishing. Kerdau in Pahang is primarily involved in rubber cultivation, though padi land is also quite extensive. Bagan in Johore is also primarily involved in rubber, with some coconut growing. Changkat Larang in Perak is again mainly rubber growing, with a few villagers employed in wage labour in nearby estates and mines, while Pahang Tua in Pahang is primarily involved in padi with some rubber and coconut as well as wage labour and petty business.

TABLE 4.8

Distribution of Estates of 102 Deceased Krian Land-owners,

1945–1954

	Size of Estate (acres)														
	½	1	2	3	4	5	6	7	8	9	10	15	25	100	Total
Total no. of estates	6	10	8	9	11	12	6	7	2	2	11	9	6	3	102
Total area (acres)	4	15	20	32	49	66	38	53	17	19	133	154	205	1,020	1,825
Per cent		1	1	2	3	4	2	3	1	1	7	8	11	56	100

Source: T. B. Wilson (1958: 66, Table 62).

TABLE 4.9
Distribution of Household Heads and Land Owned by Size of Holdings

Acreage	Kangkong Heads (%)	Kangkong Land (%)	Kerdau Heads (%)	Kerdau Land (%)	Bagan Heads (%)	Bagan Land (%)	Acreage	Changkat Heads (%)	Changkat Land (%)	Acreage	Pabang Tua Heads (%)	Pabang Tua Land (%)
0	33.3	0	7.8	0	12.8	0	0	28.5	0	0	7.4	0
½–3	34.4	19.2	18.8	6.0	43.6	11.1	½–2	40.7	18.0	0.1–1	14.7	4.4
3½–6	15.6	20.9	27.3	14.9	22.1	13.6	2½–4	13.0	14.6	1.1–2	29.5	19.7
6½–9	6.7	13.0	18.8	19.6	5.4	5.8	4½–6	7.3	14.6	2.1–3	14.7	14.7
9½–12	2.2	5.6	12.5	16.9	5.4	8.1	6½–8	1.6	4.5	3.1–4	14.7	18.1
12½–15	2.2	8.2	6.3	12.3	3.0	5.1	8½–10	1.6	5.8	4.1–5	7.4	14.1
15½–18	–	–	2.3	5.3	0.7	1.5	10½–12	2.4	10.2	5.1–7	7.4	16.4
Over 18	5.5	33.0	6.3	24.9	8.1	54.7	12½–14	1.6	7.9	7.1–10	4.2	12.6
							Over 14	3.2	24.3			
No. of Household Heads	90		128		149			123			95	
Total Acreage	354.0		958.8		1,104.7			329.0			278.1	

Sources: Husin Ali (1972: 102, Table 1; 103, Table 2); Ouchi *et al.* (1979: 116, Table 5,6).

Also available is direct and indirect evidence of the degree of concentration of land-ownership, as well as its most important corollary, landlessness. While there is little direct evidence of the overall development of padi-land ownership concentration in north Malaya,

... the indirect evidence points to the conclusion that the proprietorship of padi land is spread among a large number of owners but with a very considerable degree of concentration of the ownership of large areas into the possession of a few of them. It is estimated that not more than 2,000 families own not less than two thirds of the padi lands of North Malaya (T. B. Wilson, 1958: 67).

Unfortunately, Wilson does not offer evidence for this assertion and there is little other evidence to support his claim of such high concentration of land-ownership. In view of the relatively recent origins of peasant differentiation on the basis of land-ownership, there is little reason to expect great concentration of peasant land-ownership or a highly advanced stratification of Malay peasant society, though this does not, of course, deny the significant trends which have developed thus far as well as class differentiation along other lines which has taken place. In Locality DII in the Muda irrigation scheme, for instance, 9 per cent of all farmers in 1973 were categorized as landlords, with two-thirds of this group renting out only one parcel. In other words, only 3 per cent of all the farmers surveyed were landlords renting out more than one parcel of land (Lim Teck Ghee et al., 1974: 37).

There are no aggregate national statistics on the extent of landlessness among what may be termed the peasant population. There are also many peasant households which own very little land, e.g. less than an acre—which is rarely enough to subsist on. Nevertheless, glimpses of the extent of peasant landlessness exist. Husin Ali (1972: 102) found that among household heads, 33.3 per cent in Kangkong, 7.8 per cent in Kerdau, 12.8 per cent in Bagan, and 28.5 per cent in Changkat Larang were landless; according to Ouchi et al. (1979: 156), 7.4 per cent in Pahang Tua were in the same situation. In Locality DII in the Muda scheme area, 30 per cent of padi farmers were landless as far as padi land was concerned (Lim Teck Ghee et al., 1974: 37). In his survey of Temerloh District in Pahang, Ho (1967: 36) found that of 802 adults, 344—or 43 per cent—owned land; i.e. more than half the adult population did not own any land. In Asam Riang, Kedah, 30 per cent of the households engaged in agriculture were landless (Barnard, 1973: 114). Fisk (1961: 16) has noted that 42 per cent of the households of Genting Malik, a rubber-growing Malay reservation in Selangor, owned no land.

Land owned is not synonymous with land operated. The past dominance of certain organizational forms of padi production, especially the family's role as the basic productive unit, as well as other factors such as the fragmentation of land property, have tended to limit farm sizes previously. Through various arrangements, especially tenancy, land is distributed for purposes of culti-vation. Sometimes land-owners rent out their own land and operate land belonging to others (usually to minimize the adverse effects of fragmented ownership), but it is more usual for owners to cultivate their own land. There are many factors, however, which mediate between land-ownership and operation, though ownership nevertheless does have a considerable bearing on land operation. Many a land-hungry farmer can afford to rent only small farm areas,[36] if available, and may also supplement his income with other jobs. It does appear then that the concentration and inequitable distribution of land-ownership has a considerable influence on the distribution of farms by size.[37] The size distribution of farms (e.g. see Selvadurai, 1972a; Eddy Lee, 1976: 22, Table 6), however, reflects the distribution of farm-land ownership in a distorted fashion.

Tenancy and Peasant Strata by Tenure

Concentration of land-ownership in a situation where the peasant family remains the basic unit of production, has contributed to the development of tenancy among peasant cultivators. There is some problematic information available on the tenurial status of farmers for major crops, and in particular, padi farmers in 1960 and 1970. Employing data from the notoriously unreliable 1960 Census of Agriculture, Hill (1967: 101) found that of main-crop wet padi farmers, 33.7 per cent were (pure) owners and 31.4 per cent were (pure) tenants, whereas Goethals and Smith (1965: 18) found 45.4 per cent to be (pure) owners and 16.6 per cent to be (pure) tenants (see Tables 4.10 and 4.11)! According to the 1960 Census, padi farms comprised 29.4 per cent of all farms, and 93 per cent of all tenant farmers were to be found in the rice sector alone (Lim Chong-Yah, 1967: 168)! By 1970, 48 per cent of padi farmers owned the land they worked, whereas 27 per cent were tenants (Selvadurai, 1972: 29). While these data are highly suspect, most observers agree that tenancy rates are generally higher in padi-farming areas, compared to, say, rubber areas (also see Tables 4.13 and 4.14).

According to the Census, there was no tenancy among rubber holdings which made up 20.2 per cent of the farm total in 1960. On the other hand, a study conducted between late 1959 and early 1960, found that 79.9

TABLE 4.10

Percentages of Tenure Groups by Farm Crop, 1960

Group	Rubber	Coconut	Fruit-Residential	Mixed	Wet Padi (Main Crop)
Owner	80.1	86.8	78.9	59.8	33.7
Temporary Occupation Licencee (TOL)	1.8	3.8	7.1	1.7	4.7
Tenant	–	–	–	0.8	31.4
Other Single Tenure	5.1	3.6	8.2	3.0	5.6
Owner–tenant	1.2	0.2	1.0	11.4	15.0
Other Mixed Tenure	11.8	5.6	4.8	23.3	9.6
	100.0	100.0	100.0	100.0	100.0

Source: Hill (1967: 101, Table 2) (based on 1960 Census of Agriculture).

TABLE 4.11

Tenure of Farms Growing Main-crop Wet Padi by State, 1960[1]

State	Owner No.	Owner Per Cent	TOL[2] No.	TOL[2] Per Cent	Tenant No.	Tenant Per Cent	Other Single Tenure No.	Other Single Tenure Per Cent	Owner-Tenant No.	Owner-Tenant Per Cent	Other Mixed No.	Other Mixed Per Cent	Total No.	Total Per Cent
Federation	115,572	45.4	7,044	2.7	42,438	16.6	10,248	4.0	35,774	14.0	44,176	17.3	255,252	100.0
Johore	1,370	36.5	502	13.4	–	0.0	360	9.6	20	0.5	1,500	40.0	3,752	100.0
Kedah	22,076	31.5	704	1.0	19,634	28.0	3,664	5.2	9,850	14.1	14,146	20.2	70,074	100.0
Kelantan	19,882	42.0	102	0.3	4,460	9.4	1,294	2.7	13,342	28.2	8,230	17.4	47,310	100.0
Malacca	8,766	80.0	160	1.4	742	6.9	160	1.4	528	4.8	606	5.5	10,962	100.0
Negri Sembilan	13,804	84.6	120	0.7	340	2.1	220	1.3	860	5.3	982	6.0	16,326	100.0
Pahang	9,898	59.3	284	1.7	620	3.7	1,046	6.2	1,014	6.1	3,850	23.0	16,712	100.0
Penang & Province Wellesley[3]	3,932	29.1	260	1.9	6,200	45.9	220	1.6	2,092	15.5	814	6.0	13,518	100.0
Perak	18,968	51.2	2,470	6.7	6,020	16.3	2,222	6.0	3,236	8.7	4,100	11.1	37,016	100.0
Perlis	3,622	30.9	480	4.1	1,622	13.8	622	5.3	1,536	13.1	3,830	32.8	11,712	100.0
Selangor	4,982	44.7	1,682	15.1	1,060	9.5	140	1.3	562	5.0	2,718	24.4	11,144	100.0
Trengganu	8,272	49.5	280	1.7	1,740	10.4	300	1.8	2,734	16.3	3,400	20.3	16,726	100.0

Source: Goethals and Smith (1965: 18, Table 1) (based on Census of Agriculture, Volume 9, Tables 620–631).

[1] Only 16,526 farms reported raising dry padi in the Federation.

[2] Temporary Occupation Licencee.

[3] About 6,000 of the farms which are either tenant or owner–tenant operated appear to be in the Krian District.

TABLE 4.12

Padi Farmers by Tenure, 1970
(percentages)

	Owner	Owner–Tenant	Tenant
Perlis	45	24	31
Kedah	45	20	35
Penang	44	17	39
Perak	50	13	37
Selangor	60	25	15
Negri Sembilan	87	7	6
Malacca	52	18	30
Johore	70	20	10
Pahang	70	14	16
Trengganu	55	23	22
Kelantan	25	55	20
Peninsular Malaysia	48	25	27

Source: Selvadurai (1972: 29).

per cent of the lots in a rubber-growing Malay reservation in Batang Kali Mukim (Selangor) were operated by people other than the owners—usually on a share-cropping basis—and only 5.7 per cent of the farms were operated by the registered owner, while 14.4 per cent were run by members of the owner's immediate family (Fisk, 1961: 22). From this and other evidence, Hill (1967: 102) concludes that 'it is clear that the picture presented by the census is far from accurate' with regard to the extent of tenancy in rubber holdings.

A recent study (Gibbons et al., 1983)–see Table 4.15–of the 490,460 rubber smallholders in Peninsular Malaysia in 1977 found that 73.5 per cent of rubber smallholders operated all the rubber land they owned, while 23.0 per cent had others operating all their land and 2.7 per cent operated part and had others operating part of their land; they accounted for 70.1 per cent, 25.2 per cent, and 4.7 per cent respectively of all rubber smallholding land. The average size of rubber smallholdings was 2.65 hectares while the median size was 2.04 hectares (1 hectare = 2.471 acres). Of the rubber smallholders, 51.9 per cent owned less than 2 hectares (almost 5 acres) of land, and together their land amounted to only 24.5 per cent of all land owned by rubber smallholders, while 12.7 per cent owned at least 4 hectares amounting to 35.1 per cent of all such land. The coefficient of inequality in the size distribution of land-ownership was 0.412 for all rubber smallholders and even higher (0.424) for Malay rubber smallholders in particular. Other evidence suggests considerable variation in the extent of tenancy for land planted with different crops (e.g. Husin Ali, 1972) which in turn relates to variations in average farm size and the degree of concentration of land-ownership (see Table 4.16).

Many factors contribute to differences in the tenancy rate (see, for example, Y. Huang, 1975). Differences in income obtainable from cultivating different crops must affect the economic standing of the farmer, and thus both land-

TABLE 4.13
Tenancy in Padi-growing Areas

Place	Percentage of Land	Percentage of Operators
Province Wellesley[1]	75	–
Kedah[1]	70	–
Krian[1]	50	–
Perlis (1949–50)[2]	39	–
Perlis (1955–6)[2]	47	–
Kedah (1949–50)[2]	46	–
Kedah (1955–6)[2]	57	–
Province Wellesley (1949–50)[2]	62	–
Province Wellesley (1955–6)[2]	62	–
Kelantan (1949–50)[2]	50	–
Kelantan (1955–6)[2]	49	–
Krian (1954)[2]	43	
Temerloh District (1965)[3]	39	49
Kedah and Perlis[3]	50	41
Kelantan[3]	54	14
Malacca[3]	53	30
Selangor[3]	25	15
Malacca State (1966)[3]	–	51
Muda (1966)[3]	–	57
Tanjong Karang (1966)[4]	–	38
Central Pahang (1965)[4]	–	40
Kelantan State[4]	49	–
Padang Lalang (1964)[5]	–	44
Asam Riang (1967)[6]	70	70
Sungei Bujor, Yan, Kedah (1967)[7]	64	71
Parit Lebai Akir, Krian, Perak (1968–9)[7]	37	64
Sungei Megat Aris, Krian, Perak (1968–9)[7]	38	52
Bongor Kudong, Perlis (1975)[7]	48	67
Beseri Dalam, Perlis (1975)[7]	23	42
Pahang Tua, Pekan, Pahang (1975)[7]	9	15
Batu 12, Tanjung Karang, Selangor (1978)[7]	22	40
Gajah Mati, Pasir Mas, Kelantan (1967)[7]	–	56
DII, Muda (1973)[8]	49	54
Muda (1976)[9]	39	66
Permatang Bogak[10]	60	80
Batang Kali (rubber) (1959–60)[11]	80	–

Sources: 1. Rice Production Committee (1953: 45, 76, 88).
2. T. B. Wilson (1958).
3. Narkswasdi (1968).
4. Ho (1969: 27, Table 8).
5. Kuchiba and Tsubouchi (1967: 468).
6. Barnard (1970: 44).
7. Horii (1981).
8. Lim Teck Ghee et al. (1974: 41, 42).
9. Gibbons et al. (1981).
10. Bhati (1976: 84, 85, Table 18).
11. Fisk (1961: 17).

TABLE 4.14

Percentage of Farmers by Tenurial Status in Different Village Studies in the Muda Padi-growing Region

Tenurial Status of Farmers	Asam Riang[1] (1966/67)	Sungei Bujor[2] (1967)	Padang Lalang[2] (1964/65)	Kubang Pasu[2] (1966)	Kota Star North[2] (1966)	Yan[2] (1966)
Owner	30	29	29	42	48	31
Tenant	55	48	44	38	41	56
Owner–tenant	15	23	27	18	9	13
Others	–	–	–	2	2	–
Total	100	100	100	100	100	100
Sample Size	40	52	135	608	595	348

Sources: 1. Barnard (1970: 44, Table 2.6).
2. Lim Teck Ghee et al. (1974: 81, Table 28).
3. Horii (1981: 93, Table 7.1).
4. Gibbons et al. (1981).

ownership and tenancy. Botanical as well as other differences in the production regimes of various crops also influence the choice of mode of exploitation. For instance, the annual (and more recently, the bi-annual) padi production cycle is certainly more conducive to tenancy arrangements than land planted with perennials.[38]

Considerable differences in the extent of tenancy also exist between padi-growing areas (see Tables 4.11, 4.13 and 4.14); these differences can be substantial. For example, the Kedah Department of Agriculture (n.d.: 3) found that, of five padi-growing districts surveyed in the Muda area, the percentage of owners–operators to all operators ranged from 8.52 per cent in Batu 17$\frac{1}{2}$ and 9.23 per cent in Batu 16$\frac{1}{2}$ to 88.81 per cent in Titi Haji Idris. It has also been noted that the extent of tenancy in Malaya was highest in Province Wellesley, i.e. 62 per cent in the mid-1950s (T. B. Wilson, 1958: 97); Province Wellesley

TABLE 4.15

Tenurial Status of Rubber Smallholders by Ethnic Group, 1977

	Ethnic Group							
	Malay				Chinese			
Status	No.	Per Cent	Area (ha)	Per Cent	No.	Per Cent	Area (ha)	Per Cent
Owner Operator	275,564	75.3 (76.4)	543 596	74.3 (66.8)	77,549	69.4 (21.5)	251 933	62.8 (31.0)
Non-operating Owner	79,763	21.8 (68.4)	150 464	20.6 (51.6)	34,645	31.0 (29.7)	133 324	33.3 (45.7)
Owner operating only part of land	10,423	2.9 (78.6)	37 673	5.1 (69.1)	2,574	2.3 (19.4)	15 765	3.9 (28.9)
Total	365,750	(100.0) (74.6)	730 733	100.0 (66.3)	114,768	100 (23.4)	401 022	100.0 (34.6)

Source: Gibbons (1983: Tables 2.9 and 2.10).

TABLE 4.14 (*continued*)

Kota Star South[2] (1966)	Bongor Kubang[3] (1975)	Beseri Dalam[3] (1975)	Kubang Pasu[1] (1973)	Bukit Raya[1] (1972)	All of Muda[1] (1966)	All of Muda[4] (1976)
48	33	58	42	60	44	34
40	44	1	30	21	41	36
11	23	41	28	19	14	30
1	–	–	–	–	1	–
100			100	100	100	100
458	64	85	1,002	184	2,476	45,667

Note: A total of 41.3 per cent of farmers were landless, i.e. they did not own any of the land they operated; 24.1 per cent were pure tenants and 11 per cent were 'pure familial tenants'; 4.2 per cent were combinations of these two types, which left 23.7 per cent owners-tenants since 23.7 per cent were combinations of owners-operators, tenants and familial tenants; 2.8 per cent of the farmers illegally occupied at least part of their farm.

was, after all, the first padi-growing area in the peninsula to be colonized by the British; hence the various processes which culminate in tenancy have had more time to develop there.

Prior to the spread of irrigated double-cropping, the main trend in padi-producing areas was apparently towards increasing tenancy. Only 25 years after equal-sized lots had been distributed among settlers in the Sungei Manik irrigation scheme area, 26 per cent of the land in Stage I and 22 per cent in Stage II involved tenancy relations (T. B. Wilson, 1957: 105). He also found that between 1950 and 1955, about 40,000 acres, or approximately 20 per cent of the padi land owned in Kedah and Perlis changed from owner to tenant operation (T. B. Wilson, 1958). Malay Reservation legislation probably encouraged concentration of land-ownership, and hence growing landlordism, i.e. tenancy (J. J. Puthucheary, 1960: 7).

TABLE 4.15 (*continued*)

				Ethnic Group							
	Indian				Others				Total		
No.	Per Cent	Area (ha)	Per Cent	No.	Per Cent	Area (ha)	Per Cent	No.	Per Cent	Area (ha)	Per Cent
,416	76.1 (1.2)	11 361	66.3 (1.4)	3,007	72.7 (0.8)	6 422	67.1 (0.8)	360,536	73.5 (100.0)	812 312	70.1 (100.0)
309	22.6 (1.1)	5 422	31.7 (1.9)	948	22.9 (0.8)	2 425	25.3 (0.8)	116,665	23.0 (100.0)	291 635	25.2 (100.0)
81	1.4 (0.6)	342	2.0 (0.6)	181	4.4 (1.4)	724	7.6 (1.4)	13,259	2.7 (100.0)	54 504	4.7 (100.0)
806	100.0 (1.2)	17 125	100.0 (1.5)	4,136	100.0 (0.8)	9 571	100.0 (0.8)	490,460	(100.0)	1 158 451	100.0 (100.0)

TABLE 4.16

Average Size of Farms for Each Tenure Group by Farm Crop,
1960 (acres)

Tenure Group	Rubber	Coconut	Fruit/ Kampong	Wet Padi (Main Crop)
Owner	6.17	3.55	1.17	2.15
Temporary Occupation Licencee (TOL)	7.23	1.69	0.99	3.05
Tenant	–	–	0.63	2.80
Other Single Tenure	6.05	2.38	0.94	1.81
Owner-tenant	4.91	1.29	0.85	3.23
Other Mixed Tenure	7.07	3.21	1.32	2.73
All Groups	6.30	3.32	1.13	2.52

Source: Hill (1967: 102, Table 3).

Land Tenancy and Ground Rent

A variety of tenurial arrangements between landlord and operator can be found in Malaysian peasant agriculture.[39] Many minor variations exist in different places, and the terms used to characterize the various possible tenurial agreements between private individuals also vary to some extent.[40] Fixed rents are payable either in kind (*sewa padi* in the case of rice) or in cash (*sewa tunai*). Data on the significance of both forms of fixed rent as well as crop-sharing and leases as types of tenancy arrangements in various padi-growing areas are presented in Table 4.17. While fixed rents have predominated on the west coast, padi share-cropping appears to have been an almost exclusively Kelantanese phenomenon in the post-war period.

In padi production, it is generally believed that regardless of rental type, at least a third of the crop, or the cash equivalent thereof, accrues to the landlord. 'This proportion may rise to one half, as in Kelantan, or even more, the present writer having encountered a few farmers in Trengganu who were paying two-thirds of their crop to the landlord' (Hill, 1967: 108). However, there are other instances in which rental rates have been found to be below a third, with the proportion of cash rent to total yield ranging between 17 per cent and 26 per cent in Beseri Dalam, Perlis, and averaging around 25 per cent in Bongor Kudong, Perlis, in 1975 (Horii *et al.*, 1975: 22, 28; Ouchi *et al.*, 1977: 84, 118). But similar evidence of relatively low share-cropping rates has been disputed,[41] raising doubts about other such findings. The total magnitude of rent paid to padi landlords is estimated to be quite considerable, 'an amount in 1964 that was around $18 million—enough to pay for the installation of an irrigation work as large as the Sungei Muda Scheme, every eight years' (Hill, 1967: 109).

Practice of the various rental arrangements has not been unchanging, however.[42] As Table 4.17 shows, the ratio of rents in kind to rents in cash in Kedah for 1955 was 19 : 3, whereas in the Muda Scheme in 1976, this ratio had changed to 19 : 75. The proportion of fixed rents in Krian rose from 41 per cent in 1954 to 49 per cent in 1971; fixed padi rents declined from 35 per cent to 20

TABLE 4.17

Percentage of Tenancy Agreements by Rent Type in Padi-growing Areas and Villages
(Percentage of Areas Involved in Brackets)

Place	Cash		Kind		Total Number of Agreements
	Lease (pajak)	Rent (sewa tunai)	Fixed (sewa padi)	Share (pawah)	
Perlis, 1949[1]	–	(2)	(88)	(10)	–
Perlis, 1955[1]	7(4)	1(1)	68(82)	24(12)	9,380
Kedah, 1949[1]	(1)	(7)	(91)	(0)	–
Kedah, 1955[1]	10(11)	12(14)	76(75)	2(0)	52,640
Province Wellesley, 1949[1]	–	(1)	(99)	(1)	–
Province Wellesley, 1955[1]	9(6)	1(1)	89(88)	1(5)	10,500
Kelantan, 1949[1]	–	–	(2)	(97)	–
Kelantan, 1955[1]	0	0	3(4)	97(96)	96,040
Krian, 1954[1]	(3)	(13)	(82)	(2)	–
Malacca, 1966[2]	25		53	22	–
Muda, 1966[2]	48		49	3	–
Tanjong Karang, 1962[2]	76		24		–
Temerloh District, 1965[2]	5		95		–
Padang Lalang, 1964[3]	3	20	77		123
Padang Lalang, 1968[3]	11	42	46		124
Asam Riang, 1967[4*]	16(18)	86(80)	0	3(2)	28
Muda, 1970[5]	64		36	–	–
DII, Muda, 1973[6]	2	77	19	2	–

(continued)

TABLE 4.17 (continued)

Place	Cash		Kind		Total Number of Agreements
	Lease (pajak)	Rent (sewa tunai)	Fixed (sewa padi)	Share (pawah)	
Muda, 1976[6]	6 (5)	75 (72)	19 (22)	0 (0)	36,250
Sungei Bujor, 1967[7]	6	45	49	0	53
Parit Lebai Akir, 1968/69[7]	9	60	32	0	57
Sungei Megat Aris, 1968/69[7]	5	63	32	0	82
Bongor Kudong, 1975[7]	0	90	8	2	51
Beseri Dalam, 1975[7]	5	14	8	73	59
Pahang Tua, 1975[7]	7	77	0	16	43
Batu 12, 1978[7]	5	89	0	5	19
Gajah Mati, 1967[7]	0	0	0	100	100
Genting Malik, 1959–60 (rubber)[8]	—	14	64	22	254

Sources: 1. T. B. Wilson (1958: 35, Table 4; 36, Table 5; 39, Table 6); and Goethals and Smith (1965: 22, Table 3).
2. Ho (1969: 27, Table 8).
3. Kuchiba, Tsubouchi and Maeda (1979: 70, Table 14).
4. Barnard (1970: 44, Tables 2-6, 2-7) (including 2 farmers—7 per cent—who rented as well as leased land).
5. Doering (1970: 17).
6. Gibbons *et al.* (1981: 64, Table 28).
7. Horii (1981: 95, Table 7.3).
8. Fisk (1961: 17).

*The apparent discrepancy in the percentage distribution of farmers by tenurial status is due to the existence of 2 tenant-lessees (7 per cent) who both rent and lease land.

per cent, while fixed cash rents rose from 6 per cent to 29 per cent during the same interval (Selvadurai, 1972c: 8).

As Table 4.18 shows, cash rents were generally higher than padi rents in 1957 (except in Krian), and it is likely that the transition from rents in padi to cash rents involved an effective increase in the rental rate. The actual increase in rent involved in the transition to cash rents is in fact greater than that shown in Table 4.18. Cash rents 'are always payable in advance before cultivation begins' (T. B. Wilson, 1958: 13). This imposes a greater strain on the tenant who may have to borrow to pay rent before receiving an income from his padi crop while for the land-owner, the rent can be invested to obtain further income. The absence of a discount on payable rent—say calculated according to the market interest rate for short-term credit for the duration of the planting cycle—thus actually represents an implicit increase in the rental rate. Also, the security of tenancy associated with share-cropping or rents in kind disappear in the transition to fixed cash rents (J. C. Scott, 1976; Y. Huang, 1975: 707). Cash rents also tend to be fixed (*sewa mati*), and compensatory reduction in case of a poor harvest far less likely than if rents are paid after the harvest. Negotiable rents (*sewa hidup*) have therefore diminished with the elimination of rents in kind; risk is then borne exclusively by the tenant. Needless to say, rent increases have also occurred independently of these changes. Seven per cent of tenancy agreements in Perlis and 15 per cent in Kedah underwent rent increases of 20 per cent and 16 per cent respectively between 1949/50 and 1955/6, usually in two or more stages (T. B. Wilson, 1958: 27, 48, Table 25). In Permatang Bogak, Province Wellesley, the average annual fixed cash rent per acre rose from $15 in 1960 to $37.60 in 1963 (after the introduction of double-cropping in 1961) and to $150.38 in 1972 (Bhati, 1976: 66, Table 14).

Landlords demand a deposit as security from their tenants, colloquially known as 'tea money'. However, when another farmer offers more 'tea money' or a higher rent, the tenant may be displaced and his 'tea money' returned. Thus, 'tea money' does not actually serve to secure tenancy as alleged. So, while the tenant is still renting the land the landlord can use the 'tea money' for his own purposes, and when a change of tenants occurs, the 'tea money' from the new tenant will at least cover repayment due to the outgoing tenant: in effect, 'tea money' provides the landlord with an added source of funds (Aziz, 1958: 24; Lim Chong-Yah, 1967: 168, 169).

Concealed rent increases also take other forms, including the deliberate over-calculation of the extent of the rented land, demands that the tenant bear the costs of delivering (to the domicile of the landlord) rent paid in kind or in the payment of the Muslim tithes, including *zakat*.[43] Conditions of rent might also include obligatory labour services, the specification of the padi variety to be grown, or even the compulsory cultivation of certain off-season crops (T. B. Wilson, 1958: 19). The recent spread of double-cropping in padi production has apparently spurred the transition to cash rental (Lim Teck Ghee *et al.*, 1974: 55). Double-cropping has often resulted in the doubling of landlords' incomes with no additional effort or expenditure on their part, with rents collected on a seasonal, rather than on an annual, basis (Hill, 1967: 109; Goethals and Smith, 1965).

TABLE 4.18

Changes in Level of Average Rents in Cash and Kind in North Malaya, 1957-1965/1968

State	Cash Rents[1] ($ per acre)			Padi Rents (gantang per acre)		
	1957	1965/68	Percentage Increase	1957[2]	1965/68	Percentage Increase
Perlis	65 (8%)	70 (58%)	7.7	96 ($48)	118	22.9
Kedah	72 (28%)	93 (50%)	29.2	127 ($63)	129	1.6
Province Wellesley	70 (10%)	101 (70%)	44.3	109 ($54)	223	104.5
Kelantan	56 (1%)	66 (76%)	17.9	61 ($30)	112	83.6
Krian, Perak	86 (13%)	n.a.	—	108 ($108)	130	20.3

Sources: T. B. Wilson (1958: 54, Table 41); Y. Huang (1971: 101, Table 3a); Y. Huang (1975: 709, Table 4).

[1]Farmers paying cash rents as a percentage of all farmers paying rent (in brackets).

[2]Cash equivalent in *ringgit* in brackets at field price of $0.50 per *gantang*, $12.50 per *pikul* and $80 per *kunca*.

In the past, considerable evidence has supported the view that there is much insecurity of tenancy among padi cultivators, with this reflected in the high rate of turnover of tenants renting land.[44] Insecurity of tenure, in turn, is said to discourage good cultivation practices.[45] The Rice Production Committee (1952: 46) stated that 'in the last ten years 50 per cent of the leased lands had changed hands' in Province Wellesley. T. B. Wilson (1956: 107) found evidence of high turnover of tenants, with a third of tenant farmers in Stage I of the Sungei Manik irrigation scheme farming a given piece of rented land for only a year; another third, however, farmed for up to five years. T. B. Wilson (1958: 34, 61, Tables 58 and 59; 62, Tables 60 and 61) has studied the period of tenancy in the northern padi-growing States (see Table 4.19). Insecurity of tenure was found to vary considerably with different types of tenancy agreements and between areas, and in the case of Kelantan, he found that 42 per cent of rented padi land changed hands in 1956 alone. The median number of years the tenant was in possession of a particular piece of land was estimated to be over four for both Province Wellesley and Perlis, under three for Kedah, and less than one for Kelantan (Goethals and Smith, 1965: 27, Table 4).

Evidence emerging in recent years, however, suggests that insecurity of tenure may not be as grave a problem as previously perceived or existed. More likely, given its recent origin, it may instead suggest a slowing down in the average turnover rate among tenants, probably associated with the transition to different rental systems, or the increased application of inputs, such as fertilizers, in peasant agriculture. Barnard (1970: 47) found the average length of tenancy in Asam Riang, Kedah, to be 12.25 years. As Table 4.19 shows, in Muda Locality DII for 1973, the distribution of tenants by length of tenancy was comparable to that for Perlis and Province Wellesley in 1955 (Lim Teck Ghee et al., 1974: 51), i.e. suggesting increasing security of tenure. It has also been pointed out that while many tenancy agreements may be for only a year at a time, the rate of renewal is not necessarily low (Doering, 1970: 15).

Tenancy and Peasant Differentiation

Growing land hunger, concentration of land-ownership, tenancy (and its counterpart, landlordism) and the process of differentiation among the peasantry emerge as complex processes unfolding with the integration of the Malay peasantry into the British Empire. However, the colonial impact did not lead directly to the spread of capitalist relations of production among the peasantry. The integration of the peasant sector mainly stimulated the development of petty commodity peasant production and the related growth of circulation capital, as well as the emergence of new non-capitalist relations of production (i.e. not involving the exploitation of wage labour). Since peasant social relations of production were transformed by integration—under colonial domination—into the capitalist-dominated market, they were no longer pre-capitalist. Yet, these peasant relations cannot be termed 'capitalist'—despite subordination to circulation, especially merchant capital—in so far as they did not involve the direct exploitation of free wage labour by capital invested in agrarian production. Caught in fundamentally new circumstances created by

TABLE 4.19
Length of Tenancy on Rented Land (percentage)

Period of Tenant Possession (years)	Perlis[1] (1955)	Kedah[1] (1955)	Province Wellesley[1] (1955)	Kelantan[1] (1955)	DII, Muda[2] (1973)	Permatang Bogak[3] (1972)	Province Wellesley[4] (1968)
1 or less	14	20	8	42	14		
1–2	6	11	3	11	13	6	20
2–3	11	11	14	17	12		
3–4	10	11	11	11	7	46	35
4–5	2	7	7	3	17		
5–10	26	18	25	9		48	45
>10	31	22	32	7	37	35	
Tenants Involved:	9,380	52,640	10,500	96,040	1,418		

Sources: 1. T. B. Wilson (1958: 61, Tables 58, and 59; 62, Tables 60 and 61).
2. Lim Teck Ghee et al. (1974: 60, Table 19).
3. Bhati (1976: 66, Table 15).
4. Selvadurai and Ani (1969: 58).

colonial intervention, the peasantry survived–as peasants, in so far as they continued to have private (direct) access to land, the primary means for agricultural production–though subject to ongoing change. Hence, the peasantry, under colonialism and since, has been irreversibly transformed by its integration into the world economy and its subordination to capital. Subject to the logic of capital accumulation in its various forms, the peasantry is inextricably tied to the market and hence peasant production is dictated by the rationality of commodity production. These forces, subordinating the peas-antry to the hegemony of capital and the market, have also set in motion new processes of differentiation among the peasantry itself. Unlike the pre-colonial class structure–in which peasants were generally not significantly stratified at the village level, though they were subject to extra-local class domination–after colonial integration, peasants became subject to differentiation at the village level as well.[46] As accumulation of rural wealth on the one hand, and peasant impoverishment on the other were manifested in the growing concentration of land-ownership, peasant relations of production increasingly involved land tenancy rather than the generalization of wage labour relations.

The complex dynamics of subdivision and concentration of land-ownership, and the recent origins of peasant differentiation have a bearing on the social relations, forms and consequences of peasant differentiation. 'The concentra-tion of ownership in the three areas has not led to a clear-cut class system made up of landlords on the one hand and tenants on the other' (Husin Ali, 1975: 84). As can be seen in Table 4.20, the situation is indeed far more complex. The categories employed by others–e.g. Husin Ali (1964, 1975) and Kessler (1974)–have been adopted here. Based on the individual farmer's relationship to land, such categorization reflects his relationship to others and hence his position in peasant society.

The farmer's relationship to operated land may, however, be a doubtful criterion. Swift (1967: 262–4) has suggested that wealth differentiation within the village is both a new and unstable phenomenon. Unless a land-owner has enough property to enable his heirs to inherit sufficient wealth to accumulate successfully themselves, he argued, the divisive impact of the inheritance system can have a countervailing effect on wealth differentiation, though once the process of accumulation has advanced far enough, it is less likely that inheritance will have this retarding effect on differentiation. Also, the increasing concentration of land-ownership among those for whom land is not the main source of income, will not be checked by the inheritance system.

Landlords–those who own but do not operate land–do not themselves farm either because they can afford not to or because they hold 'better' jobs or because they are unable to due to age or illness, in which case they may be far from wealthy. Evidence suggests that landlords do not comprise a homogene-ous class clearly distinguishable from farmers (Jegatheesan, 1976: 42). Of a non-random sample of 198 resident landlords in the DII locality of the Muda region, 27 per cent (57) were 'pure' landlords, 60 per cent (128) were landlords cum owners–operators, 5 per cent (11) were rural capitalists, and 1 per cent (3) were in government service (Lim Teck Ghee et al., 1974: 119–20). While 54 per cent (114) had inherited their land, 38 per cent (80) had purchased it and 2 per cent (4)

TABLE 4.20

Breakdown of Peasant Cultivators and Landlords in Five Villages

Categories	Kangkong[1]	Kerdau[1]	Bagan[1]	Jelawat[2]	Permatang Bogak[3]
a. Landlords: income exclusively from rent of own land worked by others	6	11	14	17	2
b. Landlords cum owners-operators: income from rent of land worked by others, and from produce and labour on own land	8	15	10	18	—
c. Owners-operators: income from produce and labour on own land	17	52	34	33	9
d. Owners-operators cum tenants: income from labour on others' land and produce and labour on own land	21	28	30	68	11
e. Tenants and share-croppers: income from labour on land belonging to others	32	8	36	42	24
f. Wage-labour: income from labour supervised by others on land belonging to others	n.a.	n.a.	n.a.	29	5
Total	84	114	124	207	51

Sources: 1. Kessler (1974: 134, Table 6).
2. Husin Ali (1975).
3. Bhati (1976: 61, Table 12; 84, Table 18a).

had acquired it by forest clearance. Rent was the only source of income for 36 per cent (77),[47] a primary source of income for 21 per cent (41), and a subsidiary source of income for 36 per cent (77).

Tenancy relations also appear to be mitigated by kin relationship. Kinship ties between tenants and landlords have been found to be frequent in the Muda scheme: 78 per cent in Sungei Bujor, 66 per cent in Bongor Kudong, and 32 per cent in Beseri Dalam (Horii, 1981: 96, Table 7.4), about four-fifths in Bukit Raya (Afifuddin, 1973), 65 per cent in Padang Lalang (Kuchiba and Tsubouchi, 1967), and 52 per cent in Muda Locality DII (Lim Teck Ghee et al., 1974). In 1976, 42,279 or 71 per cent of 59,427 non-owning operators of padi parcels in the Muda region had a kinship tie to the legal owner, though the proportion of households related to one another in a village is considerably less, varying between 19 and 40 per cent; this accounted for 63 per cent of the total area of 174,022 relong cultivated by non-owners (Gibbons et al., 1981: 50). Outside the Muda region, the proportions are similarly varied, e.g. 86 per cent in Parit Lebai Akir, 60 per cent in Sungei Megat Aris, 47 per cent in Pahang Tua, 48 per cent in Batu 12, Tanjung Karang, and 35 per cent in Gajah Mati, Pasir Mas (Horii, 1981: 96, Table 7.4). Various studies argue that peasant class relations are heavily mediated by kinship, often affecting security of tenancy, time and flexibility of rent payment, rental rates, and so on, in favour of the poorer kin. As the study of Muda Locality DII shows, 16 per cent of non-kin tenancy relationships, compared to 34 per cent of those between kin, had 'social characteristics'[48] which 'soften' the 'economic' nature of tenancy relationships,[49] Horii (1972) admitted, perhaps unwittingly, that 'reciprocity' is involved where class is mediated by kinship; yet, focused his study on what he terms 'shared poverty', where kinship motivates land-owners to rent to kin at lower rentals. Reciprocity, by definition, involves a two-way or exchange relationship; for example, free labour services may be expected from kin tenants who are charged lower rentals. Such contributions or reciprocity from 'poor' kin have not been examined by most of those who have studied the influence of kinship on land tenancy. If such relationships are actually reciprocal, it would imply that while kinship may have some bearing on tenancy relations, the reciprocity involved may actually negate the existence of 'shared poverty'.

Given the recency of the forces contributing to intra-village class differentiation, and the past coherence of the village as a social unit, it is probable that kinship or similar primordial factors continue to moderate the still nascent class contradictions.[50] However the actual significance of kinship in this context needs to be more carefully examined. Although distinctions between close and more distant kin have been acknowledged, they do not appear to have been fully taken into account in the studies currently available. A study of Gelong Rambai in the Muda area (Shadli, 1978)[51] suggests that tenancy relationships are significantly affected by kinship ties involving close kin (siblings, parents, grandparents) but not significantly by those between distant kin. In any case, the significance of kinship in moderating class relations is generally acknowledged to be declining.[52]

The land-ownership pattern had a strong bearing on the pattern of income distribution in the three villages studied by Husin Ali (see Table 4.21). While

TABLE 4.21

Distribution of Land-ownership and Income by Various Tenurial Categories

	Land Ownership (acres)					Income ($)					Total
	0–3	3½–9	9½–15	15½–21	>21	0–61	61–120	121–180	181–240	>240	
Kangkong											
Landlord	–	2	–	1	3	–	1	1	1	3	6
Landlord (cum owner) operator	–	5	2	1	–	1	4	1	2	–	8
Owner-operator	7	8	2	–	–	5	7	4	1	–	17
Owner (operator cum) tenant	16	5	–	–	–	11	8	2	–	–	21
Tenant	32	–	–	–	–	29	3	–	–	–	32
	55	20	4	2	3	46	23	8	4	3	84
Kerdau											
Landlord	–	2	2	1	6	1	2	1	3	4	11
Landlord (cum owner) operator	–	5	8	1	1	2	6	4	3	–	15
Owner operator	8	32	11	–	–	18	25	5	3	–	52
Owner (operator cum) tenant	11	16	1	–	–	19	6	2	1	–	28
Tenant	8	–	–	–	–	7	–	1	–	–	8
	27	55	22	3	7	47	39	13	10	5	114
Bagan											
Landlord	–	–	1	1	12	–	–	–	3	11	14
Landlord (cum owner) operator	–	3	7	–	–	2	3	3	2	–	10
Owner operator	12	20	2	–	–	8	19	5	2	–	34
Owner (operator cum) tenant	21	9	–	–	–	3	20	7	–	–	30
Tenant	35	1	–	–	–	18	17	1	–	–	36
	68	33	10	1	12	31	59	16	7	11	124

Source: Husin Ali (1975: 86, Table 8; 88, Table 9).

TABLE 4.22

Estimated Production Returns to Muda Padi Planters,
by Tenurial Returns and Farm Size,
for Off-season Crop, 1970

Tenure Group and Farm Size	Mean Farm Size (relong)	Net Cash Returns ($)
Large Owners	9.7	1,746
Large Tenants	9.8	719
Large Owners-tenants	14.9	1,943
Small Owners	3.3	662
Small Tenants	3.7	334
Small Owners-tenants	6.3	708

Source: Doering (1973: 169, Table 5.4).

other factors have varying degrees of importance, a positive relationship between land-ownership and income is apparent in Table 4.21, and is especially strong at the poles, featuring landlords with extensive holdings at one end and landless tenants at the other. In Permatang Bogak in 1972, the highest incomes were enjoyed by landlords ($1,605.68), followed by the owner-tenants ($1,326.48), owners ($632.91), tenants ($590.34), and the landless ($192.37) (Bhati, 1976: 123, Table 34). Table 4.22 also points to a similar correlation between the tenurial status, farm size and income of farmers in the Muda region in 1970.

Technological Change and the Social Relations of Padi Production

More recent technological changes in padi production may continue to change the social relations of peasant padi production in the direction of capitalist agriculture, i.e. involving more capital-intensive padi production involving the generalized exploitation of wage labour by capital. Though the ultimate significance of this ongoing transformation remains to be seen, certain features are already distinguishable.

Basically, the Green Revolution in Malaysian padi farming—especially in Malaysia's rice bowl, the Muda region—has emphasized four new factors. First, new fast-growing and high-yielding varieties of padi, originally developed by foreign rice-breeding research organizations (such as the International Rice Research Institute at Los Banos, Philippines) sponsored primarily by United States funding agencies (e.g. the Agricultural Development Council) and introduced—often after further local adaptation—through various agricultural extension services in target padi-growing areas in Malaysia, by the relevant local government agencies, with considerable support from foreign 'agricultural development' agencies. Second, artificial irrigation systems and other related physical infrastructure prepared by Malaysian government agencies, again with heavy support from international development agencies (such as the

World Bank). Such institutional support from the Malaysian government and allied international agencies paved the way for transnational corporations to step in and profitably provide the remaining two major inputs, namely chemicals and agricultural machinery. Chemical fertilizers and pesticides have been found to be necessary for the rapid growth, high yields, and crop survival of the new varieties. The more intensive double-cropping planting schedules require field ploughing to be completed more rapidly and this has been achieved largely by substituting mechanized ploughing for buffalo-drawn ploughing.

More recently (since the late 1970s), the widespread success of the introduction of mechanized harvesting in Muda and other areas has influenced the padi-planting schedule as a whole. Whereas a certain order in the fields was required to facilitate manual harvesting, the labour required for a seedling nursery and transplanting may be rendered redundant by the new harvesting technology which no longer relies on the previously labour-intensive planting techniques. In contrast, the earlier stage of the Green Revolution had a more ambiguous effect on the social relations of padi production as the intensified work schedule associated with double-cropping increased labour require-ments, while (partial) mechanization diminished the need for labour.

These technological changes, especially mechanization, have paved the way for capitalist padi farming; while this is already emerging, there continue to be many problems (e.g. the pattern of land-ownership, the ethnicity of most existing big capitalist padi farmers, the consequent displacement of Malay agricultural labour), which may continue to hamper the generalization of this tendency. With the significant increase in productivity achieved by the Green Revolution accompanied by a government padi price-support programme, operated land area has become the key determinant of gross padi farm incomes. And in so far as padi land rentals have not kept pace with the combined effects of increases in productivity and price, it has become increasingly profitable to cultivate larger farms—even at the expense of renting land and hiring labour services. This has, of course, drastically changed the earlier relationship between tenurial status and income in the areas affected.

Higher gross incomes for padi farmers appear to have been achieved in most areas which have experienced the Green Revolution. These higher incomes, however, are not always good indicators of economic welfare. More intensive farmer involvement in padi production has generally reduced the time available for other activities—on or off the farm—some of which do not involve commodity production, and hence cash incomes (e.g. off-season fishing in padi fields and canals, which has also been undermined by pesticide poisoning). Furthermore, the increased gross incomes of padi farmers as a result of the Green Revolution have been achieved at some expense—including higher farm production costs, especially for chemical inputs, machine purchases or services, fuel costs, and sometimes hired labour, all of which have also been subject to differing degrees of inflation, especially since 1973. Hence, it is not surprising that some farmers allege that they are not economically better off after the Green Revolution (Ishak and Jomo, 1982).

To ensure the success of the Green Revolution, and ostensibly in the interest of national rice self-sufficiency, the government has introduced various subsidies (e.g. for fertilizer) and a padi price-support programme. The guaranteed minimum padi purchase price has risen from $16 in 1970 to $24-28 in 1975, $28-32 in 1979, and $36-40 in 1980. According to the government's *Fourth Malaysia Plan, 1981-1985*, the incidence of poverty among padi farmers dropped by 9.6 per cent (to 55.1 per cent), solely as a result of the 1980 price increase. This percentage had previously fallen from 88.1 per cent in 1970 to 77.0 per cent in 1975. It may well be the case that unsubsidized productivity increases have not been very significant in reducing the poverty rate among padi farmers. It seems probable that the reduction in the incidence of poverty among padi farmers is largely attributable to the price-support programme, the primary burden of which is borne by the non-rice producing population. In this connection, it should also be noted that big farmers—producing large marketing surpluses—and big land-owners—who qualify for the input (e.g. fertilizer) subsidies, which are distributed according to land area owned—are the main beneficiaries of the price-support and subsidy programmes respectively.

These recent technological changes, involving partial mechanization of the production process and requiring greater investment in padi cultivation, have also affected tenancy patterns in padi areas. The growing importance of means of production other than land has attracted capital investments, not only from the traditional centres of capital, but also from the small towns and the rural rich who can get the new inputs. With this transformation in the organization of padi production, many farms have increased in size, tenancy by the landless appears to be on the decline, the use of hired labour has risen, at least temporarily, and mechanization has remained limited. The absolute tenancy rate may not actually fall; large farmers are actually renting more land as larger

TABLE 4.23

Percentage of Farmers by Tenurial Status in
Various Studies in the Muda Area

Year	Source	Owners-Farmers	Tenant Farmers	Mixed Owners-Tenants	Others	Total
1955	E. J. H. Berwick	38	42	20	–	100
1966	Farm Economic Survey	44	41	14	1	100
1970	Doering	41	40	19	–	100
1973	Lim Teck Ghee *et al.* (Locality DII)	42	30	28	–	100
1974	Kasryno	41	31	28	–	100
1976	Gibbons *et al.*	34	36	30	–	100

Sources: Jegatheesan (1976: 28, Table 4.2); Gibbons *et al.* (1981).

areas can now be farmed with mechanization. Thus, the significance of tenancy as an indicator of land hunger is diminishing. Uneven and partial as they are, recent trends necessitate a revaluation of the role of tenancy in the social relations of padi production. Many of the land-hungry—i.e. the landless as well as those with little land property—have been tenant farmers in the past. The new trends which are raising land rental rates and otherwise reducing opportunities to rent land in padi areas, are now forcing the land-hungry into wage labour in rural as well as urban areas. This shift—from tenancy to wage labour—complements the partial transformation of some rural landlords and merchants into capitalist farmers.

This transition is still too recent to be well documented; nevertheless, in the absence of appropriate data, various studies of the Muda irrigation scheme—which, strictly speaking, are not comparable—suggest some interesting trends. Table 4.23 suggests that major shifts in the tenancy pattern may have taken place between 1970 and 1973, the early years of widespread double-cropping in the area under irrigation. While the number of pure tenant (i.e. landless) farmers appears to be declining proportionately, there has been an apparent increase in the number of 'mixed farmers' (i.e. part-owner, part-tenant), possibly also involving an increase in farm size.[53]

The State, Yeoman Peasants, and Tenancy

The relationship between the colonial state and the peasantry has been discussed in the last chapter. However, a few additional remarks should be made here on the role of the state in relation to tenancy, and its implications for peasant social relations. The importance of preserving a Malay yeoman peasantry was well recognized by the British colonial authorities: 'Malay peasants in [the British] scheme of things were yeomen and, fundamentally, yeomen were independent small land owners' (Kratoska, 1975: 209). Suggestive statements recognizing the political desirability of preserving a Malay yeoman peasantry have been made in various government documents. For example, a report released in December 1957 provided some reasons for encouraging 'the existence of a large smallholding class'. 'It is a considerable help towards political and social security; and of a great value as a basis for sound democratic government' (quoted in Aziz, 1958: 27). Likewise, T. B. Wilson justified his call for land reform and rent control in terms of counter-insurgency considerations, seeing the preservation of a yeoman peasantry as an important bulwark against the communist-led insurgency.[54]

Unlike the circumstances of the colonial era, the need for an electoral base of political power for the post-colonial governing class (see Chapter 10) necessitated significant efforts at rural development. Government efforts in the form of land development and irrigation schemes to promote double-cropping had involved over 200,000 rural households by the late 1970s while the total number of rural households rose from 858,000 in 1957 to 1,250,000 in 1970 (E. Lee, 1976: 40, Table 11). While a review of these efforts is beyond the scope of this chapter, it is also important to recognize the constraints of the ruling party's political base for its agricultural policy, especially so as not to upset the land tenancy situation through some kind of drastic land reform which could upset established landed interests.[55]

Most government rural development projects are oriented towards increasing productivity and make little attempt to fundamentally transform the social relations involving land.[56] It has also been found that the productivity of the 'hard-core' poor rubber smallholders—with holdings of less than 2 hectares for the average-sized household and no other major source of income—was 46.6 per cent higher on average than the 'non-poor'; while the former produced 99.99 kg per hectare monthly on average, the latter managed only 68.21 kg per hectare. This finding refutes the significance officially attached to low productivity as the primary explanation of peasant poverty. Instead, though gender, age, and family size were not strongly related statistically to poverty status, poverty among rubber smallholders was primarily related to the small size of their holdings; 'hard-core' poor rubber smallholders owned 1.64 hectares on average, with all poor smallholders (i.e. with incomes below the official poverty line) owning 1.75 hectares on average while other smallholders averaged holdings of 3.05 hectares (Gibbons, 1984). Ho (1968: 102) has shown that while replanting with high-yielding rubber clones can quadruple previous output per acre, total output per farmer continues to be limited by land.

In padi production, double-cropping has greatly increased costs—involving at least a general doubling of rents, purchase of chemical inputs (fertilizers, pesticides) and payment for labour and machine services necessitated by the compressed double-cropping planting schedule (see Bhati, 1976: 66, Table 14)—thus limiting the benefits obtained by the tenant farmer. After the introduction of double-cropping, the officially defined incidence of poverty among owner-farmers fell from 94 per cent to 70 per cent between 1970 and 1975, whereas the corresponding decline for tenant farmers was from 99 per cent to 84 per cent (Malaysia, 1976). Recent government efforts to promote padi 'mini estates' and settler-owned plantations under the auspices of the Federal Land Development Authority (FELDA) suggest, however, that the government may wish to promote agrarian capitalism by consolidating land at the operational—rather than at the ownership—level to realize economies of scale and increased productivity, efficiency and labour discipline through capitalist management.

The gravity of the tenancy situation among padi cultivators was highlighted by both the 1952 and the 1955 reports of the Rice Production Committee. These resulted in the colonial government's promulgation of the Padi Cultivation Control of Rents and Security of Tenure Ordinance 1955, legislating a rent ceiling and prohibiting the 'tea money' practice, among other things. Certain aspects of the ordinance, ostensibly a piece of legislation to serve the interests of tenants, raised serious doubts as to its true purpose; for example, it prohibited tenancy agreements for 'less than one season or more than one year' (quoted in T. B. Wilson, 1958: 94).[57] In a situation where agreements are not made for less than a season for obvious reasons, this maximum limit actually increased insecurity of tenure by prohibiting leases of longer duration. While rents previously below the newly legislated maxima were raised to the officially tolerated maximum levels, it was found that rents already exceeding these maxima were very rarely lowered (Lim Chong-Yah, 1967: 169). Ambiguities in legislation have tended to be resolved in favour of the stronger party, invariably the land-owners. Perhaps, most significantly, the legislation was not backed up with any effective enforcement apparatus. The Ordinance has been described as having been 'completely ineffective'[58] (Selvadurai, 1972a: 29).

The gravity of the tenancy situation was exacerbated as the 'counter-productive' impact of the 1955 Ordinance became ever more glaring. A Ford Foundation-sponsored team presented a report critically examining the 1955 legislation and recommending alternatives (Goethals and Smith, 1965). Failing to fully recognize and take account of the nature of the post-colonial state in relation to the vested interests at stake, the authors naively suggested comprehensive legislative and implementative measures for the Malaysian government's consideration; subsequently, the Padi Cultivators (Control of Rent and Security of Tenure) Act 1967, was duly passed by Parliament. Though legislatively superior (see Selvadurai, 1972a: 29–30), the Act has suffered a fate similar to that of the 1955 Ordinance: responsibility for implementation rests with State governments, which have been assigned constitutional authority over land-related matters. Rural landed interests, generally more strongly entrenched at the State level compared to the federal level, have ensured that the Act has largely remained a dead letter.

There appears to be considerable resistance from landlords to stipulations of the 1967 Act; economically and politically weak, tenants have not been in a position to ensure effective implementation (Selvadurai, 1972c: 35). Many observations have been made of rents exceeding the stipulated legal maxima (e.g. see Barnard, 1970: 49). In Sungei Bujor, 14 of the 26 cases of rent paid in kind were in excess of the legislated ceilings (Horii, 1972: 59). Findings in Muda Locality DII reflected the considerable extent of violation of legislative stipulations (Lim Teck Ghee et al., 1974: 60, 61): only 20 per cent of tenancy agreements were in writing, with only 6 per cent registered, though both written agreements and legislation are required by the Act. The small proportion of padi share-cropping still in existence appears to have been hardly affected by the law, which prohibits it altogether. Although rents are supposed to be due only two weeks after harvest, 40 per cent of cash rents were being paid in advance of planting. Rental agreements are supposed to be made for at least 3 years with the tenant having the right to renewal. Instead, 56 per cent of agreements were for an indefinite period; 25 per cent of tenants claimed not to have the right of renewal, while another 23 per cent were unsure of their rights. In sum then, existing legislation which might serve tenant interests is hardly implemented, while the bulk of legislation, together with other aspects of the state apparatus, tend, in practice, to serve landlords.

Summary

Land is the primary means of production for peasant farmers. Colonial legislation and policy radically transformed the significance of land in the peasant economy, and hence peasant relations of production. Land law in the colonial order recognized private property rights in land, rendering it a commodity to be owned, bought, or sold. The new legislation, together with several other measures taken by the colonial government, undermined the practice of shifting agriculture. More importantly, the colonial situation created the conditions for landlordism and its corollary, peasant tenancy. It also facilitated the proletarianization of poor peasants; e.g. by becoming property which could be used as collateral to obtain credit, land could also be subsequently lost through loan default.

Several large tracts of land were provided by the colonial authorities to some members of the pre-colonial ruling class, enabling them subsequently to become landlords. However, the origins of peasant differentiation are to be found in other new tendencies generated by the colonial situation. Unlike during the pre-colonial era, subsequent increase in land cultivated by peasants no longer corresponded to demographic growth. In conformity with colonial law, lawful cultivation could only be done on legally alienated land. (In the colonial economy, the best available land—in terms of soil conditions, access to communications, etc.—was alienated to capitalist interests, especially British businesses.) With Islamic inheritance law and customary Malay inheritance practices operating in this context, the outcome has been a generally increasing ratio of peasants to land, manifested mainly in greater joint ownership and subdivision of landholdings. Together with other factors differentiating the peasantry according to wealth, there has also been some concentration of land-ownership among peasants. Hence, the phenomena of landlordism, land hunger, and landlessness are primarily consequences of the peasant situation under colonialism. The integration of the Malay peasantry into the world economy has given rise to new non-capitalist relations of production fundamentally different from the pre-colonial class relations involving the peasantry.

Concentration of land-ownership has mainly led to tenancy (and share-cropping) arrangements rather than the organization of the labour process along capitalist lines. Peasant strata may be differentiated according to tenurial status, i.e. location in tenancy arrangements. The peasantry may be analytically differentiated into several related strata by using criteria including land owned, land cultivated, and the nature of the labour process. However, these divisions still appear to be somewhat ameliorated by kinship ties and there is considerable ambiguity about the nature and extent of social consciousness. While there has been a rising ground rent rate, with increases somewhat hidden by changes in tenancy arrangements and forms of rent payment, this trend does not appear to have kept pace with rising agricultural land prices. This, of course, has complex implications for capitalist investment trends in peasant agriculture; it seems, for instance, that investments in rice production will focus on means of production other than land, with the necessary concentration of land for capitalist management purposes resolved (at least temporarily) by tenancy or government-sponsored land consolidation for operational purposes, rather than by the more difficult, controversial, and more expensive route of acquiring outright ownership. In general, it seems that while the state has sought to preserve a yeoman peasantry in the interest of political stability, it has not sought to resist the tendencies contributing to peasant differentiation.

1. David Wong has comprehensively discussed the emergence and legal significance of such legislation in the Malay States. Lim Teck Ghee (1976) has provided a detailed historical account of the development of the prototype land legislation in Perak. Jacoby has also discussed the significance of the law affecting land tenure for peasant cultivation (IBRD, 1955). See also Das (1963).

2. 'The system of land-tenure as it evolved in the Federated Malay States of Perak, Selangor, Negri Sembilan and Pahang served as a model for successive British Agents and Advisers in the Unfederated Malay States of Kelantan, Kedah, Perlis, Trengganu and Johore. . . . In this it reflected the tendency of British policy towards uniformity, but the application of similar legislation to a number of disparate communities, differing in density and composition of population, methods of cultivation, the extent of the intrusion of alien economic forces, and the degree to which customary inheritance practices have been modified by Islam, resulted in a land tenure situation displaying considerable local variation' (H. Wilson, 1975: 120).

3. 'Under the terms of the new legislation, all land which had not been alienated, nor reserved for a public purpose, nor reserved forest, was considered to be State Land, the ownership of which rested in the ruler of the State in which it was located' (H. Wilson, 1975: 130).

4. '. . . in Krian, in 1874, it was difficult to get ten dollars an *orlong* for excellent *padi* land by *pulang belanja* [return of expenses], but when security of tenure and the full right of alienation of the soil were introduced in the district by the British Government, it became possible to sell the same land for $60 or $70 an *orlong*' (Maxwell, 1884).

5. '. . . the easier acquisition of state-sponsored credit by planters, the greater participation by Government and heavier investment of state revenue in plantation agricultural schemes and the lack of interest shown by Government experimental gardens in native crops' (Lim Teck Ghee, 1976: 130). Administrative actions adopted to improve peasant agriculture were few and even these 'proved to be more in the way of half-hearted, disjointed and niggardly measures rather than a concerted programme' (Lim Teck Ghee, 1976: 141).

6. In the last quarter of the nineteenth century, colonial expenditure in the Malay States was mainly oriented to the promotion of the tin industry, which British capitalists were anxious to wrest control of, and which was the most important export of the region, as far as British industry was concerned. Thus, for example, the first railways were built to connect tin-mining centres with coastal ports. Later, as rubber took the place of tin, colonial expenditure shifted accordingly. Even on the rare occasions when colonial expenditure was ostensibly to serve peasant interests, e.g. in the development of the Krian Irrigation Scheme to promote padi production, the ultimate interests served were still the capitalist employers of rice-eating workers and the colonial state which had to pay for rice imports with foreign exchange. For further discussion, see Chapter 3.

7. For example, 'Fixed rents originated as feudal dues, which were continued after the disintegration of the Raja feudalism' (T. B. Wilson, 1958: 10).

8. 'There are only one hundred and twenty titles of over thirty-five acres each (50 Kedah relong) in the whole of the west coast padi plain from the southern district boundary of Krian in Perak to the northern Siamese border of Perlis.

'These few large titles are outstanding in size, and range up to 250 acres each with an average of 95 acres, whilst throughout this area, all padi land titles averaged only five acres. Consequently this handful of titles accounts for over 11,000 acres or about three per cent of the main padi land area in which they are found.

'Each title often has more than one owner, usually the result of subdivision or inheritance. But fragmentation is less common and less advanced than on holdings of normal size, and it tends to be outweighed by plural ownership, i.e. the possession by the same owner of whole or part shares in other holdings. In one instance in Krian, six persons are named as co-owners on each of four large titles, which together total over 900 acres of padi land.

'Over all the padi lands of north-west Malaya, approximately three owners existed for each of these large titles, i.e. about 350 owners owned about three per cent of the main padi land area in the form of large holdings. Thus only a small proportion of the main padi land is shown, by the *prima facie* evidence of the cadastral sheets, to be concentrated in the hands of a few proprietors, although some of these possess some very large properties' (T. B. Wilson, 1958: 63-4).

9. Rent has been identified as the largest cost item in padi production, e.g. see T. B. Wilson (1958: 22); and Lim Chong-Yah (1967: 168). Selvadurai (1972c: 16) estimated, from a survey of padi

production in Krian, Perak, that land accounts for at least 82 per cent of total 'farm capital'. This should be viewed in the context of the extent of tenancy in padi production, since for the average farm size of 3.1 acres, only 1.6 acres is owned while the rest is rented. However, such estimates may now have to be revised downward in recognition of recent technological changes in padi and other agricultural production requiring heavy investments in machinery, chemicals, etc. Nevertheless, it is hardly likely that such increases in fixed capital investments detract from the centrality of land to peasant production.

10. 'The root cause of poverty boils down to a race between population growth on the one hand and technological progress and opening up of new lands on the other' (Lim Chong-Yah, 1967: 173).

11. '. . . overpopulation is likewise a historically determined relation, in no way determined by abstract numbers or by the absolute limit of productivity of the necessaries of life, but by limits posited rather by *specific conditions of production*.'

12. Current studies have only touched on them tangentially (e.g. see D. Guyot, 1971; Mohd. Noor, 1974; Husin Ali, 1975).

13. Kuchiba and Tsubouchi (1967: 470) mention that inheritance according to Islamic law and Malay custom (*adat*) were about equal in number in the Kedah village they studied.

14. This distinction has not been rigorously adhered to by the various writers discussing these issues in the Malayan situation, and is the source of considerable confusion (e.g. see the work of T. B. Wilson, M. G. Swift, and R. Ho). When citing such authors, what they mean, rather than what they write, will be stated, thus employing these terms more strictly.

15. '. . . in every decade of this century, an average of two-thirds of all paddy lots and about three-quarters of all kampong and rubber lots have changed hands [in Saiong Mukim]' (Ho, 1970: 87, 88, Table 3).

16. 'Changes in ownership which have resulted in an increase in the number of owners have been at least twice as numerous as those with the opposite effect' (Ho, 1970: 88). Division affected an average of 12 per cent of all padi lots, 11 per cent of *kampung* lots and 6 per cent of rubber lots in Saiong Mukim for each decade between 1890 and 1960.

17. '. . . *de jure* division of property always exceeds *de facto* or actual fragmentation, as the physical sub-division of a lot involves expensive and time-consuming re-surveys and re-registration' (Ho, 1967: 41).

18. 'The extent of the inaccuracy of official land ownership data is described for Krian, where 39 per cent of the holdings have undergone an unregistered change of ownership on average some 11 years previously' (T. B. Wilson, 1958: 97).

19. That the likelihood of a lot being subdivided into parcels increases with the size of the lot is also supported by findings from farm locality DII of the Muda irrigation scheme (Lim Teck Ghee et al., 1974: 39, Table 8). Only 4 per cent of lots under 2 *relong* were found to be sub-divided. The percentage increased to 27 per cent above 4 *relong*, 50 per cent above 7 *relong*, and to 68 per cent above 10 *relong*.

20. Swift (1965) explains the high degree of sole ownership of padi farms in Negri Sembilan by the strong influence of customary restrictions exerted by the lineage or clan on disposal of land property.

21. 'It is interesting to note that the process has resulted in a multiplication of very small shares, so that over one-quarter (26 per cent) of the shares now registered for Krian padi lands represent less than one acre of land each, and nearly one tenth (9 per cent) of the shares represent less than one-quarter of an acre' (T. B. Wilson, 1958: 83).

22. '. . . the increase in the number of joint owners, and the diminution in the size of the interests of individual owners, was a strong incentive to sell the land to someone in a position to purchase it as a composite unit. The new owners were naturally not the impoverished and landless in the reservation, but persons who already owned substantial income-producing holdings or who had other substantial sources of income' (Fisk, 1961: 21).

23. 'Thus we find co-owners with 1/127-th shares and others with 9/64-th shares and so forth' (Aziz, 1958: 23).

The Payne Land Administration Commission in Malaya stated in 1958:
'Without attempting to find fantastic cases, but merely looking through records at random, we came across nine persons having shares in a small-holding in the following proportions:

$$\frac{12522}{57024}, \quad \frac{12522}{57024}, \quad \frac{6276}{57024}, \quad \frac{3080}{57024}, \quad \frac{1540}{57024}, \quad \frac{1464}{57024}, \quad \frac{732}{57024}, \quad \frac{1569}{57024}, \quad \frac{10893}{57024}$$

In another two acres, one rood, the shares held by eight people respectively were:

$$\frac{1}{2}, \quad \frac{1}{14}, \quad \frac{1}{14}, \quad \frac{1}{14}, \quad \frac{1}{14}, \quad \frac{331737}{2286144}, \quad \frac{27909}{2286144}, \quad \frac{130242}{2286144}$$

Numerous similar illustrations could be given. In one instance we were informed that the share of rural land inherited by one beneficiary amounted to three square feet, and he insisted on having it' (quoted in Lim Chong-Yah, 1967: 171).

24. 'Co-ownership tends to result in neglect of land or use of poor techniques, lack of conservation measures and unwillingness to make long-term improvements to the land. It also tends towards land-lordism because it is simpler for the co-owners to share the value of the rent rather than any other economic arrangement' (Aziz, 1958: 24).

25. 'A consequence of sub-division is that farmers find a single piece of land too small. In order to make better use of their time and energy they try to operate several pieces of land. Generally the pieces they inherit, buy or rent will not be contiguous. This process where the pieces of land on particular farms are scattered about the village is called fragmentation' (Aziz, 1958: 23).

26. '...under the combined effects of scarcity of land, the question of the peasant's place of residence after marriage, the laws of inheritance, etc., the land owned by the peasants is geographically dispersed, and the result is a strong tendency to fragment the cultivated land holdings' (Kuchiba and Tsubouchi, 1967: 472).

27. 'In that Census, farmers were classified by the number of separate non-contiguous "parcels" or "pieces" of land in each farm, in order to reveal the extent of fragmentation. A "parcel" was defined as land entirely surrounded by land of other farmers or by land not forming part of any farm e.g. forest, river, etc., and may consist of a whole grant of land, only part of a grant or several grants' (Selvadurai, 1972a: 28).

28. 'Fragmentation is wasteful of the farmers' time, energy and equipment' (Aziz, 1958: 24).

29. Concentration of land-ownership refers to the process whereby land parcels, previously owned separately, are brought under common ownership. In so far as such land is not contiguous, it gives rise to fragmentation of land owned. Concentration, as discussed in relation to land-ownership, cannot therefore be viewed as analogous to the concentration of capital.

30. For example, Swift (1967: 251) has argued that maintenance of a certain level of 'normal' consumption is not a major cause of land sales. Instead, he suggests, land transfers are usually caused by the incurrence of extraordinary expenditure.

31. '...of the 359 householders and/or their wives in Malay households 21.4% have inherited agricultural land; 17.0% have not yet inherited agricultural land; and 60.2% have no possibility of inheriting agricultural land because none was owned by their parents' (Kuchiba and Tsubouchi, 1967: 471).

32. Frequently, land purchase prices have been depressed by the effects of Malay Reservation legislation. It has also been shown how land can be acquired by forfeiture of collateral on unsettled debts. The effective purchase prices in such cases are lower than the market price.

33. 'The total land area in these sampled estates was most unevenly distributed among the 102 owners. Half (51) of the owners each owned less than six acres, and their properties averaged only three acres each; together their property amounted to only 10 per cent of the total. The poorest three-quarters of the owners had less than 10 acres each and their total property of 313 acres formed only a small proportion (17 per cent) of the total area of all the estates.

'The owner of several titles is usually a larger landowner than average, and the several people who had died with property on at least eight separate titles accounted for half of the titles (214 titles) and had owned more than 25 acres each. Nine of the largest estates together accounted for two-thirds of the total land area. The three largest owners with more than fifteen titles each, together owned 180 land titles and their property aggregated 1,020 acres, out of the total 1,825 acres. Almost half of the land (874 acres) had been owned by two men, and it is interesting to note that of these two estates, the one acquired by inheritance belonging to a member of the Perak royal family, was smaller than the one acquired piecemeal by a Chettiar, mainly through purchase and foreclosure of mortgages: this was before the Malay Reservation Enactment prohibiting sale of padi land from Malay to non-Malay owners was applied by *Gazette* notification to Krian' (T. B. Wilson, 1958: 65).

34. Since the pioneering work of Wilson, further work has been done by various scholars on the issue of concentration of land-ownership, most notably by Husin Ali (1964, 1972, 1975).

35. The trend towards concentration of land-ownership in peasant agriculture appears to be matched by a similar trend in peasant fishing, at least on the East Coast. Raymond Firth (1966) has shown that the profound technological changes in fishing—involving changes in boats, nets as well as techniques—have involved increased investments. Control of fishing has consequently shifted from the master fishermen to the middlemen-dealers who have come to control the means of production in fishing, since the former faced considerable difficulties in mobilizing sufficient funds to make these investments. The transformation in the relations of production in fishing has also affected the relative income of the fishermen, as the rate of exploitation has risen in capital's favour. 'Much greater returns to fishing in modern conditions, accompanied by or resulting from much greater capitalization, has resulted in a marked drop in the percentage of earnings going to labour' (Firth, 1966: 323).

36. For example, pre-season rent payments economically limit the amount of land a poor peasant—who might otherwise be willing and prepared to cultivate a larger area of land—can rent.

37. Barnard has suggested that most padi farmers who are able to cultivate more than the 'economic minimum' have at least two parcels. 'This suggests that the process of accumulation of land by a minority has, in the long run, possibly as great an effect on patterns of landholding as the opposite process of the fragmentation [sic] or division of holdings into increasingly smaller units among the majority' (Barnard, 1970: 34).

38. For example, slaughter tapping of rubber trees by tenants can affect the long-term productivity of the trees, whereas similar possibilities with tenant padi farmers are more difficult to come by.

39. Tenurial arrangements between individuals differ fundamentally from those between individuals and the state, such as freehold, leasehold, and temporary occupation licences. The latter do not come into consideration here though they are not without significance for peasants.

Whether or not the ground rent claim based on ownership of land property is exploitative will not be debated here. In the view presumed here, rent is a claim to surplus labour, and is therefore necessarily exploitative. An alternative neo-classical economic perspective would deny this, e.g.: 'The existence of tenancy...cannot be automatically construed as detrimental or indicative of "exploitation". Tenancy may be an efficient means of farming by dividing labor between those who are more efficient in cultivation and those who are more efficient in management' (Y. Huang, 1975: 706).

40. The five basic types of agreements defined in terms of form of rent payment, and ownership and trust arrangements are listed here together with the most common equivalent Malay terms (T. B. Wilson, 1958: 11):

fixed rent	*sewa*
crop-sharing	*pawah*
lease	*pajak*
loan	*gadai*
mortgage	*jual janji* (literally 'promissory sale')
ownership	*sendiri*
trust	*pesaka*

41. 'A system of half-share to the landlord is so common in Malaysia, and rents as low as 1/4 are so rare, that we do not understand the apparent findings of the 1966 Farm Economic Survey that sharecropping rentals averaged only 27% for the MADA area and 25% in Kubang Pasu' (Lim Teck Ghee *et al.*, 1974: 57).

42. 'It is generally believed that with increasing reliability of water supply (removing some of the risk of bad harvests) and increasing pressure on the land there will be a transfer of rented land out of sharecropping into a fixed padi rent, which is later commuted from a fixed cash rent and eventually comes to be paid in advance of cultivation. According to Wilson, cropsharing had already declined to insignificance in Kedah as a whole by the post-war years and the process had begun of changing fixed rents from rent in kind to rent in cash, although in 1949/50 only 3% of agreements were for cash rental. By 1955/56 the proportion of cash rentals had risen to 16%' (Lim Teck Ghee *et al.*, 1974: 54).

43. *Zakat* is an obligatory Islamic tax originally intended to redistribute income in favour of the needy (see Gordon, n.d.).

44. See note 14 above.

45. For example, the use of fertilizer, which will continue to affect production for three years after application, will be discouraged if the tenant expects his tenancy to terminate before then.

46. 'Sub-division and fragmentation interact as causal factors with indebtedness, tenancy, and other features of rural poverty in a cumulative process of circular causation, not only to bring about increasing inequalities in the distribution of rural income, land and capital, but also to expedite the disintegration of the very kampong socio-economic structure itself' (Aziz, 1958: 24).

47. This includes 35 per cent of landlord-operators and 15 per cent of those in government and business!

48. The 'social characteristics' examined in the study include:
   (a) verbal, rather than written, tenancy agreements;
   (b) agreement to indefinite duration of tenancy;
   (c) negotiability of rent after harvest;
   (d) rent payment in kind; and
   (e) rent payment after harvest.

49. Though usually this means the poorer tenant is favoured, e.g. by lower rent charges, Horii argues that 'shared poverty' may also work out in favour of the kin-related landlords, e.g. in the case of aged parents renting land to their children at high rental rates.

50. In contrast to the earlier studies cited, Raymond Firth found that:
'...economic processes, which had widened the gap between capitalist entrepreneurs and propertyless fishermen, were not cushioned to any apparent degree by the elaborate network of kinship ties in the local social system... the kinship ties of these fishermen do not inhibit their economic calculation, though they may soften its intensity' (Firth, 1966: 348).

51. Shadli Abdullah (1978).

52. '...the recent rapid development in the commercial economy in the rural areas and the concomitant development of social diversification... is affecting the kinship aspect of the land tenure system by changing former "reciprocity" relationships based on kinship to purely economic relationships. The result is that differences between the land tenure arrangements based on kinship and those not based on kinship have disappeared. The effect of this has been for high rents in cash to become the rule.... In sum, while land tenure systems are essentially based on class relationships, the system in this kampong is still modified by "reciprocity" deriving from kinship relations, and does not yet have the character of a true land tenure system. On the other hand, there are indications that these "reciprocity" bonds are weakening and that the land tenure system is approaching the stage where the class aspect of landowner-tenant relations is becoming manifest' (Horii, 1972: 68).

53. 'Over the period of 1966-1974, the proportion of farmers who are full owners, appears to have remained relatively the same. There have, however, been significant trends among tenant and part-owner part-tenant (mixed) farmers. The proportion of pure tenant farmers decreased from 41 per cent of all farmers in 1966, to 31 per cent in 1974. In contrast, the proportion of farmers of mixed tenurial status doubled, from 14 per cent in 1966 to 28 per cent in 1973-74' (Jegatheesan, 1976: 27).

54. '...the need to improve the farmer's welfare... is necessary to secure social stability in rural and national life, and may gain urgency for political reasons, as in Taiwan, "in order to prevent Communist infiltration of the rural districts"' (T. B. Wilson, 1958: 93).

55. Barnard has summed up the situation pointedly, if somewhat enigmatically: 'For obvious reasons, it is politically inadvisable to carry out any radical redistribution of padi land operated, under existing arrangements' (Barnard, 1970: 53).

56. 'So far as rural development is concerned, the present policies of the Malayan government are producing a considerable effect, but in terms of this analysis they do not provide an effective answer to the fundamental problems involved' (Fisk, 1963: 173).

57. 'The Ordinance specifies the duties of tenants to practise good husbandry, but does not specify the duties of landlords to keep a clean title, make-up-to-date registration of ownership details, pay land dues and rates, and maintain survey boundary marks. The Agreement Form prescribed by the Ordinance requires tenants "to defray all expenses and perform all work necessary for the construction, and putting and keeping in order of any dams, etc." which is landlord's

responsibility as a capital improvement and, if executed by the tenant, should be subject to compensation' (T. B. Wilson, 1958: 95).

58. The exception which proved the rule took place in parts of Kedah for one season:
'Police prosecution of eight landlords for extortionate rents in four *mukim* of Kedah in 1956 and 1957, did ensure almost 100 per cent registration of tenancy agreements in the 1956/57 season compared with an overall 15 per cent registration for the rest of Kedah and Perlis' (T. B. Wilson, 1958: 96).

Part III

We, so they tell us, have built the economy,
but what good fortune is ours?

Usman Awang, 'Malaya', *1955*

THE EXPANSION OF CAPITAL IN
THE COLONIAL ECONOMY

THIS part will explore certain aspects of the broader context of class formation and contention that occurred with the development and expansion of
capital–from the sphere of circulation to production–and the subsequent
emergence of capitalist relations of production in the Malayan economy. The
proposition that capital was confined to the sphere of circulation, and hence not
directly involved in production in the colonial economy, will be examined. It
will be seen that capital was invested in production but did not give rise to
capitalist relations of production at the outset. The later emergence of free wage
labour is related to class contention and the changing needs of capital accumulation.

Chapter 5 introduces the mercantilist impact on pre-British Malaya and the
subsequent expansion of British commercial capital in the region which saw the
establishment of the Straits Settlements ports. It also locates colonialism as an
extension of the contradictions of capital accumulation on a global scale in the
second half of the nineteenth century. This establishes the broader context for
explaining British colonial intervention in the rest of the peninsular Malayan
hinterland. Expansion of commercial capital spurred the growth of trade in the
colonial economy. The ideology and policy of free trade liberalism is
interpreted in terms of the hegemony of British capital. Malaya's importance as
a British colony was linked to its large contribution–in the form of primary
commodity export earnings–to the British Empire's foreign exchange resources (especially US dollars). The hierarchical structure of commercial capital
which has developed is briefly reviewed and, finally, the early transition of
capital from circulation to production is discussed.

Chapters 6 and 7 both examine the development of commodity production
organized by capital. While there were important similarities in the development of the tin and rubber industries in Malaya–e.g. the absence of an
indigenous proletariat and the consequent necessity to import labour–the
differences between the two experiences underline the relevance of class
contention for historical analysis. In both industries, the differences in the
development of both capital and labour, the ascendance of particular forms of
monopoly capital, and the emergence of free wage labour were especially
significant for the consequent juxtaposition of ethnicity with class and
occupation.

Chapter 6 discusses the particular significance of tin-mining for colonial
intervention, the organization of Chinese capital in the industry, and the
mechanisms with which it controlled Chinese mining labour. The indirect role
of the colonial state in freeing Chinese labour eroded the competitive position

of Chinese capital in the industry and thus facilitated the ascendance of British mining capital. The chapter also briefly looks at some aspects of the subsequent fate of Chinese mining labour, particularly in terms of employment in the tin industry.

In Chapter 7 the growth of rubber planting in Malaya is situated in the context of the larger colonial system. The organization of rubber plantations is discussed and the key entrepreneurial role of existing commercial capitalist interests is identified. Encouragement and favour by the colonial state in the interests of capital were crucial, especially in coping with the challenge from peasant rubber cultivators (an issue discussed in Chapter 3 as it affected the peasantry). The development of Indian labour immigration is then related to the growth of investments in rubber growing. Finally, the role of the colonial state in mediating relations between capital and labour is discussed, with particular attention on the emergence of nominally free wage labour employed on rubber estates.

5
COLONIALISM AND
COMMERCIAL CAPITAL

THE early history of European colonialism prior to World War I may be usefully divided into three epochs (Magdoff, 1974): from the fifteenth century to the Industrial Revolution (c.1763): from then to the 1870s; and finally from the 1870s to 1914 which marked the outbreak of the first inter-imperialist war of the twentieth century. The first period saw the spread of Europeans—especially from the Italian, Spanish and Portuguese courts—in mercantilist pursuit of products from the rest of the world. The slogan 'spices, sugar and slaves' captures the essence of the motive for the global spread of the two Iberian empires—territories were occupied to obtain supplies of slaves and tropical agricultural and mineral products (Griffin, 1969); white settler colonies sprouted in the Americas and elsewhere; military, particularly naval, power secured control of the key ports and major trade routes of the period. In short, merchant capital had created a new market—a world market. Commodity production and the competition for control of raw materials for this market were thus stimulated and intensified. By and large, however, it appears that major disruptions of the internal class structures of existing societies did not occur. In fact, the mercantilist exploitation of the colonies served to consolidate rather than transform even the dominant structures of the pre-capitalist societies of Portugal and Spain.

Mercantilism and Pre-British Malaya

Well before the arrival of the Europeans in the early sixteenth century, traders from China, India and even further west had made their way to the region in search of its exotic products or to purchase goods imported from elsewhere into the region (Courtenay, 1972; Sandhu, 1973). As trade flourished, centres of long-distance commerce sprang up in various parts of peninsular and archipelagic South-East Asia (Nusantara), with such trade tending to centre on a dominant port in the region. Malacca, for example—strategically located both in relation to the monsoons during an era of sail-powered trade, and also on the important Straits of Malacca passage-way—rapidly emerged in the fifteenth century as the premier entrepôt for the region, if not the world (Meilink-Roelofsz, 1962). It is no wonder that the Portuguese—and later the Dutch—were eager to bring Malacca under their control.[1] The Portuguese capture of Malacca in 1511 was part and parcel of a larger process of Iberian rivalry and expansion all over the globe generated by the logic of merchant capital hegemony in those societies.

Inter-European conflicts, political realignments and other developments which resulted in the ascendance of Dutch naval power in South-East Asia towards the end of the sixteenth century and the corresponding expansion of Dutch commercial interests in the East, led to the virtual demise of the far-flung Portuguese empire in the region after the Dutch conquest of Malacca in 1641. Until the beginning of the nineteenth century, Dutch merchants continued to dominate the trade of the region, which centred on their monopoly of the very lucrative spice trade. By this time, however, the importance of Malacca as a commercial port was already in decline; instead it served essentially as a military outpost to control the strategic Straits. The centre of Dutch economic activities had shifted to Java, where the Dutch East India Company not only dominated trade, but also sought to organize production (Geertz, 1963).

British Commercial Capital and the
Straits Settlements Ports

The entry of British capital interests led to the creation of new patterns of commerce in the region. While the accumulation of the economic gains of mercantilism had paved the way for the Industrial Revolution of North-western Europe, the tremendous technological advances of the period also dictated certain changes in internal social arrangements for the generalization of capitalist relations of production (Dobb, 1963). This new epoch, characterized by rapid industrialization in North-west Europe, heralded the emergence of a world market and a system of trade in which the needs of capitalist interests in the industrializing 'centre' were met through a 'periphery' which served both as a supplier of raw materials for its industry, and a market for its manufactured goods. This, of course, involved a fundamental reorientation in the productive and accumulative activities of the 'periphery'—induced under colonial rule through political, economic or military means.

Dominance of British interests in the region began with the establishment of the three Straits Settlements ports—Penang, Malacca and Singapore—over a period of four decades, beginning with the Kedah Sultan's secession of Penang in 1786 (Tregonning, 1965). A British naval base in Penang provided a strategic advantage on the eastern flank of the Bay of Bengal, then an area of considerable contention between the British and the French. Through the Straits ports, the British exercised control over maritime trade through the strategically crucial Straits of Malacca—gateway to eastern South-East Asia and the Orient. Furthermore, these key Straits ports also led to control of local as well as regional trade, providing access to products of the peninsula (Wong Lin Ken, 1960).

The limited success of Penang in serving British needs for a trading entrepôt in the region and as a counter to Dutch commercial control—probably as a result of its geographical disadvantage—explains its modest progress by the second decade of the nineteenth century (Courtenay, 1972: 68). It was from the British free port of Singapore, opened in 1819,[2] that trade eventually extended to all corners of the archipelago, reaping great profits for the island's merchants. The choice of Singapore proved to be a stroke of genius for British interests (Alatas, 1971).

Malacca passed irretrievably from Dutch into British hands when Anglo-Dutch rivalry in South-East Asia culminated in a compromise Treaty in 1824 to demarcate their respective 'spheres of influence' within the region: most of the archipelago went to the Dutch, while the Malayan peninsula (including Malacca) was to be the British preserve; therefore Malacca—which by this time had lost most of its former glory—was to pass once again into British hands. The rest of the peninsula remained under the rule of local rulers, though some of them would be seen as ethnically 'Arab', 'Thai' or 'Indonesian' today. The shaping of British Malaya's territorial boundaries dates from this treaty and a subsequent one with the Siamese kingdom to the north early in the twentieth century.

Singapore's runaway success as a port soon relegated both the older ports of Malacca and Penang to a relatively subordinate status. Singapore served not only as a regional entrepôt but also conducted considerable exchange with the industrial nations as well as China and India, while the other Straits ports were more regionally oriented (Courtenay, 1972: 76). Meanwhile, British promotion of free trade through its Straits ports gradually succeeded in drawing commerce away from Dutch to British ports, a development further enhanced by the rapid establishment of various facilities serving trade and shipping. By the time the Dutch countered, setting up their own free ports, it was already too late. The dominance of the British ports prevailed. During this first period, the growth of trade and the expansion of the scope of the market further stimulated commodity production and gradually undermined and subordinated these existing pre-capitalist societies to the interests of commercial capital through trade relations. This primarily involved free trade between British capital in the colonies and capital in Britain rather than between the colonies and the rest of the world (Kay, 1975: 107; Emerson, 1937).

The second period, from after the Napoleonic Wars until around 1870, saw a relative lull in inter-European rivalry once the international supremacy of the British industry, commerce and the Royal Navy had been established. Enjoying industrial superiority, Britain could safely afford to promote free trade under the Union Jack. However, British merchant capital abroad complemented and became increasingly subordinate to industrial capital in the 'centre'. Contrasting the British and the Dutch in this regard, Furnivall (1939: 68) noted that 'whereas Dutch interest centred in the supply of Eastern produce, British interest looked also to the demand for Western produce'.

The Political Economy of Colonialism

The opening of the Suez Canal in 1869 promoted continental European interest in the East. Meanwhile, other capitalist nations, including Germany, the United States, Belgium, Italy, and Japan, were experiencing rapid industrial growth and the emergence of monopolies, while developing expansionist aspirations. The inevitable intensification of inter-imperialist rivalry eventually culminated in 1914 in World War I.

In the circumstances of the latter half of the nineteenth century, at least three kinds of conditions gave rise to a new stage of colonialism. First, economic opportunities—such as prospects for organizing mines and plantations, creating and controlling a labour force, and stimulating increased national commodity production—were clearly important factors encouraging exclusive colonial control. (This, of course, did not prevent the history of colonialism from reflecting differences and contention among rival capitalist factions or between private capital and the capitalist state.[3]) Second, inter-imperialist rivalry often necessitated the establishment of colonial control over territories as pre-emptive measures to create spheres of control and buffer areas even when no immediate economic gains were available. Long-term considerations—economic or otherwise—were certainly not alien to the colonial perspective. Third, colonial frontiers were sometimes extended to overcome actual as well as potential resistance to foreign rule, usually based in border areas. It should also be noted that the economic gains from colonialism increased as secure investment, trade, and other links developed.

'Either-or' debates over single causal factors for colonial intervention miss the point altogether. The circumstances culminating in colonial intervention typically comprise a complex set of dialectically related factors involving specific historical situations in an international context. An immediate stimulus for extending colonial control may be 'non-economic', which does not for one moment negate the overall logic of imperialism, whose 'tap-root' (the term is Hobson's) is undeniably economic.[4] The circumstances in which capital accumulation occurs must be considered in their totality. To attempt to isolate economic motives for the direct explanation of every particular colonial venture inevitably ignores the strategic and political imperatives that are crucial in the pursuit of economic interests, and reduces the theory of imperialism to a crude, mechanistic analytical device. Not surprisingly, it is precisely those wishing to discredit the theory of imperialism, who employ such caricatures (e.g. Sinclair, 1967).

British expansionism in the Malayan peninsula was no anomaly but very much in the design of the 'New Empire' established primarily over the half-century from around 1870 until the outbreak in 1914 of the inter-imperialist World War I (i.e. after the settler colony dominions and India). The significance of this new epoch stimulated explanations of the phenomenon of capitalist imperialism (Kemp, 1967). Hobson, in his pioneering 1902 work, set out to explain this 'historical fact of great significance' involving an empire whose nucleus was only 120,000 square miles, with a population of 4 million, and which dominated an area of 4,754,000 square miles, with an estimated population of 88 million.

Carefully analysing statistics of Britain's international economic position from 1870 to 1914, particularly with regard to exports, imports, commodity re-exports, and capital flows, Richard Wolff has argued that '...the late nineteenth-century British economy derived significant advantages from its colonies, that it could reasonably expect these advantages to increase absolutely and relatively, and, finally, that these advantages would most probably not have been available in the absence of a colonial tie' (Wolff, 1974: 2).

Emphasizing that trade between Great Britain and the New Empire was only a very small share of total British trade between 1870 and 1914, Fieldhouse (1961) and others have concluded that it was therefore insignificant. This line of thinking is erroneous; though trade relations may have been small, it does not follow that they were insignificant. Neither does it take into account that expansionist decisions were made before it was known or expected that the resulting trade would be small. More importantly, it ignores the historical context in which increasing protectionism by other emerging capitalist powers threatened Britain with the possibility of losing access to areas beyond its own direct (colonial) control.

Examining the significance of trade relations between Britain and the New Empire in the half century before the outbreak of World War I, Wolff (1974: 12, 17, 21) arrived at the following findings:

1. ... the role of the empire, including the new empire, was significant in providing the imports that became increasingly crucial for domestic production, employment, and consumption.
2. ... in the short run between 1870 and 1914 the absorption of British exports in the new empire at the very least significantly lessened the depressive impact of changing world trade conditions on the British economy.
3. Re-exports played an important role in the United Kingdom's balance of payments throughout the period 1880 to 1913. The bulk of re-export products ... originated chiefly in the colonies and dependencies of the new empire.

Britain's economic advantages derived from the empire would not have been available without direct control of the colonies. Colonial rule ensured ultimate control of food and raw material supplies, which would otherwise have been held by other aspiring imperial powers.[5] Regardless of the destination of exports from the colonies and the cost of alternative services, colonial dominance meant a virtual British monopoly of financing, insurance and freight, which were, of course, to Britain's international balance-of-payments advantage. Through colonial rule, British capital could affect the international division of labour by determining the nature of products and exports from its imperial realm. 'Thus, it is reasonable to conclude that, in the absence of Britain's new empire, her security, her gains from invisible exports, and both the general mix and the quantities of food and raw materials supplied to world markets would have been less favourable to her' (Wolff, 1974: 23).

After dealing with the trade account, Wolff moves on to Britain's capital account. In the century before 1914, he identifies two key characteristics of British foreign investment. First, and probably more obviously, there was a close relationship between capital outflows and the foreign links of specific British businesses. Second, the particular political alliances being cultivated by the British state also influenced the direction of capital outflows. Capital outflows to the Empire were therefore premised on interdependent economic and political considerations. The pressures of inter-imperialist rivalry, among other factors, forced a reorganization of Britain's external trade and investment situation towards the latter part of the last century. In 1914, the tendency for capital investments to flow in the direction of the New Empire was still recent in origin and could hardly have been expected to reach statistically impressive proportions. Therefore, although the fastest expanding field for British investments was clearly the New Empire, it still accounted for less than 3 per cent of total British foreign investment in 1913. While British investments continued to flow along established lines, the emerging trend in the direction of the New Empire was clear.

It is therefore in the context of British imperial expansion on a global scale that intervention in the Malayan peninsula should be situated and understood. The existence of the New Empire meant that colonial policy in Malaya also represented an extension of the rapidly increasing British experience of the new imperialism.

British Colonial Intervention in the Malayan Peninsula

The circumstances leading to British control of the Malayan peninsula have been extensively discussed elsewhere.[6] However, to locate the interests and impulse for colonial intervention in a specific historical context, it is appropriate to review some of the circumstances surrounding British intervention in the Malayan hinterland. The threat to the British of another imperialist power intervening in the peninsula—whether actual or not—was invoked by Straits business interests to persuade the British government to take interventionist action (Sardesai, 1970); in this connection, both Germany (Cowan, 1961) and France (Winstedt, 1958) have been mentioned. In any case, European rivals, especially France and Germany, had already been making significant inroads into the tin business and the Straits entrepôt trade by the mid-nineteenth century (Wong Lin Ken, 1960). Hence, it had become especially important for Straits merchant capital interests to consolidate the tenuous links with their peninsular Malay partners to ensure control of hinterland commerce. Control over the local governments in the peninsula would ensure preferential treatment for British and allied interests. In this and other respects, the inadequacy of the Colonial Office's non-interventionist policy vis-à-vis the peninsula was increasingly felt by Straits capitalist interests (Knowles, 1936). The desire to 'stabilize' political and economic conditions on the peninsula especially with regard to tin production and commerce, is generally acknowledged to have significantly influenced British intervention in the western Malay States (e.g. Khoo Kay Kim, 1972).

Between 1851 and 1860, 23 per cent of total British tin consumption was met by Malayan exports. Over the following decade, total peninsular exports more than doubled in tonnage to 34,180—about 40 per cent of the 87,120 tons consumed in Britain—or an average of almost 3,500 tons annually. In the following five years alone (1871-5), Malayan exports to Britain grew further to a total tonnage of 29,257 (Sardesai, 1970) or an average of almost 6,000 tons per annum. In the face of the decreasing proportion of Britain's tin consumption being produced in Cornwall (in the British Isles) and the tightening Dutch control of tin resources in Bangka and Billiton in the East Indies, the importance of Malayan production to British interests could not but have grown with expanding world tin consumption (see Wong Lin Ken, 1964, 1965; Yip, 1969). Protracted conflicts among mining interests in the peninsula—involving Chinese capitalists, their secret societies, and Malay territorial chiefs aligned on both sides—offered a choice opportunity for Straits-based interests to demand and obtain British intervention in the tin-rich western Malay States of Perak, Selangor, and part of Negri Sembilan during 1874.

The Pangkor Treaty of January 1874 marked the transition to a new era in Malayan history. Unlike the Straits Settlements, the peninsular States were not formally annexed; in fact they never became formal colonies till after the Japanese Occupation (Emerson, 1937). Before that, the fiction of nominal Malay rule was maintained. In the years after 1874, the rest of Negri Sembilan was brought under British control. In 1888, alleged local defiance of British authority provided a pretext for the invasion of Pahang, which met with fierce local resistance (Jang Aisjah Muttalib, 1972). As in the other States, this was put down by British might after a protracted struggle. In 1896, the four States of Perak, Selangor, Negri Sembilan and Pahang were brought under a centralized British administration in the form of the Federated Malay States (FMS).

The expectation that intervention would give British business interests in the Straits Settlements unchallenged dominance over the tin-mining industry and commerce in the peninsula was soon disappointed. Although European rivals diminished as a threat, local Chinese capitalists, who had already established themselves in both tin and trade, had still to be contended with in the years to come.

After having successfully negotiated for Singapore from an ousted ruler of the Riau-Johore Empire in 1819, the British continued to maintain a strong influence over his successors, who later opened up Johore to Chinese agricultural entrepreneurs cultivating crops for export (Trocki, 1975). A virtual economic dependency of Singapore from the early nineteenth century, Johore was actually the first Malay State to adopt a colonial-style administration even before it accepted an official Adviser to its royal court. In 1885, the British officially recognized Johore's ruler as Sultan. However, Johore was to receive an official British Adviser only much later, in 1914, the last Malay State to do so. The strong influence the British already exercised informally over the Johore sultanate made earlier assignment of an Adviser unnecessary.

Before the outbreak of World War I, the British had also gained control of the four padi-growing northern Malay States of Kedah, Perlis, Kelantan, and Trengganu, from the declining (pre-capitalist) Siamese Kingdom. Thus, the strong British expansionist impulse in Malaya upset the previous equilibrium maintained by Anglo-Siamese collaboration since their 1826 Treaty. Although the boundaries of British Malaya were already demarcated by 1914, ironically it was only governed by a unified central administration with the Japanese invasion during World War II.

Trade and Commercial Capital

In commercial terms the establishment of the Straits Settlements ports had a twofold significance.[7] First, they—in particular Singapore—became key to the East-West trade passing through the Straits of Malacca. Goods from China were exchanged for manufactures from Britain and elsewhere in Europe. Britain's colony, India, also contributed opium and textiles to this trade. The

other key role played by Singapore was in relation to the commerce of
the South-East Asian region. The establishment of Singapore in 1819 focused
the trade of the region around it, as Malacca had done four centuries before (see
Wong Lin Ken, 1960). This time, however, the goods transacted as well as the
scope of the market had changed. And as industry developed in the West, the
nature of the products demanded from the East also changed correspondingly,
the story of tin being a case in point.

While the East-West trade utilizing Singapore as a convenient transit point
enriched the Straits merchants involved, it had little direct impact on the rest of
the local economy.[8] The same, however, could not be said of the regional trade
which was developing simultaneously. While British merchants also continued
to dominate this commerce, it entailed far more involvement by local capital. It
is probable that regional trade, including that involving the peninsula, touched
the lives of the entire population residing there. The basic relations involved in
this trade, established in the early years of British colonialism, survive—to
varying extents—to this day. While there have been many changes since, the
basic contours of the market structure developed then have yet to be fundamentally transformed.

While the scope of possibilities for trade tends to widen with the expansion
of the market, this same process also diminishes the range of viable commodities which can be 'economically' produced, thus encouraging specialization. Patterns of production and trade in the South-East Asian region must
have changed considerably with the transitions from regionally-centred trade to
long-distance trade, then to trade dominated by the restrictive trade policies of
the European mercantilists, and eventually to the free-trade liberalism of British
capital. As subsistence or 'use-value' production declined in favour of increased
commodity production involving more trade, the scope for capital in the
circulation of commodities increased. Capital in circulation, especially merchant capital, thus increased its activity as the production of exchange values
(commodities) spread. Increased commodity exchanges do not, of course,
necessarily entail expanded international trade, though increased commerce in
the context of colonial integration generally tends to proceed simultaneously
with the growth of international trade, reflecting expansion of the world
market economy (Clairmonte, 1960).

It is interesting to note that in the nineteenth century, Singapore's trade with
the East Coast of the peninsula far exceeded that with the West Coast. Part of
the reason, of course, is that much of the trade with the West Coast was
conducted through the other Straits ports. Nevertheless, it is highly unlikely
that the large difference (see Wong Lin Ken, 1960: 255, Table 28) can be
sufficiently explained by this alone. Wong Lin Ken (1960: 79) explains the large
opium exports to the East Coast by pointing to the presence of Chinese mining
communities in Kelantan and Pahang. However, a careful reading of his source
for this (Purcell, 1951: 309) does not suggest a large enough Chinese presence to
account for the volume of the opium trade. Similar evidence from Kedah in the
late eighteenth century also suggests extensive commodity exchange in that
period (Wan Ibrahim, 1960). It is therefore possible that the indigenous Malay
population then (much of which was under Siamese suzerainty) was already

actively involved in commodity production for exchange (see Wong Lin Ken, 1960: 231, Table 14). Whether or not such production for exchange was still marginal to production for use cannot be easily determined, however.

The great trading agencies of Malaya generally started as modest merchant concerns in the Straits ports in the nineteenth century, though a few had origins in trade elsewhere. By the late nineteenth century, these merchant houses had come to dominate much of the international trade conducted through the Straits Settlements. Dominating the export of industrial raw materials and the import of manufactured goods, these firms earned handsome profits, also handling the financial, commercial, shipping, insurance and other related services connected with this rapidly expanding trade. Eventually these trading agencies were to diversify their activities to involve themselves, directly or otherwise, in production, especially in the rapidly growing rubber industry. (While the history of the emergence of these agencies has yet to receive comprehensive and systematic treatment,[9] the domestic commercial structure complementing this pattern of international trade has received some attention (J. J. Puthucheary, 1960).)

Free Trade and the Balance of Payments

Britain's commitment to free trade was only in so far as it served its own interests. In the early period, i.e. with the establishment of the Straits Settlements, this policy effectively undermined Dutch mercantilist practice in the region. For decades after, free-trade liberalism continued to be upheld by the world's dominant capitalist power in its quest to secure control of the Eastern trade and to develop the port of Singapore and the interests of British commercial capital located there. However, when capitalists of other nationalities began to pose a serious challenge to British interests in this free-trade situation, the colonial government did not hesitate to violate its espoused commitment to this 'cherished principle'.

This was most starkly evidenced by the example of Japanese textile exports to Malaya during the 1930s. The rapid expansion of these imports at the expense of British-manufactured textiles led the British trading agencies—who had previously benefited most from free trade—to demand that the colonial government curb Japanese textile imports. As is clear from Table 5.1, the respective British and Japanese shares of cotton piece-goods imports were dramatically altered by the imposition of discriminatory quotas in 1934. The subsequent policies of Imperial, and then Commonwealth Preference explicitly put an end to Britain's previously espoused commitment to free trade. With this preferential trade policy which in Malaysia lasted into the post-colonial era (until 1966), Britain was accorded favourable treatment as far as the importation of foreign goods was concerned, e.g. in the form of differential import tariff rates.[10]

Within the British Empire, Malaya played an important role as a 'dollar arsenal' by virtue of its voluminous exports of rubber and tin, especially to the United States. After the boom in planted rubber in Malaya, exports to the United States as a percentage of total exports from Straits ports between 1918

TABLE 5.1

Percentage of Imports of Cotton Piece-goods into Malaya by Quantity
from Major Supplying Country, 1925–1938

	1925	1926	1927	1928	1929	1930	1931	1932	1933	1934	1935	1936	1937	1938
United Kingdom	58	54	52	52	52	27	22	26	18	20	32	33	38	41
Japan	18	21	23	18	21	48	50	57	68	69	52	46	36	19
Others	24	25	25	30	27	25	28	17	12	11	16	20	26	40

Sources: 1925–32: Courtenay (1972: 130, Table 8); 1933–8: Mills (1942: 153) (his percentages for 1933 and 1936 do not add up to 100).

and 1938 fell below 30 per cent in only three years and exceeded 40 per cent in seven years. On the other hand, imports from that country over the same period never exceeded 5 per cent of total imports (Courtenay, 1972: 128, Table 7). In 1939, after the outbreak of war in Europe, the British curbed the import of non-sterling items into Malaya. This kind of policy not only saved foreign exchange, but also benefited British exports.[11] In the immediate post-war period, Malaya's contribution of export earnings in US dollars to British recovery was crucial to say the least.[12] In 1951 Malaya earned US$400 million, of which 83 per cent went into the sterling pool in London to cover Britain's international balance-of-payments deficit (Stubbs, 1974: 17). This role was not painless to the Malayan economy. Dollar earnings were loaned cheap at 3 per cent interest per annum. Meanwhile, restrictions were enforced on Malayan imports of goods from the United States. In 1948, for instance, the British colonial government banned the import of US textiles into Malaya.

The Structure of Commercial Capital

Put simply, commercial capital was, and still is, organized in two essentially pyramid-like structures, one handling imports and the other exports, which overlap at various points, especially at the top. Export-oriented producers are linked to export traders, the petty individual producers being linked by more intermediaries than the larger capitalist enterprises. The latter may even be directly linked to the exporters (e.g. through agency houses) or even to the industrial consumer (e.g. plantation subsidiaries of foreign tyre companies). The retailers who sell to consumers are similarly connected to importers, often through intermediaries, such as wholesalers. The variations within this basic pyramid structure are numerous, changing, for example, with the nature of the goods involved.

The entire import and export pyramids thus consist of the sum of the many pyramids involving particular commodities (e.g. see Figures 2.1, 5.1, and 5.2). However, the agents of both pyramids are not necessarily distinct. For instance, most major importers, except for some highly specialized ones, are also exporters. Also, retailers may be first-level produce buyers as well. The two pyramids tend to coincide at the top, e.g. in some of the bigger trading agencies. At the other extreme, the coincidence is particularly common in relation to the peasantry, as embodied by the village shop. Elsewhere in the structure, the two pyramids tend to be more distinct.

The tops of the two pyramids of commerce tend to be highly concentrated in terms of the small number of firms and the large volume of trade handled by the large firms (J. J. Puthucheary, 1960). However, at the level of the first-level buyer (Lim Sow Ching, 1968), as at retail sales level, the situation has become quite competitive, being characterized by a large number of firms. This is also reflected in the ownership structure of the retail trade in Peninsular Malaysia, in which 93 per cent and 6 per cent of all outlets in 1968 were sole proprietorships and partnerships respectively. However, even at the level of retail trade, there has been some concentration. The largest 7 per cent of retail firms engaged only 18 per cent of retail personnel, but accounted for 54 per cent of sales, while the

FIGURE 5.1

Production for Export Pyramid

PRODUCTION

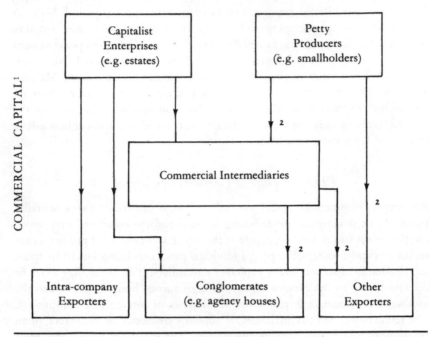

¹Commercial capital does undertake certain productive activities essential for the realization of
value, and hence profits, such as processing, packing and transportation.
²See Figure 2.1 for greater elaboration in the case of rubber smallholders.

smallest 65 per cent employed 32 per cent of workers and conducted only 32 per
cent of sales (Sieh, 1974: 52, 54).

It is a widespread belief that commerce in Malaysia is controlled by the
Chinese business community. While this view is superficial, there is apparently
much evidence in support of it. The apex of the commercial structure was,
however, dominated by British merchant capital, though much of this has been
bought up by the state in recent years. Outside the apex of the commercial
hierarchy, the personnel involved in the commercial links between importer
and consumer, as well as between petty producer and exporter, have been and
still are overwhelmingly Chinese,[13] though there is some significant non-
Chinese participation in certain sectors; Malay participation, particularly, is
growing with support from the state. Chinese capital is certainly pervasive,
though it has not and does not dominate the commanding heights of
international commerce.

While Chinese merchant capital has not been generally dominant, there have

FIGURE 5.2

Import for Consumption Pyramid

IMPORT

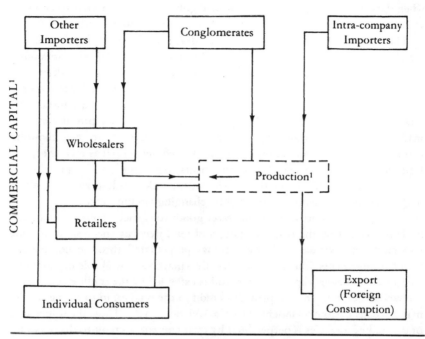

¹Capital in production is, of course, not part of commercial capital, though in certain circumstances it may well be subordinated to the interests of commercial capital.

been important exceptions. Predominantly Chinese local commercial capital is strongest for those commodities confined to local commodity circuits and not involved in international circuits, particularly with the West. Furthermore, by financing some agricultural and mining enterprises, and also by developing closer and better contacts with petty commodity producers, some of the more powerful Chinese capitalists, mostly Straits Chinese merchants, have been able to exercise control over certain sectors of the export trade. For instance, over 40 per cent of rubber exports in 1953 was accounted for by non-European companies (IBRD, 1955:499), though exports from the palm oil and tin industries were European-dominated until recently. Much of the trade with neighbouring countries, especially China and India, was developed and continues to be controlled by Malaysian Chinese and Indians respectively. A large share of the import trade for re-export from neighbours, such as Indonesia, has stayed in Chinese hands as well.

J. J. Puthucheary (1960:73) established that, for 1955, 60 per cent of Malaya's imports and between 65 per cent and 75 per cent of its exports were in

European hands. There has been increased participation by Chinese capital in such trade since the end of World War II, while there has been increased state and private Malay participation, especially since 1970. Effective control, however, has tended to remain in foreign hands,[14] and local capitalist gains in capturing a greater share of foreign trade have generally been modest, except when the solid backing of the post-colonial government has been forthcoming, as in the case of Perbadanan Nasional (Pernas), the National Corporation.

The structure of commercial capital discussed here obviously did not develop into its present form overnight. Decades passed as commodity production and commercial exchanges grew with the extension and deepening of market relations. However, the evidence suggests that the basic pyramid structure dominated by British trading agencies has remained substantially intact for well over a century (J. J. Puthucheary, 1960). Despite the inroads made—especially in some export sectors, in imports from neighbouring countries (e.g. rice), and in imports of specialized items such as machinery—by Chinese as well as smaller British merchants, the export, and especially the import trades are still under the control of the older trading agencies, albeit under new arrangements necessitated by changing circumstances.

Such effective control, especially over goods for general consumption, was initially ensured by the colonial state, and reinforced by the system of trade financing, with virtual trade monopolies perpetuated through commercial credit arrangements. Finance capital has thus played a crucial role in providing credit to commercial capital. Such credit is extended by the trading agencies to the wholesaler, who in turn provides credit to the retailer; in turn, the retailer may have his customers indebted to him (Silcock, 1956). Thus, the dominance of the trading agencies is perpetuated by their control of credit to the pyramids of commerce.[15]

Capital: From Circulation to Production

It is often argued that commercial capital has been historically incapable of transforming pre-capitalist relations of production to capitalist ones.[16] However, there is little reason to presume that such capital is necessarily confined to the sphere of circulation, and hence unable to move into production. Circulation capital is not inherently incapable of responding to attractive possibilities for profitable investment in production.[17] Not only is there no theoretical reason to believe that commercial capital necessarily always obstructs investment and participation in production, the historical evidence suggests otherwise.

In Malaya, it was not British colonial capital, however, which led the way from commerce to production. Instead, this path was pioneered by Straits Chinese capital.[18] Although Chinese merchants in Malaya predated the coming of the Europeans, most Straits Chinese capitalists followed the colonial flag to the Straits Settlements ports. The 'stable' political conditions and new economic opportunities offered by British colonial intervention especially stimulated trade and immigration. British capital wanted control of the lucrative East—West trade and had less interest in regional, and especially local, trade.

This was left to Asian traders[19]—a task to which the early immigrant Chinese businessmen in the Straits ports successfully applied themselves.

Initially, the products of the peninsula traded in the Straits ports were jungle, mineral, and agricultural goods obtained from the peasantry via Asian merchants who ventured inland. Nonetheless, while Straits capital's first and main interest was in commerce, the profitable opportunities for agricultural production were not missed. Dutch reluctance to share the spice trade prompted early British officials to encourage cultivation of certain desired commercial crops in Malaya.

In response, Chinese merchants in the Straits Settlements financed agricultural enterprises located near the Straits ports, especially in and around Penang and Singapore. Not relying much on European sources of finance, these ventures were generally poorly capitalized (J. C. Jackson, 1968: 4). Their viability thus depended heavily on rapid turnover in terms of the production schedule. Existing demand in the West for gambier and spices naturally encouraged further cultivation of these crops. Those involved became vulnerable to the price fluctuations of the world market, though this could be absorbed by the farmers because of the short life cycles of these crops and the flexibility of the shifting cultivation methods practised. The structure of financing and the supply of Chinese workers, first organized for such early commercial agricultural production, were both later extended to tin mining.

The attractions of commercial agricultural production were not ignored by the Europeans, though their record was less successful. Generally choosing crops with longer maturation periods, European agricultural practices tended to be more sedentary in nature, usually requiring heavier financial commitments. After experimenting unsuccessfully with a variety of crops in the 1840s, they turned to sugar-cane, the viability of which had already been demonstrated by earlier Chinese cultivators. Three decades later, coffee became popular with European planters. Also producing for the Western market, European agricultural enterprises tended to be far more vulnerable to market fluctuations as they were relatively less flexible organizationally, and therefore less able to adjust rapidly to changes in market conditions. The supply of labourers to work the European-owned plantations was also less effectively organized.[20]

British capital subsequently sought to and succeeded in wresting control of the tin industry from Chinese capitalists—as will be elaborated in the next chapter. Accumulated profits from commerce also contributed to the rapid growth of rubber plantations in the early twentieth century (see Chapter 7). With this stake in rubber, British plantation interests played an active role in trying to reverse the peasant adoption of rubber cultivation, discussed in Chapter 3. It was the Western rubber-using industries' desire for low-priced raw materials which ensured the existence of the rubber-growing peasantry.

As will be seen in Chapter 9, British capital's participation in production even extended to industry. Local processing of raw material exports, such as tin smelting (Yip, 1969) or preparation of sheet rubber, and local production of goods—which transport and other cost considerations strongly encouraged—offered profitable opportunities for British capital investment in industry. Subsequently, when new policies by the post-colonial state encouraged import-substitution industries, many British agency houses successfully extended their economic activities accordingly (Junid, 1975).

From the developments described, there is no reason to assume that capital was intrinsically opposed to investment in production in the colonies. There is also little reason *a priori* even to view manufacturing industry as an exception in this regard. Investments in the colonies, as elsewhere, were determined by the usual considerations of security and profitability. The point then is simply that merchant capital was not necessarily always inhibited in extending itself to direct involvement in production in the colonies.

While significant primary commodity production for export dates back to the spice trade, if not earlier, the growth of tin mining from the mid-nineteenth century and natural rubber cultivation from early this century undoubtedly marked a new phase in the economic development and transformation of Malaya. Involving the profitable investment of capital in conjunction with the exploitation of wage labour—initially subject to extra-economic coercion, and later, nominally 'free'—the systematic production of primary commodity exports for industrial use abroad subjected Malaya to a colonial-type international division of labour and greater vulnerability to the vicissitudes of the capitalist-dominated world economy. Complementing this export-dependence has been a heavy reliance on imports, resulting in an 'openness' of the economy which continues to the present despite post-colonial economic diversification into other primary commodities (most notably petroleum, liquefied natural gas, palm oil and timber) and manufactured exports (e.g. electrical goods, textiles, clothing) as well as some changes in the nature of imports in view of industrialization—especially of the import-substitution variety—and other new requirements.

Colonial Fiscal Policy

From 1922 until the 1960s, rubber and tin exports consistently accounted for more than half of all export earnings, except during the years of the Japanese Occupation and the year 1932, the nadir of the Great Depression. And although rubber's share of export earnings had exceeded tin's share by 1916, the percentage of tin export duty to total revenue greatly exceeded that for rubber in the years before the Japanese Occupation (Lim Chong-Yah, 1967). In this connection, it is interesting to note that the contribution of tin export duty to total FMS revenue declined relatively as British capital wrested control of the tin-mining industry from Chinese capital during the inter-war years. Conversely, the relative contribution of rubber export duty rose as the smallholding share of total natural rubber production grew during this period (Lim Teck Ghee, 1977). For the Straits Settlements, however, revenue from opium, liquor and tobacco—all of which were primarily consumed by the poor, especially workers—figured prominently before World War II. Together, they accounted for 64 per cent in 1901, 61 per cent in 1911, 59 per cent in 1921, 47 per cent in 1931 and 41 per cent in 1938 of annual SS revenue (see Table 5.2). The situation was not very different in the Unfederated Malay States. For instance, Kedah's share of revenue from these same items dropped from 54½ per cent in 1918/19

TABLE 5.2

Straits Settlements: Main Sources of Revenue,
1901–1938 (Selected Years)

	$ million (percentages in brackets)			
Year	Opium	Liquor	Tobacco	All Sources of Revenue[1]
1901	3.7 (53)	0.8 (11)	–	7.0
1911	5.6 (49)	1.4 (12)	–	11.4
1921	14.9 (44)	3.2 (9)	1.9 (6)	33.8[2]
1931	6.1 (23)	3.0 (11)	3.4 (13)	26.6
1938	6.4 (17)	3.7 (10)	5.0 (14)	36.6[3]

Sources: Lim Chong-Yah (1967: 256, Table 9.2); Li (1982: 20, Table 2.5).
[1]The other sources individually were very small.
[2]Excludes $5.7 million from income tax.
[3]Excludes $33.4 million Currency Guarantee Fund.

to 41 per cent in 1920/21 and remained thereabouts at least until 1929/30, when it was still 41 per cent (Li, 1982: 25–6, Table 2.7).

On the other hand, the pattern of colonial public expenditure was hardly in the interest of the bulk of the population (see Li, 1982: Chapter 2). Military expenditure's share of total expenditure rose from 20.3 per cent in 1909 to 55.7 per cent in 1919, before slipping to 12.0 per cent in 1929 and 14.9 per cent in 1938 (Li, 1982: 34, Table 2.12), while education's share remained fairly constant at 4.7 per cent in 1909, 3.8 per cent in 1919, 3.9 per cent in 1929, and 6.1 per cent in 1938 (Li, 1982: 33, Table 2.11). The size of the military expenditure should be seen against the following: the internal and external military threat to Malaya between 1909 and 1938 was virtually non-existent; the extraordinarily high expenses in 1919 essentially subsidized Britain's involvement in World War I, an inter-imperialist war; when the Japanese invasion began in December 1941, British defences collapsed pathetically. Public expenditure outside the SS varied considerably: for instance in Trengganu in 1917, 37 per cent went to the traditional Malay ruling class, compared to 5 per cent for public works (Li, 1982: 31), while in Kedah in 1906, public works took up almost 16 per cent and the Sultan 10 per cent (Li, 1982: 31).

Postscript: Dependence Despite Diversification

Despite achieving political independence in 1957, or perhaps because of the limited economic ramifications of this formal transfer of sovereignty, the post-colonial Malayan and then Malaysian economy has continued to be very open to, i.e. dependent on, the world economy, especially its industrial and financial centres. Despite significant economic diversification after independence—e.g. large-scale planting of oil palm and import-substituting industrialization in the 1960s, and petroleum production and export-led manufacturing in the 1970s—the export orientation and consequent openness of the Malaysian

TABLE 5.3

Peninsular Malaysia: Exports and Imports as Percentages
of Gross Domestic Product, 1957, 1970, and 1980

	1957[1]	1970[1]	1980[2]
Exports of Commodities and Services	47.1	44.5	51.8
Imports of Commodities and Services	37.5	39.3	53.8
GDP in Current Prices ($ million)	4,985	9,945	46,790

Sources: 1. V. V. Bhanoji, Rao (1976).
          2. Ministry of Finance (1982).

economy remains very strong. Hence, for instance, as Table 5.3 shows, exports have increased as a percentage of GDP (at current prices) from 34.9 per cent in 1947 to 47.1 per cent in 1957, 43.8 per cent in 1970, and 59.2 per cent in 1980, before declining to 54.4 per cent in 1983. Meanwhile imports as a percentage of GDP also rose from 25.1 per cent in 1947 to 37.5 per cent in 1957, 39.6 per cent in 1970, 56.6 per cent in 1980, and 59.0 per cent in 1983.

This growing openness of the economy is all the more remarkable because of the declining significance of traditional exports, such as rubber and tin, especially after the 1960s. As Lim Chong-Yah (1967) clearly shows, except for the years of the Great Depression (in the early 1930s) and the Japanese Occupation (early 1940s), rubber accounted for at least a third of pan-Malayan exports from 1923 to at least 1967, even touching 65 per cent in 1952, at the height of the Korean War boom. Yet in the last decade and a half, this percentage has dropped from 40 per cent in 1969 and 34 per cent in 1973 to only 9 per cent in 1982! The role of tin has been even more volatile, but has clearly declined in recent years from 23 per cent in 1965 to 5 per cent in 1982.

Summary

The expansion of European commercial capital was first felt in Malaya in the early sixteenth century with the advent of first Portuguese and then Dutch mercantilism. Subsequently, British commercial expansion saw the establishment of the Straits Settlements ports. These were important in being on the naval route to China and in encouraging regional and local trade. Colonial intervention into the rest of Malaya was part of a general global trend involving the creation of a 'New Empire', partly in response to the growing rivalry among industrializing Western European powers.

The initial expansion of British commercial capital owed much to the colonial policy of free-trade liberalism. However, when these policies began to work against the interests of British capital, e.g. as it did with the rise in imports of Japanese textiles in the inter-war period, they were adjusted accordingly. (Malaya's contribution to the British Empire's foreign exchange reserves was very considerable.) The hierarchical organization of commercial capital has always been largely dominated by the agency houses but—even at the level of retail trade—there has been significant unevenness in development. It should also be noted that the accumulation of capital from commercial activities has contributed to the development of production capital in Malaya. Finally, the bias in the sources of government revenue collection and the pattern of public expenditure clearly reflect class interests operating through the fiscal instruments at the disposal of the colonial state.

1. In the words of a contemporary Portuguese observer, Tomé Pires:
'Malacca is a city that was made for merchandise, fitter than any other in the world; the end of monsoons and the beginning of others. Malacca is surrounded and lies in the middle, and the trade and commerce between the different nations for a thousand leagues on every hand must come to Malacca' (quoted in Wheatley, 1961: 313).

2. It should be noted that Raffles was no naïve advocate of free trade. He violated the principles of economic liberalism when this was advantageous to British interests (see Allen and Donnithorne, 1954: 22).

3. Sinclair (1967) can barely conceal his glee in concluding that:
'The Colonial Office, far from being manipulated by investors, was unresponsive to their needs, and treated them with a coolness which did not always stop short of contempt.'
Instead,
'In areas not yet fully under British control, like Johore, their attitude might best be described as seeking to preserve a future estate.'
But as he also reveals,
'Later, they did encourage British investment in states already under British control.'
Suggesting 'that British officials were not tools of British capitalists and, indeed, were often hostile to them', he eventually lets the cat out of the bag:
'One after another, ex-governors and officials, often the same individuals who had opposed concessionaires in Johore, engaged in speculation there upon their retirement.'
How the existence of competing capitalist interests, manifested in the discriminatory use of state power, is supposed to be a refutation of the 'Hobson-Lenin thesis' [sic] is beyond this writer's comprehension.

4. See Kemp (1967) for a discussion of the theory of imperialism.

5. For example, the New Empire's share of British tin imports rose from 49.1 per cent in 1870 to 94.8 per cent in 1913.

6. See Knowles (1936); Emerson (1937); Thio (1957, 1967); Parkinson (1960); Cowan (1961); MacIntyre (1961); Tarling (1962); Chew (1969); Sardesai (1970); Courtenay (1972); Rubin (1974a, 1974b).

7. 'The Straits Settlements were essentially centres of exchange, and grew wealthy by their transit trade. Their prosperity was the result of two causes, their situation on the great trade route through the Straits of Malacca, and their system of free trade. The manufactures of Europe and India were brought to the Straits Settlements, and above all to Singapore, for transhipment to China, or for distribution throughout Indo-China and the East Indian islands. Conversely, they were the great depots where the products of Siam, the Malay Peninsula, and the Archipelago were collected to be sent to Great Britain, India and China. The history of the Straits Settlements is in its essence the expansion of their commerce from Burma to Australia and from Java to China' (Mills, 1960: 219).

8. 'Despite the much closer economic relationships with their peninsular hinterlands that were possessed by the Straits ports at the end of the nineteenth century compared with those held in the early years of their existence, Penang and Singapore (and to a lesser extent, Malacca) continued to develop as foreign enclaves, having less in common with the indigenous societies on whose geographical margins they were located' (Courtenay, 1972: 106).

9. While comprehensive and systematic treatment has been lacking, various published company histories are quite revealing. They proudly and romantically proclaim the glorious stories of how

British fortunes were made at the expense of the producers and consumers in the colonies (e.g. see Harrisons and Crosfield, 1943; see also Allen and Donnithorne, 1954: 53–7; Cunyngham-Brown, 1971).

10. 'In the colonial period and right up to August 1966 when the Commonwealth Preferential System was abolished, Great Britain had a great advantage over her European and American competitors in selling manufactured goods to West Malaysia. Consequently, she captured a large share of the West Malaysian market' (David Lim, 1973: 263).

11. 'Although introduced to conserve foreign exchange, this canalization of imports provides a great opportunity for English manufacturers' (Jago, 1940: 135).

12. 'In the period after World War Two, Malayan rubber exports saved the United Kingdom from bankruptcy after the war by earning more dollars in the critical 5 years from 1946/7 to 1951 than all the industries and trades of the metropolitan country put together' (Fisher, 1964: 610).

13. 'Essentially, the present (middleman) position of the Chinese originated in the free trade period of British imperialism and was consolidated by political colonialism' (Lee Poh Ping, 1974: 15).

In this connection, a British observer noted in 1863 that:

'The details of the great European trade of these settlements are managed almost exclusively by Chinese.... Here the Chinese step in as a middle class and conduct business, apparently on their own account but really as a mere go-between' (quoted in Song, 1923: 106).

The present situation remains substantially similar:

'Largely because British trade firms dominated Malaysian imports, exports, and distribution, most Chinese in commerce were left historically at the lower level of retail trade. [In Malaysia today, there are] perhaps 400,000 Chinese shopkeepers....

'Within the perspective of the enormous wealth [in the country], the rural Chinese shopkeeper is only a step above the modest Malay rice farmer, his wealth often consisting of no more than a shop-house with a small inventory of goods and three months credit from his supplier' (Grace, 1976).

14. Sime Darby, long considered the most 'Asian' of the big agency houses, finally had its first Malaysian chairman in 1976.

15. For example, as a matter of policy, James Guthrie (of Guthrie and Co., the oldest agency house) gave financial help to enable many Chinese immigrants to set up business, undoubtedly with the hope of enlarging his markets and improving his access to supplies of produce (Allen and Donnithorne, 1954: 54).

16. 'But historically merchant capital has never been able to effect this transition to capitalism proper itself.... Merchant capital is trading capital and the surplus value it seizes is used to expand trade[,] not the forces of production' (Kay, 1975: 95).

17. For instance, the new technological conditions identified with the 'Green Revolution' generally attracted capital to agricultural production and, in some instances, resulted in the reorganization of the relations of production along capitalist lines.

18. '...the British capitalist refused to risk even small capital in the Malayan states until the enterprising and industrious Chinese opened the (tin) mines there and began to exploit them' (Swettenham, 1948: 262–3).

19. These were not exclusively Chinese but also included Indian, Arab, and Malay traders (Wong Lin Ken, 1960: 77).

20. The problems encountered in this regard probably contributed to the colonial government's subsequent encouragement of the indenture system to recruit workers for capitalist enterprise in Malaya.

6
TIN: CAPITAL
AND CHINESE LABOUR

Tin Mining and Colonial Intervention

THE case of tin mining in Malaya provides a clear illustration of colonial intervention to secure control of raw material supplies. Until the mid-nineteenth century, Dutch merchants had maintained tight control over the tin mined in the Malay archipelago through various agreements with the local rulers concerned. Employing threats of armed intervention, the British forced free-trade treaties upon some rulers in the Malay peninsula, which allowed Straits Chinese and European traders access to, and eventually control of tin supplies.

The Malays had been mining tin for centuries. However, the discovery of substantial deposits in Perak, in the context of rapidly growing industrial tin consumption in the mid-nineteenth century, led to an influx of Chinese miners who quickly took over and developed the mining industry utilizing the superior mining techniques they had acquired elsewhere (Wong Lin Ken, 1964). As there was no Malay proletariat who could be set to work on the mines, the existing Malay rulers agreed to arrangements from which they obtained large commissions from Chinese miners.

The Chinese population grew rapidly with the expansion of the mining industry and by the late 1870s, a few years after British intervention, about four-fifths of the immigrant Chinese in the FMS were directly involved in mining (Arudsothy, 1968: 57). With the increasing and concomitant growth in Chinese tin mining and immigrant labour, the Malay ruling class lost control of the industry and the ability to effectively exact dues.[1] The increased demand and commercial network for food and other supplies greatly encouraged commodity production by Malay peasants, leading to the expansion of commercial activities by Straits merchants and their agents in the hinterland.

Because the significance of export-oriented productive activity in the Western Malay States actually preceded the British flag, it has been argued that subsequent colonial intervention served only to consolidate these developments (Khoo Kay Kim, 1972; Drabble, 1974). However, this view overlooks the significance of intervention by the colonial state, which by 'stabilizing' a very turbulent situation arising from preceding changes, paved the way for subsequent development under colonial auspices in the service of specific class interests. British capital had learnt, often from bitter experience, the importance of government control and support in providing a stable and attractive investment environment, in terms of 'law and order', as well as economic infrastructure.[2]

TABLE 6.1

Tin Prices, Production of Tin-in-Concentrates, and Mine Employment,
1874–1941 and 1946–1983

Year	Tin Price ($/Pikul)	Tin Price (5-yearly Average)	Employment ('000)	Output ('000 tons)
1874	30			4
1875	23			9
1876	21	22		10
1877	18			3
1878	18			8
1879	21			11
1880	26			12
1881	28	27		11
1882	31			12
1883	30			17
1884	25			18
1885	23			17
1886	34	32		20
1887	37			24
1888	42			24
1889	36			27
1890	32			27
1891	(31) 33	35		32
1892	(35) 37			34
1893	(31) 38			40
1894	(33) 38			48
1895	(30) 35			50
1896	(28) 32	37		49
1897	36			44
1898	43			41
1899	73			39
1900	74			43
1901	68	76		47
1902	79			47
1903	84			51
1904	77			52
1905	82			51
1906	90	80		49
1907	85			48
1908	67			51
1909	68			51
1910	78			46
1911	94	89		47
1912	103			50
1913	100			51
1914	73			51
1915	78		164	50
1916	86	99	139	47
1917	109		123	43
1918	151		145	40

Year	Tin Price ($/Pikul)	Tin Price (5-yearly Average)	Employment ('000)	Output ('000 tons)
1919	121		113	39
1920	151		90	37
1921	85	108	86	36
1922	81		82	37
1923	102		97	39
1924	124		106	47
1925	132		107	48
1926	145	132	110	48
1927	145		122	54
1928	114		109	65
1929	104		104	72
1930	73		81	67
1931	60	81	57	55
1932	70		41	29
1933	100		43	25
1934	114		55	38
1935	111		63	42
1936	100	108	80	67
1937	120		88	77
1938	95		58	43
1939	114		73	47
1940	n.a.		n.a.	83
1941	n.a.		n.a.	79
1946	170		23	88
1947	218		28	27
1948	281	266	44	45
1949	294		50	55
1950	367		37	58
1951	527		44	57
1952	480		40	57
1953	363	418	38	56
1954	354		35	61
1955	365		40	61
1956	387		40	62
1957	373		38	59
1958	369	384	26	38
1959	397		21	38
1960	394		27	52
1961	447		31	56
1962	448		34	58
1963	445	532	33	59
1964	619		35	59
1965	702		43	63
1966	645		49	68
1967	600		48	71
1968	565	620	49	74
1969	626		45	72
1970	665		45	73

(continued)

TABLE 6.1 (*continued*)

Year	Tin Price ($/Pikul)	Tin Price (5-yearly Average)	Employment ('000)	Output ('000 tons)
1971	632		45	74
1972	627		44	76
1973	686	809	41	71
1974	1,134		43	67
1975	964		41	63
1976	1,147		36	62
1977	1,588		36	58
1978	1,743	1,719.4	38	62
1979	1,960		40	62
1980	2,159		40	60
1981	1,956		34	59
1982	1,818		32	52
1983	1,826		27	40

Sources: Thoburn (1971: 391, Appendix 4.2; 394, Appendix 4.4; 416, Appendix 5.3); Wong Lin Ken (1965: 250, 254); Fermor (1939: 76); *Bulletin of Statistics of Mining Industry*, 1939–66; *Monthly Bulletin of Statistics*, 1967–82 (various issues); *Monthly Tin Mining Industry Statistics*, 1982–3 (various issues).

Notes: 1. Prices for 1874–90 are annual values of tin imported into the Straits Settlements from the FMS. Wong derived these figures from Straits Settlements trade returns.

2. Prices for 1891–6 which are bracketed are from Wong (1965).

3. Prices for 1891–1903 are for Straits refined tin in Singapore.

4. Values for 1904–83 are Straits ex-works prices.

5. Data were not available for 1942–5.

An increased demand for tin, produced by expansion of the British tin-plating industry and the decline of Cornwall tin production, encouraged Straits merchants to invest in the Malay States. From 1844 onwards, they applied increasing pressure on the colonial authorities to intervene in the Malay States to 'stabilize' conditions for better security of their investments in tin production. A suitable opportunity arose when a minor war between two Chinese mining groups in Perak, who were backing rival claimants to the throne, caused some disruption in mining activities[3] and provided the final pretext for British 'intervention' to take over Perak. Before the end of 1874, similar 'interventions' were also conducted in Selangor (on the pretext of uncontrollable piracy) and part of Negri Sembilan. Over a decade later, in 1887, after alleged harassment of British economic interests in Pahang, the pretext of the murder of a Sino-British subject was used to coerce the Sultan there to accept a British Resident.

'Direct' colonial rule—as practised in the Straits Settlements—was never imposed in the Malay States. Nominal autonomy, embodied in the personage of the indigenous ruler, was maintained throughout. The ruler's acceptance of a British Resident ensured the advancement of British interests; after all, the Resident's advice was to be 'asked and acted upon on all questions other than those touching upon the Malay religion and custom'.

With conditions in the tin-producing States thus 'stabilized' and demand for tin still rising in the world market (see Table 6.1), mining grew rapidly in what were to become the Federated Malay States.[4] The Chinese population of these States almost doubled from 163,000 in 1891 to 300,000 a decade later, while in the Straits Settlements, it increased more slowly from 228,000 to 282,000 over the same period. Tin exports from Perak rose from 650 tons in 1874 to 18,810 tons in 1893, while the other States produced 18,930 tons (Yip, 1969: 60, 61).

The Organization of Chinese Mining Capital

The organization of capital for the pioneering tin industry was similar to the earlier experience described for agriculture (J. C. Jackson, 1968; Lee Poh Ping, 1974; Trocki, 1975). Straits Chinese capital was very responsive to the profitable opportunities in tin mining. However, though the bulk of early Chinese investments were made by Straits merchants, they generally remained cautious and were not directly involved in production. Rather, through middlemen called 'mines advancers', funds were advanced, thus securing control of the ore produced, offering prospects of further profits from smelting and the export trade.

In the early organization of Chinese tin mining, the middleman or mines advancer 'could at the same time be a tin-mine owner, a shopkeeper, a tin-ore dealer, an operator of "revenue farms" and, if he was a successful man, often an advancer to smaller mines advancers' (Yip, 1969: 90). The advancer usually provided the tin-mine owner-cum-employer with his 'variable capital' needs, i.e. to feed, clothe, and house the workers, and sometimes additional loans above that in return for an exclusive right to purchase the output. With the emergence of this 'tribute system' (which will be discussed later), dependence of the poorly capitalized mine headman on the mines advancer increased. The advancer thus enjoyed the greatest control, and hence profits, and also stood to gain otherwise from his many different roles.[5] It has even been suggested that under this system, 'the Chinese tin miner could seldom make a fortune' (Yip, 1969: 91).

Despite various efforts by British capital to capture control of tin production in Malaya, Chinese dominance did not diminish significantly until around the turn of the century. Various technological conditions favoured Chinese mining methods as the shallow deposits needed little expensive equipment and were not usually abundant enough to adequately utilize the larger-scale, more expensively equipped European enterprises. In such an environment, the large, heavily capitalized European establishments, with their complex equipment and relatively highly paid staff, were a poor match for the financially modest, but flexible, Chinese mines. Low investment requirements and the availability of financing by mines advancers and their Straits merchant backers contributed to the relative ease of entry into the industry. With so many small mines competing, the resulting low prices for tin ore suited tin traders in the Straits Settlements and industrial consumers in the West. Perhaps what was most decisive in favour of Chinese mining enterprise during the early years was the labour situation.

Chinese Capital's Control over Chinese Labour

Chinese capitalist control of tin mining persisted long after British intervention in the tin producing Malay States because of effective and exclusive control over Chinese labour. Relying on 'labour-intensive' production techniques, the minimization of the wage bill was key to their viability and profitability.

Early Chinese pioneers to South-East Asia, who had generally financed their own emigration, went mainly into commerce or artisan production. However, the demand for labour, caused by the rapid expansion of tin mining and related developments, required a large labour force, which was met by the inflow of indentured labour. In the absence of a local proletariat, Chinese capitalists chose to employ an immigrant proletariat they controlled by a variety of economic and extra-economic means. Initially imported under the onerous 'credit-ticket' system, the traffic in indentured workers came to be known as the 'pig-trade'. Under the 'credit-ticket' arrangement, a Chinese coolie-broker paid the expenses of the *sinkheh*[6] (new immigrant), who was held on arrival in the Straits Settlements, until the debt incurred was paid off by an employer in exchange for a contractual obligation on the *sinkheh*'s services for a specified period. This transaction was conducted between broker and prospective employer, with the labourer usually unaware of his employer, place or conditions of work. The prices offered for *sinkheh* varied with labour requirements and after arrival they were often retained in terrible conditions for speculative purposes. As this business was very lucrative to the labour brokers, trickery and even kidnapping were sometimes resorted to in China to obtain emigrants. The charge for a junk voyage was relatively high compared to the maintenance costs during the journey. As income was obtainable only on the number of *sinkheh* landed, this was often maximized by having as many emigrants as possible on board a junk. The deaths of *sinkheh* because of poor conditions on board cut into profits, but overloading the junks cost little more otherwise.

Not surprisingly, the first Straits Settlements legislation in 1877 affecting Chinese labour 'protected the coolie-brokers and employers more than the immigrants' (Wong Lin Ken, 1965: 70). The sentiment in government circles was that legislative involvement in labour matters might reduce the flow of labourers, who were then in great demand by employers. In fact, legislation was introduced 'for the protection of the employer' against crimping, and to ensure contract enforcement (Blythe, 1947: 76). Eventually, however, strong competition for labour from outside the British realm[7] necessitated increased 'protection' of Chinese workers to ensure a labour supply. Nevertheless, the mounting difficulties in meeting capital's labour needs led to a Commission being appointed in 1890 to inquire into the 'state of labour in the Straits Settlements and Protected Native States, with a view to devising a scheme for encouraging immigration and thereby supplying the demand of [*sic*] labour' (Blythe, 1947: 77). New steps were taken to supervise the immigration and contractual conditions of Chinese indentured labourers. 'But the labour laws were honoured more in the breach than in the observance' (Wong Lin Ken, 1965: 74). With the absence of an adequate enforcement apparatus serving to perpetuate this state of affairs, Chinese labour conditions were undoubtedly deplorable.[8] The weak Manchu government was unlikely to intervene, having signed a treaty with Britain in 1904 depriving China of any say in the recruitment of Chinese indentured labour. British subjects, including Straits Chinese businessmen, could recruit as many workers as they wanted, who could subsequently be repatriated if and when Britain wished.

This cheap source of labour enabled Chinese-owned mines to produce at low cost, making competition by use of less labour-intensive techniques difficult (see Table 6.2). When increasingly exorbitant prices were charged—by the small number of coolie-brokers—for indentured labourers under the credit-ticket system, employers began to recruit for themselves, usually by sending foremen and supervisors back to their own villages in China. The recruit's passage to Malaya would be covered by the boss, who would employ him on arrival. Thus, kinship and village bonds came to be used to control workers. With this development, indentured labour on the credit-ticket system declined in importance. A 1910 colonial government commission to investigate working conditions for Chinese workers, especially indentured labourers, painted a terrible picture. Yet it recommended extending the use of indentured labour to the largely British-owned rubber industry, then at an early stage of rapid growth and in great need of labour. By the time the importation of indentured Chinese labour was banned in 1914, indentured labour had practically ceased to exist anyway.

Another important means by which Chinese capitalists controlled Chinese workers was the secret society. Secret societies had emerged in China on a quasi-religious basis to become important in the resistance against the Manchu (Ching) Dynasty. In Malaya, however, they were transformed into quasi-welfare organizations serving multifarious functions in the uncertain frontier society and embracing most strata of the Chinese community.[9] It has been claimed that membership of secret societies was often obligatory, and to resist could be suicidal. A society would offer protection—against other societies among others—and established its own law and code of conduct, while requiring complete loyalty from members. In mining areas, Malay chiefs, and later the British, dealt with the Chinese communities through the *Kapitan China*, who was usually head of the most powerful local secret society as well as the leading capitalist in the area. Through these societies, Chinese capitalists exercised almost exclusive control over Chinese labour. It has been noted, for instance, that 'western companies had great difficulties in getting labour owing to the opposition of the Chinese mining capitalists through the agency of the secret societies' (Wong Lin Ken, 1965: 53). 'These capitalists, it is believed, were the headmen of the various secret societies into which the newly arrived immigrants were inducted', wrote R. N. Jackson (1961: 46), a colonial official-cum-historian.

Yet another widespread, if not universal, characteristic of the organization of Chinese labour communities in Malaya was the 'truck system', by which workers usually received their wages at long and irregular intervals. In the interim, a worker would be advanced items for personal consumption (usually including opium) at higher than usual prices. As he usually had no savings on

TABLE 6.2

Tin-mining Labour Force by Mining Method, 1903 and 1910–1968

Year	Dredging	Gravel Pumping	Hydraulicing	Opencast	Underground	Total All Mining	Total Tin	Dulang Washers and Other
1903	—	22,391		143,028	20,918	186,337	...	...
1910	—	28,521		122,686	19,154	170,361	...	10,257
1911	—	30,881		150,439	15,107	196,427	...	10,907
1912	—	35,494		157,081	18,834	211,409	...	12,031
1913	228	36,681		167,669	20,454	225,032	...	14,155
1914	508	32,373		124,015	14,793	171,689	...	14,877
1915	1,521	33,089		118,454	11,393	164,457	...	15,859
1916	1,918	31,403		94,890	10,932	139,143	...	14,007
1917	2,156	28,922		81,660	10,602	123,340	...	13,870
1918	2,562	33,384		97,082	11,593	144,621	...	15,774
1919	2,734	27,781		73,632	9,960	114,107	...	15,553
1920	2,844	35,139		41,854	9,722	89,559	...	12,867
1921	5,608	29,973		40,699	10,058	86,338	...	13,418
1922	5,189	31,947		36,545	8,514	82,195	...	12,753
1923	5,606	45,401		43,024	11,631	105,662	...	7,849
1924	6,584	39,295	12,068	40,491	8,041	106,479	...	7,794
1925	7,497	49,575	13,818	29,379	6,988	107,257	...	7,792
1926	9,057	54,592	11,659	28,556	6,429	110,293	...	5,923
1927	11,120	64,567	12,476	28,417	6,308	122,888	...	7,536
1928	14,212	59,834	10,108	19,087	5,900	109,141	...	10,409
1929	16,817	59,160	9,003	13,338	6,150	104,468	100,039	8,947
1930	12,293	41,076	9,111	12,202	5,846	80,528	76,796	7,784
1931	9,214	25,599	5,574	12,731	3,920	57,038	53,919	8,739

1932	6,991	16,555	4,991	12,494	3,424	44,455	41,014	8,975
1933	6,545	17,616	4,809	10,616	3,276	42,862	39,380	9,028
1934	8,935	28,759	4,616	7,818	4,491	54,619	50,464	9,696
1935	10,537	31,070	4,993	11,467	477	62,844	57,263	9,701
1936	15,506	42,197	4,822	10,951	6,742	80,218	73,468	9,851
1937	16,154	47,382	4,664	13,378	6,707	88,285	80,648	9,858
1938	12,934	23,246	3,797	11,623	6,063	57,663	50,402	9,687
1939	16,438	36,555	...	11,389	4,952	69,334	65,556	9,822
1946	8,184	7,882	2,726	3,647	2,345	24,784	23,026	22,973
1947	12,493	19,418	2,830	3,516	3,510	41,767	39,362	21,109
1948	15,235	23,611	3,040	4,195	4,434	50,515	46,861	20,281
1949	15,776	23,584	2,568	3,622	6,438	51,988	47,107	19,306
1950	15,732	23,968	2,489	3,403	5,940	51,532	47,201	18,702
1951	15,486	23,707	1,471	3,484	6,766	50,914	45,931	6,400
1952	14,882	23,179	1,465	6,411	4,740	50,677	44,659	6,659
1953	13,488	17,172	1,310	4,923	4,243	41,136	36,899	7,801
1954	14,077	19,327	1,344	4,719	3,780	43,247	39,715	7,742
1955	14,442	19,163	1,283	5,223	3,859	43,970	55,559	8,762
1956	14,322	18,917	1,435	5,814	3,283	43,771	39,459	7,775
1957	13,781	16,854	1,529	6,072	3,342	41,578	36,585	7,957
1958	9,555	9,292	1,201	4,678	2,496	27,222	23,153	7,945
1959	8,593	10,703	1,024	5,704	2,588	28,612	23,778	7,937
1960	11,334	12,771	1,241	7,892	2,807	36,045	29,242	7,889
1961	11,438	15,471	1,235	8,690	2,663	39,497	32,459	8,379
1962	10,933	16,567	1,211	9,930	2,678	41,319	33,373	11,266
1963	11,156	17,984	239	8,347	2,549	40,275	33,650	13,529
1964	10,910	22,646	256	7,742	2,615	44,169	38,387	14,797

(continued)

TABLE 6.2 (continued)

Year	Dredging	Gravel Pumping	Hydraulicing	Opencast	Underground	Total All Mining	Total Tin	Dulang Washers and Other
1965	10,676	29,292	136	7,365	2,672	50,141	45,345	15,663
1966	10,785	33,608	120	7,919	2,542	54,974	48,800	16,945
1967	10,520	32,290	130	7,160	2,630	52,730	49,224	...
1968	10,673	32,514	141	6,159	2,534	52,021	48,675	20,794
1969	10,340	30,570	150	810	2,460	49,560	44,700	370
1970	10,230	31,230	120	890	2,440	50,030	45,110	200
1971	10,000	31,340	42	940	2,530	46,642	45,162	310
1972	9,710	30,450	26	1,080	2,690	45,311	44,236	280
1973	9,320	27,520	—	1,490	2,420	42,030	40,980	230
1974	9,080	29,700	—	1,320	2,340	43,490	42,700	260
1975	8,900	27,690	—	1,530	2,230	41,070	40,600	250
1976	8,550	23,210	—	1,380	2,130	35,810	35,500	230
1977	8,720	23,840	—	1,240	2,030	36,580	36,050	222
1978	8,680	26,210	19	1,360	1,980	38,879	38,449	250
1979	8,720	26,310	—	2,220	2,070	40,703	40,310	990
1980	8,920	25,970	—	2,370	1,830	40,493	40,080	990
1981	9,060	21,120	—	1,920	1,670	34,338	33,850	80
1982	9,230	18,710	—	2,070	1,700	32,148	31,800	90
1983	7,705	13,411	—	—	—	27,043	26,705	—

Sources: Thoburn (1971:392, Appendix IV-3), Ministry of Labour, *1969 Handbook of Labour Statistics*; Department of Statistics (1983), *Monthly Tin Mining Industry Statistics*, July.

Notes: 1. Figures for 1983 are preliminary and subject to revision.
2. Figures after 1969 are only given for 'Dredging', 'Gravel Pumping', 'Total All Mining', 'Total Tin', and 'Others'.
   The figures for the last column for 1969–82 are for other tin-mining methods.
3. Figures for 'Total All Mining' have been amended to tally with total obtained by adding figures for 'Dredging', 'Gravel Pumping', 'Hydraulicing', 'Opencast', and 'Underground'.

which to fall back, the labourer had no choice but to meet his needs by taking items on credit from the supplier-cum-employer. This practice—distinct from indenture—often bound labourers to employers in perpetual debt. Thus, in his capacity as merchant-creditor, the employer recovered a considerable portion of wages paid. It also increased the resilience of the mining entrepreneur, who was therefore less likely to close down as soon as his direct income from tin production failed to meet the wage bill; in effect his income exceeded the difference between production and wage payments since a large part of the latter was usually retrieved in his capacity as merchant-creditor. The arrangement was also attractive to the Straits capitalists and mines advancers financing the mining operations, who thus obtained a share of the output and had first option to purchase the ore, besides profitably providing consumption items. In fact, the financier's actual contribution often barely exceeded these provisions since Chinese mining techniques then utilized relatively little equipment.

A related operation which further strengthened employers' control over labour was the revenue farm system. For a certain fixed fee, the colonial administration awarded these farms to selected Chinese businessmen, who then had control of lucrative operations such as opium sales and gambling. Once indebted, many labourers were forced to pledge their labour services to the revenue farmer for a certain period in settlement of such debts. Indentured labourers were often unable to 'free' themselves despite having completed the initial period of their contracts because of these additional debts. Even 'free' workers could become bonded after becoming similarly indebted.

Another important aspect of late nineteenth-century Chinese tin mining in Malaya was the tribute system. To minimize the risks of mining his property a mine-owner would allow a gang of labourers to work the mine under a headman, who was usually too poorly capitalized to independently gain access to mining land. The tin extracted would then be divided in fixed proportions among all concerned. Thus, with minimal effort on his part, the owner could collect an income, comparable to a rent, usually amounting to at least a tenth of output.[10] The headman could also arrange with a mines advancer, if the owner was not already one, to supply consumption items to workers. This kind of production arrangement relied primarily on manual work, since investment in equipment was unlikely, given the nature of the financial arrangements. The development of the forces of production, including technology, was thus retarded by both the organization of production, as well as concentration of the bulk of profits in the hands of those with no direct involvement in production. Hence, the tribute system was viable only as long as easily accessible surface deposits were still in abundance. The possibility of striking it rich—because of the sharing arrangement in the tribute system—attracted many labourers who had completed or absconded from their indentured service. By 1903, when 77 per cent of the labour force were in opencast mines, half of all mine workers were working under the tribute system, with only 15 per cent receiving wages, and the other 35 per cent still indentured (Yip, 1969: 79, 83). However, the conditions which had initially led to this system of production were beginning to change, thus undermining the basis for its continued operation.

The Colonial State, Labour, and the Decline of
Chinese Mining Capital

One factor contributing to the decline of Chinese mining after the turn of the century was the exhaustion of known accessible surface deposits. The mining of deeper deposits involved different techniques requiring heavier investments in equipment and less use of direct labour. Together with the strengthening position of labour, giving rise to increased labour disputes and higher labour costs, this encouraged greater investment and use of equipment and reduced reliance on labour among Chinese mining capitalists. Obviously, only the better-funded and more successful Chinese mines could adopt new techniques, particularly gravel-pumping. The smaller operations relying on more labour-intensive techniques continued, but became increasingly marginal to the industry as a whole.

Perhaps most decisive in the struggle over the tin industry was the Chinese capitalists' control of labour—which had enabled them to keep wage rates low[11]—a constant source of frustration to other prospective employers, especially British investors.[12] Also, by supplying consumption items to workers, i.e. by paying in kind, Chinese capitalists further reduced the expenditure required to maintain their labour force. The loosening of this control over Chinese labour, achieved through a combination of measures by the colonial state, resulted in a further weakening of the position of Chinese mining capitalists.

Various legislative measures were taken to 'free' the Chinese labour market and to 'protect' Chinese workers. Indentured labour was increasingly super-vised and, by the time it was legally abolished in 1914, it had ceased to be of much significance.[13] The Federated Malay States Labour Commission Report of 1910 observed that improvements in communications and rapid economic growth offered alternative employment opportunities, which encouraged absconding and thus diminished the efficacy of the indenture system. It also encouraged employers to improve working conditions, including wage rates, in order to retain their labour force.

Meanwhile, the credit-ticket system of indentured labour recruitment had been abolished in Perak in 1894, and in Selangor and Negri Sembilan the following year. This too had begun to decline in significance before 1890. While 36.7 per cent of Chinese emigrants arriving at Singapore and Penang in 1881 had their fares paid for, this proportion fell to 10.9 per cent by 1890 (Yip, 1969: 70, Table 1.5). Even 'assisted' immigration of Chinese to Malaya declined, though it continued to meet labour requirements until 1928. Employers increasingly turned to the system of private recruitment mentioned earlier by which trusted employees were sent back to China to recruit fellow villagers and kinsmen who came as nominally free labourers but were obliged to be 'loyal' to their employers (Yip, 1969: 77). Another recruiting system, using inter-connected lodging houses in the ports of emigration and immigration, was similar to indenture in various respects, involving many of its worst attributes.

The successful campaign waged by the colonial administration after 1891 to wipe out secret societies facilitated the ascendance of British mining interests.[14] In 1896, for example, 70 per cent of the Chinese in Krian, Perak, belonged to a single secret society, whereas only two years later, a mere 5 per cent of the population belonged to any at all. In Selangor, total secret society membership is said to have involved less than 5 per cent of the Chinese population by 1898 (Wong Lin Ken, 1965: 219). The 'freeing' of labour encouraged mobility in search of higher wages, generally to foreign mines, raising wages all round. Thus, competing interests within the capitalist class served to ease the oppressive labour conditions, though labour struggles certainly played no small part in bringing about these transformations.

Within Malaya, the challenge to colonial authority embodied by Chinese secret societies and their control of Chinese labour drove the administration to actively attempt to destroy their power. The role of the 'Protector of Chinese' (a British official) was to assert the authority of the British government and to police the Chinese community. Ostensible colonial concern for the welfare of Chinese workers actually sought to wean them away from exclusive Chinese capitalist control. Despite the decline of the secret societies however, the Chinese community continued to remain organized across class lines in craft-guilds, clan groups, dialect associations, and similar organizations. The separate system of Chinese vernacular schooling continued to expand, training a labour force for almost exclusive employment by Chinese capital.

The decline of the truck system has been linked to, among other things, the decline in Chinese smelting in the wake of the ascendancy of British smelting companies, most notably the Straits Trading Company (Yip, 1969: 107). The Company first made headway with those mining enterprises which did not rely on Straits Chinese capital for financing, since Straits-financed mines were usually obliged to send their product to their financiers for smelting and export (Yip, 1969: 107). Eventually the Company successfully competed for tin ore from the larger group of Straits-financed mines, by also offering to finance mining operations indirectly through tin ore dealers. Before 1890, all tin exports from the Federated Malay States were in the form of metal, smelting being done on the peninsula. The Straits Trading Company opened a large new smelting plant in Singapore in 1890 and closed its smelters in the FMS. By 1901, only 46.4 per cent of tin exports from the FMS were in the form of metal, declining further to 22.5 per cent by 1910, which reflected the rapid capture of the smelting business by the large foreign-owned smelters in the Straits Settlements (Yip, 1969: 108, 109). These rapid changes in the location of smelting were encouraged by the different freight rates introduced for ore and metal on the state-owned railway and also by the different export duties exacted. The metal content of the ore was consistently under-assessed to make it more profitable for mines in the FMS to export tin in the form of ore rather than metal (Yip, 1969: 117). Train charges were similarly biased. The Company was also given the exclusive right to export ore from Selangor and Sungei Ujong for a period of time. A Chinese smelting works started in Penang in 1898 to take advantage of this situation also proved successful and was eventually bought over by European interests in 1911. Simultaneously, the British took legislative measures to make smelting a British preserve in the face of competition from outside the Straits Settlements, Australia, and Britain, where British-owned smelting works were sited. An export duty on tin ore was imposed after United States tin interests sought to break the British monopoly over smelting (Wong Lin Ken, 1965: 229).

The British hold on the smelting industry undermined the Straits Chinese merchants' financing and control of tin mining, and hence the truck system as well. The Truck Enactment of 1908 barred debt-bondage of mining labour under the truck system, giving workers the option of receiving cash instead of consumption items as part of their wage. Wage payments in the form of opium were forbidden and the prices of goods which could still be provided on credit under truck arrangements were to be fixed by the colonial government.

Opium smoking was a widespread indulgence among Chinese—particularly workers—in Malaya. Most acquired the habit only after arrival in the country, and those who did strenuous physical work were especially encouraged by merchant–employers involved in the opium trade. It has been estimated that the average Chinese worker, employed for 360 days in a year, spent two-thirds of his income on opium (Li, 1955: 95)! While this staggering proportion may appear somewhat implausible, high worker expenditure on opium is undeniable. The rights for the preparation and sale of opium—which were initially farmed out, mainly to Chinese businessmen—were retracted in the last decade of the nineteenth century when the administration of the Federated Malay States gradually began to eliminate the revenue farms. Opium farms were stopped by 1901 and the last of the gambling farms ceased in 1912, further weakening Chinese employers' control of workers.

But opium smoking had already begun to decline among the Chinese before the abolition of the revenue farms. The emergence of the tribute system contributed to this trend since opium-smoking partners were expected to be less productive. The anti-opium sentiments of some employers were believed to be genuine by at least one colonial official who attributed this to the deleterious effects of addiction on productivity. Nevertheless, many capitalists continued to indulge in the business outside their own mines because it was very lucrative (Wong Lin Ken, 1965: 224-5). The abolition of the farms eliminated an important source of income for the mining capitalist, who gained his profits through a variety of other operations. While all profits ultimately came from the labour of the mine workers, only part of this was derived directly from production (i.e. after deducting wages), whereas the rest was obtained indirectly (i.e. from wages and other incomes) from commerce and usury.

Although opium farms were ostensibly abolished for moral and health considerations, opium was not prohibited in pre-war Malaya. Instead, the new opium policy rendered it a very important source of revenue for the colonial administration, at the expense of the opium-smoking Chinese population, of course. In response to tremendous local and foreign (both in Britain and China) public pressure, a Commission (of five Englishmen and one Chinese) was appointed to investigate the matter (Li, 1955: 96-7). Its report in 1909 advocated the continued availability of the drug, on such grounds as the likely 'law-abiding' character of the addict because of its addictive properties and the threat of opium deprivation in prison. Also, opium addiction was found not to adversely affect worker productivity. The Commission's recommendation for a government monopoly of the import, preparation, and distribution of the drug was implemented. The opium price increased fourfold from $3 a *tahil* (1⅓ oz.) in 1910 to $12 in 1919. The largest single source of government revenue for the British administration in Malaya from 1874 to World War II was from neither tin nor rubber, but from opium. For over half of this period, between 40 per cent and 60 per cent of the Straits Settlements' revenue was from opium.[15] Such considerations probably affected the Commission's deliberations.

The Colonial State and the Ascendancy of British Mining Capital

Changing technological conditions in the tin-mining industry (see Table 6.2), which increasingly favoured the better-financed enterprises, offered British mining capital a clear advantage, and resulted in significant British inroads. However, far more important than greater financial backing was the role of the colonial state in promoting British participation in the industry.[16] Despite strong criticism 'that the British administration had been doing too much to encourage the growth of the western (particularly the British) tin mining industry', colonial policy actively supported foreign investment (Yip, 1969: 151). From the end of the nineteenth century, new legislation gave the colonial government virtually complete control over tin mining. The Perak Mining Code of 1895, which was a prototype for subsequent mining legislation in the rest of the FMS, strongly favoured the subsequent development of mining with more technically advanced methods—in effect, the more highly capitalized foreign investors. Mining land policy was also changed to favour those with strong financial backing,[17] hence discriminating against the bulk of Chinese mining enterprise, which tended to be relatively small in terms of capital. Large areas of land, much of which had been appropriated from Chinese and Malay owners, were issued to Europeans at low cost, a policy generalized to all the Federated Malay States in 1913 after the introduction of the tin dredge necessitated larger mining land concessions.

The British colonial administration facilitated the British take-over of the tin industry in other ways besides labour policy. From 1909, mining interests were officially represented in the Federal Council—the colonial legislative body—to thus ensure favourable legislation and policy in all relevant areas. When the price of tin fell in 1920, the FMS government predictably intervened in a timely fashion, buying up nearly 10,000 tons of tin in a dramatic price-support effort. This entire effort involved an initial commitment of about twenty million Straits dollars and was later estimated by the 1924 FMS Annual Report to have cost over two and a half million Straits dollars, or about 4 per cent of annual revenue then. British capital, which historically had been relatively inflexible organizationally, and hence more vulnerable to the market, was thus rescued from an extremely difficult situation by timely government intervention.

As European companies increased their share of tin output, the colonial government's fiscal policy changed accordingly (see Table 5.4). Export duty

rates on tin declined considerably from previously higher levels[18] (see Lim Teck
Ghee, 1971: 290, Appendix 2.3). Between 1889 and 1906 when the industry was
still predominantly in Chinese hands, export duty on tin contributed between a
third and a half of the total revenue of the FMS (Yip, 1969: 112-14). The
percentage of tin export duty to total revenue declined rapidly in the remaining
pre-World War I years and never exceeded 20 per cent between 1914 and 1938,
except in 1937, which was an exceptional year for the tin market (Lim Chong-
Yah, 1967: 350). Nor can it be said that the proportional decline in tin revenue
was being compensated for by taxes on rubber. Rubber exports, which rapidly
grew to exceed tin, contributed more than a tenth of total revenue in only two
years (1925 and 1926) before 1938 (Lim Chong-Yah, 1967: 350).

    The Great Depression in the world economy from the end of the third
decade of the present century had important repercussions on the international
tin market in which the United States of America had been, by far, the largest
single national consumer since the latter part of the nineteenth century (see
Tables 6.1 and 6.3). It was a dramatic reminder of the vulnerability of the
industry to the vicissitudes of industrial monopoly capitalism. By 1925, the
United States accounted for 76,000 of the 150,000 tons consumed in that year
(Lim Chong-Yah, 1967: 39, 40). British capital, which had strong interests in tin
mining all over the world—including Bolivia, Nigeria, the then Netherlands
East Indies, and Siam initiated international tin control measures to
'rationalize' world production in accordance with profit-maximization considerations. Low release quotas were desired to keep prices high. Three
agreements affecting Malaya were made and implemented from the early 1930s
until the outbreak of the Pacific War. Mining interests in the FMS, represented
by predominantly British interests, agreed to lower release quotas for the world
market. The small, predominantly Chinese, producers preferred large quotas,
knowing that when the quota was small, the bigger European producers could
fulfil it themselves by pooling and manipulation, whereas small producers
supplied tin only when the quota was large, hence their 'marginal' status. They
would be the last to produce and the first to shut down under conditions of
restriction. Whether or not the Malayan quota as a whole was under-assessed

TABLE 6.3

Some Effects of the Depression on Tin Mining in British Malaya,
1929-1933

Year	Number of Mines in Operation[1]	Tin Output[1] (tons)	Tin Mine Workers Employed[1]	Price per Pikul[1] ($)	Net Tin Exports[2] ($ million)
1929	1,286	69,366	100,000	104.37	117
1930	1,234	63,974	75,000	72.89	77
1931	1,188	54,908	52,000	60.29	51
1932	1,068	29,742	40,000	69.76	31
1933	1,013	24,904	34,000	99.99	37

Sources: 1. Siew Nim Chee (1953), in Silcock (1961: 426, Table 8).
           2. Bauer (1944), in Silcock (1961: 185-200, Tables 2, 3, 5, 7, and 9).

relative to productive capacity, remains a moot point.[19] While total Malayan tin output did not increase significantly during the 1930s, the European consumption of Malayan tin output rose from 52 per cent in 1930 (the last year before international control) to 63 per cent a decade later (Lim Chong-Yah, 1967: 59, 66). As can be seen from Tables 6.2 and 6.3, the consequences for employment in the tin industry were dramatic. For those who managed to retain jobs, wages dropped to minimal levels of subsistence.[20] 'Chinese migration was extremely sensitive to fluctuations in tin prices and employment. For instance there was a net efflux of 112,965 in 1931, compared with a net influx of 228,285 in 1926' (Caldwell, 1977b: 48).

British dominance of the tin industry in Malaya translated into more than mere statistics in terms of nationality of ownership.[21] The considerably higher capitalization of British-owned tin enterprise and the reduction in the number of firms in the industry as small-scale Chinese enterprises lost out, together brought about a more monopolistic structure in the tin mining industry in Malaya. However, actual concentration of control over the industry was even greater owing to the organizational structure of British-owned tin-mining companies in Malaya. For 1954, it has been shown that three managing agencies, Anglo-Oriental (40), Neill and Bell (24) and Osborne and Chappel (10), managed 74 of the 108 dredges in Malaya on behalf of a total of 47 companies which accounted for 73 per cent of total European-owned mine output. Eleven years later, in 1965, the industry had been considerably reorganized. Three mining agencies, Anglo-Oriental (11), Osborne and Chappel (10) and Associated Mines (4), controlled the operations of 25 of the 43 public limited tin-mining companies (Sumitro, 1968: 171). The picture is further complicated by the fact that a few British-based holding companies controlled a good part of world tin production as well as many Malayan public companies. While some of the mining agencies were subsidiaries of these holding companies,[22] there was no necessary correspondence between the holding company and the managing agency of a tin-mining enterprise. These ownership and control patterns have changed considerably since the late 1920s (Knorr, 1945). The recent take-over and reorganization of the London Tin group by the Malaysia Mining Corporation, and the apparent potential of the Selangor-based Perangsang group point to an important new trend of encroachment by interests closely linked to government. Available evidence— e.g. reflected in the pattern of interlocking directorships in the industry— suggests a high degree of concentration of ownership, secretarial functions and management among European-established tin companies, most of which are now owned by Malaysian public enterprises (see J. J. Puthucheary, 1960: Chapter 4; Tan Tat Wai, 1977: 242-7).

Chinese Labour and Employment

A few years after the introduction of the dredge in 1912, employment in mining dropped rapidly from a high of 225,405 in 1913 to 82,195 only nine years later (Kinney, 1975: 99). Employment picked up again with a revival of the world tin market, but more importantly, due to the growing popularity of the relatively labour-intensive gravel pump method. By 1926, half of the total mining labour force of 110,000 was in gravel-pumping (Lim Chong-Yah, 1967: 53). The number of tin-mine workers generally continued to decline to around 40,000 in the early 1950s (see Table 6.2). Recession conditions—e.g. during the Great Depression, World War II and in the late 1950s after the Korean War boom, and most recently in the early 1980s—have drastically reduced the size of the labour force, reflecting the vulnerability of the industry to world market conditions (see Table 6.2).

The expansion of the European-owned portion of the tin industry also saw an increase in the non-Chinese percentage of the work force. The efficacy of the racial 'divide and rule' managerial policy was, of course, not novel to the experienced British.[23] Chinese employment in mines dropped from 189,100 in 1911 to 61,310 in the late 1930s. The percentage of Chinese in the mining labour force declined from 96 per cent in 1911 to around 81 per cent before the war, and to 61 per cent by the early 1960s (see Table 6.4). Pre-war expansion of the non-Chinese mine labour force consisted mainly of Indians, reflecting the general British preference for Indian labour.[24] Post-war growth, though, has primarily involved Malays.

Despite the dramatic decline in the number of Chinese employed in the tin industry, Chinese immigration into Malaya continued. Immigrants were drawn by the opportunities of a rapidly growing colonial economy, which contrasted greatly with then existing conditions in China, though many came to Malaya only to return to China after accumulating some savings.[25] Richer Chinese, on the other hand, had little difficulty obtaining land; hence, Chinese-owned land-holdings have tended to be larger in size than those held by Malays. Thus, non-Malay land-ownership in the agricultural sector has a stronger representation of capitalist and petty capitalist interests, who generally own areas far larger than the small self-employed peasant, whether Malay or non-Malay. Officially discouraged from owning land, non-Malay peasants often operate in uncertain, and sometimes illegal, conditions.

With only limited access to land and finding wage employment opportunities limited and unattractive (especially with labour no longer being in short supply), many Chinese turned to self-employment or to small enterprises, becoming, for example, self-employed small-scale producers, traders, and fishermen. Usually financed by financiers or with locally accumulated savings, such enterprises have more often than not been organized along kinship lines. Others, including those linked by kinship or other ties to bigger Chinese merchants, were often 'sponsored' as agents in remote areas away from the hub of commerce. Usually buying produce from peasants for the market beyond, they also sold goods, and often offered credit facilities as well. *Thus, a considerable portion of the Chinese population in Malaya filled many of the new occupations generated by development of the colonial economy which did not interest foreign capital.* The ability of the Chinese to achieve this appears to result largely from their creative use of kinship, dialect group and other ties for economic collaboration. The consequent economic inter-connections reinforced such relationships, which might otherwise have withered away under the impact of social change, and

TABLE 6.4

Employment in Tin Mining in Malaya, by Race, 1911–1965 (annual average)

Quinquennial Average	Chinese		Indian		Malay		Others		Total
	No.	Percentage of Total	No.	Percentage of Total	No.	Percentage of Total	No.	Percentage of Total	
1911	189,100	96.2	4,630	2.4	2,580	1.3	210	0.1	196,520
1931–5	44,530	85.1	5,130	9.8	2,270	4.3	430	0.8	52,360
1936–40[1]	61,310	81.3	9,420	12.5	4,010	5.3	650	0.9	75,390
1946–50	30,980	68.5	6,660	14.7	6,690	14.8	880	2.0	45,210
1961–5[2]	26,700	60.9	5,060	11.5	11,470	26.2	610	1.4	43,840

Source: Yip (1969: 384, Table V-19).

[1] Average for three years, 1936–8; the figures for other years are not available.

[2] Average for two years, 1962 and 1964.

also consolidated the significant trade and occupational specialization which has existed along such lines.[26]

From 1930, the British administration applied quotas on the immigration of Chinese males because of the employment situation during the Depression and the growing militancy of Chinese labour. Chinese women, however, were still encouraged to immigrate to 'stabilize' the Chinese population. The era of immigrant labour was virtually over, and a settled, permanent Sino-Malayan working class was being consolidated. In fact, contrary to the position maintained by the colonial government in the 1930s, available demographic evidence indicates that 'the increase of permanent Chinese settlement was in fact quite rapid some time before official policy was shaped to an acceptance of Malaya as a country with a permanently settled multi-racial population' (Smith, 1964: 174). This incorrect official characterization of the actual situation became the basis for official condonation and encouragement of racially divisive policies and practices, such as in education.[27]

Compared to the Indians, whose progress had been 'slower and less continuous', the Chinese in Malaya had made fairly continuous progress towards permanent settlement, at least since the turn of the century. Presumably, this difference was influenced by the different political conditions in India and China and by respective differences involved in the cost, ease, and distance of travel, as well as by conditions in Malaya. The far greater scale of Chinese investments and the relatively insignificant role of Indian capital must also not be discounted. The greater socio-cultural isolation of the estates must have affected its inhabitants, the bulk of whom were Indian labourers. The 'loosening' of the ties of the Chinese working class to the Chinese capitalists eventually became reflected in exclusively labour organizations, which increasingly expressed themselves in working-class militancy and political radicalism.[28]

Postscript: The Current Fate of Mining Labour

As can be seen in Tables 6.1 and 6.2, employment in the tin-mining industry has experienced a long-term decrease since employing over 225,000 in 1913, with the decline of opencast mining (see Table 6.2). Since the onset of the Great Depression in the early 1930s, employment in tin mining has never exceeded 100,000, and since 1970, employment has declined from about 50,000 to only 27,043 in 1983.

Trends in the tin-mining industry in the late 1970s suggest that despite increasing productivity and a rising tin price, the incidence of poverty among mine workers actually increased in both absolute and relative terms. During the period 1976–80, the mining and quarrying sector experienced the highest sectoral average annual growth rate for value added per worker, i.e. of 8.6 per cent. Yet in this period, the mining sector also had the dubious distinction of registering an absolute as well as relative increase in poverty incidence. Over the same period, the tin price rose from $15,075 per tonne in 1975 to $36,040 in 1980 (i.e. at an average annual growth rate of about 19 per cent), before slipping to $30,093 in 1983 (Malaysia, 1984: 48, Table 2.4). Yet, the incidence of poverty among mine workers rose over that period from 31.8 per cent in 1975 to 33.0 per cent in 1980 and 41.0 per cent in 1983 (Malaysia, 1984: 80, Table 3.2).

Summary

British intervention in peninsular Malaya in the 1870s was partly motivated by the desire to bring order to the tin industry, and hence tin supply, and to establish British control of tin production. In the nineteenth century, the abundance of surface alluvial deposits of tin ore and the prevalence of uncomplicated mining techniques fostered the establishment of numerous small mining ventures. Usually financed by Straits merchants, the success of Chinese mining entrepreneurs was largely contingent on maintaining effective control—exercised in a variety of ways—over the Chinese mining labour force.

Despite many attempts to wrest control of tin production from Chinese capital before the turn of the century, British capital was largely unsuccessful in spite of being favoured by the colonial state, e.g. in allowing the alienation of mining land and undertaking the construction of the transportation network. However, with the exhaustion of surface deposits, the financial requirements for profitable mining increased. More importantly, from the last decade of the nineteenth century, the colonial state took measures to weaken the control that Chinese capital exercised over Chinese labour. Having done this, the government intensified its policies favouring British mining capital, thus ensuring control of the industry. Besides involving the transfer of ownership and control of the industry, the industry, as a whole, also became more monopolized.

For Chinese labour, the implications of these changes were very important. A variety of means for exercising control over Chinese labour had been utilized by Chinese capital, including indenture, the 'personal' recruitment system, kinship links, clan ties, provincial connections, vernacular schooling and other forms of patronage. The existence of a permanently settled Chinese population, growing labour discontent, intervention by the colonial state in the interest of British mining capital, and the declining need for extra-economic forms of labour control were factors that contributed to the emergence of Chinese free wage labour. (While nominally free wage labour emerged significantly early in the twentieth century, some of these 'primordial' forms of labour control exist up to the present.) Freed from the tight control of Chinese capital, Chinese labour was in a position to organize itself. As the British take-over of the mining industry also resulted in a drastic reduction of the mining labour force, as well as the proportion of Chinese labour, Chinese immigrant settlers turned to alternative occupations in the colonial economy.

1. For example, the Chinese population of Larut rose from 3 in 1848 to 40,000 in 1872, while the district ruler, the Menteri of Larut, retained a police force of only 40 (Yip, 1969: 58).

2. '[The] many failures and disappointments for European investors in the Malay States ... had taught businessmen with local experience two painfully acquired lessons: first that modern political

administration was essential 'if ambitious projects with long maturation periods were to have reasonable prospects of success; and, second, that capital could only be risked in greater volume when appropriate infrastructure (roads, railways, ports, storage facilities and the like) had been provided, and when suitable land and company law, banking and credit facilities, and so on, had been made available. These necessary tasks could only be undertaken by, or under the auspices of, western style government' (Caldwell, 1977a: 21-2).

3. 'But strife between contending Malay chiefs, each with his private army and each supported by the Chinese miners dependent upon him for livelihood and protection, broke out in a serious form in the late 1860s in Selangor and elsewhere in the tin belt.... Malay States tin imported into the Straits Settlements, having climbed to 4,713 tons in 1871, shrank to 2,335 in 1873 ...' (Caldwell, 1977a: 19).
This resulted in a drop of nearly a million dollars in 'returns of the value of imports at Penang during the years 1872 and 1873' (Yip, 1969: 59).

4. Other parts of Malaya have not produced significant quantities of tin.

5. 'It is therefore apparent that the mines advancer occupied a very important position in early Chinese tin mining. A successful mines advancer who held at the same time the roles of miner, mine owner, tin-ore dealer, shopkeeper and "revenue farmer" was almost in control of all the economic activities of the mining district. Through his advances to mines he secured a monopsony of the local tin market and a monopoly of the local market of foodstuffs and other provisions to the mining labourers, and through his gambling and opium-smoking dens, he extended his hold over the mining labourers. His position in the local mining industry was a unique [sic] and a powerful one' (Yip, 1969: 93-4).

6. The early immigrants under this system were almost entirely, if not exclusively, male.

7. Particularly from the neighbouring Dutch colony, Sumatra.

8. 'As late as 1898, it was "by no means infrequent" for employers in Ulu Selangor to work their sick labourers to the point of death and then throw them out of the mines to die by the roadside. In 1890, it was reported that employers in Jelebu sent their labourers to the government hospital on the verge of death because it was more convenient to let them die there, as they would avoid funeral expenses.... So deplorable were the conditions in the mines that in 1892 it was stated that the indentured labourer was better fed and housed in the government prison in Jelebu than in the mines' (Wong Lin Ken, 1965: 74).

9. 'At least in Singapore Chinese society of the late nineteenth century, leadership and control of the secret societies in the pioneer agricultural population was apparently not in the hands of the Straits Chinese merchants. The Straits Chinese were the most "desinicised" segment of the Chinese community and therefore had little "cultural" claim to leadership. Further, involvement would involve too great a risk to the conduct of their business which relied greatly on the goodwill of the colonial authorities who frowned upon the secret societies' (Lee Poh Ping, 1974).
While no comparable study of the early tin-mining community is available, similar circumstances suggest that secret societies there were probably also not dominated by the Straits Chinese merchants. This probably allowed the predominantly China-born entrepreneurs involved in production a certain measure of autonomy despite their financial subordination to Straits capital.

10. This aspect of the system was also comparable to the piece-rate wage payment system and to agricultural share-cropping.

11. 'The rising rate of wage resulting from the loss of control over the tin mining labour market was also a significant factor which led to the decline in the Chinese control of the industry, as Chinese mining methods depended to a large extent on the availability of cheap labour' (Yip, 1969: 151).

12. Ethnic employment preferences were also true of the Malays and Indians. However, there was no British working class in the colony.

13. '... recently it has practically disappeared in mining districts and has been confined almost entirely to the sugar estates in Krian' (quoted in R. N. Jackson, 1961: 147).

14. 'It was only with the destruction of the Chinese secret societies in the 1890s that one of the primary obstacles to the entry of Western enterprise was removed' (Wong Lin Ken, 1965: 237).

15. For more detailed discussions of opium revenue, see Li (1955: 28-30) and Lim Chong-Yah (1967: 253 60).

16. 'The factors which enabled the foreign companies to gain control of the industry over

Chinese miners were not all economic; they were also political. Apart from the advantage of having large amounts of capital and more efficient methods of mining and prospecting than Chinese miners, the foreign companies also had the advantage of a British colonial government in Malaya whose official policy definitely worked towards their benefit. Beginning with the present century, a series of enactments established official control over tin mining in all stages and no one was allowed to open a mine without the permission of the government. In the granting of licences to mines, the amount of capital which a mining firm could raise was one of the most important factors which influenced official decisions. Thus, as soon as this standard was applied, the foreign companies with their heavy investments in fixed capital had an advantage over the small Chinese miners' (Yip, 1969: 20-1).

17. 'To enable European companies to obtain large areas of mining land at practically no cost, the Perak Government decided in 1906 to take back all (idle or inadequately exploited) properties from the Chinese and Malay owners and alienate the resumed land in large areas for redistribution. When it came to granting this resumed land, the amount of capital that an application could raise became the most important criterion in influencing official decisions' (Yip, 1969: 152).

18. '... the greater the extent to which tin production became a British enterprise, the less important the duty on tin was to the local revenues' (Li, 1955: 50).

19. See Knorr (1945); Li (1955: 55-6); Lim Chong-Yah (1967: 59-60); and Yip (1969: 275-9).

20. 'Imagine ... the suffering that was inflicted on thousands of Chinese labourers working many hundreds of miles from their homes who, even when earning, lived close to the margin of subsistence' (Yates, 1943, as quoted in Caldwell, 1977b: 43).

21. Since the capital for early Chinese tin mining was raised neither in China nor in Europe but from accumulation by merchant capital in the Straits Settlements, generation of profits from tin mining did not entail an outflow of reinvestable funds as became the case with British capital. Remittances by some immigrant Chinese did occur, though this may be conceived of as a necessary cost of reproduction for an immigrant labour force.

22. Lim Chong-Yah and Knorr (1945: 89) apparently see the direction of control otherwise: 'Anglo-Oriental ... controlled, among others, the British Tin Investment Corporation and the London Tin Corporation' (Lim Chong-Yah, 1967: 69).

23. An 1895 issue of the *Selangor Journal* advised:
'To secure your independence work with Javanese and Tamils and, if you have sufficient experience, also with Malays and Chinese; you can then always play the one against the other. ... In case of a strike, you will never be left without labour ...' (quoted in R. N. Jackson, 1961: 104).

24. 'Western companies found it easier to manage Indian labourers than Chinese, and learned that they could always break up Chinese labour rings by employing Indians' (Wong Lin Ken, 1965: 219).

25. For example, during the 1920s, for every 100 arrivals, there were 80 departures.

26. For example, see Yong (1968).

27. 'In fact, the majority of the children born in Malaya in this century have remained in the country, and educational policy in the colonial period certainly did nothing to encourage any sense on the part of Chinese children of belonging to the country rather than belonging to an outpost of the larger Chinese community' (T. E. Smith, 1964: 180).

28. See Hanrahan (1954); Parmer (1962, 1964); Stenson (1970); Yeo (1976). Parmer (1964: 157) suggests that, from 1936, 'virtually no section of Malaya's labour force was without some kind of organization or was free of industrial disputes'. Pye (1965: 61) similarly observes that, by 1937, 'the principle of organized labour and collective action was no longer completely foreign to the minds of Malayan workers and the groundwork was prepared for the subsequent development of labor unions'.

7
PLANTATION RUBBER: CAPITAL AND INDIAN LABOUR

Rubber and the Colonial Economy

BESIDES their interest in seeing a profitable, preferably British-owned, extractive mining industry, the colonial authorities were also keen to develop export-oriented capitalist agriculture[1] (see J. C. Jackson, 1968; Lim Teck Ghee, 1976). After different degrees of success with experimental and commercial cultivation of various crops, the rubber plant—specifically *Hevea brasiliensis*—was brought to Singapore in 1877.[2] It was not an instant success, and H. N. Ridley, the Director of the Singapore Botanical Gardens, who was very active in promoting its cultivation in the peninsula, gained the nickname 'Mad Ridley' for his efforts. The first attempt in Malaya (in 1896) to plant rubber on a plantation basis[3] was by a Straits Chinese capitalist, Tan Chay Yan, from Malacca.

By 1900, there were still only about 5,000 acres of planted rubber in the East, even though early field trials had proved successful. Most of the supply for industrial use in the West still came from wild rubber in Brazil (Allen and Donnithorne, 1954: 111). Soon, however, cultivated rubber production in the world rose phenomenally from 11,100 tons in 1910 to 305,100 tons in 1920 (Lim Chong-Yah, 1967: 75). With the growth of the motor-car and other rubber-using industries in the West towards the close of the nineteenth century, British interests were increasingly frustrated by American control of the Brazilian rubber supply. Young rubber plants were brought, often smuggled, to London from Brazil and sent to its tropical colonies to promote rubber production within the British Empire. At that time, the most important crop cultivated on European farms in Malaya was coffee. In the 1890s, the coffee price dropped dramatically. As the demand for rubber continued to rise with the growth of the pneumatic-tyre industry, British investments shifted to rubber.[4] This alternative was encouraged by the generous support provided by the government, especially for plantation interests, e.g. by waiving land rents and duties and subsidizing the importation of Indian labour (Thoburn, 1971: 272). Estate planting and output, and with it, estate employment, grew rapidly with occasional setbacks, usually due to price drops (see Table 7.1).

The gains offered by investment in the rubber-growing industry during the first two decades of the twentieth century were described as 'tremendous' and 'beyond imagination', and for good reason too.[5] In 1910 and 1911 alone, 640,000 acres were planted. In 1910, some British rubber companies paid as much as 300 per cent in annual dividends. In 1912, sixty rubber companies offered dividends of 68 per cent. Between 1905 and 1906, for example, the average rubber price rose from 61 cents to $1.50 per lb. In spite of the violent

TABLE 7.1

Rubber Prices, Estate Output, and Employment, 1905–1983

Year	RSS 1 Price (cents/lb.)	Net Export Unit Value[1] (cents/lb.)	Estate Output[2] (tons)	Estate Employment[3]
1905				
1906			385	
1907			889	58,073
1908			1,425	57,070
1909			2,716	77,524
1910			5,632	128,446
1911			9,736	166,015
1912			14,193	188,050
1913			20,226	201,207
1914			26,100	161,379
1915			36,859	180,395
1916				196,123
1917				220,788
1918	64.3	66.3		201,862
1919	80.7	79.3		237,128
1920	75.7	78.7	107,557	216,588
1921	31.1	31.9	–	156,341
1922	28.8	25.9	–	167,259
1923	51.2	50.2	66,685	163,105
1924	49.0	46.7	54,077	159,357
1925	114.0	103.5	65,158	184,354
1926	80.5	83.1	112,547	246,760
1927	64.3	64.6	92,289	225,218
1928	36.8	33.5	100,233	223,044
1929	34.6	34.2	144,578	258,780
1930	19.1	19.3	140,789	170,620
1931	9.8	11.3	141,457	142,484
1932	7.0	7.9	140,525	126,235
1933	10.2	10.1	137,363	123,924
1934	20.6	25.7	147,417	161,408
1935	20.2	20.5	133,067	145,899
1936	27.0	26.4	125,005	153,455
1937	32.1	32.5	166,255	199,119
1938	24.1	23.9	129,728	170,932
1939	31.0	31.0	243,000	174,084
1946	n.a.	n.a.	173,500	332,300
1947	37.3	37.5	359,865	289,200
1948	42.1	42.3	402,907	287,000
1949	38.2	37.5	400,009	275,000
1950	108.2	108.1	375,853	281,600
1951	169.5	167.9	327,956	282,800
1952	96.1	95.4	341,078	280,000
1953	67.4	67.7	341,117	281,390
1954	67.3	60.7	344,851	267,981

(continued)

TABLE 7.1 *(continued)*

Year	RSS 1 Price (cents/lb.)	Net Export Unit Value[1] (cents/lb.)	Estate Output[2] (tons)	Estate Employment[3]
1955	114.2	108.7	351,802	278,200
1956	96.8	96.5	350,805	280,200
1957	88.7	90.2	367,909	276,740
1958	80.2	79.1	389,409	281,900
1959	101.6	99.4	407,170	282,510
1960	108.1	108.4	413,195	285,300
1961	83.5	82.9	428,153	285,560
1962	78.2	78.5	438,261	286,220
1963	72.4	73.6	458,304	286,320
1964	68.1	69.1	476,841	275,410
1965	70.0	69.4	490,944	270,160
1966	65.4	66.9	584,472	249,500
1967	54.1	56.5	517,472	231,900
1968	53.1	53.2	554,145	206,680
1969[4]	69.8	68.7	593,374	202,321
1970	56.4	57.6	611,188	202,572
1971	46.1	47.6	651,147	200,266
1972	42.4	42.2	648,883	193,010
1973	75.1	70.3	662,957	188,853
1974	81.4	85.6	649,080	181,225
1975	62.0	62.1	571,623	189,073
1976	90.2	85.1	641,403	199,023
1977	92.0	90.8	617,684	172,219
1978	104.3	100.3	608,236	167,577
1979	126.7	122.0	597,705	162,092
1980	141.7	134.1	577,529	158,086
1981	116.9	108.9	565,226	151,719
1982[5]	91.23	n.a.	567,588	141,972
1983	112.13	n.a.	551,250	132,979

Sources: 1. Thoburn (1971: 414, Appendix V-3).
    2. Thoburn (1971: 412, Appendix V-1).
    3. Thoburn (1971: 413, Appendix V-23); Parmer (1960: 273).
    4. 1969–81: Department of Statistics, *Rubber Statistics Handbook*.
    5. 1982–3: Department of Statistics, *Rubber Monthly Statistics*.
Notes: Estate output and employment figures for 1900–39 are for the FMS only.
The production and employment figures for 1982 and 1983 are preliminary.
Net export unit values for 1969–81 are from Ministry of Agriculture, *Statistical Digest*. From 1978 to 1981, net export unit values refer to RSS (ribbed smoked sheets) only.

fluctuations in the price of rubber from the outset, and its general decline through the 1910s, the price (see Table 3.4) remained attractive enough to put a total acreage of 779,100 under cultivation by 1920.

But the over-enthusiastic response of rubber producers soon backfired. Heavy planting during the boom period was characterized by the anarchy of capitalist competition and, hence, a lack of planning of output for future requirements. As global cultivated rubber production increased by over twenty-five times during the 1910s, the rubber price plumetted from 8s. 9d. per lb. in 1910 to 2s. 6d. in 1915 and to 1s. 10½d. by 1920 (Lim Chong-Yah, 1967: 75). For 138 sterling rubber companies in Malaya, the average dividend rate fell from 22.36 per cent in 1919 to 3.23 per cent in 1920 (Whittlesey, 1931: 75). New planting was reduced drastically, labour sacked (the number of estate workers dropped from 237,128 in 1919 to 156,341 in 1921), and a voluntary curtailment of production by 25 per cent was undertaken by most of the larger planters who were members of the Rubber Growers' Association (see Table 7.1). Smaller independent planters and smallholders were less willing to cooperate because they were less dependent on wage labour, operationally more flexible (in the face of declining prices), and more short-term oriented.

The commodity market in rubber developed a notorious reputation for severe price fluctuations which alarmed rubber-growing interests. Keynes calculated in 1938 that 'there has only been one year in the last ten in which the high price of rubber exceeded the low by less than 70 per cent' (quoted in Arudsothy, 1968: 119). Comparing price variations for several raw materials between 1921 and 1938, Bauer (1961: 186) showed that rubber was the most susceptible to fluctuations: average annual variation in prices was 47 per cent, while the lowest price as a percentage of the highest price for the entire period was only 3 per cent. These vicissitudes were the crux in the struggle between capital and labour over the wage rate which commonly declined in 'slippery' correspondence with price drops, but tended to be 'sticky' in response to rubber price rises.

Organization of Plantation Rubber Capital

As rubber production gained popularity in Malaya, the existing small proprietary plantations were soon unable to exploit the new opportunities that arose. Having fitfully developed over the years, the limited resources of these concerns were not enough to respond rapidly to the new circumstances; in fact, they were not even sufficient to ride out previously depressed price conditions in agriculture without considerable difficulty. Merchant capital in the Straits Settlements, in the form of the trading agencies which had prospered from the commerce of the colony, became the key to much of the expansion of the rubber industry in Malaya. New limited liability joint-stock companies were floated in London by the agency houses, thus mobilizing considerably greater funds. These included shares of original proprietors, the agency houses' own investments, as well as capital subscriptions of the British public and London finance companies. It was usual for the agency house to be appointed managing agent and/or company secretary for the new plantation enterprise, while the original proprietors were appointed managers, an arrangement to the mutual benefit of both parties concerned.[6] The transition from proprietary to corporate ownership corresponded to the emergence of more monopolistic forms of capital, with various implications for industrial organization.[7] Such reorganization provided access to the London finance market, which greatly contributed to the rapid expansion of the Malayan rubber industry in the first decade of the century (Allen and Donnithorne, 1954: 112). After 1914, however, the flotation of new rubber companies declined and the years from 1914 to 1921 were essentially a period of financial consolidation as existing companies significantly increased their investments. Rubber investments in Selangor, Negri Sembilan, and Kedah doubled over this period (Voon, 1976: 56-7).

Of course, agency houses were not solely responsible for this growth, although they played the most outstanding role by far. Some important groups of estates were formed independently of these firms. Nor was British capital alone—continental European investors, as well as rubber-using Western industrial companies, joined the rubber investment boom, although their involvement was of less significance.[8] The enthusiasm which American and Japanese capital showed in investing in plantation rubber in Malaya led in 1917 to the Rubber Lands (Restriction) Enactment (Drabble, 1973: 137-8), by which all lots of rubber land exceeding 50 acres could be alienated only to British nationals, subjects of the Malay rulers, corporations registered in the British Empire or residents in the peninsula of at least seven years' standing.

The predominantly Chinese local capitalists, as well as poorer Malay and Chinese peasants, also responded to the new opportunities. While European acreage grew from 168,000 in 1907 to 1,050,000 in 1918, 'Asian' rubber acreage rose from 2,000 to 836,000 over the same period (Caldwell, 1977b: 39). In terms of size, some Chinese-owned plantations were comparable to the European-owned ones, but the bulk of local capital, being small and fragmented, generally could only acquire small acreages.[9] Some of the smaller 'Asian' capitalist holdings which were less than 100 acres in size[10] were subsequently classified together with peasant holdings as smallholdings, while estates were defined as those over 100 acres in size.

The transition from proprietary to corporate ownership dominated by agency houses also set the dominant, though not exclusive, pattern for control of the industry. After sponsoring the formation of a rubber company, the Straits agency would normally be appointed managing agent in Malaya and also company secretary in London. The managing agency supervised estate management in Malaya and handled marketing through the Straits agencies' trading connections. Besides thus enjoying operational control, the agencies generally also possessed significant direct financial interests in the rubber companies controlled, and were usually represented on the company directorates (J. J. Puthucheary, 1960: 33).

Despite the large number of directorships, from the outset, the control of British rubber companies was highly concentrated in the hands of a few directors linked to several agency houses. In 1921, for all of South-East Asia, 77 directors, representing 7 per cent of all directors, controlled 30 per cent of all directorships, with each holding 5 to 22 directorships (Voon, 1976: 77), a high proportion of these being of companies located in Malaya. In 1953, concentration of control was still a strong feature of the Malayan rubber industry; 700 European-owned estates were managed by 20 managing agencies, of which 11 were agency houses. 'About 25 persons, some of whom are directors of agency houses, sit on the board of directors of nearly 200 rubber companies which own nearly a million acres of rubber in Malaya' (J. J. Puthucheary, 1960: 44-5).

Through amalgamations and similar devices, the number of agency responsibilities held by certain houses has actually increased since (Lim Mah Hui, 1980).

Rubber companies managed by different agencies have also been linked through interlocking directorships. In the early 1950s, fourteen managing agencies, which managed over 85 per cent of the 1.4 million acres of European-owned rubber, were thus connected (J. J. Puthucheary, 1960: 46). Such cohesive control enabled British rubber plantation interests to 'take joint action against any labour or political problems, and meet the challenge of an almost united body of American consumers' (J. J. Puthucheary, 1960: 47). The fact that 78 per cent of the planted rubber acreage in the East was either British-owned or in British-controlled territory, encouraged British rubber interests to embark unilaterally on a restriction scheme in 1922 to boost sagging prices (Voon, 1976: 180). The scheme also served to curb the challenge from the smaller 'Asian' rubber growers in Malaya, especially the Malay peasantry[11] (see Table 3.4). However, despite some success in raising the world market price for rubber and thwarting the challenge from peasant production, British ownership and control of the industry worldwide actually diminished because of Dutch refusal to cooperate.

The structure of control in the industry was important, not only in terms of control, but also for the distribution of surplus value created by the rubber plantations. Agency houses were in an excellent position to reap tremendous profits from charges on freight, insurance, brokerage and management commissions; correspondingly, their directors collected considerable fees. Costs at the London end of operations were very high since it was usually 'notoriously badly organized' (Voon, 1976: 163). Agency houses also gained considerable promotion profits when floating rubber companies (Drabble, 1973: 85). It has been argued that the proliferation of rubber companies and the structure of their control hindered subsequent amalgamation of these companies because of the vested interests involved (Bauer, 1948: 11). But on the whole, the agency house system is recognized to have been a considerable financial burden on the Malayan rubber industry, which was also weighed down by the highly salaried European staff. The British-owned estate sector's high-cost operations also rendered it especially vulnerable to declines in rubber price—hence, the plantation capitalists' desire for restriction schemes to prop up the price of the commodity. It should be noted that, in the 1950s, for example, only about 16 per cent of net rubber profits were being reinvested in the industry (Chou, 1966: 156). The low rate of reinvestment apparently dates from the years after the initial rapid expansion of rubber plantations early this century.

The Colonial State and British Plantation Interests

British investments in rubber planting were strongly encouraged by the British administration through: attractive land alienation policies which made choice land available at nominal rates with a minimum of restrictive conditions; the availability of government loans at low interest rates; negligible taxation in the Federated Malay States; minimal export duties in the Straits Settlements;

provision of important infrastructure, especially roads, railways (charging low freight rates), and harbour facilities; and, above all, the active encouragement and subsidization of the immigration of low-wage Tamil labourers. In general, the colonial state served to facilitate British investment, and to ensure and maximize their profitability.

Capitalist influence on decision-making by the colonial state was strong. The United Planting Association of Malaya, 'an influential organization of employers... is represented by its members on the State Councils of the Federated States, on the Federal Council, on the Legislative Council of the Straits Settlements and on the Johore Council of State' (Aiyer, 1938: 25). Retired senior colonial officials were often appointed to directorships, or even chairmanships, of rubber companies, to enhance the influence exercised by the particular companies over government.

The provision of infrastructure by the state effectively subsidized the costs of production for capitalists. When provided selectively, it was an important means of discriminating between various interests, as was, for example, the case in advancing plantation rubber interests over peasant interests, and, more particularly, in favouring British capital. Such discrimination has been discussed in Part II, especially in Chapter 3, and at this juncture, only a few additional remarks need to be made on land matters.

'Ridiculously cheap' land was made available in abundance for alienation to European interests. The Land Enactment of 1897 for the Federated Malay States especially facilitated the alienation of land for capitalist agriculture. The process of land alienation was initiated by the prospective planter, freely allowing him to 'select the most accessible, well-drained and topographically favourable land for planting purposes' (Voon, 1971: 89). The construction of communications infrastructure also played a crucial role in determining the location of rubber estates, and though plantations sprouted all over, Selangor emerged as the clear favourite (Voon, 1971; 1976: 49). The earlier development of the transportation network was strongly influenced by the needs of the tin industry. Equally, rubber companies sought to locate their plantations in accessible proximity to the emerging road and railway transport patterns. In many cases, land adjoining newly built roads was reserved for acquisition by plantations on the official pretext that this was the most rational mode of resource distribution.

A quick way of acquiring land was to buy over existing cultivated land. The common practice for expanding plantations to absorb neighbouring land attained serious proportions when much 'traditional' Malay agricultural land was bought over by the heavily financed foreign-owned rubber companies from peasants eager to enjoy windfall profits. The concern generated by such sales led to a series of legislative measures, beginning from 1913, designating certain areas to be owned only by Malays[12] (Drabble, 1973: 73). Besides peasant land, British companies also took over established Asian-owned estates. The 'general tendency was that foreign companies gained control and ownership of Asian-owned estates or smallholdings and hardly the reverse happened in the pre-World War II period' (Voon, 1971: 93). Even before the introduction of restrictions on purchase of Malay peasant land, Asian-owned estates were already being bought over since these were larger than peasant lots and hence more easily integrated into large plantations.

Rubber and Indian Labour Immigration

The main source of labour[13] for British interests in Malaya had been their colony, India.[14] As in other British colonies lacking an available indigenous or local proletariat, Indian labourers were imported to work for the colonial state and in the British-owned capitalist sector. But for a long time, immigration into Malaya was much less than desired by the colonial authorities and British capital. This was mainly due to the prospective emigrants' lack of funds, the Indian administration's dissuading stance, and the existence of alternative opportunities in other relatively more attractive British colonies, many of which even received the Indian colonial government's blessings. Often, these other colonies—Fiji, Burma, Ceylon, Southern and East Africa and the British West Indies—offered higher wage prospects, better living conditions and a greater chance of landing as a free man, unlike the immigrant to Malaya who was usually indentured, especially during the nineteenth century.[15] Emigration to Malaya was monopolized by a few private recruiting firms which restricted supply in order to obtain higher commissions. Labourers flowed from one British colony to the other, though not without considerable trickery and even abduction (Geohagen, 1873:63). An Indian contractor testified in 1890 that 'if the men in India knew exactly what they were coming to here under the existing conditions, they would prefer to remain there' (quoted in Thompson, 1947:90). Initially, employment for Indians in Malaya was primarily in the colonial government machinery where they occupied low, poorly paid positions as labourers, domestic servants, soldiers, policemen and clerks. Subsequently, as British agricultural enterprise became more important, Indian labour became identified with sugar-cane cultivation and then coffee growing. The British colonial experience in India dating from the mid-eighteenth century almost certainly affected the ethnic choice of personnel. The absence of a local Malay proletariat, and especially of trained personnel for clerical tasks, necessitated an alternative source of labour. As British-owned enterprise emerged, Indian labourers were recruited for this as well. In the Malayan context, this choice was further encouraged by the difficulties the British encountered with Chinese labour, discussed in the preceding chapter.[16] Also, emigration of Javanese wage labour, as distinguished from peasant settlers, was greatly constrained by Dutch government controls (Shamsul Bahrin, 1965). The availability of an assured supply of labour from India provided one solution to British capital's labour problem in Malaya.

With the rubber boom, it became imperative to have a considerably enlarged labour supply.[17] Therefore, conditions of service (passage, accommodation, remuneration, etc.) had to be improved, and, in 1887, the governments of the Straits Settlements and of several Malay States agreed to provide a steamship subsidy for transporting Indian labour immigrants. The colonial government in India was persuaded to encourage emigration to Malaya. Regulations in both India and Malaya were changed to break the monopoly of the

Indian recruiting agents, labour depots for collecting and clearing Indian emigrants were set up in South-east India, and an intense propaganda campaign was mounted to increase labour recruitment.

Not unlike the experience of the Chinese working class, the transition to free wage labour[18] for Indian workers went through several phases.[19] Indenture was most important in the early stages of labour recruitment, giving way around the turn of the century to the *kangany* system, which also eventually diminished in importance, marking the decline in significance of recruited Indian labour. Thereafter, Indian workers, who were not recruited but whose passages were subsidized, continued to arrive until 1938, when all assisted immigration to Malaya was finally prohibited. While unassisted Indian labour immigration had existed right from the start of British rule, it became significant only after the Depression, when a quota was imposed on assisted labour immigration. In 1938, when the Indian government banned the emigration of all unskilled labour, virtually all remaining labour immigration into Malaya consisted of either skilled workers or labourers returning to the peninsula.

By the time Indian indentured labour was officially banned in Malaya in 1910, its inflow had trickled down considerably; whereas in 1889, over 70 per cent of 8,994 immigrant Indian labourers were indentured, by 1910, only 6 per cent of 55,463 immigrant workers were (Sandhu, 1969: 308). Between 1900 and 1911, the Indian population in Malaya doubled, and over the next decade it doubled again (Arasaratnam, 1970: 28–9). Indentured labour was proving to be quite uneconomic as many such workers were physically unfit and died before the end of their contract period.[20] In 1910, the FMS government appointed a Commission to inquire into the conditions of indentured labour; it reported that 'there was a tremendous difference between the death-rates of indentured and unindentured labourers' (quoted in R. N. Jackson, 1961: 112). The work conditions of indentured labourers were very poor, and it has been noted that before its prohibition, on some estates, 'as many as 60 rising to 90 per cent of the labourers died within a year of arrival' (Sandhu, 1969: 171).

Actually, large investments in rubber necessitated a greater labour supply than could be met by the indenture system. The competition from alternative employment opportunities in the rapidly growing colonial economy therefore forced the rubber industry to improve employment conditions. Also, with the advances in communications came greater opportunities for absconding from bonded labour. Even administrative innovations to increase Indian labour immigration failed to keep up with the growing labour requirements. Under the circumstances, the abolition of indenture, as well as other concessions to labour, were inevitable. Moreover, estate employers bitterly resented the virtual monopoly exercised by recruiting agencies in India which profited handsomely from the trade in indentured labour. The widespread opposition to indenture in Malaya, India, and even Britain, also helped to bring about its eventual demise. Between 1870 and 1910, 249,832 indentured Indian labourers in all arrived in Malaya, though the first decade of the twentieth century accounted for less than 40,000 (Sandhu, 1969: 308).

The *kangany* system for Indian labour recruitment introduced in Malaya in the 1890s was first tried in other British colonies. In its essentials, it was similar to the system of personal recruitment of Chinese labour discussed earlier. Rapidly taking over as the main source of supply of Indian labour, in 1907 *kangany* recruitment came under the control of the Indian Immigration Committee. Part of its appeal to the prospective employer was the relatively lower cost involved in sending a *kangany*, or Tamil foreman, back to his village to recruit labour compared to the price of indentured labour obtained from recruiting agencies. British employers also thus broke the monopoly of Indian recruiting firms, which were believed to have restricted labour supply. Further, as with the Chinese system of personal recruitment, the likelihood of absconding was less compared to indentured labour, especially since the *kangany* usually had a vested interest in ensuring that the labourer did not abscond. For example, a *kangany* often received 'head money' from each recruited coolie for every day worked, which would be forfeited if the coolie absconded (Sandhu, 1969: 101). Apart from being his labour overseer, the *kangany* frequently also related to the labourer as shopkeeper and money-lender, leading, all too frequently, to the labourer being indebted to the *kangany*. This indebted state was often prolonged because of the difficulty the labourer had in ridding himself of the debt burden, and the lucrativeness of this arrangement to the creditor. As the *kangany* was directly involved in production on the plantation, he also had a greater interest in the quality of labourers recruited. Restricted, by regulations, to recruiting only from around his native village, he was obliged to rely more on persuasion, rather than deception, unlike professional recruiters. But: 'it must, however, be emphasized that the Kangany system was only a variant of the indenture system, as in effect, the debt-bondage relationship between servant and master still remained, although indirectly' (Arudsothy, 1968: 75). After the 1920s, assisted immigration, including that of *kangany*-recruited labour, practically ceased with the onset of the rubber slump. When assisted immigration was revived in 1934, *kangany* recruitment continued to account for only a small fraction of the Tamil labourers coming to Malaya (Parmer, 1960: 270).

At the height of expansion of the rubber industry, even *kangany* recruitment was inadequate to meet labour needs. The problem was compounded by desertion of recruited workers, especially indentured labourers (R. N. Jackson, 1961: 124). Capitalists faced with common labour supply problems increased collaboration through the agency house system discussed earlier. The Indian Immigration Committee was set up in 1907 to provide assistance, similar to that for *kangany* recruits, to individual labourers who volunteered themselves at Malayan depots in India. 'Crimping', i.e. the employment of a labourer who had broken a contract elsewhere, was prohibited by law. Gross mistreatment of labour, which had the effect of discouraging immigration, was to be curtailed, and offending employers penalized. In 1908, a Tamil Immigration Fund, to which employers contributed according to the number of workers employed, was started to provide free passages for labourers to Malaya. All employers of Indian labour were required to contribute annually to this fund to subsidize the costs of immigration to Malaya. This recruiting system was even cheaper than the *kangany* system since no inducement to a recruiter was necessary. Further, the hold of the *kangany* over the labourer was diminished. Increased supervision

TABLE 7.2

Ethnic Breakdown of FMS Estate Labour Force, 1907-1938[1]

Year	Indians	Chinese	Javanese	Others	Total	Indians as Percentage of Labour	No. of Estates
1907	43,824	5,348	6,029	2,872	58,073	75.5	287
1908	43,515	6,595	4,999	1,961	57,070	76.2	300
1909	55,732	12,402	6,170	2,778[2]	77,524[2]	71.9	n.a.
1910	n.a.	n.a.	n.a.	n.a.	128,446	–	n.a.
1911	109,633	31,460	12,795	12,127	166,015	66.0	711
1912	n.a.	n.a.	n.a.	n.a.	188,050	–	n.a.
1913	142,476	25,081	12,197	8,496	188,250	75.7	n.a.
1914	120,144	24,000	10,115	7,120	161,379	74.4	n.a.
1915	126,347	27,446	8,356	8,592	170,741	74.0	719
1916	138,295	42,831	7,485	7,496	196,123[2]	70.5	797
1917	148,834	55,240	7,746	8,902	220,758[2]	67.4	920
1918	139,480	46,372	8,249	7,821	201,954[2]	69.1	1,003
1919	160,658	61,089	7,861	7,492	237,134[2]	67.7	1,087
1920	160,966	40,866	8,918	5,808	216,588[2]	74.3	1,105
1921	121,644	25,712	5,732	3,353	156,341[2]	77.8	1,001
1922	122,589	27,575	4,996	3,724	158,794	77.2	1,052
1923	121,463	31,957	4,791	4,894	163,105	74.5	1,204
1924	119,242	30,884	4,516	4,715	159,357	74.8	1,068
1925	137,761	37,879	4,165	4,549	184,354	74.7	1,206

1926	176,114	61,064	4,760	4,822	246,760	71.4	1,403
1927	172,466	44,239	4,550	3,963	225,218	76.6	1,421
1928	162,460	50,647	5,149	4,788	223,044	72.8	1,509
1929	181,205	65,617	5,316	6,642	258,780	70.0	1,651
1930	132,745	30,860	3,665	2,411	169,681	78.2	1,757
1931	104,767	32,916	2,464	2,357	142,504	73.5	1,800
1932	90,003	31,349	1,920	2,328	125,600	71.7	1,912
1933	96,138	35,188	2,207	3,318	136,851	70.3	2,030
1934	119,443	40,305	2,521	4,153	166,422	71.8	2,178
1935	118,591	29,950	1,941	2,658	153,140	77.4	2,345
1936	123,595	30,760	1,924	2,979	159,258	77.6	2,419
1937	155,725	37,200	2,371	3,823	199,119	78.2	2,519
1938	137,353	28,925	1,762	2,892	170,932	80.4	2,388

Source: Parmer (1960: 273).

[1]The estimates of FMS estate labour differ from those provided in Table 7.1 because of the different primary sources used by the respective authors.

[2]The total number of workers does not tally with the sum of the ethnic columns in the original work cited.

of emigration by the Indian government also tended to curb *kangany* recruitment.

Capital's efficient organization of inexpensive systems of immigration kept labour costs low.[21] In this scheme of things, the Indian Immigration Committee played a key role. In 1938, all assisted immigration to Malaya was banned by the Indian government. However, this had been anticipated by the Malayan authorities, who had built up 'an Indian labour force to meet the requirements of the rubber industry at full production' (Parmer, 1960: 257) by late 1937, two years after the Government of India had threatened to restrict emigration when employers refused to raise wages. Of all Indian immigration to Malaya up to 1941, 1,910,820 had been assisted, while 811,598 had come unassisted (Sandhu, 1969: 305).

At the outset, British interests regarded Indian immigrant labour as transient to the Malayan scene, generally encouraging working-age Indian labourers to work in this other British colony for a few years before eventually returning. Permanent settlement for labourers was not encouraged. Hence, 'in the earlier phases of the growth of the Malayan population, economically active persons tended to form an unusually high percentage of the total population' (Arudsothy, 1968: 198). Such employment of immigrant Indian, as well as Chinese and Indonesian, labour (see Table 7.2) provided capital with many of the advantages of utilizing migrant labour (Arrighi, 1973; Burawoy, 1977; Castles and Kosack, 1973). This labour trade also meant that the necessary costs of labour reproduction were largely borne outside the country of employment; by employing young labourers, in the prime of their working life, the bulk of the costs of upbringing (and of retirement, if that age was reached) of a labourer were borne in India. Since migrants were usually from peasant families (Arasaratnam, 1970: 27), so-called 'subsistence' peasant production actually 'subsidized' the costs of reproduction of the labour required by capitalists.[22]

While total Indian emigration to Malaya between 1860 and 1957 has been estimated to total about 4 million, 70 per cent of this number left Malaya over the same period. The practice of repatriating retired and aged labour has been compared to the disposal of 'sucked oranges'. A very high proportion of the net immigration of 1,234,283 Indians 'appears to have [been] wiped out by disease, snake-bite, exhaustion and malnutrition, for the Indian population of Malaya in 1957 numbered only 858,615 of which 62.1 per cent was local born'[23] (Sandhu, 1962: 68). Also, about 60,000 are estimated to have died working on the notorious Siamese 'death railway' during the Japanese Occupation (Gamba, 1962: 131).

Two official views emerged on the role of Indian immigrant labour in Malaya. One advocated the permanent settlement of Indian labour in Malaya to ensure the permanent availability of a pool of workers. When repatriation of unemployed immigrant workers was being contemplated during the Depression by colonial authorities, for instance, it was thought better to allow unemployed workers to remain in Malaya since their presence would depress wage rates. Many employers were even prepared to retain workers on estates at reduced wages. Otherwise, they usually preferred government provision of relief works rather than repatriation.

The other view, which was especially persuasive among the colonial authorities, held that international migration should be a tool for regulating labour supply in Malaya; in other words, that immigration should cater to manpower requirements, and that repatriation would be the means for displacing unemployment to India. This strategy generally prevailed, especially during the Great Depression, when employment in the rubber industry fell by half and the government anticipated having to bear the costs of retaining a pool of unemployed workers and the political implications of their presence in Malaya.[24]

The permanent settlement of Indians in Malaya was largely precipitated by the emergence of 'free' wage labour. Indenture, recruitment and assisted immigration were undoubtedly important systems for supplying labour to serve British interests. After the early rubber boom years, however, though still fluctuating, labour needs were no longer increasing as rapidly as in the past. Further, rising nationalist sentiments in India and elsewhere were resulting in pressure on the Malayan colonial authorities to improve Indian labour conditions. More importantly, it was recognized that recruitment was no longer necessary to ensure an estate labour force: a proletariat had been created in Malaya, partly by immigration, and also by the gradual impoverishment of certain segments of the Malay peasantry. It was also clear that even though 'free', the bulk of the estate labour force was unlikely to contemplate alternative options: mainly educated in their vernacular language (Colletta, 1975), socialized almost entirely in the plantation subculture (Jain, 1970) and equipped with few, if any, transferable skills, Indian workers had little scope for occupational mobility open to them except to similar manual jobs, e.g. in the government services.[25]

The direct employment of Indian labour by British interests—both the colonial state and British capitalist employers—rendered it far more subject (compared to Chinese labour) to British designs. Colonial labour policy, easier access to India and other factors explain Indian labour's relatively weaker inclination to permanent settlement in colonial Malaya (Smith, 1964). Nevertheless, the possibilities for female employment on estates and elsewhere brought about increased immigration of women, the establishment of families, and increased permanent settlement in Malaya. Such stabilization of the immigrant labour force was especially significant in the 1930s (see Sandhu, 1969: 186, Table 8b), as was the case with Chinese immigration. With the decline in importance of indentured and *kangany*-recruited labourers, the emergence of free wage labour and the employment of both parents, as well as children on plantations, a new and more favourable official attitude towards the permanent settlement of Indian labour developed.

Capital, the State, and Labour

There was a constant struggle between capital and labour over the wage rate in the rubber industry.[26] Although labour agitation, occasionally supported by the Indian colonial government,[27] generally improved wage conditions, capital effectively used the frequent and severe vicissitudes of the world rubber market

TABLE 7.3

Some Effects of the Depression on Rubber in British Malaya, 1929-1933

Year	Total Rubber Output[1] (tons)	Output per Acre[1] (lb.)	Estate Employment in SS and FMS[2] ('000)		Male Wage Rate[3] (cents/lb.)	Ribbed Smoked Sheet Price[1] (cents/lb.)	Net Rubber Exports[1] ($ million)
			Indians	Others			
1929	200,000	485	205	53	.50	34.48	202
1930	197,000	460	154	51	.40	19.31	108
1931	197,000	445	121	43	.30	9.96	54
1932	177,000	385	104	41	.26	7.01	37
1933	220,000	465	111	49	.32	10.23	58

Sources: 1. Bauer (1944), in Silcock (1961: 185–200, Tables 2, 3, 5, 7, and 9).
2. Arudsothy (1968: 133, Table 4.7).
3. Kinney (1973: 294).

to curb and lower them.[28] This can be illustrated by what happened during the Great Depression (see Table 7.3). In the boom year 1925, after the price of rubber had risen following the imposition of the Stevenson Restriction Scheme, estate wage levels went up by 10 per cent due to the increased demand for labour. But when the Great Depression set in, the rubber price plummetted dramatically in 1932 to one-fortieth of its 1925 peak price. The number of Indian labourers employed on estates halved from the 1929 figure of 205,000 to 104,000 by 1932.[29] Total payrolls fell by about 80 per cent between the end of 1929 and the middle of 1932 owing to reduced employment and wages (Bauer, 1948: 193). Between 1930 and 1932, 190,356 unemployed Tamil labourers were repatriated at government expense. By 1934, the rubber industry had recovered, but wages remained at Depression levels. Two years later, a representative of the Indian government observed that despite the return to prosperity, there had been no commensurate increase in wages. Only in 1938 was the pre-Depression wage rate reintroduced, just four months later, wages dropped again (Li, 1955: 90).

The labour policies of the colonial state, as has been implicit in the discussion, were aimed at ensuring a cheap and abundant supply of labour for capital. The colonial authorities were frequently under pressure from British capital to keep wages low, and readily obliged, being themselves the largest single employer of Indian labour. 'In spite of allegations to the contrary, wages on public works were seldom higher than plantation wage rates except in the early days of road and railroad building' (Parmer, 1960: 225). In general, the colonial government supported private capitalists in their endeavours to keep the wage rate low. During the rice shortage of 1919-20, for example, it provided large subsidies to keep the price of rice—the estate labourers' major expense item—low.

Conditions of work generally improved as workers in Malaya became increasingly class-conscious, better organized and more militant. However, important differences continued to exist between the colonial government's treatment of Chinese and Indian labour. Because the colonial government in India continued to maintain an active interest in the welfare of Indian immigrants in Malaya, the government in Malaya was forced to take a special interest in the welfare of Indian workers in particular. In 1911, a Labour Department was established, mainly to 'look after' the interests of Indian labour[30] (Parmer, 1960: 130-2). From 1922, a committee was set up to determine standard wage rates for Indian labour.[31] Colonial labour policy and administration developed primarily for Indian labour and their European employers.

Despite the racial plurality of the population, labour became better organized and more militant. Especially after the 1930s, when free wage labour had emerged, economic conditions were fluctuating, and anti-colonial sentiments were rising (Stenson, 1970). Banishment ordinances for Chinese and Indians were enacted in response by the colonial authorities, and for a long time, while 'harmless' organizations—such as those for religion, gambling or smoking—were allowed, labour unions, working-class based and politically oriented groups were proscribed and could not be registered. Finally, in the late

1930s, despite strong protests by many less enlightened capitalists, union registration, industrial courts and collective bargaining were legislated, largely in response to intensifying labour agitation, and to counteract the growing influence of more militant labour leaders; however, government employees, many of whom were Indian, were still denied the right to unionize. However, all strikes were banned by the colonial government in 1940.

Few colonial labour regulations affected work conditions of Chinese labour, e.g. on the mines, and even these served to sanction existing Chinese employment practices. There was also minimal government involvement in determining the wage rates of Chinese workers in the pre-war period. Unlike Indian workers, Chinese labourers were usually hired on a contract basis by British capital,[32] and were therefore not under the direct control of estate owners. Though Indians on the whole received less wages for similar work,[33] they were often provided with housing, clinics and certain other welfare services, reflecting the preoccupation of the colonial Labour Department with the affairs of Indian labour. In many respects, the colonial authorities tended to treat Indian labour in a patronizing manner. Such differences in the treatment of different ethnic components of the labour force had some effect on their subsequent organizational independence and political expression.

Postscript: Post-war Trends

After the Japanese Occupation ended in 1945, militant nationalist and labour organizations organized effectively to agitate for independence and better work conditions. After reaching a peak around 1947, the heavy arm of the colonial state came down hard on labour and other activists, crushing militant organizations as well. Hence, it is not at all surprising that wage levels actually dropped after 1947 before picking up during the Korean War boom (see Table 7.4). The establishment of the pliant National Union of Plantation Workers (NUPW) in the early 1950s did not do much to improve conditions for estate workers. In fact, as Table 7.5 shows, the real wage of tappers was 19 per cent less in 1975 and 8 per cent less in 1981 compared to 1960. This is especially remarkable considering the increase in average output during the period from 2 247 kg to 5 083 kg. Though rubber prices, and hence wage levels, peaked in 1960 and fell in both 1975 and 1981, the wage decrease is all the more staggering in view of the 126 per cent increase in worker output, i.e. labour productivity, over the period. Despite low prices around 1975 and again around 1981, Table 7.6 suggests that profits, on average, accounted for more than half of total revenue on the medium-sized estates surveyed during 1975–81.

The vulnerability of the poverty rate to the rubber price also suggests that increasing productivity has not benefited estate workers very much, if at all. Average output rose from 3 879 kg in 1970 to 4 680 kg in 1975 and 5 116 kg in 1980. Meanwhile, the rubber price rose negligibly from $1.28 per kg in 1970 to $1.39 in 1975, before increasing to $3.03 in 1980, and then declining to $1.93 in 1982 and recovering to $2.34 in 1983 (Malaysia, 1984: 48, Table 2.4). Not surprisingly then, the official poverty rate among estate workers increased from 40.0 per cent in 1970 to 47.0 per cent in 1975, before decreasing to 35.1 per

TABLE 7.4

Peninsular Malaysia: Rubber Estate Wages, 1946–1983

Year	(i) Average Monthly Wage ($)	(ii) Employment	(iii) Annual Wage Bill (i × ii × 12) ($'000)	(iv) Annual Wage Bill Including Management and Professional Salaries (iii × 1.2) ($'000)
1946	...	332,300	...	...
1947	61.12	289,200	212,111	254,533
1948	52.58	287,000	181,085	217,303
1949	44.24	257,800	146,417	175,700
1950	...	281,600	...	...
1951	*85.80	282,800	291,171	349,405
1952	*74.10	280,000	248,976	298,771
1953	62.77	281,390	211,954	254,345
1954	64.35	267,981	206,935	248,322
1955	70.50	278,200	235,357	282,429
1956	75.88	280,200	255,139	306,167
1957	78.77	276,740	261,586	313,903
1958	*78.00	281,900	263,858	316,635
1959	78.74	282,510	266,938	320,326
1960	92.24	285,300	315,793	378,951
1961	80.48	285,560	275,782	330,939
1962	83.39	286,220	286,402	343,683
1963	79.02	286,320	271,517	325,820
1964	88.35	275,410	291,990	350,388
1965	85.88	270,160	277,444	332,933
1966	91.95	249,500	275,308	330,370
1967	92.89	231,900	258,476	310,171
1968	97.68	206,680	242,262	290,714
1969	103.02	202,321	250,128	300,154
1970	100.79	202,572	244,996	293,995
1971	98.59	200,266	236,937	284,324
1972	101.01	193,010	233,961	280,754
1973	119.57	188,853	270,979	325,175
1974	127.25	181,225	276,731	332,078
1975	148.54	189,073	337,027	404,432
1976	148.73	199,023	355,197	426,237
1977	175.70	172,219	363,113	435,735
1978	183.84	167,577	369,693	443,631
1979	203.73	162,092	396,279	475,535
1980	223.63	158,086	424,239	509,087
1981	226.32	151,719	412,045	494,454
1982	241.06	141,972	410,678	492,813
1983	245.95	132,979	392,478	470,974

Sources: 1946–68: Thoburn (1971: 420, Appendix V–6); 1969–81: Department of Statistics, *Rubber Statistics Handbook*; 1982–3: Department of Statistics, *Rubber Monthly Statistics of Malaysia* (figures are preliminary and subject to revision).

*Estimated.

TABLE 7.5

Peninsular Malaysia: Number of Tappers, Productivity, and Real Wages
on Estates, 1960–1981 (Selected Years)

| | | | Average Daily Tapper's Wage | |
Year	No. of Tappers	Average Output (kg)	Current Prices	1960 Prices
1960	186,800	2 247	3.40	3.40
1965	181,800	2 744	3.15	3.07
1970	160,100	3 879	4.00	3.65
1975	124,100	4 680	4.30	2.76
1979	116,759	5 201	7.20	3.95
1980	114,700	5 116	7.90	4.07
1981	113,000	5 083	6.70	3.14
Change (%)				
1960–75	–33.6	108.3	26.5	–18.8
1960–81	–39.5	126.2	97.1	–7.6

Sources: Calculated from Department of Statistics, *Rubber Statistics Handbook, Malaysia* (various years); Bank Negara (1984), *Money and Banking in Malaysia*.
Note on Consumer Price Indices:

1959–100	*1967–100*	*1980–100*
1960 : 99.8	1970 : 101.3	1981 : 109.7
1965 : 102.3	1975 : 144.0	
1967 : 108.0	1979 : 168.3	
	1980 : 179.5	

TABLE 7.6

Profit Margins on Estates,[1] 1975–1981

Item	sen/kg	Per Cent
Total revenue[2]	153.0	100.0
Expenditure		
Management	8.4	5.5
Other overheads	6.5	4.2
Field maintenance	11.3	7.4
Latex collection and transport	1.5	1.0
Tapping wages	42.1	27.5
Sub-total	69.8	45.6
Net profit	83.2	54.4

Source: Ariffin bin Mohd. Nor and James Nayagam, 'Incentive Wage Concept: An Alternative Strategy for Land Development Schemes', RRIM reprint 5, October 1983, p. 12, Table 5, cited in Table 2 of Ozay Mehmet, 'Inter-regional Labour Migration, Poverty and Income Distribution: the Case of Peninsular Malaysia,' Paper presented at the seminar on 'Current Population Policy and Research', Port Dickson, 3–5 December 1983.

[1] Average adopted from nine to seventeen well-organized estates of less than 200 planted hectares surveyed by the Rubber Research Institute of Malaysia (RRIM) Costing and Management Study Group.

[2] Net of manufacturing cost, export duty, and research cess.

cent in 1980, and then jumping to 54.6 per cent in 1983 (Malaysia, 1984: 80, Table 3.2).

Summary

The related transformations of capital and labour in Malaya are reflected in the history of the rubber industry. Though several different cash crops had been experimented with in the nineteenth century, the rubber boom early in the twentieth century evidenced a dramatic expansion of production capital in agrarian activities, largely organized by the leading merchant capitalists in the colony, the agency houses. True to form, the colonial state stepped in to help, e.g. by alienating the best available land to British capital, providing infra-structural facilities, especially in communications, and undertaking botanic and other related research. The colonial state also played a key role in upholding the interests of capital over the peasantry.

Confronted with the non-availability of an indigenous proletariat, British capital turned to another colony, India, for labour. Various forms of labour control—e.g. the indenture system and *kangany* recruitment—were used by British capital. These forms, which involved extra-economic coercion of involuntary labour, had certain disadvantages which were partly overcome when the state stepped in to coordinate a labour immigration system at less cost to plantation owners. As the planting boom subsided and labour requirements stabilized, the settlement of Indian labour in larger numbers in Malaya, the increasing availability of workers of other ethnic groups, as well as the growing clandestine organization of Indian labour, all encouraged the British to abandon the remaining forms of extra-economic coercion of labour. Instead, with the spread of free wage labour on plantations, the colonial state turned to other means of disciplining Indian labour, using both the carrot (e.g. in the form of the Labour Department's patronizing treatment of Indian labour) and the stick (e.g. by curbing the growth of radical labour leader and by repatriating labour militants).

1. A British Secretary for the Colonies wrote to the Governor of the Straits Settlements in 1895: '... The point of greatest importance appears to me ... to be the encouragement of agriculture in order that the prosperity of these (Malay) States, which has hitherto depended so largely upon the plentiful supplies of tin, may still be assured, if, and when, their mineral sources in the course of years show signs of depletion ...' (quoted in Sandhu, 1969: 49).

2. The introduction and spread of rubber-planting enterprise in South-East Asia as a whole has been studied by Voon (1976). Drabble (1973) has written a fairly comprehensive economic history of the early development of plantation rubber cultivation in Malaya until 1922, the first year of operation of restriction schemes on rubber production.

3. In his book dealing with plantations as an organizational form of production, S. B. D. de Silva argues that economies of scale are not important for plantation production. Instead, the large size of individual units is attributed by him to special circumstances connected with foreign ownership, including the high costs of management by agency houses. No change in production technique or a significantly different division of labour is involved in plantation, compared to petty capitalist, rubber cultivation. The allegedly scientific nature of plantation, in contrast to peasant

agriculture was largely a sham pretext with which the plantations succeeded in gaining real advantages from the state. He further maintains that neither the existence of large-scale cultivation units nor export orientation *per se* are basic attributes of plantation products.

Another interesting perspective on plantation agriculture is provided by Beckford (1972). In this connection, it is useful to note that while an official view in 1936 held that a London price of 8d. per lb. was the bare minimum required to ensure a 'reasonable return to efficient growers', small local producers exported 150,000 tons at a price of about 1d. per lb. (Bauer, 1948: 252).

4. 'Development of the industry in the early period was primarily pioneered by enterprising but somewhat desperate coffee planters who interplanted rubber among coffee, or ex-planters who applied for land for planting the new crop on their own or through local syndicates' (Voon, 1971: 83).

5. 'The tremendous profits made in the rubber industry were sometimes beyond imagination. . . . The profit to the producer, after he had paid the government tax, which amounted to £3 an acre, was £60 an acre. In 1910 some of the British rubber companies paid dividends of as much as over 300%. In 1912, there were sixty companies in the Federated Malay States which paid dividends ranging from 20% to 275%, and the average dividend for those sixty companies was 68.8%. It was estimated that rubber shareholders in Great Britain received an average annual dividend of 225% during the nine years from 1911 to 1919, while at least eleven companies showed an average dividend of 117% during that period. From the point of view of the British shareholders, no dividend of less than 100% of capital invested could be considered satisfactory' (Li, 1982: 87).

6. 'Properties were rarely purchased outright, the transfer being one of control more than ownership, for a substantial part of the purchase price was paid in shares, guaranteeing the vendors' stake in the new company' (Voon, 1971: 85).

7. 'The transition from proprietary to corporate ownership brought about significant alterations in ownership and management patterns and changed the scale of operation. Proprietary estates, once acquired by planting companies, did not remain static in size or shape' (Voon, 1976: 168).

8. Of 1,034 rubber company directors in Malaya in 1914-15, 1,025 were British by nationality while the remaining nine were Belgian and French, from the Socfin group. This was in sharp contrast to the distribution of directorships in the Netherlands East Indies where 414 of the total of 979 directors were British, with 287 Dutch and 226 Belgian or French (Voon, 1976: 150).

9. 'The larger estates, with a few exceptions, were owned by Europeans. The estates larger than 500 acres in size were virtually controlled by the British. Most of the estates owned by Chinese and Indians were of smaller size, generally between 100 and 499 acres' (Li, 1955: 61).

10. From the first national Agricultural Census in 1960, Cheng Siok Hwa (1970: 49) found that, 'though 65 per cent of the estates came under the private person form of ownership, only 20 per cent of the estate acreage came under this type of ownership indicating that estates owned by private persons were generally much smaller than estates owned by limited companies'. All estates exceed a hundred acres by definition, of which the private ones averaged 331 acres each while corporate estates averaged 2,386 acres each. While many changes before 1960 affected the pattern of ownership, the general trend has tended to be in the direction of decreasing personal ownership, with the important exception of the many subdivisions of estates which occurred especially during the 1950s, just before and after Malaya obtained political independence in 1957 (see Aziz, 1962). There is little reason to doubt that the substantial differences in acreage between private and corporate estates have been long-standing, though not in the proportions of 1960.

11. A fuller discussion of the class bias of the restriction schemes is provided in Chapter 3.

12. The significance of the establishment of Malay reservations by the 1913 Malay Reservations Enactment and subsequent legislation is discussed in Part II.

13. Initially, this was often in the form of penal labour. It has been suggested that the use of ostensible criminals was probably subject to considerable abuse: '. . . the requisite number of men are fined for some imaginary offense and must work off the fine without pay other than their food' (Lasker, 1950: 188). The terrible conditions of convict labour were reflected in a very high mortality rate:

'Between the years 1820 and 1824, for example, for every 192 new convicts entering the Colony, there were 103 deaths each year. In some years, the number of deaths in fact exceeded the arrivals, as for instance in 1859–60 when there were 236 deaths amongst the convicts compared with 171 new arrivals' (Sandhu, 1969: 134).

14. Partly due to the destruction of India's rural industries under the colonial impact, nineteenth-century India witnessed widespread poverty and in certain circumstances, famine. From 1876 until the end of the nineteenth century, deaths from famine totalled 26 million. In 1918–19, 10 million died from starvation (Clairmonte, 1960: 111). Thus, not unlike nineteenth- and early twentieth-century China, the 'push' element for emigration was also very strong.

15. The indenture system was once described as the 'new system of slavery' by an English lord. For an overview of the indenture system involving Indian labour in the British Empire, see Tinker (1974). He shows it to be intimately bound up, as slavery under capitalism had been (Williams, 1964; Patterson, 1977), with the development of plantation agriculture (Beckford, 1972).

16. In the words of the Governor of the Straits Settlements in 1887:
'I am . . . anxious for political reasons that the great preponderance of the Chinese over any other race in these Settlements, and to a less marked degree in some of the Native States under our administration, should be counter-balanced as much as possible by the influx of Indian and other nationalities . . .' (quoted in Sandhu, 1969: 58).

17. The Federated Malay States' annual report for 1896 stated:
'. . . the number of large estate [*sic*] now being opened in Malaya increases so rapidly that the scarcity of labour is likely to be increasingly felt.

'With the extension of planting operations, the labour question has become one of such importance that, if the Government of the Malay States really meant to encourage planters, it was evident that something must be done to supply them with labour' (quoted in R. N. Jackson, 1961: 95).

18. '. . . the laborer's freedom was of doubtful value as long as the advantage of freedom, viz. to improve his terms of employment, was frequently negated by employer combinations' (Parmer, 1960: 253). The sentiment expressed in this statement is not to be ignored, especially if the low mobility prospects of Tamil-educated workers is considered. Nonetheless, the termination of involuntary forms of labour has important implications, both for capital and labour.

19. Detailed discussions of Indian immigrant labour in Malaya can be obtained in Marakayyar and Marjoribanks (1917); Jackson (1961); Arudsothy (1968); Sandhu (1969); and Arasaratnam (1970). Considerable attention is correctly given to the immigrant labourers, who were derogatorily referred to as *kaletheh* (donkeys).

20. 'The health of the indentured Indian labourers always gave cause for concern' (R. N. Jackson, 1961: 132). Even after the abolition of indenture, health conditions of Indian estate labour remained deplorable. However, there was gradual improvement with the growing recognition by employers that healthier workers would diminish costs (owing to the deaths and debility of workers), as well as increase productivity.

21. 'The Indian immigration machinery was usually able to meet labor demand quickly and thus blunt tendencies for wages to rise by maintaining pressure on jobs. The immigration machinery was devised with this object in mind' (Parmer, 1960: 254).

22. Snodgrass (personal communication) has correctly pointed out that the degree of subsidization depends on the wage rate and savings rate of plantation workers. While Jain (1970) claims that savings were high in the 1960s, it is unclear how much this was a result of specific rubber price conditions. In any case, wage rates and labour conditions improved slowly, especially after labour became 'free', which was at a time when Indian immigrant labour was becoming more settled in Malaya. As labour settled and the supply of labour became decreasingly immigrant in nature, the plantations increasingly bore the costs of reproduction of estate labour. The present discussion, however, refers to an earlier period when labour needs were being met primarily by immigration of predominantly Tamil ex-peasants. Yet, in so far as these migrant workers were mainly transient and dreamed of returning to settle in India with some savings, Snodgrass's comment is of some relevance. Available data, however, does not allow a more detailed picture of its significance.

23. It was a long-standing practice for Indian workers to return to India upon retirement. Therefore, presumably, many deaths in Malaya involved younger workers. A more in-depth

analysis of the Indian labour situation would have to take greater account of the age and sex cohorts involved. Some of this can be obtained from Sandhu (1969), Smith (1964), and various government census reports.

24. 'Repatriation was also preferred because it was cheaper than the alternative suggested, relief works. Further, the colonial government knew that half the costs of this measure would be borne by the Indian Immigration Fund sustained by employers. As long as labor could again be obtained from India, repatriation remained feasible and remained as the policy preference during the twenties and thirties' (Parmer, 1969: 260).

25. Vernacular education and other related factors have contributed to a phenomenon of labour market segmentation along racial lines (see Mehmet, 1972). In so far as considerable economic activities developed under the aegis of Chinese capital, vernacular Chinese education offered more opportunities than schooling in Malay or Tamil. However, Chinese vernacular schooling also ensured the existence of a labour pool for almost exclusive employment, and hence exploitation, by Chinese capital.

26. It was estimated in the 1920s that for every £109 sterling in profit which went to British capital, the tapper earned about £15 in money wages, and possibly the equivalent of about £10 in the form of accommodation, food, and other services provided. Assuming an average workday of 8 hours, this meant that the labourer worked about $6\frac{1}{2}$ hours creating surplus value for capital (Labour Research Department, 1926: 35).

27. Much credit has been given to the role of the Indian colonial government for its paternalistic concern for the fate of Indian labour overseas, e.g. see Li (1955); Sandhu (1969); Arasaratnam (1970). There should be no illusions, however, as to its basic class bias:
'The attitude of the Government of India was fundamentally sympathetic toward Malayan officials and employers. Although subject to political pressure, India managed to maintain what was, from Malaya's point of view, a broad-minded approach to emigration problems' (Parmer, 1960: 253).

28. 'Laborers' wages were to be kept from rising too high but were permitted to fall as low as they might. When it suited employers' interests, the labourers' liberty was defended' (Parmer, 1960: 254).

29. Caldwell (1977b: 45) provides different figures suggesting a halving of estate employment from 258,780 in 1929 to 125,600 in 1932.

30. The head of the Department, the Controller of Labour, is recognized to have generally served the interests of capital, though differences with particular capitalists over method and style were not unknown.
'Because he possessed considerable political power, employers were sometimes anxious lest the Controller or his officers exercised that power arbitrarily. Their anxiety was unwarranted. The Controller was unlikely ever purposely to exercise his power in such fashion. He was part of a government which was fundamentally in harmony with the objects of capitalist enterprise. When differences did occur between government and industry, it was usually over the means to an agreed goal. . . . Sometimes, the Controller found that his role of the laborers' protector conflicted with his role of the employers' friend. In such situations, he usually decided in favour of the employer, although generally taking the action advocated by the most enlightened and progressive employers' (Parmer, 1960: 265, 267).

31. 'Broadly stated, the Indian immigration machinery was designed to keep wages from rising higher than the employers wished while the standard wage inquiries aimed to keep wages from falling lower than the Government of India thought desirable' (Parmer, 1960: 256).

32. After the abolition of Chinese indentured labour in 1914, European employers of Chinese relied almost solely on indirect methods of employment, such as contract labour (Parmer, 1969: 254). This practice enhanced the control of Chinese labour contractors over their workers and kept European contact with Chinese labour to a minimum. Such an arrangement provided the British employer a certain amount of flexibility in dealing with price fluctuations, labour problems, etc.

33. During the Depression, many Chinese workers were prepared to work for lower wages than Indians who had a stronger bargaining position owing to their officially recognized right to repatriation (Arudsothy, 1968: 134-5).

Part IV

If the misery of the poor be caused not by the laws of nature,
but by our institutions, great is our sin.

Charles Darwin

CAPITALIST FRACTIONS AND
POST-COLONIAL DEVELOPMENT

THIS last section examines the significance of internal differentiation among the local capitalist class for post-colonial development. Within the capitalist class as a whole, these class fractions share interests which set them apart from other fractions. The existence of class fractions therefore involves contradictions and contention within the capitalist class in post-colonial development. Contention involving these fractional interests in some issues of economic development, and consequently class relations, are addressed in the following chapters.

In the colonial era, the economic hegemony of British capital was clearly maintained and advanced by the colonial state. Hence, the most relevant distinctions among particular local capitals would be on the basis of their relationships to the world market and foreign, especially British capital. This is taken up in Chapter 8. In the post-colonial period, the development of capitalist interests has attained very significant proportions. The condition for such development has been the very breakdown of the colonial system, i.e. new alignments among foreign capital, the post-colonial state, and local capital. Industrial capital and statist capital have become significant fractions in post-colonial Malaysia; the criteria for distinguishing these two fractions are discussed in Chapters 9 and 10 respectively.

The relevance of the distinction between national and comprador capital suggested in Chapter 8 has continued to develop since the colonial period (upon which many of the details of the argument are based), since the hegemony of foreign capital still remains, and the Malaysian economy is still part of the world economy. Chapter 8 discusses the development and organization of local capital and suggests two criteria by which it can be differentiated. One is on the basis of involvement with either the national commodity circuit or the international commodity circuit. The other distinction is based on the complementary or competitive relationship of particular local capitals to foreign capital. The nature of local, predominantly Chinese, capital in the Malayan economy is discussed and the suggested distinction between national capital and comprador capital is addressed in light of the preceding discussion on local capital.

A brief review of industrialization in colonial Malaya in Chapter 9 reveals that colonialism was not inimical to industrialization *per se*, although it undoubtedly constrained its development in many directions. The role of the post-colonial state in relation to industrial capital and the evolution of industrial policy, including some aspects of government taxation, tariffs and incentives, are briefly examined. An evaluation of certain features of industrialization in post-colonial Malaya identifies the implications of both the initial import-substitution impulse and the more recent shift to export-oriented manufacturing. The ownership and control situation in the industrial sector are outlined, with particular attention given to the foreign–local distinction and some of its implications. Finally, the discussion returns to the role of the post-colonial state with an assessment of policies affecting capital–labour (i.e. industrial) relations.

The ascendance of the statist capitalists is the subject of Chapter 10. The historical beginnings of the political basis of this class fraction, including the political developments culminating in independence and the character of the post-colonial ruling Alliance Party, enter into the discussion. The British-groomed, predominantly Malay administrative petty bourgeoisie, whose class origins could often be traced to the pre-colonial ruling class, emerged in the post-colonial situation as the governing group. The nature of the class compromise, upon which the post-colonial state was first constituted, limited early government efforts to promote Malay capitalism. After over a decade of independence, the maldistribution of income was exacerbated for all three major ethnic groups, most of all among the Malays. Over the same period, the rising aspirations for greater wealth accumulation among the increasing number of bourgeois Malays were unsatisfied. At the same time, popular resentment against their use of government privileges was growing, especially among non-Malays, since these privileges were supposed to be ethnically exclusive. These growing class-based contradictions fuelled the racial conflagration of May 1969, and this event in turn provided the opportunity for a more assertive faction within the ruling party to take over the reins of state power. Various government policies and activities since then, including the New Economic Policy, are seen here as the manifestation of the governing group's efforts to consolidate and advance itself as a class fraction through the use of state power. New contradictions which have emerged with the rise of statist capitalist interest are discussed.

8

LOCAL CAPITAL: THE NATIONAL-COMPRADOR DISTINCTION

The Organization of Local Capital

IT is clear that the activities of capital which developed in the Malayan economy under British colonialism were largely dominated by foreign, especially British, capital. However local capital, which was predominantly Chinese, developed considerably as well (see Part III). Local Chinese capital, which had its beginnings with Chinese merchants based in the Straits Settlements, grew rapidly in commerce, but remained subordinate and complementary to British capital in the emerging commercial circuits. Gradually, with increased commodity circulation encouraged by British free-trade liberalism, Straits-based Chinese merchant capital not only established an important niche for itself, but with capital accumulated from trade, sponsored Chinese pioneer agriculturalists and miners on the peninsula. Through its involvement as financier, it gained some control over and profits from commodity production, which was primarily for the external market.

Capital-financed commodity production grew rapidly as colonial rule was extended throughout the peninsula. The political conditions established by the colonial state encouraged the interests of capital in general, with British capital particularly favoured. Thus, it was not long before British capital established its dominance in tin, largely at the expense of Chinese capital (see Chapter 6), and in rubber, primarily over peasant interests (see Chapter 3).

Because of the absence of a readily available local proletariat and the largely petty nature of early Chinese investments, much of the early economic activity organized by Chinese capital did not involve free wage labour (see Chapter 6). In fact, besides utilizing bonded labour, Chinese businessmen also controlled and manipulated trade guilds, clan organizations and dialect associations for their own ends (Simoniya, 1961: 50). Historically, the internal organization of Chinese businesses has been on 'feudal' lines, i.e. in the form of enterprises in which workers are socially constrained from freely selling their ability to work for a wage[1] (Huang Chih Lien, 1971). Instead, kinship links, clan ties and provincial or dialect commonalities serve as criteria for employment preferences. In other words, the labour market is 'segmented'. The enterprise itself is not run on strictly modern capitalist lines. For instance, patronage, as well as 'pre-capitalist' practices, such as the apprenticeship system, plays an important role.[2]

The demise of the indenture system and the weakening of the secret societies did not mean the end of the 'personal' system of labour recruitment from native villages. Rather, it assured the development of 'feudal' or 'traditional' kin based forms of labour organization, which especially benefited from the 'personal' labour recruitment system. Thus, the demise of indenture and secret societies gave rise to new forms of labour recruitment and control serving the needs of Chinese capital at that time. Some of these continue to this day in modified forms. Although the development of monopoly tendencies among Chinese capital has contributed—albeit somewhat ambiguously—to the reorganization of Chinese enterprises along more 'modern' capitalist lines, e.g. with the emergence of the corporate form, many Chinese concerns, especially petty ones, continue to be run along more 'traditional' lines. More recent circumstances—such as increasing state intervention,[3] and the challenge of 'modern' business organization by both foreign and local capital—have necessitated the organization of many businesses along more 'modern' capitalist lines.

There is little doubt that socio-cultural organizations, such as trade guilds, clan groupings and dialect associations, served the interests of Chinese capital (Simoniya, 1961; Huang Chih Lien, 1971). For instance, the *pang* society, based on association by common surname or place of origin or even by virtue of personal friendships, was 'characteristically a group based on the close relations between the economy at the native place and the economy at the place of settlement' (Suyama, 1962: 198). Even in 1958, the Singapore Chinese Chamber of Commerce was still comprised of various *pang* of fellow provincials, the membership of these *pang* reflecting considerable business and occupational specialization. This clearly suggested that 'surname organizations are not merely groups for ancestor worship but also undertake economic activity.... Thus, kinsmen scattered over a large area often utilize their related clans for economic and business purposes' (Suyama, 1962: 207).

Similarly, evidence from the history of Chinese banking in Malaya (Tan Ee Leong, 1953; Lee Sheng-Yi, 1966, 1974; Dick Wilson, 1972) shows that all the early Chinese banks in Malaya were organized on clear provincial or dialect lines: Kwong Yik for the Cantonese; Sze Hai Tong for Teochews; three early Hokkien banks later amalgamated to form the Oversea-Chinese Banking Corporation (OCBC), and so on. These banks played an important role in financing the activities of Chinese business, especially in commerce.

A combination of factors—including the emergence of a permanently settled proletariat (Smith, 1964), intensifying labour struggles (Hanrahan, 1954; Parmer, 1962; Yeo, 1976), intervention by the colonial state in the interest of British capital, and, perhaps most importantly, the declining efficacy of and need for extra-economic forms of control—brought about a gradual 'freeing' of Chinese labour by the 1930s. Although some means to preserve 'communal unity' across class lines still remained—e.g. Chinese vernacular education and the manipulation of 'communal' issues—the previously strong hold exercised by Chinese employers through secret societies, clan associations, dialect associations and other formal and informal ties was slowly, but surely, being eroded. Nevertheless, kinship, clannishness and provincial loyalties have continued to figure in contemporary Chinese capital's activities, especially in smaller scale enterprises (Huang Chih Lien, 1971). To this day, considerable labour market 'segmentation' continues, mainly along ethno-linguistic lines,[4] this being perpetuated partly by the unintegrated systems of vernacular education inherited from the colonial period. As before, such labour market segmentation favours the interests of capital in facing the challenge from labour and in keeping wages low.

While it is undoubtedly true that Chinese labour immigration, especially under the indenture and assisted immigration systems, was dictated primarily by the needs of Chinese capital, there was also considerable voluntary emigration from China to Malaya and other parts of South-East Asia. Much of this was encouraged by economic conditions in China and the turbulent state of Chinese political and social affairs for about a century from the mid-nineteenth century.[5] Emigration, previously restricted under Manchu rule, became easier after the defeat of the Chinese imperial regime by British and other European powers. First, the declining Manchu state and then, the beleaguered Guomindang government had neither the interest nor the strength to intervene in the emigration of the Chinese population to the colonial economies of South-East Asia, especially Malaya, which offered far better opportunities than the unstable Chinese economy. The frontier conditions prevailing in the rapidly expanding Malayan economy attracted enterprising pioneers. While most were eventually marginalized, many emerged as successful entrepreneurs, though often subordinate to the already established Straits Chinese capitalists and British commercial capital.

In contrast to the substantial and ubiquitous, though not dominant, presence of Chinese capital in the colonial Malayan economy, capital identified with other local ethnic groups was even more marginal, if not altogether negligible. Indian immigration to Malaya, in contrast to the Chinese influx, was primarily in tune with the specific labour requirements of British capital and the colonial government, and hence under greater British supervision and control. The bulk of Tamils were brought to man estates and government work gangs while other South Asians came to serve in other more privileged capacities in the state machinery, e.g. Sikhs in the armed forces and Ceylonese as junior professionals and petty officials. Indian merchants mainly grew in specialized branches of commerce such as the trade in Indian textiles. As commodity circulation developed, usurers from India extended their activities to Malaya. Partly financed by British banks, these *chettiar* thrived on the indebtedness of a wide range of people, from small Chinese capitalists to Malay peasants and Indian workers. In conditions of economic depression, when defaults ran high, they accumulated considerable property. Few, however, actually made the transition to involvement in production. Thus, Indian capital was mainly confined to the sphere of circulation—commerce and usury—where it was usually subordinate to British capital.

Forfeiting control of trade in return for tribute from Arab, Chinese and other traders, the pre-colonial Malay ruling class never quite became commercial capitalists. Instead, by British design, they were successfully integrated in a complementary but subordinate role in the colonial administrative apparatus. Comfortably salaried, they did not consider becoming entrepreneur capitalists, though property ownership and rentier capitalism (e.g. from land-ownership) were certainly not beyond them. The mass of the Malay peasantry were left on the land and no Malay proletariat was readily available for wage employment. Malay capitalists, therefore, also remained negligible in the colonial era.

Local Capital, Foreign Capital, and the Commodity Circuits

Chinese capital which was the only significant local capital, in ethnic terms, was under pressure on at least two fronts–from British capital, and from Chinese labour. The former, and other related observations, have led to a recognition of fractions of local capital, distinguished on the basis of their relationship to foreign capital and the world market. Before moving to a more detailed discussion of such fractions and their common interests, some of the more important contradictions among local capitalist interests need elucidation.

It is possible to distinguish two distinct, but related, commodity circuits. The production of commodities for consumption within the national economy–or the national commodity circuit–is distinguishable from production of commodities for external consumption–or the international commodity circuit. The historic role of foreign capital in the colonial epoch was to stimulate production for the latter and, where necessary or feasible, to limit national commodity production so that its existence would not interfere with production for the international circuit. Production and circulation in the colony were very clearly subordinated to the requirements and logic of accumulation of capital at the colonial centre. This was expressed in the expansion of international commodity circuits, including export-import trade–a key feature of the 'open' colonial economy.

Since the different interests of capital in circulation also determined their production preferences–for example, commercial capital involved in the international circuit would generally prefer export-oriented production and the importation of local consumption requirements from the centre, while capital in the national circuit would tend to encourage local production for local consumption–the implications of such differences for industrialization would hence be correspondingly different. Therefore, while foreign capital in general would not necessarily be opposed to industrialization *per se*, it was to be expected that industries related to the export-import trade were promoted by foreign capital in the colonial epoch. These included processing of raw material exports, e.g. tin smelting and rubber smoking, as well as the final preparation of certain imported consumer items, such as food and beverages, for retail.

Of course, foreign capital is quite capable of extending its involvement in industrial production in response to changing circumstances. The post-colonial import-substituting industrial impulse reflected the interests of both foreign industrial capital anxious to retain or expand markets in the post-colonial era as well as the interests of local capital involved in the national circuits. Just as this latter fraction of local capital had had an interest in bringing about the demise of the colonial order, it sought to continue to influence post-colonial economic development policy to serve its own interests. However, foreign capital, especially industrial capital, has generally been more successful in influencing government policies. Nevertheless, it is this somewhat new and uneasy alliance between foreign industrial capital and local capital in the national commodity circuits that has encouraged and gained from import-substituting industrialization. This is qualitatively different from the old alliance of the colonial era between foreign commercial capital and local capital linked to the international commodity circuits. The extent of the difference between the old and new alliances is a historically concrete question, to which the available information does not as yet permit an answer. While there may not be much difference in the parties involved, this in itself does not deny the new interests underlying the alliance and its implications for economic development.

Another important distinction to be made in the circulation of commodities concerns the different levels of participation and concentration within the hierarchy of commercial capital (see Chapter 5). Since commercial operations at all levels tend to be financed and controlled from the apex of the structure, various aspects of the structure of commercial capital clearly have some bearing on control over commerce and the distribution of surplus value among various levels of commercial capital.

Since British trading agencies, especially the great agency houses, ultimately controlled much of the import and export sectors in Malaya, it is probable that the predominantly Chinese local capitalists, who either dealt directly with them or who were financed by them, have been the most dependent portion of the Chinese commercial bourgeoisie. On the other hand, there have also been local merchants who bypassed the European agencies in their trade links, being connected instead to independent national and regional commercial circuits. These merchants—who included the numerous retailers, shopkeepers, and first-level produce buyers involved in the circulation of commodities—have almost invariably become dependent—through various arrangements, especially credit—on both types of more strategically placed Chinese merchants mentioned here.

The number of Chinese merchants dealing directly with European commercial agencies was probably very small in the late nineteenth century (Lee Poh Ping, 1974: 32) and there is little reason to believe that the proportion has fundamentally changed since then, though the range of goods transacted has widened. What has changed is the degree of concentration among the agencies, with the great agency houses now clearly dominant (see J. J. Puthucheary, 1960), as well as among the Chinese commercial capitalists dealing with them (see Tan Tat Wai, 1977).

These comments on commercial capital can be extended to include consideration of capital as a whole, including production capital. Competition has long been identified as intrinsic to the workings of capital; it is also considered a necessity, so that the forces of production develop, ensuring the survival of some capitalists at the expense of others. In this, and other ways, competition eventually begets monopoly—its own negation. One development identified with colonialism is the imposition of monopoly capitalist domination with the support of the colonial state. In those sectors of the economy in which foreign capital participates directly, monopolistic structures are especially stark[6] (see Edwards, 1975). Thus, foreign capital, and the fractions of local capital identified with it, tend to be located in the more concentrated sectors of the economy, especially in the form of monopoly firms and the like. This explains the relative profitability of these foreign and local firms. The 1971 *Financial Survey of Limited Companies* found that though foreign firms accounted for only 53 per cent of total sales, they had 70 per cent of gross profits and 78 per cent of net profits after direct taxation.[7] This dominance is manifested in the size, investment, and organizational form of the firm.[8]

Chinese Capital in the Colonial Economy

Crucial to the operations of capital is the role of the state. There is little doubt that since the colonial state generally favoured the interests of British capital over others, local capitalists who collaborated with British capital were generally better placed than others to expect support from the state. Foreign capital in Malaya was primarily 'expatriate' in character and only those who might conceivably be termed 'settler' capitalists—i.e. 'alien' locals such as the Chinese, Indians, Arabs, and Indonesians—accumulated capital locally, generally reinvesting their profits locally rather than repatriating them. In this context, favour for British capital therefore had an explicit racial bias. However, racial distinctions could not be a viable criterion for discriminating among the local Chinese capitalists cooperating with foreign capital. Instead, favour and discrimination have tended to be along cultural lines, identifiable with schooling and therefore language, following from British merchant capital's preference in choice of local trading partners.[9] Evidence of favour along such lines is strong, especially among local Chinese capitalists.[10]

When secret societies—and hence this means of labour organization and control—were officially abolished, the Chinese community in late nineteenth-century Malaya witnessed the emergence and strengthening of clan societies, district organizations, and dialect associations (Yong, 1967). By the early twentieth century, however, the Chinese bourgeoisie had also become more cohesively organized on class lines. In Singapore, the Straits Chinese British Association (SCBA) and the Singapore Chinese Chamber of Commerce (SCCC) made their appearance within the first decade of the century. The SCBA included English-educated Straits-born Chinese in business and the professions and 'invariably pledged their loyalty to the British Crown' (Yong, 1968: 267). The SCCC, on the other hand, represented 'mainly Chinese speaking and Chinese educated merchants ranging from small storekeepers to rich shippers and rubber magnates', who 'being more China-oriented, were normally less-favoured by the Colonial Government' (Yong, 1968: 272). While SCBA leaders contributed to activities such as English education, most SCCC leaders were actively involved with Chinese schools.

Despite their different outlooks, there was apparently little conflict; in fact, a certain amount of cooperation (e.g. in the formation of various banks) existed between the two groups, who even shared some leaders in common. Conditions in the colonial economy—e.g. government encouragement of raw material production for export and consumption of manufactured imports—allowed little opportunity to establish businesses exclusive to the national commodity circuits. Hence, ironically, as late as 1923, the chairman of the ostensibly

'Chinese-oriented' SCCC was actually working as a comprador in a British bank (Lee Poh Ping, 1974: 178).

The tin and rubber slump of 1923 and the far more traumatic one at the end of the 1920s badly shook the confidence of Chinese merchants involved in international commerce, not least because of manipulations at their expense by British capitalists. Shocked into recognition of their heavy dependence on the export–import trade, many Chinese capitalists subsequently sought and found alternative investment opportunities tied into the national commodity circuit.[11] These were 'in what may be called nationally-based businesses, businesses not directly dependent on the import and export trade', such as light consumer industries utilizing locally available raw materials and readily accessible production techniques (Lee Poh Ping, 1974: 218; see also Simoniya, 1961: 51). In contrast to 'expatriate' British capital, 'some of the Chinese funds were invested in real estates connected with service trades such as theatres, restaurants and office buildings in urban districts, reflecting the Chinese tendency to domiciliate'[12] (Suyama, 1962: 211). Practically all the SCCC members who joined in 1928 and after had some involvement in nationally-based businesses, such as the manufacture of medicinal products, biscuits, cement and building materials, dealings in local produce 'and so on, whereas those joining before that year were very strong in tin, rubber, gambier and pepper, silk, sugar, rice and other products which were dependent on the Westernized import and export sector' (Lee Poh Ping, 1974: 221). Despite some diversification, the Chinese capitalist class was not completely transformed by the Depression, on the whole continuing to reflect its reliance on traditional export-oriented economic interests. While the limited change which took place merely allowed for a lesser degree of dependence on international commodity circuits and hence the world economy, the significance of the experience was that it encouraged the emergence of industrial capital producing for the national market.[13]

After the Depression, British commercial capital reasserted its hegemony, once again curbing Chinese capitalist expansion. The situation changed again during the war when Malaya was integrated into the Japanese empire. Though the racist policies of the occupying Japanese troops discouraged Chinese capitalist expansion, local production to replace previously imported goods was stimulated somewhat. Following the reimposition of British rule which unsuccessfully attempted a return to the pre-war order, the new political compromise underlying post-colonial rule opened new opportunities for local capital, though non-Malay capital has become increasingly constrained once again by the expansion of Malay capital, especially since the 1970s.

The National–Comprador Distinction?

Is it possible then to identify the relationships of particular capitals to the international circuits and to foreign capital?[14] In practical terms, it is no easy task as the usual criteria invoked for distinguishing between 'national' and 'comprador' fractions of capital do not yield neat and distinct categories, reflecting the complex nature of the relationships involved. What have been termed 'comprador' and 'national' capital are usually defined by their respective relationships to the world economy. Yet, it is these very relationships which are ambiguous, and this in turn explains the somewhat ambivalent character of these fractions of capital.

The significance of some of these criteria needs comment. The analytical distinction most often suggested refers to the differing involvements in the national and international circuits of commodities. To imply that this is the sole basis of the contradiction between 'comprador' and 'national' capital would be erroneous. For one thing, such a distinction only takes account of the sphere of circulation and involves the often difficult distinction between national and international commodity circuits. Chapter 5's discussion on the emergence of the structure of commerce in Malaya suggests that merchant capital as a whole undoubtedly shared certain common interests, e.g. in relation to both consumers and producers, including capital in the sphere of production. In at least some respects, almost the entire local commercial bourgeoisie is linked in various ways to the import-export trade, i.e. to international commodity circuits. In its entirety, this not only includes competition for business and therefore for profits, but also struggles between the different (more or less concentrated) levels of the structure of commercial capital over distribution of commercial profits. And in so far as the highly concentrated sectors of export-import trade are controlled by foreign capital, these struggles may take on a nationalist (though nonetheless inter-capitalist) character.

Moving beyond the criterion of commodity circuits, which essentially lies at the level of circulation, to the sphere of production, possible arenas of conflict involving large versus small capital, British versus others, etc., have already been mentioned. For example, the historical development of the tin industry in Malaya, discussed in Chapter 6, involved protracted struggles between big British capital and smaller Chinese capital. Likewise, the post-Depression and post-colonial industrial impulses initiated by segments of local Chinese capital have given rise to certain conflicts with vested foreign capitalist interests. Conversely, many post-colonial investments in manufacturing by transnational corporations have threatened local industrial capital.

Yet in production, as in circulation, the relationships are not only those of conflict. In fact, it appears that collaboration is very much the order of the day, and that conflict and competition occur within a context of shared class interests. The conditions for such collaboration continue to change, however. The basis for cooperation is becoming increasingly technological, i.e. organizational and technical. Correspondingly, the significance of ownership is declining, while the locus of control and the means of extracting surplus value are adjusting to new conditions. What is important to recognize then is that while there undoubtedly is contention between local and foreign capital, shared class interests encourage a great deal of collaboration, especially in dealing with other interests, such as labour.

There are undeniably many export-oriented capitalists who are not tied to foreign capital as suggested above. These, for example, would include tin miners, estate owners, and manufacturers who can produce quite independently of foreign capital. However, in so far as they are producing for external markets—and this is especially true for those involved in primary export production and processing—they are bound up with the international commodity circuits and probably with foreign commercial capital as well. Manufacturers, too, may be similarly connected to obtain their means of production (machinery as well as raw materials), and possibly for the export of certain manufactures. Such capitalists, though undoubtedly more independent of foreign capital in the production sphere, are nevertheless inextricably bound up with international commodity circuits.

All this leaves only a small proportion of local capital really independent of foreign capital and the international commodity circuits. These would involve those producing independently—of foreign capital, foreign technology, and international commodity circuits—for the national commodity circuits. Although their current contribution to national production is presumably small because historical and contemporary circumstances have not favoured their growth, their numbers are greater since this sector comprises many small enterprises.

The preceding discussion points to some of the difficulties in establishing unambiguous criteria for distinguishing capitalist fractions on the basis of relationships to international commodity circuits and foreign capital. Only very small groups can be unambiguously identified as clearly being either 'comprador' or 'national' in character. The bulk of local capital is more ambiguously situated, and this, too, to varying degrees.[15]

Summary

While British capital dominated activities in the colonial economy, local, predominantly Chinese, capital grew as well. Beginning in the sphere of circulation, local capital soon moved into the sphere of production. Hence, local capital may be further differentiated on the basis of its relations to the commodity circuits and to foreign capital. Capital engaged in the international commodity circuits (the world market) can be distinguished from capital engaged in the national commodity circuits (the national market). The former would be interested in deepening ties with the world economy, whereas the latter would be concerned primarily with the development of the national economy. (Here, the distinction between the sphere of production and the sphere of circulation is not emphasized.) Alternatively, it may be suggested that only local commercial capital directly subordinate to foreign commercial capital is comprador in nature. There are other criteria (e.g. relative size and degree of monopoly) which complicate the picture even more.

Examination of the relationship of the colonial state to Chinese capital suggests that while British capital favoured business collaborators, Chinese capital did not appear to be in serious conflict on this score. The Depression offered some limited opportunities for establishing nationally oriented industrial activities, but without the support of the state, this trend could not be sustained. The proportion of local capital neither subordinated to foreign capital nor tied to the international commodity circuits is small. On the other hand, local commercial capitalists who are completely subordinate to foreign capital are also not a majority. This leaves the bulk of local capital linked more ambiguously to foreign capital and the world market. Correspondingly, the contradictions among local capital, and hence the resulting contention, have been subject to other influences—especially ethnic concerns—and have been very complex in nature. However, in so far as all the fractions belong to the capitalist class, their relationship to labour is less ambiguous, being based on shared common interests.

1. These social constraints do not constitute legal limitations. Juridically speaking, the worker can try to sell his ability to work on the labour market. Although in reality he may have few alternative opportunities open, this does not negate his juridically 'free' status. Therefore, the persistence of such 'traditional' organizational forms does not in itself deny the existence of 'free' wage labour. Rather, despite his nominal 'freedom', the wage labourer is 'coerced' by the economic environment to seek employment in an enterprise organized along such 'traditional' lines.

2. Huang Chih Lien (1971) discusses the functioning of the operation of these relations as well as the 'abuses' to which it remained open. He also suggests that such organization of production impeded technological progress and that the colonial authorities 'protected' these enterprises, thus consolidating Chinese capital in relatively backward organizations with non-capitalist relations of production.

3. For example, in the 1970s, the Malaysian government passed legislation requiring that employment in large firms 'reflect the multi-racial composition of the population'.
'The evidence is strong that not only are most Chinese business establishments small, but also that the forces restricting easy expansion, both physical and psychological, are considerable. Some firms have indeed made the transition successfully, but the numbers are few. Nevertheless, the MCA must come down strongly in favour of the view that Chinese must move from family businesses to larger combines run on a modern and efficient basis' (Milne, 1976: 252).

4. For example, see Mehmet (1972). Huang Chih Lien indicates that occupational specialization amongst Chinese is along even more exclusive lines, such as clan groupings or dialect/provincial ties. (See also Suyama, 1962.)

5. Periodic famines, other calamities, and the socio-political upheavals of the times encouraged large-scale emigration, especially from southern China. A famine in 1849 claimed about 13.75 million lives while another from 1875 to 1878 killed about 9.5 million more. The decade-long Taiping Rebellion against Manchu rule from 1854 is estimated to have had a casualty rate of about 20 million fatalities.

6. The subordination of petty local (competitive) capital to large foreign (monopoly) capital is starkly demonstrated in an example cited by Huang Chih Lien. Carpenter handicraftsmen in Singapore were confronted by the prospect of a British financial group investing in a furniture company in Singapore. One response could have been for the local carpenters to set up a modern woodwork factory by themselves. However, according to Huang, this possibility was rendered unfeasible by their inability to cooperate in the face of the external threat. The result was that many carpenters eventually left their occupation while many of those who remained competed for contracts to supply the new foreign-controlled factory.

7. Department of Statistics (1975), *Financial Survey of Limited Companies 1971*.

8. Most Chinese capitalist enterprises are modest in terms of size, especially in comparison to European establishments. Differences in enterprise organization have been attributed to such differences in size (J. J. Puthucheary, 1960: 134). However, the same author has also noted that 'even the very big Chinese capitalists operate through private firms or at best private limited companies' (J. J. Puthucheary, 1960: 125), though a recent study suggests that there has been considerable change in the organization of Chinese capital in the post-colonial period (Tan Tat Wai, 1982).

It is suggested that the corporate form of ownership is necessary for foreign investment by 'expatriate' capitalists, particularly by those unable to participate directly in the organization of production. There is really little choice in the matter. Chinese 'settler' capitalists, who can be directly involved in production, have often preserved personal forms of ownership and thus maintained direct control. The difference in organizational form then is not due to cultural reasons (e.g. 'backwardness' or 'feudalism') but rather to the different operational requirements of 'settler' in contrast to 'expatriate' capital investments.

9. 'In the context of a pioneer Chinese society in Singapore, so culturally different from the West and possessing so many adventurers, those Chinese with some westernization and some roots in the area would make more appealing partners than those Chinese with none' (Lee Poh Ping, 1974: 34).

10. For example, see Sim (n.d.); C. S. Wong (1963); Yong (1967, 1968); Lee Poh Ping (1974).

11. 'Chinese capital . . . succeeded in retaining and even consolidating its position in the sphere of domestic trade' (Simoniya, 1961: 39).

12. There actually is little reason to assume otherwise, i.e. to suggest that Chinese capital had an 'expatriate' character. However, to consider it 'settler' capital may also be erroneous since there was generally little prior capital accumulation by the Chinese businessmen who emerged in Malaya. 'One of the characteristics of Chinese capital in Southeast Asia is that the entire process of accumulating that capital took place within the countries of Southeast Asia' (Simoniya, 1961: 39).

13. '. . . Chinese capital is realizing an economic structure independent of European capital by fixing its funds in the form of long-term investment in these industries for the purpose of opening stabilized markets in the vicinities through related banking organizations' (Suyama, 1962: 212).

14. Simoniya's position—which is at great variance with the current Soviet view—is worth quoting at length:
'The Chinese bourgeoisie in Southeast Asia is not homogeneous. Its largest segment consists of petty and middle-class bourgeoisie and only a small part is represented by big capital. The specific method of formation of the Chinese bourgeoisie in Southeast Asia under conditions of colonial domination left its imprint on the nature of its various strata. . . .

'By its economic positions in the countries of Southeast Asia the Chinese bourgeoisie is divided into two groups: comprador and national. The rich trading bourgeoisie comprises the basic nucleus of the comprador group. The interests of this segment of the Chinese bourgeoisie are closely interwoven with those of foreign capital. . . .

'The economic situation of the middle class and petty Chinese trading bourgeoisie is radically different from that of the rich trading bourgeoisie. The overwhelming majority of the petty bourgeoisie own only small stores and do not exploit any hired labor. On the contrary, they are themselves exploited [sic] both by foreign capital and the rich Chinese bourgeoisie and usurers. . . .

'The non-comprador group of the Chinese bourgeoisie in Southeast Asia consists of representatives of industrial and business capital connected with the domestic commodity circulation. That group is part of the national bourgeoisie . . . whose interests lie in the development of the national economy, as distinguished from the comprador bourgeoisie which is in the service of foreign monopolies' (Simoniya, 1961: 54–5).

15. Any hope for a committed 'anti-imperialism' among local capitalists should therefore be confined to a limited few, at most. In a sense, 'imperialism' itself thwarted the development of such interests. The limited influence of such interests in a colony further renders it incapable of leading any 'anti-imperialist' movement.

When such leadership is provided by the larger exploited classes under 'imperialism', the class basis of such a movement provides it with a momentum beyond mere 'anti-imperialism'. The existence of such class interests in the leadership of the anti-imperialist movement calls capitalism itself into question. This in turn threatens the alignment of national capital with other 'anti-imperialist' forces, thus rendering it an even more ambiguous and unreliable partner in 'anti-imperialist' movements.

The relationship is rendered even more problematic by the conditions of existence of the 'national' capitalist sector. Constrained by 'imperialism', its weak existence in the colonial economy is associated with the especially deplorable conditions of the working class it exploits. Poorly 'capitalized' as it usually is, this sector tends to have a low 'capital-labour ratio' (hence it employs proportionately more workers in relation to total investment) and to pay lower wages. Their employees are unlikely to have a special love for their capitalist employers, especially as kinship and other 'traditional' relations decline in significance. Yet, profitability remains low owing to the lower 'organic composition of capital' or capital-labour ratio, and the lower productivity usually associated with this sector.

Finally, Chinese predominance among national capitalists in Malaya renders the position of national capital even more problematic in a society where the ethnic dimensions of class exploitation have coloured and distorted the development of class consciousness.

9
INDUSTRIAL CAPITAL AND
POST-COLONIAL INDUSTRIALIZATION

Industry in Colonial Malaya

MUCH handicraft production in pre-colonial Malaya did not survive long under colonialism. With the exception of various exotic or unsubstitutable products, local production of many items was displaced by cheap manufactures from abroad. In this matter, it has been shown that imports of British products were favoured over other imports. All sectors of production in Malaya became increasingly geared to producing raw materials for Western manufacturing needs and basic consumption items for the producers themselves (see Chapter 3), though these requirements did not altogether preclude industrial development (see Thoburn, 1975a; Junid, 1975). The processing of raw materials (especially rubber and tin) for export[1] and some processing of food and other items for local consumption were the main features of early local industry. It has been suggested that lowly capitalized light engineering industries also emerged to serve export-oriented primary production[2] (Thoburn, 1975b). High transport costs, which presented a high degree of 'natural' protection, appear to have been a significant factor urging such development. Otherwise, with a few exceptions, the growth of local manufacturing was effectively discouraged by colonial protection of British manufactures. As in many other colonies, the momentum of industrial development in colonial Malaya was greatly influenced by the colonial presence and British interests.

The Depression of the early 1930s disrupted trade connections with the West and temporarily reduced foreign investment in the colony. This traumatic experience provided local capitalists with an opportunity to reorientate their economic activities away from the external market, i.e. the international commodity circuits, and gave rise to the emergence of new industries more oriented towards the local market (Lee Poh Ping, 1974). Similarly, the Japanese Occupation of the early 1940s, which again disrupted commercial ties with the West, also revived local handicraft production to replace imports from the West.

Nevertheless, before Malaya achieved its independence in 1957, incentives for industrial growth were few. Suggestions for protection policies to encourage local industrialization were resisted by the colonial administration on several grounds (see Wheelwright, 1963b: 71) and several attempts by local industrialists to alter this policy, e.g. by 'protecting' the emergence of local industries, were ignored by the colonial government (Kanapathy, 1970: 125). Capitalists involved in primary production opposed protection which they expected would raise wages and other costs. Trading agencies were against their import trade being exposed to competition from local production, while the colonial government had no wish to lose revenue from import taxes. Nevertheless, the developments encouraged some industrial development and the agency houses, among others, were quick to involve themselves in some of these industries and thus retain control over the local market. Junid (1975) has argued that most British industrial investors in the post-colonial period were specially motivated by the desire to protect their share of the local market previously met by imports handled by the agency houses. The trading agencies thus diversified to promote local manufacturing, either on their own or in partnership with British industrial capital.

The little industry which developed during the colonial epoch was mainly concentrated in the major ports, particularly in Singapore. J. J. Puthucheary's discussion (1960: Chapter 4) of Singapore industry in 1958 has shown that while the vast majority of enterprises were small and most of the employers Chinese, 74 European firms, comprising 3.1 per cent of the total number of firms, employed 31 per cent of the workers.[3] The 2,327 Chinese firms employed 24,337 workers. The 1959 Census of Manufacturing for the Federation of Malaya found that large units, i.e. those employing over 20 full-time workers, comprised only 13 per cent of the total number of establishments, but accounted for 77 per cent of gross sales and 68 per cent of employees (Wheelwright, 1963a: 213). This Census ignored more than half of those categorized by the 1957 Population Census as being in the manufacturing sector, i.e. those in the numerous, very small establishments were not enumerated.

At the time of independence, the picture of industry in Malaya and Singapore was one of numerous, small, privately owned enterprises on the one hand, and a few large establishments usually owned by limited companies on the other. Though a strong European presence dominated the latter group, local capitalist participation in industry was generally higher than in large-scale, export-oriented primary production. Many industries catering to the domestic market were dominated by foreign-controlled firms such as Fraser and Neave, Unilever, and Bata. Industry in Malaya at that time was 'mostly either associated with primary industry in various forms of processing or catering for the naturally protected section of the home market' (Wheelwright, 1963a: 214). 'Apart from a few locally manufactured items such as soap, aerated waters, rubber shoes and some simple rubber products, there were [sic] no manufacturing sector to speak of' (Mohar, 1976: 2).

The Evolution of Post-colonial Industrial Policy

In contrast to colonial practice, the post-colonial state almost immediately introduced incentives to promote industrial development, though this process was noted as rather erratic and haphazard (Lo, 1972: 86; Edwards, 1975: 289). With the imminence of 'independence' through a fairly smooth transfer of power from the British to a government representing an alliance of the local élite, a World Bank mission issued an influential report (IBRD, 1955) making comprehensive recommendations for post-colonial economic development. Diversification of production in the national economy was encouraged, including attempts at import-substitution, though the 'openness' of the economy was not to be challenged. Industrialization was to be promoted with depreciation allowances and some (but not much) tariff protection, but tax holidays for pioneer industries were discouraged as being undesirably 'discriminatory'. The primary role of government was to provide infrastructural facilities—especially transport, communications and power—for such development. State enterprise and economic nationalism were out of the question. Various financial and other inducements were suggested for the promotion of private enterprise; specifically, new arrangements for industrial finance were strongly urged, and this eventually bore fruit in 1960 with the establishment of Malayan Industrial Development Finance Limited (MIDFL). In its election manifesto for the first (1955) general election, the Alliance Party—which won 51 of the 52 seats—accepted and incorporated the basic principles of the industrial policy recommended by the Bank report. The manifesto demonstrated the Alliance government's commitment to encourage local industrial capital, attract foreign capital, introduce new income tax incentives, provide industrial estate facilities, further infrastructural development, train labour, etc. (Lo, 1972: 76).

In 1957, the government-appointed Industrial Development Working Party reiterated most of the recommendations of the earlier World Bank report. To reassure foreign investors, it added provisions for free transferability of investment funds and profits, and explicitly made guarantees against nationalization (Lo, 1972: 76). However, the Working Party also favoured tax relief for pioneer industries, and in the following year, the first Pioneer Industries Ordinance was legislated to provide income tax relief for varying periods, depending on the size of investments. The espoused rationale for the 'open door' approach was to attract foreign industrialists to establish factories in the country to produce items previously imported. 'Foreign investors were allowed to own one hundred percent of the equity even when they had the full protection of the domestic market for their products' (Mohar, 1976: 4).

To protect the emergence of new industries in Malaya, a Tariff Advisory Committee was established in 1961 within the Ministry of Commerce and Industry. In this respect, post-colonial policy represented a departure from the colonial experience in so far as the state now actively intervened to promote industrialization. An observer remarked: 'What exists is very largely a promotional effort, geared to the provision of an investment climate favourable to private enterprise, especially foreign private enterprise' (Wheelwright, 1963b: 69). By direct and indirect subsidization of new manufacturing concerns and protection of the national market by various means, the post-colonial government sought to promote import-substituting industrialization.

In 1963, a second World Bank mission submitted a report in anticipation of the formation of Malaysia, a federation envisaged as embracing all the former British colonies in the region. Eventually, Malaya and Singapore, as well as Sabah and Sarawak on the island of Kalimantan (Borneo), i.e. all the British territories with the exception of oil-rich Brunei. Besides endorsing the thrust of post-colonial Malayan industrialization policy and urging that a Tariff Advisory Board be established to work out a common external tariff after the formation of Malaysia, possibly the most important recommendation of the Report was to set up a new body specifically for industrial promotion. Consequently, in 1965, the establishment of the Federal Industrial Development Authority (FIDA) was approved by the government. The different incentive systems developed by the various State governments in the pre-Malaysia days were also harmonized through fresh legislation.

Within a decade of independence, the limits to import-substitution and the disappointing results achieved under this policy were becoming clear. In response, to accelerate the pace of industrialization and to diversify the type and location of new industries, as well as to attract greater foreign and local investments, the government appointed the Raja Mohar Committee to study the possibilities. Its recommendations led to the Investment Incentives Act of 1968, described by the Minister of Commerce and Industry as providing 'a variety of incentives to induce a greater and more rapid flow of investments' (quoted in Lo, 1972: 89). This Act was thus promulgated partly in response to the disappointing and deteriorating industrialization record in the decade after independence.[4] The 1968 Act's incentives were intended to encourage investments 'not only in the manufacturing and agricultural based industries but also other enterprises and to encourage the expansion of export in manufactures' (quoted in Lo, 1972: 89). It signalled a shift away from import-substitution towards export-oriented industrialization.[5]

Taxes, Tariffs, and Treats

While the dominance of foreign commercial capital was not undermined at independence, the establishment of the post-colonial state undoubtedly represented certain shifts in the alignment of the dominant classes in Malaya. The rise of industrial capital, while not involving a clean break with merchant capital, did nevertheless have important implications for government policy. By focusing one's attention on some of the outcomes of post-colonial industrial policy, it will be possible to identify more specifically the particular kinds of interests (i.e. the fractions of capital) which were favoured by state actions.

It has been argued that the post-colonial government provided excessive and unnecessary tax exemptions to encourage industrial, especially foreign, investment in the country[6] (David Lim, 1973: 261; Edwards, 1975: Section 5.2). This has been clearly reflected in the differential incidence of taxes on foreign and local firms. For example, among limited companies in the manufacturing sector in 1971, the effective rate of direct taxation on profits was 67.6 per cent and 39.9 per cent for local and foreign companies respectively. While the difference is substantial, it is certainly not atypical: for all limited companies in the same year, the rates were 59.8 per cent and 39.5 per cent respectively.[7]

While it has often been argued that tariff protection in Malaya has been low compared to other similar economies (e.g. see David Lim, 1973), Edwards (1975: Sections 2.3 and 3.1) has argued that most post-colonial manufacturing in Malaya was established behind tariff and quota protection and enjoyed a particular advantage in the latter phase of the import-substitution period between 1962 and 1966. The average effective rate of protection for the enumerated manufacturing sector rose from 15 per cent in 1962 to 45 per cent in 1966 and 55 per cent in 1972 (Edwards, 1975: 293). Profit levels were naturally very sensitive to such increases in protection which, furthermore, assured manufacturers of virtually monopolistic markets.[8] The cost of such protection has been high in various instances,[9] although the overall impact remains difficult to assess.

A brief review of the experience of the Malayan (later Malaysian) Industrial Development Finance Limited (MIDFL) during the 1960s provides revealing insights into the role of the post-colonial state and international aid agencies in relation to foreign and local industrial capital. Proposed by the IBRD Report of 1955, the MIDFL was incorporated in 1960 and subsequently reorganized in 1963.[10] Its initial share capital was held by the Malayan government, the principal banks in Malaya, various insurance companies, the Commonwealth Development Corporation (the former Colonial Development Corporation), the Commonwealth Development Finance Company, and the International Finance Corporation (IFC) of the World Bank group (Drake, 1969: 160). While the foreign equity in MIDFL brought in some funds from abroad, the existence of MIDFL also allowed foreign corporations to 'tap' the Malaysian 'capital market' more efficiently. In this manner, a relatively small initial investment of foreign government funds resulted in a substantial amount of local finance becoming available in the form of loans to foreign private corporations.

The establishment of an official stock market in Malaya was also made possible by MIDFL. MIDFL's services were first used to float stock issues by Dunlop Malayan Industries and Malayan Tobacco Company Limited, both subsidiaries of foreign companies. The floating of stock issues in the local market by subsidiaries of foreign companies was favoured for a number of reasons. Dividend payments for equity financing could be adjusted and would hence be more flexible, whereas loan financing would require fixed repayment schedules. While risks involved for the foreign company were minimized since the financial outlay required could thus be reduced, effective control could be maintained since stocks were usually sold to a large number of small investors. Thus, by various techniques, such as transfer pricing, licensing and management contracts, surplus value could still be discreetly transferred abroad. Profitable companies could also be identified by foreign and local speculators watching their performance on the stock market. The coming together of local and foreign capital through the medium of the stock market also establishes a commonality of class interests important for foreign capital operations in alien situations.

MIDFL also provided loan funds to investors without seeking management control—an arrangement attractive to any investor. However, restrictive conditions for loan eligibility ensured that mainly large, highly capitalized, often foreign, industries were served, since few local enterprises were big enough to qualify (Drake, 1969: 164). Up to 1967, the MIDFL made 145 loans amounting to $60 million. Of this, however, 64 loans for less than $50,000 each totalled less than $2 million (Drake, 1969: 164). Rather than help finance smaller local industrial enterprises as it was ostensibly intended to, the MIDFL was in effect mainly financing large foreign industries. Although the MIDFL was primarily financed by share capital in its early years, after 1964 the bulk of financing was from the Malaysian government, and to a lesser extent from the International Finance Corporation, following the recommendation of a joint World Bank–IFC mission (Drake, 1969: 161).

Industrial Performance in Malaya

Industrial growth proceeded at a fairly quick pace after independence. The percentage of the Gross Domestic Product in real terms accounted for by manufacturing rose from 8.5 per cent in 1960 to 10.4 per cent in 1965, 13.1 per cent in 1970, and 17.9 per cent in 1982 (David Lim, 1973: 109, Table 7.7; Treasury, 1983: 7). Employment in manufacturing doubled from 135,700 or 6.4 per cent of the labour force in 1957 to 270,000 or 9.2 per cent in 1970, before rising to 796,000 or 15.5 per cent in 1982 (David Lim, 1973: 112, Table 7.8; Treasury, 1983: 9). Nonetheless, in comparison with investments in other sectors, the labour employing capacity of the manufacturing sector was found to be rather low (David Lim, 1975). Edwards (1975: Appendix 3, Table 3) has shown that the number of workers employed per $1 million of final demand in the agricultural sector was about thrice that for the manufacturing sector. At least up to the mid-1960s, industrialization was unable to grow sufficiently so as to reduce the unemployment rate (Wheelwright, 1965). A 1970 report by the Malaysian government's Economic Planning Unit anticipated 'sharply rising unemployment despite output growth of nearly 7 percent a year' (quoted in Edwards, 1975: 318). Large-scale industry grew more rapidly than small-scale industrial enterprise, while those industry groups with high capital utilization rates expanded fastest. Obviously, such trends have tended to be less favourable to employment creation (McTaggart, 1972: 22). Manufacturing output rose at the average annual rate of 17.4 per cent between 1959 and 1968, and even more rapidly between 1968 and 1980 (before the global recession badly hit this sector's growth. Meanwhile, the share of agricultural product processing fell from 28.9 per cent in 1959 to 10.5 per cent in 1968, before rising again to 12.3 per cent of total net manufacturing output in 1982, reflecting the more recent emphasis on resource-based industrialization (David Lim, 1973: 247, Table 12.1; Treasury, 1983: xxvi, Table 3.5).

Most industrial growth between 1959 and 1968 was of an import-substituting nature; while domestic demand expansion was substantial, export expansion was negligible over the period (Hoffmann and Tan, 1975). Government statistics also suggest that the 'rate of exploitation' rose between 1963 and 1968. While employment increased by 50 per cent and total wages and salaries rose by 74 per cent, output value rose 82 per cent and value added 108 per cent (McTaggart, 1972: 10). Regional imbalances have been exacerbated by the tendency for industrial capital to prefer location in already developed areas, except where special considerations, such as access to raw material supplies, determine otherwise.

'Import-substitution' industrialization is often misunderstood in at least one important sense. Generally, such development, rather than eliminate or lessen reliance on imports, usually only succeeds in altering the pattern or nature of imports. As such industries are often little more than assembly and repackaging plants heavily reliant on imported raw materials and equipment,[11] the primary outcome of such industrialization then has been to change the nature of imports from finished goods to unfinished goods and equipment (to 'finish' them). For instance, while the value of local manufactures rose from $444 million to $1,471 million, the value of imported semi-manufactured goods and machinery plus equipment rose from $473 million and $458 million to $768 million and $1,344 million respectively between 1961 and 1971 (Junid, 1975: 80, Table 2.11). David Lim (1973: 253, Figure 12.2) has shown that, between 1959 and 1968, 'the annual rates of growth of the producer-orientated industries as a group tended to decline over the years whereas those for the consumer-orientated industries tended to increase', reflecting the nature of the industrialization that took place. Over the same period, annual growth rates for manufacturing did not display any significant tendency to rise, while annual growth rates of pioneer industries actually declined quite rapidly (David Lim, 1973: 251).

While the aggregative nature of the data does not permit any conclusive assessment of these tendencies, it does suggest the limitations of import-substitution industrialization in a small, 'open' capitalist economy (Hirschman, 1968; Sutcliffe, 1971, 1972). The local market, which defines the scope for import-substitution production, is limited not only by the nation's small population and relatively low average income, but more importantly, by the skewed distribution of wealth and income. The latter results in a national consumption pattern which seriously constrains the potential for import-substitution industrialization.

After the first post-colonial decade's emphasis on import-substituting industrialization, the government's industrial policy shifted to export-oriented industrialization.[12] Faced with the limitations of import-substitution industrialization, this re-direction provided a fresh impetus to the slackening industrial growth rate in the late 1960s. By the early 1970s, export-oriented industries were strongly encouraged as a matter of government policy.

This new emphasis was spurred by the New Economic Policy's commitment to redistribute wealth ownership along ethnic lines within the context of an open industrializing capitalist economy. It was correctly recognized by the authorities that increasing local (including state) ownership of productive assets, especially in primary production, and even reduced foreign ownership (but continued foreign control) of industry were far from incompatible with continued participation in the world capitalist economy.

By the early 1970s, government efforts to attract and encourage export-oriented industries were in full swing. The Federal Industrial Development Authority (FIDA) (now known as the Malaysian Industrial Development Authority, MIDA)—originally proposed for establishment in the mid-1960s, but only activated later in that decade—had sprung into action. Various new measures—notably the establishment of 'free trade zones' (also known as 'export processing zones')—were introduced to facilitate Malaysia's integration into the emerging new international division of labour as transnational enterprises began globally relocating various parts of their production processes in secure locations abroad offering lower wage and other (e.g. energy) costs.

Two main types of export-oriented industries have developed. The first kind—often called resource-based industries—involve the increased processing of older (e.g. rubber, tin) and newer (e.g. palm-oil, timber) primary commodities for export. While there is still considerable scope—from a technical point of view—for expansion in this area, the severe constraints on export prospects due to foreign protection, as well as insurance, transport and other taxes and fees imposed by the dominant economic interests of the industrialized economies of the 'North', continue to favour the export of less-processed raw materials. The other kind of export-oriented industrialization has been far more impressive in terms of growth and employment generation. Typically, it involves the relocation of certain labour-intensive aspects of industrial processes in politically stable and (relatively) low-wage environments such as those offered by the free trade zones in Malaysia and elsewhere in the Western Pacific rim. The most spectacular example of this is, of course, the electronics industry. While the employment-generating consequences of the location of such industries in Malaysia can hardly be denied, it is also important to note other consequences of such industrialization, which further integrates the Malaysian economy into the world capitalist economy, albeit on different terms consistent with the emerging new international division of labour.

Whereas the value of manufactured exports grew from $131 million to $343 million during 1963-9, it jumped to $846 million in 1971 and $6,307 million in 1981. Manufactured exports' share of all exports rose from 4.9 per cent in 1963 to 8.8 per cent in 1969, 16.9 per cent in 1971 and 29.8 per cent in 1983 (see Table 9.1). In examining the indices for industrial production for the period 1968-78 (in the *Monthly Industrial Statistics, Peninsular Malaysia*), there are four specific industry types which have registered average annual growth rates above 15 per cent—namely oil-palm processing (29.6 per cent), electrical appliances and related equipment (24.1 per cent), transport equipment (23.4 per cent), and

TABLE 9.1

Malaysian Manufactured Exports
(Selected Years)

Year	1963	1969	1970	1971	1976	1980	1983
Total manufactured exports ($ million, current prices)	131	343	615	846	2,526	6,107	9,797
Manufactures as percentage of all exports	4.9	8.8	11.9	16.9	18.9	21.7	29.8

Sources: H. Osman-Rani (1982: 270, Table 12.3); Junid (1980: 276, Table 9.15); Malaysia (1984: 49, Table 2.4).

textiles (16.0 per cent) (Osman Rani Hassan, 1980). Furthermore, whereas electrical and electronic machinery and appliances accounted for only 3 per cent (worth about $17 million) of Malaysia's total manufactured exports in 1970, by 1982 these exports accounted for 52 per cent, worth $3,864 million. Meanwhile, exports of textiles, clothing, and footwear rose from $40 million (7 per cent) to $819 million (11 per cent) (Treasury, 1983: Table 3.5).

But the change of strategy from import-substitution to export orientation has apparently affected wage rates, and hence real wages. The *Census of Manufacturing Industries* for the years 1963, 1968, and 1973 provide the most comprehensive data available on wages paid in the industrial sectors in Peninsular Malaysia for the relevant years. Changes over the period 1963-8 can be seen as reflecting the consequences for wage levels of the latter phase of the import-substitution period, while trends in the period 1968-73 may be viewed as the initial outcome of the switch to an export-led industrialization strategy.

Table 9.2 shows the average monthly wage rates of all full-time paid employees for the years 1963, 1968, and 1973, in current and 1968 prices respectively. Wages for factory workers—as expressed in 1968 prices—rose from $125 in 1963 to $132 in 1968 and then declined to $111 in 1973, whereas the average wages for non-factory employees in the manufacturing sector were $305, $346, and $336 respectively. Average monthly wages (in 1968 prices) for all (including part-time) paid workers in the manufacturing sector were $161, $176, and $152 respectively for the relevant years. The increase in real wages between 1963 and 1968 was 5.6 per cent for full-time factory workers, 13.4 per cent for full-time non-factory workers, and 9.3 per cent for all (including part-time) workers in the manufacturing sector, whereas between 1968 and 1973 average real wages actually declined by 15.9 per cent, 2.9 per cent, and 13.6 per cent respectively. It is clear then that wage rates in the manufacturing sector generally rose between 1963 and 1968 and then declined between 1968 and 1973, and that non-factory workers fared relatively better than factory workers in both periods.

Available evidence also suggests increasing inequality in the distribution of wages *within* the manufacturing sector between 1963 and 1973. Taken in conjunction with the preceding observation on the growing differentials between factory and non-factory workers, one may deduce that the share of wages accruing to factory workers has declined relative to that obtained by non-factory workers in the sector. (And if factory labour is identified with productive labour and non-factory labour with unproductive labour, the implications are clear.) According to Table 9.2, wages and salaries as a proportion of value added declined from 0.37 in 1963 to 0.31 in 1968 and to 0.25 in 1973.[13] In Table 9.3, which breaks this down according to the number of full-time paid employees in the enterprise, one can discern a tendency for this proportion to decline as the number of employees increase in those enterprises employing twenty or more workers. For smaller enterprises employing less than twenty, the wage proportion of value added increases with the number of employees, presumably because of the declining significance of unpaid and part-time—usually family—labour utilized as the enterprise size grows.

TABLE 9.2

Average Wages, Value Added and Fixed Assets per Worker
in the Peninsular Malaysian Manufacturing Sector, 1963, 1968, and 1973

		1963	1968	1973
Av. Monthly Wages of All Full-time Paid Factory Workers	(current prices)	119	132	131
	(1968 prices)	125	132	111
Av. Monthly Wages of All Full-time Paid Non-factory Workers	(current prices)	290	346	395
	(1968 prices)	305	346	336
Av. Monthly Wages of All Paid (Full-time & Part-time) Workers	(current prices)	153	176	179
	(1968 prices)	161	176	152
Av. Wages per Worker / Av. Value Added per Worker		0.370	0.305	0.252
Av. Value Added per Worker / Av. Fixed Assets per Worker			0.98	1.01

Sources: Osman Rani Hassan and Jomo Kwame Sundaram (1980), derived from
(i) Census of Manufacturing Industries, 1963, 1968, 1973, and
(ii) Khoo Kay Jin and Ikmal Mohd. Said (1979).

TABLE 9.3

Wages and Salaries as a Proportion of Value Added by Employment
Size of Enterprise for the Manufacturing Sector
in Peninsular Malaysia, 1963, 1968, and 1973

Number of Paid Full-time Employees in the Enterprise	1963	1968	1973
1–4	0.342	0.316	0.285
5–9	0.397	0.363	0.289
10–19	0.424	0.402	0.327
20–29	0.432	0.421	0.304
30–49	0.425	0.369	0.301
50–99	0.365	0.353	0.257
100–199	0.362	0.259	0.244
200–499	0.310	0.270	0.234
500 and above	0.350	0.283	0.240

Source: Osman Rani Hassan and Jomo Kwame Sundaram (1980), calculated from Census of Manufacturing Industries, 1963, 1968, and 1973.
Note: The omission of unpaid and part-time labour from the above is an important qualification especially relevant to family-type enterprises, which tend to employ relatively few full-time paid employees. It is suggested here that this may at least partly explain the apparently lower wage share of value added for firms with the smallest number of employees.

The data offered by the *Monthly Industrial Statistics* is not as comprehensive as the information from the various *Census of Manufacturing Industries* (1963, 1968, 1973) used to obtain Tables 9.2 and 9.3. Nonetheless, Table 9.4 provides some indication of trends after 1973. While total employment in the manufacturing sector rose from 159,259 in 1973 to 296,378 in 1979 and 323,861 in 1983, the export-oriented electronics, textiles, and clothing industries together accounted for 116,789 (39.4 per cent) in 1979 and 135,877 (42.0 per cent) in 1983, with electronics alone accounting for 65,949 (22.3 per cent) in 1979 and 81,936 (25.3 per cent) in 1983. During 1973-9, employment grew by 435.5 per cent in electronics, by 98.2 per cent (17,018) in textiles, and by 107.8 per cent (8,461) in clothing, compared to 47.6 per cent (57,917) for other industries, though growth slackened in the early 1980s. Nevertheless, it is quite clear that the export-oriented industries have contributed significantly to employment growth in the industrial sector.

It is also quite clear from Table 9.4 that the average earnings of employees in these three export-oriented industries were below the average for the manufacturing sector as a whole. While wages in these industries have risen slightly higher than in other industries, in 1979 they continued to be below the average for the manufacturing sector as a whole. The ratio of earnings in these export-oriented industries to earnings in other manufacturing industries improved only slightly over the period, and this may well be due to the influence of other export-oriented industries categorized under 'Others'.

Perhaps, most significantly, if the growing inequality of earnings within the manufacturing sector itself—already noted above for the period 1963-73—continues to widen thereafter, it is very possible that a substantial portion of the

TABLE 9.4

Employment and Earnings in the Peninsular Malaysian Manufacturing Sector, 1973-1983

Industry	1973 (June) Employment (No.)	1973 (June) Average Monthly Earnings ($)	1973 (June) As Percentage of Sectoral Average	1979 (June) Per Cent Employment Increase 1973-9	1979 (June) Employment (No.)	1979 (June) Avg Monthly Earnings Current Prices ($)	1979 (June) 1973 Prices ($)	1979 (June) As Percentage of Sectoral Average	1983 (June) Per Cent Employment Increase 1973-83	1983 (June) Employment (No.)	1983 (June) Avg Monthly Earnings Current Prices ($)	1983 (June) 1973 Prices ($)	1983 (June) As Percentage of Sectoral Average
Electronics and electrical goods	12,316	165.56	87.3	435.5	65,949	295.46	203.79	92.3	565.3	81,936	517.90	282.52	98.8
Textiles	17,425	126.89	66.9	88.2	34,533	243.48	167.94	76.0	87.6	32,697	374.83	204.47	71.5
Clothing	7,846	104.00	54.8	107.8	16,307	191.82	132.31	59.9	170.8	21,244	322.82	176.10	61.7
Others	121,672	206.67	108.9	47.6	179,589	355.76	245.38	111.1	54.5	187,984	575.31	313.84	109.8
Total Manufacturing	159,259	189.70	100.0	86.1	296,378	320.24	220.88	100.0	103.35	323,861	523.98	285.83	100.0

Sources: Monthly Industrial Statistics (various issues).

Note: The Official Consumer Price Index (1967: 100) for 1973, 1979 and 1983 were 117.6, 170.5, and 215.6 respectively.

real increase in earnings noted for the manufacturing sector as a whole, and for the export-oriented industries in particular, may actually accrue to the relatively few high-earning managerial and technical personnel.

It is clear from the foregoing that real wage levels in the manufacturing sector in Peninsular Malaysia rose between 1963 and 1968 and then declined over the next half decade. It is generally agreed that the former period is identifiable with the mature phase of the import-substitution era in Malaysian industrialization, while the latter period represents the first phase of the subsequent export-oriented industrialization era. It is suggested that the wage trends described above can be explained as a direct result of the change in industrialization strategy, which also entailed greater curbs imposed upon labour.

Import-substitution has by and large involved the domestic assembly, packaging, and final processing of finished goods—previously imported from abroad—by domestic labour operating machines still largely imported from abroad. The employment-generating ability of such industrialization has generally been limited by the typically 'capital-intensive' foreign technology appropriated, and also by the small domestic market available for the relevant goods as determined by the limited and skewed purchasing capacity of the population. In these circumstances, capital in such industries has generally been more capable of conceding real wage increases to labour since the wage bill accounted for a relatively small proportion of the costs of production.

In contrast, the success of export-oriented industrialization has been partly contingent on the state's ability to attract foreign investors seeking to lower production, especially labour, costs in order to be more competitive on the international market (see Table 9.5). It is precisely because of their use of 'labour-intensive' production techniques that these industries tend to be more employment-generating (in a direct sense) as well as more sensitive to changes in the wage bill. A considerable number of such industries, often characterized as 'footloose', are easily capable of relocation elsewhere if sufficiently deterred by domestic conditions or sufficiently attracted by circumstances there.

TABLE 9.5

Average Hourly Earnings in Electronics and Garment Manufacturing
Industries in Selected Countries
(US$)

Country	Year	Electronics	Garments
Hong Kong	1980	0.97	1.03
Korea	1980	0.91	0.59
Malaysia	1980	0.42	–
Philippines	1978	0.30	0.17
Singapore	1980	0.90	0.80
Sri Lanka	1981	–	0.12
Japan	1980	5.97	3.56
USA	1980	6.96	4.57

Source: Gus Edgren, *Spearheads of Industrialisation or Sweatshops in the Sun? A Critical Appraisal Of Labour Conditions In Asian Export Processing Zones*, ILO ARTEP, Thailand, 1982, p. 17.

Therefore, the proponents of an export-oriented industrialization strategy, hinging primarily on being able to attract and retain certain industries, are necessarily committed to policies maintaining a relatively low-wage, 'disciplined' labour force, and other aspects of a 'stable and attractive investment climate'. Although a low-wage policy does not completely preclude the possibility of real wage increases, its compelling logic tends to keep wages low and even to depress real wage levels—as was the case in Peninsular Malaysia between 1968 and 1973. Given the state's continuing commitment to an export-oriented industrialization strategy (since the late 1960s), the apparent rise in the real wage after 1973 has probably been preceded by at least a commensurate increase in labour productivity. As was also found for the 1968–73 period, an increasing capital intensity in relation to labour productivity (as measured by the ratio of fixed assets to value added per worker) does not in itself ensure real wage increases.[14] More precisely, the wage increases after 1973 probably reflect the improved bargaining position of labour, due primarily to the declining unemployment rate in the labour force, at least until 1980, after which real wage levels declined once again as unemployment began to rise again as labour laws and government policies towards labour tightened up.

Ownership and Control

The issue of ownership and control of the industrial sector has understandably generated much interest and concern. Contrary to the popular view (IBRD, 1956) of Chinese-dominated small industrial enterprise dominating the manufacturing sector, J. J. Puthucheary (1960) found that in Singapore's manufacturing sector, large firms dominated, while European companies were very significant in terms of market share and even employment. In the absence of similar data for the peninsula, Puthucheary suggested that the ownership pattern there was probably not too different. This was confirmed by Wheelwright (1965), who found that the top 156 companies there in 1959 accounted for more than half of all sales and employed about a third of the sector's labour force. Foreign dominance was pronounced with half the share capital in the top 83 companies being owned overseas.

Compared to foreign capital, local capital has historically tended to limit its activity to the national and, at most, the regional economy. Quite naturally, it had a particular interest in import-substituting industrial growth. New policies were introduced in the 1960s which, while continuing to encourage and benefit foreign investment, sought to impose certain conditions in the interest of local capital. Thus, for example, the government began to demand local equity participation in industrial ventures initiated by foreign capital, especially in those producing for the local market. Joint ventures with local capitalists were especially encouraged, as was the floating of public companies in which local investors could purchase shares. It has been said that an unwritten condition of the 1968 Act was to require pioneer companies to have a minimum of 51 per cent local ownership (Lo, 1972: 90). However, it still remains unclear whether increasing local ownership actually had any significant impact in terms of increasing local control over these industries. Needless to say, local participation in the ownership of these industrial ventures has been limited to the small minority in a position to invest.[15]

The pattern of concentration and foreign dominance in the manufacturing sector mentioned above has been confirmed by other studies. The World Bank report on the occasion of the formation of Malaysia noted that the top 2 per cent of manufacturing firms accounted for 40 per cent of value added (IBRD, 1963: 27). The *First Malaysia Plan* (Malaysia, 1965: 124) observed that 60 per cent of new manufacturing output came from firms employing at least 50 workers, i.e. only 4 per cent of all manufacturing establishments. Hirschman[16] (1971) confirmed that while most manufacturing establishments are quite small, the sector is dominated by a few relatively large establishments. Furthermore, this pattern of dominance has become more pronounced over time. Firms with annual sales of over $1 million comprised less than 5 per cent of all establishments and accounted for two-thirds of the sales of manufactured goods, whereas over 75 per cent of all manufacturing firms had less than $100,000 worth of sales in any year. The 97 largest establishments with over 200 employees accounted for over 35 per cent of sales and 38 per cent of value added, while two-thirds of all establishments had less than 5 paid full-time employees each. While 85 per cent of establishments were found to be either individual proprietorships or partnerships, limited companies comprised 10 per cent of all establishments and accounted for 76 per cent of all sales. And although citizens owned 94 per cent of all manufacturing establishments, these firms accounted for only 52 per cent of sales and also of value added.

Recent data [17] indicate that while foreign firms accounted for only 15 per cent of the 3,685 enumerated firms, they employed a third of all workers, possessed 49 per cent of all fixed assets, and accounted for 56 per cent of total value added. The average assets per foreign firm were worth $1.5 million, almost six times as much as the local firm average of $270,000. The average number of workers per $1,000 of assets was 489 for local firms and 44 for foreign firms, reflecting the greater 'labour-intensity' of techniques utilized by local firms.[18] There also seems to be a strong correlation between foreign investment and the degree of concentration in an industry (Edwards, 1975: Section 5.3).

Sieh's (1977) study of the official shareholders lists of the largest 98 Malaysian-incorporated companies engaged in manufacturing during 1974-5 revealed an extremely high degree of concentration of equity capital in a small number of large holdings, with an overall Gini coefficient of 0.91. One per cent of the over 100,000 shareholders accounted for almost 80 per cent of the shares held, worth a total of about $1,200 million. Overall ownership is divided fairly evenly between citizens and foreigners, but while local holdings tend to be small and scattered, foreign investors usually maintain controlling interests, so that foreign control tends to exceed the foreign share of ownership, even when owning less than a majority share.

The rates of reinvestment of firms have also been compared in terms of nationality of ownership by Hirschman[19] (1971: 26, 30, Table 6). He found that, for 1968, Malaysian-owned manufacturing establishments had a reinvestment rate of 26 per cent; Singapore-owned establishments were slightly lower at 21 per cent while British and American establishments were much lower at 13 per

cent and 11 per cent respectively. Khor (1979: 192, Table 4.4) found the annual
reinvestment rates[20] of local firms and foreign subsidiaries and branches to be
200 per cent and 34 per cent respectively on average during 1967–72. Hirschman
(1971: 27, 30, Table 7) calculated the ratio of 1967 investments to 1966 profits to
be 142 per cent for locally controlled firms, 5 per cent for foreign-controlled
firms, and 12 per cent for branches of foreign companies. (Using figures for
1967 profits as well as 1967 investments instead, the ratios were 89 per cent, 5
per cent, and 2 per cent respectively.) Similarly, for pioneer industries for the
late 1960s, Lindenberg (1973: 203) found:

Ownership	1967 Investments 1966 Profits	1968 Investments 1967 Profits	1969 Investments 1968 Profits
Malaysian	69.2	94.8	67.4
Foreign	17.0	5.8	3.2
Total	22.0	9.6	13.6

In 1972, for instance, foreign firms in manufacturing accounted for 52 per
cent of sales, 75 per cent of gross profits, and 84 per cent of net profits in
manufacturing; the average gross profit rate was 8.2 per cent for local
manufacturing firms compared to 15.7 per cent for foreign firms, while the
average net profit rates were 3.9 per cent and 9.6 per cent respectively (Khor,
1979: 190, Table 4.3).[21] These figures reflect not only the higher profitability of
foreign companies, but also the lower incidence of taxation to which they were
subject in Malaysia. It is highly probable that there has been a net outflow
abroad of funds from the manufacturing sector in Malaysia[22] (Edwards,
1975: 329).

Lindenberg (1973) studied the pioneer industry programme over the
duration of the First Malaysia Plan, i.e. from 1965 to 1970. Pioneer firms
qualified for a good many privileges from the Malaysian government and
accounted for a substantial portion of the industrial growth during the Plan
period: 64 per cent of gross sales value, 62 per cent of value added, and 43 per
cent of new employment; also, more than 12 per cent of the increase in gross
national product was attributable to pioneer industries. As of 1968, pioneer
industries were less labour-intensive than the manufacturing sector as a whole
(McTaggart, 1972: 13). The development of pioneer industries tended to
consolidate the pre-existing racial composition of the capitalist class as, in fact,
they did not fulfil the government stipulation that 10 per cent of the shares
should be in Malay control. In fact, in 1968, less than 1 per cent of shares in these
firms were held by Malays. In general, Lindenberg found foreign pioneer firms
less likely than local pioneer firms to provide Malays with ownership and
directorship opportunities. In his 1968 sample, 77.1 per cent of shares in pioneer
firms were held by foreigners, a percentage greater than the foreign share in
manufacturing as a whole, which was 59.6 per cent in 1970 (Malaysia, 1973: 83,
Table 4.7).

Joint ventures and fully foreign-owned industries demonstrably dominated
the growth of pioneer industries.[23] Local participation was quite limited and

involved mainly Chinese capitalists from major family and ownership groups, many of whom had 'political connections'. The few Malay directors were drawn mainly from the top echelons of the civil service and from among prominent politicians, with some even holding directorships in several companies (Grace, 1976). In other words, the pattern of concentration of ownership which emerged and became identified with the colonial era was extending into the emergent manufacturing sector as well.

Ownership and control are no longer—if they ever were—directly related in the contemporary epoch of monopoly capital. International monopoly corporations utilize their organizational and technical superiority to effectively control foreign subsidiaries even when in a position of minority ownership. In such situations, it is common for the appropriation of surplus value to take place via means other than the 'normal' distribution of profits, as in the form of dividends. David Lim suggests that a great variety of means are utilized by foreign firms to transfer surplus value discreetly out of Malaysia[24] (see Edwards, 1975; and Khor, 1983b). These practices are being developed routinely all over the world by transnational corporations whose interests are sometimes contrary to or constrained by the policies and interests of host governments, or their local business partners. Thus, the decreasing proportion of foreign ownership, e.g. in the corporate sector of the economy, involves the replacement of equity-based control (through direct investments) by organizational and technical control as the means to ensure the outflow of surplus value.

The Post-colonial State and Labour

In its professed role of promoting the interests of particular capitals, the state intervenes, mediates and often defines the terms of the relationship between labour and capital. In doing this, it attempts to simultaneously serve two, sometimes contradictory, ends: while it facilitates the process of capital accumulation by maintaining the conditions for continued exploitation, it also seeks legitimacy as the embodiment of the collective social interest. During both the colonial and post-colonial periods in Malaya, however, the priorities of the state have clearly emphasized the former. To create an environment attractive to investors, restriction and control of labour, dating from the colonial era, have been continued by the post-colonial state.

Trade unions were never officially recognized by the colonial authorities before 1940 (Gamba, 1962). Mounting labour and nationalist militancy in the immediate post-war period led to the colonial government's declaration of a state of 'Emergency' in mid-1948 (Stenson, 1970; Morgan, 1977; Caldwell, 1977c). By the end of that year, government deregistration of the more militant unions and other repressive measures had reduced total trade union membership to about a third of what it had been at the beginning of that year (Edwards, 1975: Appendix 4). While independent union organization was discouraged by various government measures, 'responsible' unions were being groomed under colonial tutelage.[25] Fresh legislation was introduced by the British authorities to further curb labour agitation and the unions: for example, the Trade Disputes Ordinance of 1949 severely curtailed the right of workers to strike, while the Employment Ordinance of 1955 provided for summary dismissal of workers on vague grounds of 'misconduct'. In 1956 and 1957, the government deregistered 45 unions. Despite all this, union membership grew and strikes increased. Meanwhile, the prospects for independence were becoming increasingly imminent.

In 1959, the post-colonial Malayan government passed the Trade Union Ordinance which embodied previous legislation passed since the declaration of Emergency in 1948. Another declaration of a state of emergency during the period of *konfrontasi* with Indonesia from 1963 to 1966 also saw the reimposition of many of the severe restrictions of the previous Emergency. Further labour legislation was introduced in 1965, including requiring compulsory arbitration (i.e. effectively limiting the right to strike) for a wide range of 'essential services', with the definition of 'essential services' including even the pineapple industry among others. Government employees were effectively barred from industrial action following several disputes involving railway, postal and fire-fighting service workers. The Industrial Relations Act of 1967 subsequently incorporated and tightened up existing legislation regarding industrial disputes.

After bloody communal riots broke out in May 1969, a third state of emergency was declared. In October, the government introduced amendments to the Industrial Relations Act to preclude issues, such as management rights regarding dismissal and transfers, from negotiation, etc. Procedures for collective bargaining and for settlement of industrial disputes by conciliation and arbitration were stipulated. In 1971, when Parliament was reconvened for the first time after the May 1969 post-election riots, these and other regulations were incorporated into new legislation of fairly comprehensive scope including among other things, specific provisions to prevent union officials from being office-bearers in political parties and unions from having political funds.[26] The 1971 legislation further limits the right to strike[27] (e.g. by designating various issues, such as union recognition, as 'non-strikable' issues), extends the power of management (e.g. by not requiring employers to state reasons for dismissal), fragments labour unity, bolsters 'responsible' unions and curbs the emergence of new independent unions (e.g. strengthening the powers of the authorities concerned in matters such as union registration).

There is still no minimum-wage legislation in Malaysia. The government's Malaysian (formerly Federal) Industrial Development Authority assures investors in pioneer industries of safeguards during their first five years of existence or 'for any such extended period' against 'unreasonable demands' from unions (FIDA, 1975: 13-14). While there is no legislation explicitly prohibiting unions in pioneer industries,[28] as is sometimes mistakenly alleged, it is indeed telling that the many workers in the electronics assembly industry, which has existed in the country since the end of the 1960s, still remain completely non-unionized.[29] In general, state actions have been consistently pro-capital, although efforts are made to project a neutral image, ostensibly presenting these undertakings as in the 'national interest'.

The nature and implications of industrial relations legislation accurately conveys the state's interests in mediating relations between capital and labour. The latest round of legislative amendments is sufficient to dispel any doubts about the state's role in these matters. The thrust of these amendments, apparently in response to the historic Malaysian Airlines System (MAS) industrial disputes of 1978-9, set the stage for the role envisaged for labour in the country's development strategy for the 1980s, which, by the government's own admission, is unlikely to be fundamentally different from that pursued into the 1970s. When unions—already docile by international standards—need to be further circumscribed, this can no longer be dismissed as 'irrational overkill'; on the contrary, the amendments represent a somewhat systematic effort to anticipate and curb all possible threats to the industrial order envisaged for the 1980s.

In the early 1980s, even more official emphasis has been given to increasing productivity, as well as labour discipline and subservience, in the context of a selective attempt to emulate Japanese economic practices, especially in the area of industrial relations. This campaign has largely involved appeals for labour to 'cooperate' with management, accept greater discipline and work harder, though little mention is made of the various material incentives enjoyed by privileged Japanese workers.

Hence, labour can be expected to be more 'disciplined' than ever in the 1980s (e.g. as manifested by the number of man-days lost because of industrial actions) because of the threatened consequences for behaving otherwise. Despite the increased importance of even the docile 'responsible' unions on narrow economic issues this does not necessarily signify the end of the labour movement. The circumstances imposed by legislation may actually backfire and engender a more militant (and political) challenge to capital and the state, as 'moderate' union leaders have been warning the government.

Summary

Industrialization in the colonial period was constrained by the domination of British commercial capital. The processing of raw materials for export and other industries enjoying 'natural protection' developed in this context. When domination by foreign capital was temporarily weakened, e.g. during the Depression, nationally-oriented industries sprouted, though in the colonial context, such trends were always shortlived.

Post-colonial industrial policy initially sought to promote import-substituting industrialization, a strategy resulting in some change in the composition of imports, with finished goods giving way to means of production and unfinished goods (e.g. unassembled car parts). With the exhaustion of these opportunities by the late 1960s, the state switched to an export-oriented industrialization policy. This recent emphasis on export-oriented growth has broadened the Malaysian economy's ties to the world economy, adding manufactures to the older list of exports comprising mainly raw materials.

On the advice of foreign consultants, the post-colonial state has encouraged industrialization, primarily by creating 'hot house' conditions to protect new industries. A variety of incentives have been proffered by the government to promote industry. Besides direct and indirect forms of subsidy (e.g. by preparing industrial estates and by making available easy loan facilities at low interest rates), the government also employs tariff and taxation policies towards this end. To ensure an attractive 'investment climate', it has developed a variety of measures, including labour legislation, to facilitate the disciplining of industrial labour and to minimize the wage bill for the industrial capitalists.

Foreign capital has successfully extended its domination of the Malaysian economy to the manufacturing sector. While some agency houses and some other capitalists involved in commerce or raw material production have made the transition to industry, much of the new industry also involves capital previously uninvolved in the Malaysian scene (e.g. electronics). However, while foreign control in the industrial sector is quite secure, this is not necessarily reflected in the pattern of ownership. In fact, foreign ownership of assets in manufacturing may decline as foreign industrial capital becomes increasingly capable of exercising control through its technological and organizational advantages. On the whole, while the post-colonial industrialization impulse was partly promoted by local capitalist interests—which had long been frustrated by the colonial state—industrial capital has successfully turned the new opportunities to its advantage.

Although the colonial and post-colonial state have discouraged labour unionization, when this has been inevitable they have sought to weaken the unions through segmentation by trade and enterprise on the one hand and by patronizing 'responsible' leaders with conciliatory and economistic orientations on the other. Even though import-substitution generated relatively few employment opportunities, the relative capital intensity of the operations involved allowed real wage rates to rise. The subsequent switch in the late 1960s to export-oriented industrialization initially depressed the real wage rate because low wages and production costs were the main attraction for international capital's relocation in countries like Malaysia. However, as the unemployment level fell in the mid-1970s, real wages began to rise again, before the recession of the early 1980s caused unemployment to rise and depressed real wages once more.

1. Edwards (1975: Section 6.7) has shown how the freight rate structure of various Western-dominated shipping conferences and the tariff system of the consuming industrialized economies discouraged the further processing of raw materials in Malaya.

2. The existence of such light engineering—mainly for assembly, repair, and maintenance—would repudiate the claim that export-oriented primary production in a colonial context is intrinsically antithetical to industrialization. Nevertheless, the nature of such development reflects the basic external orientation of production in such an 'open' economy. Production is either directly for export or to serve the needs of the export sector (see Thoburn, 1975b).

3. The influential World Bank Report of 1955 stated:

'... very small enterprises is the rule.... With only a score or so of important exceptions, the capital, management and skill in Malayan industrial enterprises are Asian. European capital had tended to concentrate on the plantation, mines and commerce of Malaya, while the Chinese have taken a leading part in the industry' (IBRD, 1955: 305).

4. 'There is evidence to suggest that, in the middle and late 1960s, peninsular Malaya was approaching the end of the import-substitution phase of industrialization and was seeking to move into the second, and more difficult, phase of industrial growth' (Courtenay, 1972: 173).

5. Such an industrial orientation has been very strongly advocated by several foreign and local economists. For example, see David Lim (1973); Kasper (1974); and David Lim (1975: Parts 4 and 5). Such a position is usually accompanied by a plea for continued foreign investment.

6. One specific result has been that the post-tax profitability of British manufacturing companies in Malaya between 1955 and 1964 was substantially greater than that of British companies in the rest of the world. The subgroup 'other manufacturing' in Malaya had a post-tax profitability almost thrice that for the world as a whole, while the ratio in other manufacturing subgroups, including food, chemical and electrical engineering products, was almost twice (see David Lim, 1973: 264, Table 12.8).

7. Calculated from Department of Statistics (1975a: 5, Table F).

8. The Malaysian Treasury (1973: 36) noted 'a tendency for the price of some commodities under tariff protection to increase towards the price of similar imported commodities which had been subjected to a high import duty'.

9. Focusing on the car assembly industry, for example, Edwards (1975: 342) concludes that 'Malaysia would gain if the plants were closed down, the cars imported under the present tariff structure and the employees paid from the tariff proceeds for doing nothing'.

Since food price increases in the early 1970s have been higher than general price rises (40 per cent and 28 per cent respectively between 1970 and 1974), lower-income groups have presumably been the hardest hit by the inflationary situation (Edwards, 1975: 319). In so far as food and beverage processing has been an important component of industrial growth under protection, it may be suggested that the industrial promotion policy has affected the low-income classes adversely in this respect.

10. The author is grateful to A. Ritchie for his insights on the nature and role of the MIDFL.

11. It has been suggested by David Lim (1973: Chapter 12) 'that the overall rate of growth of the producer-oriented industries was considerably greater than that of the consumer-oriented industries'. Further, he notes that the former group tends to have greater linkages—both backward and forward—with other industries in the national economy. However, it is unclear what bearing these have on the argument that much import-substituting industrialization has been heavily reliant on imported inputs. Of the producer-oriented industries considered by Lim, the group 'basic metals and metal products', primarily meaning tin, is almost entirely for export, whereas 'non-metallic mineral products', mainly petroleum and its products, were largely imported in crude form during the period considered. This suggests that export-oriented raw material processing continued to play an important role in industrial growth in the post-war period.

12. In 1974, $2,000 million worth of goods manufactured in Malaysia were exported (Grace, 1976).

13. The decline in wage levels between 1968 and 1973 after the rise in wages between 1963 and 1968 also begs explanation. Unfortunately, available information does not permit any conclusive findings on this matter. An orthodox neo-classical economist, however, might suggest that this can be explained by a rise in the marginal productivity of labour in the first period and its subsequent decline in the second.

Other traditions in economics would offer different explanations for the observed wage trends. It is suggested that the following factors are probably of relevance in this matter. As pointed out earlier, the 1963-8 period represents the mature phase of the import-substitution period. Since this strategy has generally been associated with 'capital-intensive' industries employing relatively little labour, it would be more likely in these circumstances to expect industrial capital to concede real wage increases since the wage bill would then typically comprise a relatively small proportion of production costs. In the second period, with the advent of export-oriented industrialization—usually identifiable with more 'labour-intensive' industries—one can reasonably expect the converse to be the case, i.e. that capital can be expected to seek to depress real wage rates, though not necessarily money wage rates (as expressed in current prices). Hence, in Table 9.2, one finds the average monthly wage rate to be $132 and $111 respectively in real price terms.

Another factor which probably has some bearing on this matter relates to the particular inflationary experience identified with the year 1973. After many years of low inflation, the price index rose rather dramatically from 1973. While this may have some significance for the estimation of the deflator index for 1973, the important point here is that labour may not have had sufficient time and opportunity to try to offset the price increases in the wage rate. The time issue may have been significant in the unusual inflationary circumstances of 1973, and if it is the case, it can reasonably be expected that the dramatic decrease in real wages between 1968 and 1973 would be somewhat ameliorated in subsequent years, for which strictly comparable data is not yet available.

However, the time factor may not be very relevant if the strength of labour relative to capital (and the state, of course) diminished. The preceding discussion of trends in industrial relations legislation suggests that this may well be the case. Again, there is no way to prove this conclusively, but information on the unionization of employees (especially in the manufacturing sector), incidence of strikes, and number of man-days lost in the post-colonial period is highly suggestive. In this connection, it is worthwhile to note that the major decreases in real wages apparently occurred between 1969 and 1970 (5.3 per cent) and then between 1971 and 1972 (6.5 per cent). The real average monthly incomes of directly employed factory workers (in 1967 prices) for the years from 1968 to 1973 were $132 (1968), $133 (1969), $126 (1970), $124 (1971), $116 (1972), and $112 (1973) respectively.

In other words, the industrial relations environment, which has been increasingly unfavourable to labour, can be expected to continue to inhibit wage increments, especially those which would offer real wage increases. In this regard, a continued commitment to 'labour-intensive' export-oriented industrialization can be expected to frustrate efforts to raise real wages. For instance, the tremendous growth of the electronics industry in Malaysia has mainly involved non-unionized female labour whose real wage gains, if any, have apparently not been commensurate with their productivity increases.

14. The real issue here is, what meaning to attribute to all this. A significant tendency in the classical economic tradition, based on the labour theory of value, measures capitalist economic exploitation in terms of the rate of surplus value (S/V) which is the ratio of surplus value created (S) to the value of variable capital (or the wage bill) involved (V). This is, of course, formulated in abstract value terms and not in terms of prices. However, it may be suggested that 'value added minus wages' may be used as an imprecise but perhaps suggestive price indicator of surplus value. (This exercise should be done with great reservation as there are other serious methodological issues involved as well, e.g. the method of computation of value added used by those preparing official statistics and the disregard for the problems raised by 'transfer pricing'. If so, the decline in the wages and salaries (W) proportion of total value added (X) between 1963 and 1973 suggests a probable increase in the rate of surplus value (S/V) over the period. The findings from Table 9.3 then suggest that for medium and large industrial enterprises and probably for small ones as well— if unpaid and part-time family labour is taken into account—there appears to be a tendency for this rate to increase with the number of employees in the enterprise concerned.

It can, of course, be argued that the preceding argument is predicated on a particular perspective in economics and that the trends noted with regard to the declining wage share of value added can be alternatively explained by the increasing capital-labour ratio observable between 1963 and 1973 (and this can again be misleadingly 'demonstrated' by reference to the declared prices of fixed assets in relation to the wage bill). In this connection, it is often stressed, for example, that the capital-labour ratio generally tends to rise with enterprise size in the Malaysian manufacturing sector, and that this can provide an alternative interpretation of the second tendency discussed above. It is undoubtedly true, of course, that there is a fundamental difference of approach and method involved, though it is not possible to engage in the relevant debates here. It is sufficient, however, to observe here that the declining wage share of value added has been accompanied by a rising ratio of value added to fixed assets per worker. For instance, as shown in Table 9.2, this ratio rose from 0.98 in 1968 to 1.01 in 1973.

15. Recent work by Hirschman (1971), Lindenberg (1973), Lim Mah Hūi (1980), Tan Tat Wai (1977), and Sieh (1977) point to a high degree of concentration of ownership in the national economy in general and in manufacturing in particular. Concentration of control is even greater.

16. Hirschman utilized the 1968 *Census of Manufacturing Industries* and the 1967 *Report on the Financial Survey of Limited Companies* to obtain a picture of the ownership pattern in the Malayan

manufacturing sector and to compare rates of reinvestment by nationality of ownership.

17. Recent trends in foreign investment in manufacturing have been surveyed by Khor (1983b). An earlier observation still seems relevant:

'Foreign investment in manufacturing is growing rapidly alongside that of the Chinese. Until the 1975 recession, foreign companies had invested nearly $300 million in manufacturing or about 45 per cent of all paid-up capital. Much of this investment had come in the past years and for different reasons. Some finance had come in because of various tax incentives. Other investment was seeking availability of raw materials. And some of it was seeking availability of low wage labor. In any event, in the early 1970s Malaysian industrial growth was heavily dependent on this foreign capital' (Grace, 1976).

18. See also David Lim (1973: 159) and Edwards (1975: 334).

19. Ratio of net capital expenditure (purchase of new and used fixed assets minus sale of fixed assets) to operating surplus (value added minus wages and salaries) for Hirschman.

20. The rate of reinvestment is defined here as the ratio between net fixed investment and net profits (Khor, 1979: 193). The 200 per cent average annual rate of reinvestment implies that local companies were not only ploughing back all their profits for further productive activity, but were also borrowing an equivalent amount to invest.

21. For 1972, the average gross profit rate was 11.6 per cent for all local firms and 22.8 per cent for foreign firms, while the corresponding net profit rates were 5.6 per cent and 14.4 per cent respectively. While the foreign companies' share of all assets was 50 per cent, they enjoyed 66 per cent of gross profits and 72 per cent of net profits (Khor, 1979: 190, Table 4.3).

22. The available data does not readily lend itself to precise measurement of this phenomenon. For example, Edwards (1975) has emphasized the significance of transfer pricing in obscuring such empirical verification. Emphasizing the distinction between ownership and control of industrial enterprises, he suggests that the incidence of transfer pricing is probably greatest in joint ventures, the result being a higher actual profit rate for foreign capitalists than for local partners.

23. New foreign corporations were attracted by new opportunities for investment, though those established during the colonial era were not to be left out. Not only did agency houses turn to investments in the protected manufacturing sector, e.g. Harrisons and Crosfield moved into the cement industry and Sime Darby into paints, but even rubber estate companies diversified, e.g. Dunlop started tyre production for the national market.

24. '... there have been instances where foreign investors have made immense profits by charging exorbitant prices for capital and technology by passing reconditioned second-hand and technologically obsolete machinery as new.... Every year about $350 million are recorded as being remitted overseas though the actual amount must be considerably greater than this. The practice of over-invoicing and underbilling, the retention of export proceeds by parent companies abroad and the remittance to West Malaysian branches only that amount required by the local management, and the exploitation of whatever deficiencies that exist in the West Malaysian tax system are only some of the other ways in which capital can be transferred out of West Malaysia' (David Lim, 1973: 265).

25. The most important success in this regard was the amalgamation of several regional estate unions to form the National Union of Plantation Workers (NUPW), which remains the largest union in the country to this day.

'According to a Government report, the Union (NUPW) maintained a cordial relationship with the Department of Labour.... Employers also welcomed this union, presumably because of its "responsible" and non-militant attitude...' (Ali Raza, 1969: 358).

26. Besides legislation specifically directed at labour, a host of other laws also serve to limit the power of labour. For example, the Internal Security Act (1960) consolidated regulations passed during the colonial period allowing for unlimited detention without trial of persons deemed to be security risks.

27. 'It is not surprising then that any action taken by the unions is likely to be illegal. The 1972 Annual Report of the Malayan Employers' Consultative Association listed industrial action taken against its members and in every case the industrial action was claimed by the Annual Report to be illegal' (Edwards, 1975: Appendix 4).

28. Legislation does exist requiring key trade union officials to have been employed in the industry concerned for at least three years.

29. The *New Straits Times* of 28 April 1977 reported the refusal of the Labour Ministry to permit the Electrical Industry Workers' Union (EIWU) to unionize the 33,000 predominantly female work-force in the industry then on the grounds that the EIWU catered for a different category of workers, even though the International Labour Organization approves of the grouping of electrical and electronics workers in the same union. As of late 1982, electronics industry workers in the country remain non-unionized.

10

THE ASCENDANCE OF THE STATIST CAPITALISTS[1]

Politics and the Post-colonial State

WITH the achievement of independence in Malaya on 31 August 1957, the Alliance—a coalition of the United Malays National Organization (UMNO), the Malayan Chinese Association (MCA), and the Malayan Indian Congress (MIC)—took over the reins of government of the new nation. UMNO had emerged in 1946 as a coalition of different Malay organizations formed specifically in opposition to the British proposal to establish a Malayan Union for the perpetuation of colonial rule. After its left-wing, largely in the form of the Malay Nationalist Party (Parti Kebangsaan Melayu Malaya or PKMM) broke away to later organize the Malay-based Pusat Tenaga Rakyat (PUTERA) coalition, UMNO—led by the so-called Malay 'administocrats'[2]—increasingly symbolized what has been termed 'moderate' Malay nationalism. As the independence of Malaya became inevitable, the British initially supported the Independence of Malaya Party (IMP), and later the Partai Negara (PN). Both these parties were closely identified with Dato' Onn Jaafar, UMNO's founder president who had resigned in 1951. But, unlike UMNO, which was persistent in its demand for a politically independent non-communist Malaya, neither the IMP nor the PN was successful in mobilizing much Malay support. Eventually, realizing they were backing sure losers, the British swung over to UMNO.

Paving the way for independence were severe repressive measures taken against the more militant anti-imperialists, including radical Malay nationalists, most of whom were associated with the PKMM which was banned in 1948. Its youth wing, Angkatan Pemuda Insaf (API) was the first political organization to be banned in early 1948. In that year, the British colonial government began conducting a counter-insurgency campaign—euphemistically called the 'Emergency'—against radical nationalist guerrillas led by the Communist Party of Malaya (Parti Komunis Malaya or PKM). Not until the mid-1950s—in the twilight of British rule, but also after the height of the Emergency was over—did the colonial authorities permit the legal organization of radical Malay nationalist political groupings in the form of the Partai Rakyat. By this time, however, UMNO's hegemony had been established among the Malays and its credibility was greatly enhanced by the achievement of political independence from formal colonial rule in 1957.

The MCA was formed in the late 1940s after the declaration of the Emergency as an anti-communist alternative to the predominantly Chinese PKM (see M. Roff, 1965). From its inception, it has tended to reflect the interests of big Chinese businessmen; hence limiting its following among other classes in the Chinese community from the outset. The MIC, too, was formed in the late 1940s and went through various 'radical' twists and 'pan-Indian' turns before emerging in the mid-1950s as a moderate party led by Indian professionals and businessmen.[3]

After the formation of an electoral coalition between the UMNO and the MCA to contest the Kuala Lumpur municipal elections in the early 1950s, the Alliance Party—its three components claiming to represent the three major ethnic communities in Malaya—was formed and soon put to the test in the 1955 general election which it won overwhelmingly in a limited electorate. In the next general election four years later, two years after independence, major inroads were made by opposition parties—primarily the Pan-Malayan Islamic Party (Partai Islam SeMalaya or PAS) in the northern States, and the Socialist Front[4] (SF) in the larger west coast towns.

The formation in 1963 of the Malaysian federation incorporating most of Britain's former colonial realm in South-East Asia (except Brunei) led to a state of 'confrontation' with the Indonesian government under Sukarno,[5] providing the pretext for further repression of the Left in Malaya which had viewed the formation of the new federation as serving British 'neo-colonial' designs (Wheelwright, 1974). Portrayed as national traitors collaborating with the Indonesian enemy, the SF suffered badly in the 1964 election. Even after the end of confrontation, pressure against the non-clandestine Left persisted; very notable in this regard was the crippling of the Labour Party after its call for a national *hartal* (strike) to protest the devaluation of Malayan currency in line with sterling's devaluation in late 1967.

The Political Economy of the Alliance

The policies of the Alliance government reflected the nature of the post-colonial state. While it lies beyond the scope of this book to provide a detailed analysis of the character of the post-colonial state, nevertheless, some discussion of the contradictions involved is essential for understanding the ascendance of the class fraction of 'statist capitalists', often termed 'bureaucrat capitalists'.

UMNO's dominance in the Alliance coalition was ensured by the stronger support it commanded compared to its partners. UMNO claimed to represent the interests of the Malays, who comprised the largest ethnic community in the new nation; it had successfully mobilized Malay mass opposition against specific colonial designs, particularly the Malayan Union proposal. After the withdrawal of the Malay Left from UMNO, and the subsequent repression of the Left by the colonial and post-colonial authorities, UMNO faced very little competition in mobilizing Malays politically. Through a combination of measures—including 'patronage' (e.g. Guyot, 1971), 'ethnic corporatism' and successful 'crisis management'—UMNO preserved and advanced its political predominance after independence, and even more so after 1969.

Another important factor contributing to UMNO's predominance was the effect of past colonial policy towards the bulk of the Malays, who were peasants. While the colonial government unhesitatingly served the interests of foreign capital in its policies affecting the peasantry, it otherwise directly intervened minimally in Malay peasant society. This policy of 'benign neglect' was frequently garbed in paternalistic pronouncements of concern for the plight of the Malays at the hands of the immigrant Asians.[6] The ideology of alien Asian subjugation of the Malays was thus fostered by the colonial state as a ploy to obscure the primary role of colonial interests in maintaining the conditions responsible for the plight of the Malay peasantry. Such propaganda escalated from the 1930s, and particularly after the defeat of the Malayan Union proposal when the British also enunciated a concept of Malay 'special rights' quite late in the colonial era[7] (Means, 1972). This self-serving ideology whitewashed the cumulative consequences of colonial policy, especially the colonial state's promotion of the interests of British capital, and also influenced government planning for the post-colonial Malayan nation.

The other important element contributing to UMNO's position within the Alliance was the nature of its leadership. After overcoming early resistance from certain quarters of the pre-colonial Malay ruling class, the British sought to co-opt this class by recruiting it to man the middle echelons of the colonial state apparatus. These 'administocrats' generally occupied positions immediately subordinate to those held by British administrators.[8] The machinery for the preparation of this stratum evolved over the years, initially centring on the élite Malay College at Kuala Kangsar, Perak (Tilman, 1961). It has been observed that 'while their presence is most apparent in the Civil Service, many graduates of the College can be found among the political elite...' (Tilman, 1969: 232). Indeed, the 'administocrats' and those who led UMNO share a common social background; in fact, many of the latter actually began their careers in the colonial administration.

Conspicuous by its virtual absence at the morrow of independence was a Malay bourgeoisie. It has often been observed that the ethnicity of many ostensibly Malay businessmen can usually be traced to Arabs, Indians and those who are now termed 'Indonesians'. Many reasons have been put forward to attempt to explain the low participation of Malays in capitalist activities during the colonial era.[9] In this connection, it is interesting to note that Chinese specialization in certain economic and occupational roles often involved sub-ethnic specialization as well, i.e. following dialect group or kinship lines (see Chapter 8). This suggests that the organization of capital in the frontier economy relied greatly on kinship and other similar relationships. Having secured niches in the colonial economy, the reproduction of these class and occupational roles tended to preserve the sub-ethnic, and therefore the ethnic, patterns of specialization as well. In fact, the very nature of social organizations involving those conducting petty business activities in Malaya has tended to reproduce such patterns. The pre-colonial Malay ruling class, subsequently ensconced in the colonial administrative apparatus, did not have much reason to take such initiatives; the steady and relatively high remuneration offered by their vocations discouraged them from seeking alternative occupations. Malay peasants, on the other hand, had insufficient funds, and few, if any, connections to engage in business. Usually possessing land, there was little reason for them to offer themselves as wage workers. The 'alien Malays' among the Malays–i.e.

the Arabs, Indians, and Indonesians—had poorer access to administrative positions but were also less tied to the land. Consequently, they were in the best position to participate in capitalist production, both as capitalists and as wage labourers.

In other words, a Malay bourgeoisie failed to emerge during the colonial era because those who might have comprised this class under different circumstances were incorporated into the colonial bureaucracy at middle-echelon positions.[10] Still, it was not unknown for highly salaried Malay administrators, as well as others who had accumulated wealth and had high incomes,[11] to invest and further increase their incomes. But this small minority was rarely directly involved in production, and such incomes were primarily of a 'rentier' nature. Except for the marginal 'alien Malay' groups mentioned earlier, a Malay entrepreneurial bourgeoisie did not exist. The only local bourgeoisie to speak of was mainly Chinese.

In marked contrast to the class composition of the Malay community and the character of the UMNO leadership, the MCA was primarily a party of businessmen from the outset.[12] Though led mainly by English-educated elements, at least until the early 1970s, the MCA has not been altogether oblivious to the interests of other segments of Chinese capital.[13] Its previous inability to mobilize widely beyond the Chinese business community, relatively large though this is, has undermined its electoral appeal. Consequently, and for other reasons as well, its stature within the ruling coalition, particularly in relation to UMNO, has declined since the 1950s.

Nevertheless, its economic strength enabled the MCA to bargain for a *modus operandi* which enabled important segments of Chinese capital to preserve as well as expand their interests in the first decade after independence. This was often represented in the formula: 'politics for the Malays, the economy for the Chinese', which was essentially false, since Malays with significant political power comprise only a small minority, while only a small proportion of Chinese have considerable economic assets. This popular caricature ignores the domination of the national economy by foreign capital, the influence of capital over political decisions, and the systemic constraints on the scope for state intervention. Nevertheless, this catchy representation did capture the tone of the apparent compromise underlying the post-colonial government's policies. Development on such a fragile and unstable basis was plagued with contradictions which had unfolded by the end of the 1960s, putting an end to the 'Alliance contract'. It is to the main class dynamics of this process that attention will now be focused.

The 'Administocrats' as Governing Group

It has been argued that, in certain circumstances, the social group (including the bureaucrats themselves) in control of the state apparatus can constitute a class in itself (Gandy, 1976). Specific historical circumstances have enabled the Malay 'administocratic' stratum of the colonial era to emerge as the 'governing' or 'reigning' class[14] in post-colonial Malaya. How developments in post-colonial Malaya contributed to the ascendance and consolidation of this class and, correspondingly, to its increasing use of state power to further its interests will now be discussed.

The situation in Malaya immediately after independence, where a governing group dominated the state without an economic base of its own, was necessarily fragile and untenable in the long run, though not altogether unusual. In fact, it has been the common lot of many ex-colonial societies in which the hegemonic fraction of the bourgeoisie was foreign and hence absentee.[15] The local bourgeoisie therefore comprises only a portion, and a weak one at that, of the bourgeoisie. The particular circumstances of colonialism in Malaya, as in many other places,[16] set the stage for the emergence of a post-colonial governing group, economically, socially, culturally, and otherwise poorly integrated with the local bourgeoisie. British capital and the colonial state enhanced their hegemony by mediating between Chinese capital and Malay administrators.

The post-colonial ascendance and dominance of the Malay 'administocratic' stratum in the state apparatus was not entirely without popular Malay support, originally harnessed in opposition to the 1946 'Malayan Union' proposal, then sustained by the promise of independence from British colonial rule. In the early years after independence, the post-colonial state continued to serve the interests of British capital in particular, and foreign capital in general. The governing stratum, spawned by the colonial state, had little reason to be distrusted by the hegemonic fraction of the bourgeoisie, i.e. foreign ('expatriate') capital: the Malay 'administocrats', as represented by UMNO, were in alliance with Chinese capital, or at least with its dominant groupings represented through the MCA, and partly derived their initial position of dominance in the post-colonial order from compromises and arrangements acceptable to the colonial state, and British as well as Chinese capital. This stratum therefore had a stake in and, consequently, a respect for the capitalist status quo, though the economic assets it had accumulated at the time of independence were limited. Hence, the Alliance Party was also an alliance of class fractional interests,[17] sharing a common stake in the preservation of the capitalist order. Constrained by a limited social and economic base, the 'administocrats' were hardly in a position to mount a strategic challenge to the more established capitalist interests at the time of independence in 1957. This governing group used the state apparatus in post-colonial Malaya not only to serve the interests of the dominant classes in general, but also to expand its social bases and to consolidate itself economically. In this context, the governing or reigning 'administocratic' group developed a particular class fractional identity in relation to other classes and class fractions.

Early Government Efforts to Promote Malay Capitalism

The first government-initiated efforts at creating a Malay capitalist class can be associated with the results of some proposals made by the early UMNO leadership.[18] In 1953, the colonial government established a statutory corporation, the Rural and Industrial Development Authority (RIDA), primarily oriented towards 'economic development' programmes for Malays. When independence was proclaimed in 1957,[19] the policy of creating a Malay capitalist class through state assurance of 'special rights' was given constitutional recognition (Means, 1972: 40). At the end of the 1950s, responsibility for rural development was taken over by the newly created Ministry for Rural Development, leaving RIDA with 'responsibility for Malay development in commerce and industry' (Beaglehole, 1969: 221). Up to this point, RIDA's record—with some exceptions, like training schemes—remained unimpressive, especially in the promotion of Malay industry, mainly undertaken through credit provision and technical assistance. Intensified demands by the incipient Malay bourgeoisie in the post-colonial era resulted in the establishment of a Malay Secretariat in the Ministry of Commerce and Industry. Despite being given a more specific task for the first half of the 1960s, RIDA's achievements continued to remain minimal, apparently due to the lack of sustained and solid government support. Elsewhere in the economy, the pattern of ownership and control inherited at the time of independence was not changing substantially, and the few changes that were taking place were barely affecting the Malays. As was to be expected, the limited Malay advances in the capitalist sector were by the already wealthy.[20] Except in the transport industry where some gains were made due to the government's preferential policy, Malay ownership in the capitalist sector of the economy generally remained negligible. The post-colonial Alliance government's paltry efforts at promoting Malay capitalism can be attributed to the less dominant position of UMNO in the Alliance compromise then, and the social character of UMNO's support. By the mid-1960s, these limited measures had yet to bear much fruit.

By 1965, things were beginning to come to a head.[21] Malay expectations had been raised by the achievement of independence and the now dominant position of UMNO in the Alliance government. The issues of the ethnic balance involved in the formation of Malaysia (Wheelwright, 1975a) and the political-territorial re-inclusion of Singapore, the regional economic centre, presented a new opportunity for the case for Malay capitalism to be pressed home.

A number of developments distinguish 1965 as a watershed year in the development of Malay capitalism. Early that year, the Majlis Amanah Rakyat (Council of Trust for the People) or MARA was formed, along lines proposed by the then Deputy Prime Minister, Tun Abdul Razak Hussein, to replace the failing RIDA. RIDA itself was merged with the above-mentioned Malay Secretariat, which was transferred from the Ministry of Commerce and Industry (then headed by a Chinese minister) to the powerful Ministry of National and Rural Development headed by the increasingly assertive Deputy Prime Minister then. In June of that year, the first ever national Bumiputra[22] Economic Congress was held. This conference—which reflected the emerging coherence and consolidation of the aspiring Malay governing group—and the proposals and resolutions emerging from it, expressed many of the frustrations of the participants with regard to government policy in relation to the Malay economic status quo.[23] In the same year, Bank Bumiputra Malaysia Berhad[24] was established with government assistance to serve as a financial centre for the accumulation of Malay capital.

Despite the far more substantial measures taken by the government for the promotion of a Malay capitalist class after 1965, actual progress remained disappointing for the remainder of the decade. The significance and efficacy of these post-1965 measures in promoting Malay capitalism continued to be limited by the class compromise underlying the Alliance arrangement. Changes in ownership of the established capitalist sector were not significant. As noted earlier (see Chapter 9), in manufacturing—the sector with the fastest growth rate in the post-colonial period—Malay capital did not fare well. The Malays who made inroads into the industrial sector were few in number and were mainly prominent politicians and former senior civil servants who had retained useful connections with government (Lindenberg, 1973; Grace, 1976).

Class, Race, and Income Distribution

Besides the frustrations felt by the nascent Malay bourgeoisie and petty bourgeoisie, economic conditions for most of the rest of the population had also been deteriorating in the decade after independence. Popular frustrations were mounting, but with official suppression and proscription of class-based organizations and ideologies transcending ethnic lines, political mobilization on ethnic lines prevailed. It is therefore important to survey briefly the economic circumstances which contributed to this displacement of class-based frustrations with particular attention on the income distribution pattern as symptomatic of the growing economic inequality during the 1960s.

Between 1957 and 1970 income inequality in Malaya apparently increased for the population as a whole, and especially among the Malays.[25] The Malaysian Treasury (1974: 84) has reported[26] that the average per capita income increased by 25 per cent over the 13-year period. In 1957, the top 20 per cent of households received almost half the total income, whereas in 1970 they accounted for 56 per cent; conversely, the bottom 60 per cent of households accounted for 30 per cent in 1957, but for only 25 per cent in 1970. The Gini coefficient[27] also increased over the period, from 0.41 in 1957 to 0.50 in 1970, reflecting the regressive trend in income distribution (see Table 10.1). Class, rather than race, appears to better explain the pattern of income inequality[28] (Anand, 1982). The first dozen years after independence saw the lot of the poor actually decline in absolute terms. For example, the average monthly income of the bottom 10 per cent declined from $48 to $33, i.e. there was a drop of 31 per cent. The monthly income of the bottom 30 per cent declined by $9.33 per capita on average, while the bottom fourth and fifth deciles managed to record increases of only 4 to 6 per cent in their mean incomes. Despite the low inflation rate in Malaysia in the 1960s, they would hardly have been able to improve on their previous standard of living (Treasury, 1974: 85). Income inequality affected all three major ethnic groups. While most marked for the Malay community as a whole, the relative position of poorer Indians declined most, while the income distribution pattern within the Chinese community also regressed.

The mean income of Malay households declined from 68 per cent of the national average in 1957 to 64 per cent in 1970 (Treasury, 1974). As for income distribution within the Malay community, the top 20 per cent of Malay households accounted for 42.5 per cent of total Malay household income in 1957, compared to 51.3 per cent in 1970. On the other hand, the percentage

TABLE 10.1

Peninsular Malaysia: Rural-Urban Size Distribution of Household Income

	All Households				Rural Households				Urban Households			
	1957/8	1967/8	1970	1973	1957/8	1967/8	1970	1973	1957/8	1967/8	1970	1973
Income share of												
Top 5%	22.1	23.6	28.1	26.4	19.0	19.2	23.9	n.a.	20.7	23.4	27.5	n.a.
Top 20%	48.6	51.3	55.9	53.7	44.5	46.8	51.0	n.a.	49.6	51.8	55.0	n.a.
Middle 40%	35.5	34.4	32.5	34.0	37.3	36.7	35.9	n.a.	33.2	34.0	32.8	n.a.
Bottom 40%	15.9	14.3	11.6	12.3	18.2	16.5	13.1	n.a.	17.2	14.2	12.2	n.a.
Mean Income	215	240	264	324	172	185	201	n.a.	307	360	407	n.a.
Median Income	156	154	167	n.a.	131	134	145	n.a.	216	246	283	n.a.
Gini Ratio	0.41	0.44	0.50	0.50	0.38	0.40	0.46	0.46	0.42	0.45	0.50	0.48
Theil Index	0.30	n.a.	0.48	0.43	0.25	n.a.	0.40	n.a.	0.30	n.a.	0.45	n.a.
Sample Size	2,760	6,696	26,310	7,285								

Sources: Snodgrass (1975); Ishak Shari and Rogayah M. Zain (1978).

n.a.: not available

TABLE 10.2

Peninsular Malaysia: Size Distribution of Household Income by Ethnic Group

	Malay Households				Chinese Households				Indian Households			
	1957/8	1967/8	1970	1973	1957/8	1967/8	1970	1973	1957/8	1967/8	1970	1973
Income share of												
Top 5%	18.1	22.2	23.8	22.7	19.2	19.9	25.4	18.8	19.4	22.3	28.4	25.6
Top 20%	42.5	48.2	51.3	50.8	46.0	46.7	42.3	48.6	43.6	48.1	53.6	51.3
Middle 40%	37.9	34.8	35.7	35.5	35.9	36.3	33.5	35.5	36.6	35.6	31.5	33.7
Bottom 40%	19.6	17.0	13.0	13.7	18.1	17.0	14.2	15.9	19.8	16.3	14.9	15.0
Mean Income	140	163	172	222	302	349	381	444	243	260	301	365
Median Income	112	120	122	n.a.	223	261	269	n.a.	188	191	195	n.a.
Gini Ratio	0.34	0.40	0.46	0.45	0.38	0.39	0.46	0.42	0.37	0.40	0.47	0.44
Theil Index	0.21	n.a.	0.40	0.36	0.35	n.a.	0.39	0.31	0.23	n.a.	0.39	0.35

Sources: Snodgrass (1975); Ishak Shari and Rogayah M. Zain (1978).

n.a.: not available

received by the bottom 40 per cent of Malay households dropped from 19.6 to
13.0. Over the 13-year period (1957-70), the Gini coefficient for Malay
household incomes rose from 0.34 to 0.46 (see Table 10.2).

As the income distribution trends reveal, income inequality among the
population as a whole widened in the post-colonial period. Since the position of
Malays as a whole deteriorated in relative terms, and the higher-income group
among Malays enjoyed absolute as well as relative increases in income, poorer
Malay households must have suffered absolute as well as relative declines in
incomes. For the peasant sector, there is little reason to believe that the
tendencies towards impoverishment, class, and income differentiation—which
emerged during the colonial era—were reversed or even checked in the post-
colonial period despite the government's avowed commitment to 'rural
development'. In fact, the nature of rural development programmes and other
aspects of government policy affecting the peasantry appear to have favoured
those among the peasantry in a position to accumulate.

The general unemployment situation in the country apparently deteriorated
as well. Government unemployment statistics are widely suspected to be
underestimated; nevertheless, these do indicate increasing unemployment. For
example, the official unemployment rate rose from 6.5 per cent in 1965 to about
8.0 per cent in 1970 (Malaysia, 1971: 102, Table 7.2). The forces contributing to
peasant landlessness continued unabated in the post-colonial years, while the
pace of land settlement on government schemes in the 1960s remained slow.[29]

Meanwhile, developments in the capitalist sector—involving sluggishness in
manufacturing, plantation and mining employment growth—could not absorb
the rapidly growing labour force. The visibly ethnic patterns of employment
were an immediate source of frustration among the unemployed, as well as
those aspiring to upward occupational mobility. The apparently non-Malay
(especially Chinese) character of the private capitalist sector appeared impreg-
nable to Malays, who were encouraged to perceive their exclusion from jobs as
being racially motivated. Confronted with an avowedly 'pro-Malay' government which appeared to be advancing the interests of Malays over those of
other races—e.g. by provision of 'special privileges' and ethnic employment
quotas—non-Malay resentment against the system and especially against state
policies inevitably took on an ethnic character.

Capital and Ethnicity before 1969

At this juncture, it seems useful to review some of the complex developments
involving class and race which eventually culminated in the 13 May 1969
events, the 'palace coup' which followed, and the New Economic Policy which
emerged in its aftermath. As shown earlier, the development of the colonial
economy in Malaya resulted in the economic dominance of 'expatriate' foreign
capital. The end of the colonial epoch and the emergence of the post-colonial
state did not immediately involve the promotion of new class interests at the
expense of established propertied interests. Foreign dominance of the economy
meant, among other things, that the domestic bourgeoisie was relatively weak
(see Golay, 1969). Further, the ideological basis of the post-colonial state,

designed by the departing colonialists and dominated by UMNO, involved 'protection of the Malay community'[30] (Chandrasekaran, 1974) and provision of 'special rights' ostensibly for development of the Malays (Means, 1972), an arrangement which limited the political power of the local non-Malay (primarily Chinese) bourgeoisie. Policies pursued by the post-colonial government, under the general rubric of Malay 'special privileges', expanded the ranks of the Malay petty bourgeoisie, resulting in heightened aspirations for more of the same. Preference to Malays in the award of scholarships and recruitment into the civil service swelled the ranks of this politically powerful group in control of the state apparatus[31] (Gibbons and Zakaria, 1971).

In situation in Malaya after independence, the governing group in control of the state machinery owned relatively little of the modern capitalist sector.[32] This situation was simply unstable in the long run and the status quo could not be maintained forever. The post-colonial ascendance of the Malay petty bourgeoisie to state power unveiled a new stage in class contention as this group sought to utilize political power to develop its own economic base.

The disappointing results of the early efforts to create a class of Malay capitalists frustrated the few existing Malay capitalists as well as those with such class aspirations. Their frustrations were, understandably, directed primarily at their competitors among the already entrenched bourgeoisie, typically identified with the Chinese bourgeoisie. Also, since it was mainly Chinese businessmen who occupied those less-monopolized positions in the economy to which a newly emerging bourgeoisie could aspire, frustrations stemming from inter-capitalist rivalry were increasingly expressed in ethnic terms. Furthermore, they were often also the capitalists who dealt directly with the Malay masses, especially in commerce and credit, i.e. the sphere of circulation, and hence were a convenient target for mobilizing of popular resentment. That this Chinese bourgeoisie did not actually dominate the economy was therefore quite irrelevant to Malay bourgeois aspirations.

Given such a strong identification of ethnicity, or 'race', with classes and class fractions, the most convenient ideological banner with which to mount a political and economic challenge was obviously ethnic. One consequence of the prevalence of racial ideologies in Malaysia has been a tendency for intra-ethnic inter-class divisions to be played down compared to inter-ethnic differences. Furthermore, differences within particular class fractions tend to be minimized, thus uniting different strata or segments within a class fraction, which often is identified with a particular ethnic group. One common expression of racial ideology is the frequently expressed identification of the (usually Chinese) 'middleman' as exploiter.[33] This gains widespread acceptance in a popular consciousness where all too often class divisions are associated with ethnic distinctions.

Much of the non-Malay bourgeoisie successfully adjusted to most of the early efforts to promote the economic interests of the Malay petty bourgeoisie in control of the state apparatus, to the mutual benefit of both parties involved. By collaboration,[34] bribery and corruption, and through business acumen and other abilities derived from long experience and necessitated by the new conditions, it continued to thrive in the early post-colonial era. Given the initial economic weakness of the statist petty bourgeoisie, compared to the established capitalist class, existing business interests continued to be well served since business interests could continue to buy political influence.[35]

In the pre-1969 period, the state did not explicitly or aggressively promote Malay advances into the capitalist sector.[36] Thus, before the New Economic Policy (NEP), announced in 1970, Malay penetration of the capitalist sector was limited, though this does not mean that no inroads had been made. For instance, it has been noted that, though still very small, Malay ownership of locally incorporated tin dredging companies in Malaya was expanding fastest compared to other ethnic groups (Yip, 1968). It has also been noted that Malay investors had some, though not many, interests in the pioneer industries of the 1960s (Lindenberg, 1973).

As this implies, a firm economic basis for Malay capitalists had yet to be established by the late 1960s. For example, in 1969, twelve years after independence, Malays and so-called 'Malay interests'[37] owned only 1.5 per cent of all share capital of limited companies in Peninsular Malaysia, while Chinese and Indians accounted for 22.8 per cent and 0.9 per cent respectively. Local branches of foreign incorporated companies, non-residents, and foreign-controlled companies in Malaysia accounted for 29.7 per cent, 26.4 per cent, and 6.0 per cent respectively, while most of the rest was held by 'other individuals and locally controlled companies' (10.1 per cent), nominee companies (2.1 per cent), and the federal and state governments (0.5 per cent) (Malaysia, 1971: 40, Table 3-1).

Meanwhile, as government measures enabled growing numbers of Malays to acquire a higher education, the numbers of those aspiring to be part of the new Malay 'middle class' grew. Their frustrations were not directed solely at non-Malay capitalists. In their view, the state, ostensibly in the hands of the UMNO-led Alliance, was not doing enough for them. One expression of such sentiments within the ranks of UMNO was the emergence of the so-called 'ultras' or 'Young Turks',[38] who precipitated the UMNO party crisis in 1969 and have been credited with the downfall of the then incumbent prime minister, who was personally very strongly identified with the policies of the preceding period.

May Thirteenth 1969 and Its Aftermath

In the absence of strongly influential, class-oriented ideologies and organizations capable of forging a multi-racial, class-based solidarity, the opposition towards some of the felt consequences of post-colonial development surfaced in inter-racial antagonism. The 'Malayness' of the government and the 'Chineseness' of the ubiquitous local bourgeoisie encouraged long-existing, apparently ethnic, class-based frustrations to take on a racial complexion. The culmination of the first dozen years of post-colonial development came in the form of the ugly post-election race riots of May 1969.[39]

The 10 May 1969 election results demonstrated the extent of popular disillusionment with the ruling Alliance Party. In the predominantly non-Malay urban areas, opposition parties made huge inroads, largely at the expense of candidates from the MCA. In primarily Malay rural areas, the vote also swung against the Alliance, marking a decline in Malay electoral support for the dominant UMNO. While there is no way to confirm the view that the outbreak of violence was premeditated before the election results were known, it is generally agreed that the first skirmishes were apparently precipitated by the tension between elated non-Malay supporters of the opposition and youthful UMNO supporters ostensibly defending Malay interests. With the outbreak of riots, parliamentary rule was suspended and military rule imposed until early 1971.

Under mounting pressure from within UMNO, its president and the Prime Minister of the country since independence, Tunku Abdul Rahman, was forced to step down in mid-1970. He was succeeded by his long-time deputy for both these positions, Tun Abdul Razak, in what many believe to have been a 'palace coup' of sorts. Razak had been heading the National Operations Council which ran the country after the May riots. He had been personally identified with various government programmes and policies ostensibly meant to uplift the Malays, having served as Minister in the key Rural and National Development portfolio which had taken over much of RIDA's functions; he was also instrumental in the reorganization of RIDA in the mid-1960s and therefore in the establishment of MARA. After becoming the Prime Minister in 1970, he rapidly rehabilitated those identified with the 'Young Turks' of the late 1960s, who had been widely credited with ousting the Tunku.[40]

In the aftermath of the May 1969 election and riots came a drastic reorientation of some government programmes and policies. The inclusion of more component parties in the ruling coalition resulted in its political base being broadened considerably as well as the greatly enhanced dominant status of the UMNO within the coalition. The Gerakan Rakyat Malaysia (Malaysian Peoples Movement) which had captured control of the Penang State government soon isolated and expelled its social-democratic and labour wing and began cooperating openly with the Alliance central government. Another primarily non-Malay based opposition party with considerable electoral support in parts of Perak State, the People's Progressive Party (PPP), also joined forces with the Alliance. The Malay-based Partai Islam SeMalaya formed a coalition with UMNO as well. Meanwhile, the Democratic Action Party (DAP), which drew support mainly from the Chinese community, conducted (then secret) negotiations with the MCA to explore the possibilities of coalition. Other former opposition parties in Sabah and Sarawak were co-opted as well. In 1974, the new coalition of ruling parties was formally reorganized for the general election under the rubric of the Barisan Nasional (National Front), successor to the previous Alliance arrangement.

The bargaining position of the MCA had been considerably weakened by its especially poor performance in the 1969 election and its decision to opt out of the government after the election. Furthermore, all the new coalition partners from the peninsula had been brought in primarily on the initiative of UMNO leaders, whereas the MCA effort to negotiate with the DAP was unsuccessful. The co-option of PAS meant that Malay opposition at the parliamentary level hardly existed, whereas non-Malay opposition—in the form of the DAP and the Partai Keadilan Masyarakat (Social Justice Party) or Pekemas—continued. In these circumstances, and with the strengthening of the organization under its new leadership, UMNO further enhanced its already pre-eminent position within the ruling coalition.

The New Economic Policy

The strengthened position of UMNO, and more so of those elements within it that stood for a more active promotion of Malay capitalism, produced new policies and programmes on the economic front[41] (Von Vorys, 1975). The most important embodiment of this trend was in the formulation of the New Economic Policy, first launched in association with the Second Malaysia Plan for 1971–5.[42] The NEP contains two prongs, namely to eradicate poverty 'irrespective of race', and to 'restructure Malaysian society to reduce and eventually eliminate the identification of race with economic function'.

As officially elaborated, the first poverty eradication prong of the NEP is certainly not to be achieved by eliminating class exploitation. The established interests of the property-owning classes are respected, at least in principle.[43] Efforts to improve the lot of wage earners, beyond employment promotion measures, are virtually non-existent. The measures for poverty eradication that have been announced do not offend existing propertied interests—hence, no land reform, for example. Acceptable measures include land settlement for some of the landless, job creation for the unemployed, as well as productivity and commodity price increases for the peasantry. Even these have been constrained by the economic environment; for example, the government has been able to implement successfully a guaranteed minimum price scheme for padi produced for the domestic market. However, it cannot do likewise for rubber, which is sold on the international market. The available measures which may be employed by government are certainly far from exhausted, though the actual range of choices available is limited by the framework within which the government is operating. In so far as poverty is rather arbitrarily defined by the government in terms of an undisclosed poverty line,[44] poverty eradication is also subject to similar interpretation. In any case, the official view of poverty does not necessarily involve reducing income inequality at all. It is in fact possible for poverty to be reduced, or even eradicated, according to such a definition, in a situation of unchanging or even growing income inequality.

Table 10.3 suggests that this may well have been the case in the 1970s. While official data suggest that the mean household incomes of the poorest 40 per cent of the population of Peninsular Malaysia rose between 1970 and 1979, these sources also point to the growing disparity (in proportionate terms) between mean and median incomes in Peninsular Malaysia over the same period for all ethnic groups except Indians separately considered. Such a disparity is, of course, only a rough indicator of constant or growing income inequality, but it appears to be supported by data from several other surveys, which point to growing income inequalities between 1970 and 1976 (Ishak Shari and Jomo Kwame Sundaram, 1981). The overall Gini coefficient is estimated to have declined almost negligibly from 0.513 in 1970 to 0.508 in 1979 (Malaysia, 1984:94). In this connection, it appears that the state may have enhanced

TABLE 10.3

Peninsular Malaysia: Ratio of Mean and Median Incomes, 1970-1979 ($ per household per month)

		In Constant 1970 Prices					In Current Prices				
		1970	1973	1976	1979	Annual Growth Rate 1971-9 (%)	1973	1976	1979	Annual Growth Rate, 1971-9 (%)	Annual Growth Rate (1971-9) of Mean Income of Bottom 40 Per Cent (%)
Malay	Mean	172	209	237	296	6.2	242	345	492	12.4	10.6
	Median	120	141	160	197	5.7	163	233	327	11.8	
	Ratio	1.43	1.48	1.48	1.50	1.1			1.50	1.1	
Chinese	Mean	394	461	540	565	4.1	534	787	938	10.1	8.4
	Median	268	298	329	373	3.7	343	480	620	9.8	
	Ratio	1.47	1.55	1.64	1.51	1.1			1.51	1.0	
Indian	Mean	304	352	369	455	4.6	408	538	756	10.6	9.9
	Median	194	239	247	314	5.5	277	360	521	11.6	
	Ratio	1.57	1.47	1.49	1.45	0.8			1.45	0.9	
Others	Mean	813	1,121	870	1,147	3.9	1,299	1,268	1,904	9.9	14.8
	Median	250	306	270	331	3.2	355	394	550	9.1	
	Ratio	3.25	3.66	3.22	3.47	1.2			3.46	1.1	
All	Mean	264	313	353	417	5.2	362	514	693	11.3	10.5
	Median	166	196	215	263	3.2	227	313	436	11.3	
	Ratio	1.59	1.60	1.64	1.59	1.0			1.59	1.0	
Urban	Mean	428	492	569	587	3.6	570	830	975	9.6	
	Median	265	297	340	361	3.5	345	495	600	9.5	
	Ratio	1.62	1.66	1.67	1.63	1.0			1.63	1.0	
Rural	Mean	200	233	269	331	5.7	269	392	550	11.9	
	Median	139	159	180	222	5.3	184	262	369	11.4	
	Ratio	1.44	1.47	1.49	1.49	1.1			1.49	1.0	

Sources: Malaysia (1981: 37, Table 3.3; 36, Table 3.9); Malaysia (1984: 94, Table 3.8). Derived from Post Enumeration Survey of 1970 Population and Housing Census, Household Income Survey 1973, Labour Force Survey 1974 (reference 1973), Agriculture Census 1977 (reference 1976), and Labour Force Survey 1980 (reference 1979).

inequality in income and in the economic welfare of the population with its increasingly 'regressive' tax incidence structure and inequitable public expenditure pattern (Ismail Mohd. Salleh, 1977; Meerman, 1979; Ishak Shari and Jomo Kwame Sundaram, 1981; Jomo, 1983c, 1984). Hence, the evidence points to declining absolute poverty measured in terms of a fixed poverty line occurring in a context of virtually unchanging inequality, with this combination made possible, of course, by the high economic growth experienced in Malaysia over much of the 1970s.

Perhaps even more ominous are the reasons for this success in poverty reduction. As Table 10.4 shows, the poverty rate among rubber smallholders fell from 64.7 per cent in 1970 to 59.0 per cent in 1975 and to 41.3 per cent in 1980 before rising to 61.1 per cent in 1983, while the average export price of rubber rose from $1.28 per kg in 1970 to $1.39 in 1975 and $3.03 in 1980, before falling to $2.34 in 1983 (Malaysia, 1981: 18). Hence the dramatic reduction in the percentage of poor rubber smallholders in 1980 was achieved by favourable export prices which—as the smallholders are painfully aware—are continually subject to the vicissitudes of the international market situation. The same is equally true for other export commodity producers. The poverty rate among estate workers (the majority of whom work on rubber plantations), for instance, rose from 40.0 per cent in 1970 to 47.0 per cent in 1975 before dropping to 35.1 per cent in 1980 and jumping to 54.6 per cent in 1983.

The poverty rate among padi farmers declined from 88.1 per cent in 1970 to. 77.0 per cent in 1975, 52.7 per cent in 1980 and 54.0 per cent in 1983. While the productivity increases related to the introduction of high-yielding padi varieties and double-cropping have been significant, these were largely accomplished in the late 1960s and early 1970s. Subsequent net income gains in the face of rising production costs are primarily attributable to government and consumer subsidization of the purchase price of padi, which was raised for example, by more than 30 per cent in mid-1980 following demonstrations in Alor Star, capital of the rice-bowl State of Kedah, in January 1980 by padi farmers experiencing declining net incomes. (In this connection, it should be noted that such padi subsidies favour bigger farmers who produce larger marketable surpluses.) In other words, the apparent improvement in the economic welfare of the largest poverty groups may prove to be quite hollow if, for instance, world rubber prices dip or state-organized price subsidies fail to stay ahead of rising padi production costs.

From this angle, it is interesting to look at the case of mine workers, the bulk of whom are to be found in tin mines. The incidence of poverty among this group dropped from 34.3 per cent in 1970 to 31.8 per cent in 1975, before rising again to 33.0 per cent in 1980 and 41.0 per cent in 1983. Over the same period, the price of tin rose from $10,777 per tonne in 1970 to $15,075 in 1975, $36,040 in 1980 and $30,093 in 1983, while value added per worker in this sector rose by 8.6 per cent annually during 1975–80 to register the highest growth rate for any sector for this period (Malaysia, 1981: 18, Table 2.3; 86, Table 4.7). This does suggest that neither higher export commodity prices nor higher worker productivity in themselves necessarily ensure higher net incomes for producers, especially if they are wage earners, rather than petty commodity producers, who

TABLE 10.4

Peninsular Malaysia: Incidence of Poverty by Sector,
1970, 1975, 1980, and 1983

	Total Households ('000)	Total Poor Households ('000)	Incidence of Poverty (%)	Percentage among Poor
	1970			
Rural				
Agriculture:	852.9	582.4	68.3	73.6
Rubber smallholders	350.0	226.4	64.7	28.6
Oil palm smallholders	6.6	2.0	30.3	0.3
Coconut smallholders	32.0	16.9	52.8	2.1
Padi farmers	140.0	123.4	88.1	15.6
Other agriculture	137.5	126.2	91.8	16.0
Fishermen	38.4	28.1	73.2	3.5
Estate workers	148.4	59.4	40.0	7.5
Other industries	350.5	123.5	35.2	15.6
Sub-total	1,203.4	705.9	58.7	89.2
Urban				
Mining	5.4	1.8	33.3	0.2
Manufacturing	84.0	19.7	23.5	2.5
Construction	19.5	5.9	30.2	0.7
Transport and utilities	42.4	13.1	30.9	1.7
Trade and services	251.3	45.4	18.1	5.7
Sub-total	402.6	85.9	21.3	10.8
Total	1,606.0	791.8	49.3	100.0

(continued)

TABLE 10.4 (continued)

	Total Households ('000) 1975	Total Poor Households ('000)	Incidence of Poverty (%)	Percentage among Poor
Rural				
Agriculture:				
Rubber smallholders	915.1	576.5	63.0	69.0
Oil palm smallholders	396.3	233.8	59.0	28.0
Coconut smallholders	9.9	0.9	9.1	0.1
Padi farmers	34.4	17.5	50.9	2.1
Other agriculture	148.5	114.3	77.0	13.7
Fishermen	157.4	124.1	78.8	14.9
Estate workers	41.6	26.2	63.0	3.1
Other industries	127.0	59.7	47.0	7.1
	433.3	153.4	35.4	181.4
Sub-total	1,348.4	729.9	54.1	87.4
Urban				
Mining	5.3	2.0	37.7	0.2
Manufacturing	120.4	21.0	17.4	2.5
Construction	25.5	6.1	23.9	0.7
Transport and utilities	64.4	13.8	21.4	1.7
Trade and services	337.4	62.3	18.5	7.5
Sub-total	553.0	105.2	19.0	12.6
Total	1,901.4	835.1	43.9	100.0

	1980			
Rural				
Agriculture:	924.8	422.5	45.7	66.5
Rubber smallholders	409.0	168.9	41.3	26.6
Oil palm smallholders	23.6	1.8	7.7	0.3
Coconut smallholders	32.8	12.8	38.9	2.0
Padi farmers	145.0	76.4	52.7	12.0
Other agriculture	165.0	106.1	64.2	16.7
Fishermen	41.1	18.6	45.3	2.9
Estate workers	108.0	37.9	35.1	6.0
Other industries	524.7	119.6	22.8	18.8
Sub-total	924.8	422.5	45.7	66.5
Urban				
Mining	5.2	1.7	33.0	0.3
Manufacturing	175.0	23.5	13.4	3.7
Construction	32.6	5.7	11.4	0.9
Transport and utilities	81.6	15.7	19.2	2.4
Trade and services	449.1	47.2	10.5	7.4
Sub-total	743.5	93.8	12.6	14.7
Total	2,193.0	635.9	29.0	100.0

(continued)

TABLE 10.4 *(continued)*

	Total Households ('000)	Total Poor Households ('000)	Incidence of Poverty (%)	Percentage among Poor
	1983			
Rural				
Agriculture:	906.6	497.6	54.9	69.4
Rubber smallholders	405.8	247.9	61.1	34.6
Oil palm smallholders	23.0	1.5	6.5	0.2
Coconut smallholders	31.0	10.1	32.7	1.4
Padi farmers	138.9	75.0	54.0	10.5
Other agriculture	161.7	87.3	54.0	12.2
Fishermen	40.5	18.1	44.7	2.5
Estate workers	105.7	57.7	54.6	8.0
Other industries	1,489.5	619.7	41.6	86.4
Sub-total	906.6	497.6	54.9	69.4
Urban				
Mining	5.2	2.1	41.0	0.3
Manufacturing	222.2	28.0	12.6	3.9
Construction	38.0	5.2	13.7	0.7
Transport and utilities	92.3	14.4	15.6	2.0
Trade and services	523.5	48.2	9.2	6.7
Sub-total	881.2	97.9	11.1	13.6
Total	2,370.7	717.6	30.3	100.0

Sources: Malaysia (1981: 33, Table 3.2); Malaysia (1984: 80, Table 3.2).

Notes: 1. The calculations took into consideration the effects of programmes implemented during 1971–80 as well as changes in other factors, such as prices and costs.
2. Data from studies conducted by the Economic Planning Unit and the Socio-Economic Research Unit in the Prime Minister's Department, Ministry of Agriculture, Department of Statistics and other agencies were used in the computations.

stand to gain from increased productivity, all other factors remaining equal. This, of course, has serious implications for the distributional consequences one can expect from higher commodity prices or increased labour productivity, both of which (especially the latter) are often touted as solutions to poverty in Malaysia. The examples involving estate, industrial and mine workers cited in this book suggest that increases in commodity price or productivity are appropriated primarily by capital (employers) and are less likely to benefit wage earners than self-employed petty commodity producers. Hence, with the development of the capitalist sector, and therefore the proportion of wage earners (in relation to petty commodity producers), increases in either commodity prices or productivity in themselves will be even less likely to raise worker incomes.

The second major prong of the NEP proclaims an intention to eventually erase the identification of race with occupation, and, by implication, with social class as well. One important element towards this has been to establish ethnic employment quotas. One effect of this was the reduction of the unemployment rate for Malays in the 1970s to a level lower than that for the labour force as a whole,[45] though the unemployment rate among Malays has become the highest once again in the early 1980s. Besides increasing the proportion of Malays in the working class, it has also resulted in greater numbers of Malays at supervisory and managerial levels. It is the latter, who have achieved previously unimagined upward social mobility, who provide important support for the present regime and its economic policies.

The state has greatly expanded tertiary educational opportunities for Malays, thus enlarging the social bases for continued long-term support for statist or bureaucrat capitalism. Since the Malay community is highly differentiated, the increase in educational opportunities for Malay is essentially class biased; it is those with relatively privileged class origins who have been best able to take advantage of this post-colonial policy, which has been greatly emphasized under the NEP.[46] The importance of cultivating such strata, obligated to and therefore allied with the statist bourgeoisie, has been recognized by government leaders.[47] Currently available data does not empirically distinguish between the Malay bourgeoisie and petty bourgeoisie, but there is little doubt that the Malay petty bourgeoisie has benefited, together with the Malay bourgeoisie, from the NEP.[48]

The most important element of this second prong of the NEP, however, has been the stated goal of 'rectifying' the inter-ethnic imbalance in the ownership and control of wealth in the country. This is viewed primarily in terms of the creation of what is tantamount to a Malay bourgeoisie. The government's proclaimed target is that by 1990, or two decades after the announcement of the NEP:

... at least 30% of the total commercial and industrial activities in all categories and scales of operation should have participation by Malays and other indigenous people in terms of ownership and management. The objective is to create over a period of time, a viable and thriving Malay industrial and commercial community which will operate on a par and in effective partnership with non-Malays in the modern sector (Malaysia, 1971: 158).

TABLE 10.5

Malaysia: Ownership and Control of the Corporate Sector, 1970–1990 ($ million)

	1970		1971		1975	
	$ m.	*Per Cent*	*$ m.*	*Per Cent*	*$ m.*	*Per Cent*
Malaysian residents[2]	1,952.1	36.7	2,512.8	38.3	7,047.2	46.7
Bumiputra total	125.6	2.4	279.6	4.3	1,394.0	9.2
Bumiputra individuals[3]	84.4	1.6	168.7	2.6	549.8	3.6
Bumiputra trust agencies[4]	41.2	0.8	110.9	1.7	844.2	5.6
Other residents[5]	1,826.5	34.3	2,233.2	34.0	5,653.2	37.5
Foreign residents	3,377.1	63.4	4,051.3	61.7	8,037.2	53.3
	5,329.2	100.0	6,564.1	100.0	15,084.4	100.1

Sources: Malaysia (1976: 86, Table 4.16); Malaysia (1981: 62, Table 3.14; 176, Table 9.7); Malaysia (1984: 101, Table 3.12).
Derived from Annual Ownership Survey of Limited Companies conducted by the Department of Statistics (1971-6) and records of the Registrar of Companies (1977-9).
[1]Estimated.
[2]Classification is by residential address of shareholders, not by citizenship. It includes foreign citizens residing in Malaysia.

The Malaysian government has announced various measures to be taken towards achievement of this target. Since the publication in 1971 of the *Second Malaysia Plan 1971-1975*, this strategy has been elaborated by subsequent government pronouncements, e.g. the subsequent two five-year plans and the various mid-term reviews. While modifying and redefining government policy in some areas, these documents reaffirm the state's commitment to advance the interests of statist capital. Many new measures have been intended to broaden the scope and range of government support activities for private Malay capitalists, previously the preserve of MARA and similar agencies in the pre-NEP period. Efforts to promote the interests of private Malay capitalists have not only been continued, but have actually increased recently with the government's new commitment to privatization.

The novel aspect of the restructuring strategy previously, however, was the greatly expanded use of the 'public enterprise' form[49] for advancing Malay capitalism, ostensibly in trusteeship for the Malay community as a whole.[50] Of the targeted 30 per cent of shareholdings to be held by Malays by 1990[51] (see Table 10.5), the *Mid-Term Review of the Second Malaysia Plan* (Malaysia, 1973) projected about three-quarters to be accounted for by 'Malay interests' and only the remaining quarter to be held by Malay individuals. The Fourth Malaysia Plan revised these projections and expects only 17 per cent of the Bumiputra share of the corporate sector to be held by individuals in 1990. This contrasts with the situation in 1969 when only a third of the 1.5 per cent of total share capital held by Malays was in the hands of 'Malay interests'. This seemed to suggest the means by which Malay ownership of the economy was to be

TABLE 10.5 (continued)

1980		1983[1]		1990 Third Malaysia Plan Target		1990 Fourth Malaysia Plan Target	
$ m.	Per Cent	$ m.	Per Cent	$ m.	Per Cent	$ m.	Per Cent
18,493.4	57.1	33,010.6	66.4	56,022.6	70.0	52,193.9	70.0
4,050.5	12.5	9,274.7	18.7	24,009.7	30.7	22,368.8	30.0
1,880.1	5.8	3,762.2	7.6	5,914.2	7.4	3,891.4	5.2
2,170.4	6.7	5,512.4	11.1	18,095.5	22.6	18,477.4	24.8
14,442.9	44.6	23,735.9	47.7	32,012.9	40.0	29,825.1	40.0
13,927.0	42.9	16,697.6	33.6	24,009.7	30.0	22,368.8	30.0
32,420.4	100.0	49,708.2	100.0	80,032.3	100.0	74,562.7	100.0

[3]Includes institutions channelling funds of individual Bumiputra such as Lembaga Urusan dan Tabung Haji, Amanah Saham MARA and cooperatives.
[4]Shares held through institutions classified as 'Bumiputra trust agencies' such as PERNAS, MARA, UDA, SEDCs, Bank Bumiputra, BPMB, FIMA and PNB.
Previously this item was classified as 'Bumiputra interests'.
[5]Includes shares held by nominee and other companies, including Bumiputra interests.
[6]Excludes government holdings other than through trust agencies.

increased.[52] The strategy emphasized increased direct participation by the state, ostensibly on behalf of all Malays, to expand the share of the economy under Malay ownership.

It has been suggested that 'if the government of Malaysia wishes to increase the share of total wealth owned by Bumiputra the sole feasible policy by which this can be realized is state capitalism' (Moore, 1975: 56). Moore claimed that the government's choice of organizational form for Malay economic advancement was inspired by equity concerns.[53] However, the government has never suggested that public enterprises are to be an end in themselves. Instead, it has always insisted that they are only a temporary means for advancing Malay economic interests until such time that they can be taken over by private Malay interests.

The existence of public enterprise in Malaysia predates the introduction of the NEP.[54] Most public enterprises established during the NEP period have been set up to promote Malay capitalist interests,[55] though, as a means to this end, they sometimes involve contradictory purposes.[56] It is not necessary to make the case that the post-NEP public enterprises are actually instruments for the advancement of Malay capitalism since this is openly stated to be their purpose. Unlike governments claiming to be socialist, such as Tanzania (Shivji, 1976), the Malaysian government makes no pretence about its intention to develop a Malay bourgeoisie through this medium.[57] Instead, it has sought to justify this policy on the basis of disproportionate ethnic representation among capitalists, as well as among other classes.

Until the NEP, the role of the post-colonial state had been largely confined to administrative, supportive, and regulatory activities. While undoubtedly important, these did not represent direct and active efforts in promoting the interests of the governing group. With the NEP, the state no longer merely played a supportive role for private capital; it moved to centre stage to become a medium for capital accumulation serving the particular interests of the governing class. At least in this important sense then, it can be suggested that the statist bourgeoisie crystallized with the announcement and implementation of the NEP. With the growth of public enterprises,[58] political power and control over capitalist enterprise have converged in the hands of the statist bourgeoisie. Ministers, other ruling-party politicians, and senior bureaucrats in government service share control of these new instruments of class interest.

The extension of statist capitalist interests is not, however, confined only to the new 'public enterprises' which claim to represent 'Malay interests'. Continued support by the state for private capital accumulation by Malays can be seen in similar light.[59] Joint ventures involving Malay and non-Malay partners (so-called 'Ali-Baba' arrangements), appointment of Malays to company directorships, and the securing of government contracts by politically well-connected businessmen are all manifestations of expanding Malay private capital. Private companies, for example, recognize the advantages to be gained from having politically well-connected directors.[60]

The ascendance of the statist bourgeoisie with the NEP is also reflected in the scale and nature of expansion of public development expenditure since the Second Malaysia Plan. Such expenditure expanded tremendously in the 1970s from $4,242 million in 1966–70 to $9,793 million in 1971–5 and an estimated $24,937 million in 1976–80 and a projected $42,830 million for 1981–5. Perhaps more interesting than the aggregate increase is the percentage accounted for by the commerce and industry sector which jumped from 3.3 per cent during the First Malaysia Plan period (1966–70) to 14.6 per cent for the Second Malaysia Plan period (1971–5), and estimated 13 per cent for the Third Malaysia Plan period (1976–80), and allocated 16.5 per cent for the Fourth Malaysia Plan period (1981–5).

As Table 10.6 shows, there has also been a clear trend in terms of the relative emphasis given to the two main 'prongs' of the NEP. Since the NEP's inception, the government has increasingly shifted emphasis in terms of allocation of funds from poverty eradication to restructuring of society. The ratio of allocations for restructuring compared to poverty eradication rose from 21.6 per cent during 1971–5 to 37.3 per cent during 1976–80. The ratio of the original allocations under the Fourth Malaysia Plan, 1981–1985 rose to 47.2 per cent (Malaysia, 1981), but with the Mid-Term Review, it has risen again to 62.7 per cent. However, the estimated ratio of actual expenditures during 1981–3 was even higher, at 80.7 per cent (Malaysia, 1984). The allocation directed towards 'poverty eradication' was 4.7 times that for 'restructuring' (by the government's own definition) during the Second Malaysia Plan period; this ratio declined to 2.7 for the Third Malaysia Plan period (1976–80) and has been projected to decline further to 2.1 for 1981–5 by the Fourth Malaysia Plan, and to 1.6 by the Mid-Term Review of the Fourth Malaysia Plan. Equally

TABLE 10.6

Malaysia: Development Plan Allocations for Poverty Eradication and Restructuring Society, 1971–1985
($ million)

	Second Malaysia Plan	Third Malaysia Plan	Fourth Malaysia Plan (Original)	Expenditure, 1981-3	Fourth Malaysia Plan (Revised)
1. Poverty Eradication	2,350.0	6,373.4	9,319.2	6,699.1	10,497.0
2. Restructuring Society	508.3	2,376.0	4,397.6	5,406.8	6,576.8
3. Overlapping	3.4	149.0	300.5	184.7	464.5
Total	2,861.7	8,898.4	14,017.3	12,290.6	17,538.3
Allocation for Restructuring Society as Proportion of Allocation for Poverty Eradication [(2) ÷ (1)]	0.216	0.373	0.472	0.807	0.627

Sources: Malaysia (1981: 127, Table 6.3; 245, Table 13.2); Malaysia (1984: 213, Table 7.3).

significantly, the allocations for 'restructuring' alone rose from $508.3 million in 1971-5 to $2,376.0 million in 1976-80 and was originally projected in 1981 to rise to $4,397.6 million during 1981-5, before this was revised upward to $6,576.8 million in 1984. The allocation for 'commerce and industry' alone accounted for 71 per cent of the 'restructuring' allocation for 1971-5, rose to 81 per cent for 1976-80 and was projected to be 79 per cent for 1981-5. Since over half the Malay population is officially considered poor, theoretically, Malays would comprise the majority of the beneficiaries of poverty eradication measures regardless of race. On the other hand, the most well-to-do, probably comprising no more than 3 per cent, of the Bumiputra community, benefit directly and substantially from efforts to restructure society. Hence, shifting emphasis from poverty eradication to restructuring society would tend to increase inequality within the Malay community.

It is important to emphasize that, unlike the rest of the bourgeoisie, the statist capitalists are not involved in capital accumulation solely based on their own private property. The statist capitalists also use the state apparatus to accumulate.[61] Such a mode of accumulation may eventually lead to fiscal crisis and even foreign 'debt bondage' (Khor, 1983a), though a debt crisis still appears some way off, given Malaysia's considerable foreign assets and previously healthy trade balance. With capital accumulation taken care of by the state, private appropriation by statist capitalists is conducted through the high salaries and other forms of remuneration available to those in government service or in public enterprises. This is supplemented by numerous other supplementary income opportunities arising from access to the state, including various forms morally characterized as corrupt, some of which are disallowed by the letter of the law. Growing state intervention and the strengthening of the governing class, both related to the rise of statist capitalism, have also created opportunities and encouraged activities contributing to the spread of corruption.

Statist Capitalism and Its Contradictions

Who, then, are the statist capitalists? The complex origins and nature of this class or fraction of the capitalist class do not permit neat definition. It certainly includes those social groups who control capital accumulation by virtue of their access to state power. These then would certainly include powerful ruling-party politicians and others in control of the state apparatus, such as senior bureaucrats, as well as politically well-connected businessmen. Ethnically, it appears that this class is predominantly Malay, though it is important to recognize that it is not exclusively so.[62] The statist capitalists are popularly identified primarily with Malay politicians, bureaucrats, and businessmen. Many powerful Malay politicians as well as senior government bureaucrats can trace their social origins to the 'administocrats', i.e. the Malay administrative stratum in the colonial state apparatus which has its roots in the pre-colonial ruling class[63] (Tilman, 1969; Nordin, 1976). Many successful Malay businessmen are also from similar social backgrounds (e.g. see Lim Mah Hui, 1980; Tan

Tat Wai, 1982). However, it has also been noted that a high proportion of successful Malay entrepreneurs are from long-standing business families[64] (Popenoe, 1970).

Though the statist bourgeoisie has consolidated itself as a class, especially at the political level, this hardly means that it has transcended the contradictions of its present situation. Reference to some of these can suggest the kinds of problems into which it will run and which may eventually prove to be its undoing. The potential for statist capitalist development is constrained by its social base. Tracing its origins to the pre-colonial ruling class as well as rural landed interests which were consolidated by colonial laws and policies, the statist bourgeoisie continues to maintain strong connections with landed interests. In so far as they continue to ally with such interests, the statist capitalists will be incapable of initiating thorough-going land reforms, even those of a 'capitalist' variety, which more 'populist' statist capitalists elsewhere have been able to achieve. This incapacity will continue to hinder its ability to mobilize broad Malay peasant support for its policies.

Having their origins in the colonial state, and being relatively deficient and inexperienced in entrepreneurship, statist capitalists in Malaysia have few constraints against collaboration with foreign capital, especially since their ascendance has not even involved populist anti-imperialist rhetoric. The creation of new partnerships, often ostensibly in the interests of technology transfer or employment creation, have shaped new alliances with foreign capital. Accumulating successfully within the context of the world economy, statist capital also has had little reason to reduce the openness or dependence of the Malaysian economy though this would not preclude efforts to obtain better terms within this context, e.g. by supporting demands associated with the New International Economic Order. And in so far as its primary mode of capital accumulation is via the state, it has tended to favour measures enhancing accumulation by the state,[65] though as this class consolidates itself, pressure for increased private accumulation will mount. In this context, the announcement of the official privatization policy in 1983 can be seen not only as an initiative necessitated by the fiscal crisis (see Khor, 1983a), but also as a response to such interests. The pervasive ideology of Malay economic rivalry with the Chinese has also strengthened the alliance of statist capital with foreign capital. The post-colonial state run by statist capitalists therefore tends to continue to be essentially dependent or comprador in nature though perhaps on a more selective basis and not necessarily with the same old partners from the colonial era. Thus, the 'openness' of the economy as well as the hegemony of foreign capital[66] continue to be guaranteed by statist capitalism. Nevertheless, in its vigorous pursuit of capital accumulation, it is also capable of encroaching into the domain of established capitalist interests. In certain instances, statist capital may find portions of the foreign-owned sector the only or the choicest sector to take over.[67] Constrained by its essentially 'comprador' character, such decisions usually lead only to 'gentle' nationalization—'by the back door', i.e. by purchase or with compensation—or to the establishment of joint ventures, 'turn-key' arrangements, etc.[68] Foreign (as well as local) capital cooperating with statist capitalist interests usually gain from such developments, e.g. foreign capital may thus be better protected and made more secure, and can have access to privileges otherwise enjoyed solely by statist capitalists.

National capital is obviously not favoured by statist capital's essentially comprador nature. Its economic weakness implies that it has relatively little to offer partners, while its lack of political clout prevents it from substantially influencing developments in its favour. Established local comprador elements are also threatened by the aggressive intrusion of statist capital, though particular capitalists in a position to strike mutually profitable bargains are constantly seeking to do so, thus undermining the potential unity of such capital in facing statist capital. Thus, the accelerated pace of advance of statist capitalist interests also challenges the predominantly Chinese, established local capitalists. Generally, the ethnic dimensions of these fractional configurations of the capitalist class in Malaysia further stimulate rivalry along ethnic lines.[69] The resistance of both foreign and local capital to statist capitalist intrusion is well captured, for example, in statements by spokesmen of such interests about the 1975 Industrial Coordination Act[70] (e.g. Philip Khoo, 1977). The Act is widely believed to have been intended to control the growth of the Malaysian manufacturing sector so as to ensure advancement of Malay capitalist interests in this sector.[71]

However, another potentially problematic area for the statist capitalists may be the student, youth, and intellectual components of the Malay petty bourgeoisie. The situation in Tanzania of 'increasing saturation of the "bureaucratic bourgeoisie" coupled with its arrogance resulting in the frustration of student aspirations to the high bureaucratic posts' (Shivji, 1973: 85) may also take place in Malaysia.[72] Malay students, whose expectations have been raised by their access to opportunities for higher education, are likely to be increasingly disenchanted with statist capitalism, while the cultural and moral corruption accompanying it has encouraged a morally-inspired religious opposition. It has also been suggested that Malay university graduates, who dominate the humanities, social science and other less technical programmes in the local universities, may soon saturate employment opportunities in government service. However, the new opportunities offered by the NEP, including the imposition of ethnic quotas for employment at the management level in the private sector, may solve or at least postpone the problem temporarily. Yet, as these opportunities are filled, a graduate employment-mismatching problem is anticipated. The *Third Malaysia Plan 1976–1980* (Malaysia, 1976: 155) pessimistically estimated that, by 1980, 'there will be a growing surplus of graduates in the non-technical disciplines with supply exceeding requirements by about 41%'. Though apparently alarmist in retrospect, the problem may only have been postponed rather than overcome. The kind of change such frustrations can engender remains unclear, however.[73]

The accelerated integration of Malays into the working class is probably even more significant. Relatively poorly equipped in terms of educational credentials, encouragement of Malay wage employment[74] has resulted in the bulk of Malay workers occupying lower-status and lower-paid positions in the work force. For many Malays from peasant backgrounds, the experience of working for a wage together with other employees is a profoundly new experience. As this experience accumulates, it is probable that Malay labour militancy will grow.[75] In so far as Malay workers choose to cast their lot with their class rather than with their race, it will pose a growing threat to the capitalist class as a whole, including the statist bourgeoisie.

It has also been suggested that the long-run elimination of the historical identification of race with class, as envisaged by the NEP, will implicitly highlight class rather than ethnic divisions. Correspondingly, class contention would involve increasing class-consciousness. In this regard, however, it is necessary also to bear in mind that since 'these processes cannot be instant and are bound to be drawn out, it would be unrealistic to dismiss completely the possibility of the racial ideology intensifying occasionally before its final death' (Shivji, 1973: 81). Unlike in East Africa, possible recourse to 'repatriation' of non-Malays from Malaysia is unlikely because of the relatively large proportion of the population involved, and, perhaps more significantly, its strong representation in classes other than the bourgeoisie, especially the working class. This means that since the racial identification with class cannot be simply displaced abroad, it necessitates resolution locally.

Summary

In the colonial period, the hegemony of British capital had limited the expansion of local capital. The colonial state, which advanced British interests, co-opted the pre-colonial Malay ruling class to serve in the middle echelons of its administrative apparatus. In the post-colonial period, this statist petty bourgeoisie—termed the 'administocrats'—emerged as the governing group, mediating between the interests of foreign capital, the fractions of local capital, the upper strata of the peasantry, and the urban petty bourgeoisie on the one hand, and the dominated classes—mainly the working class and the lower strata of the peasantry and the urban petty bourgeoisie—on the other.

The efforts of the governing Malay statist petty bourgeoisie to use the state to promote Malay capital were constrained by the class compromise underlying the ruling Alliance Party arrangement. Government encouragement of private Malay enterprise was tolerated as long as this did not really threaten the established capitalist interests. Consequently, the rapid growth of the Malay petty bourgeoisie in the first twelve years following independence was not matched by success in developing a Malay capitalist class. From the mid-1960s, the efforts of this governing petty bourgeoisie secured some new gains, but these did not go beyond stretching the framework of the prevailing Alliance compromise. By this time, growing income inequalities among all ethnic groups had sharpened (class-based) frustrations, which, however, were increasingly perceived in ethnic terms.

In the absence of concerted mobilization across ethnic lines by class-based organizations, these frustrations led to a disenchantment with the Alliance government (as reflected in the 1969 general election results), and exacerbated ethnic tensions, culminating in the May 1969 racial conflagration. These circumstances enabled the so-called 'Young Turks' within UMNO, the dominant partner in the Alliance coalition, to ease out the 'Old Guard' associated with the Alliance policies of the 1960s.

Hence, the new order is very much a response to as well as a product of the old one. In the new order, the development of Malay capitalism has been advanced by placing the onus of capital accumulation on the state. Having access to state power, the governing group controls this accumulation. As a class, these primarily Malay statist capitalists have been ascendant since independence and dominant since 1969. Initially, though private capital accumulation was encouraged, public enterprises were designated to advance the interests of this class. On the one hand, the state has been bearing the costs of capital accumulation, while on the other, private accumulation and consumption by statist capitalists has been enhanced by attractive salary structures, expense allowances, and other pecuniary benefits, as well as other forms of appropriation, including corruption. The rise of statist capital has also involved the emergence of new contradictions with other capitalist fractions, the dominated classes and sometimes even with the growing Malay petty bourgeoisie. In fact, the more pronounced forms of class contention in contemporary Malaysia are outcomes of class contradictions generated by the rise of the statist bourgeoisie.

1. This section has been somewhat influenced by the work of Issa Shivji (1973, 1976). There are, of course, many important differences between the Tanzanian and the Malaysian cases.

2. See Chandrasekaran Pillay (1974). The term 'administocrats' is used to refer to the Malay administrative stratum recruited from the ranks of the pre-colonial Malay 'aristocratic' class by the British colonial regime.

3. See Stenson (1980).

4. The Socialist Front (SF) initially comprised the Partai Rakyat (People's Party) and the Labour Party. Originally modelled along the lines of Western European social-democratic parties, the latter became increasingly radicalized from the late 1950s by its primarily working-class base. Later, the National Convention Party, led by Abdul Aziz Ishak, who had been an UMNO minister, joined the SF. The SF coalition subsequently broke down in the mid-1960s apparently over differences on language and cultural policy, i.e. over the 'national question'.

5. For various interpretations on the formation of Malaysia and the subsequent confrontation, with Indonesia, see Pluvier (1965) and Wheelwright (1975).

6. In this regard, Skinner's observation on the Thai experience is suggestive:
'The Chinese middleman, though in fact only a part or function of the total economic system was the most visible reason for the misery and indebtedness of the Thai peasantry. It became advantageous, therefore, for the Thai government to divert attention from the limited results of its economic policies by pointing to the Chinese middlemen as the cause of rural problems' (Skinner, 1957: 248).
For some discussion of similar actions by the colonial government in Malaya, see Kratoska (1975).

7. 'Special rights in regard to land law were designed to preserve the traditional life style of the Malay peasants, while special rights in matters of education and entrance to the public services were designed to effect selective social changes within Malay aristocracy which would preserve the status and role of the *raja* class in Malay society and make them more effective junior partners in the colonial system' (Means, 1972: 36).

8. '... in time, it became increasingly difficult and uneconomic to fill the lower and routine administrative positions with Europeans. At about the same time that it became apparent that local people were needed for the lower levels of the public service, the Malay Rulers were also expressing

concern about their loss of powers. As a consequence, the initial scheme for local recruitment had as its primary objective the selection of Malays from the aristocratic raja class for training and eventual recruitment into the public service....

'While indigenous non-Malays were recruited to the public service, they generally became clerks or peons, or they entered the technical and professional services, rather than the more politically sensitive administrative positions which were monopolized by the Europeans and aristocratic Malays' (Means, 1972: 34).

9. For example, see Freedman (1961); Alatas (1972a); and Parkinson (1975).

10. For many years, civil service positions were reserved exclusively for the British, who occupied the most senior and strategic positions, and Malays, who were allowed to take the less important, intermediate-level positions.

11. For example, members of the royal family received handsome and regular salaries from the colonial government, thus ensuring their commitment to maintaining the status quo.

12. Increased participation from professionals as a social grouping (and not merely in their individual capacities) has been a relatively recent and not especially smooth development.

13. It would not be wrong to assert that the economic interests of Chinese capital are also embodied by the Chinese Chambers of Commerce, though their leadership has not been identical with that of the MCA. The Chambers are essentially business-oriented in their activities and do not organizationally participate in the state's policy-making apparatus. Its only medium for doing so would be its representation through MCA leadership. Yet in so far as the leadership of the Chambers has historically been somewhat different (e.g. involving far more Chinese-educated businessmen), it suggests that they may organizationally represent business interests different from those represented by the MCA leadership. However, as with the case of the SCBA and SCCC (see Chapter 8), such differences are not to be over-emphasized.

14. 'By reigning class or fraction is meant that one from which the upper personnel of the state apparatuses is recruited, i.e. its political personnel in the broad sense. This class or fraction may be distinct from the hegemonic class or fraction....

'The distinction between hegemonic class or fraction and reigning class or fraction, which depends ultimately on the strategy of alliance and compromises necessary for the establishment of hegemony, is important. Its neglect leads to two consequences. It becomes impossible to reveal the real hegemony lying beneath the appearances of the political arena, the conclusion being that that class which occupies the top of the state apparatus is the hegemonic class or fraction...' (Poulantzas, 1973: 45-6).

15. Here only those situations where colonial capital took a primarily 'expatriate' form are being referred to. Where colonial capital was mainly of a 'settler' nature, and where the original indigenous population was not totally subjugated or eliminated (e.g. as in North America and Australia), the preservation of colonial rule has been most tenacious (e.g. as in Algeria, Kenya, and the Portuguese colonies), and has even become embodied in racist ideologies for the maintenance of class/race rule (as in South Africa).

16. In East Africa and in parts of the West Indies, for example, former British colonies also inherited similar fractions within the local ruling class, which in most cases also have an ethnic manifestation.

17. The nature of the partnership is reflected in some practical aspects of electoral participation by the Alliance: '... although the back-bone of the voting power of the Alliance is the Malay rural vote, the financial basis of the party is the economic resources of... MCA' (Beaglehole, 1969: 218).

18. Chandra (1977) has shown that important ideas for the promotion of a Malay capitalist class emerged well before 1957, the year of independence.

19. In 1957, Aziz (1957) observed that, 'A new class of Malay rentiers is being created.' He added, 'I fail to see how this will help the 3 million Malays to improve their economic condition.'

20. For example, for locally incorporated tin-dredging companies, Yip (1968: 78) found that: 'Most of the Malay shareholders are members of the royal family of each state, titled Malays (for example, Datos and Hajis), government officials (including a number of ministers), and landowners.'

21. 'The pressure on Government to launch a more determined policy also reflected the increased strength and influence of the Malay business community whose existence was partly the result of the opportunities created for the Malays by government policy. In view of the structure of

Malay society, the realities of political power in Malaysia after 1957, and the extent of political and administrative control of economic activity, it was to be expected that many of those best placed to take advantage of the new opportunities would tend to be drawn along [sic] the Malay political and administrative class. For these reasons, in spite of the weakness of its organization, Malay business opinion is able to exercise substantial influence as a result of the informal political channels available to its leadership' (Beaglehole, 1969: 227-8).

22. 'Bumiputra', literally meaning 'prince of the land', has come to be officially used in the Malaysian context to refer to those also termed the 'Malays and other indigenous people', i.e. excluding 'immigrant races' such as Europeans, Chinese and Indians, but not Arabs and Malays from Indonesia.

23. 'The first Bumiputra Economic Congress held in Kuala Lumpur in June 1965 for instance not only sought to identify the areas of economic participation Malays consider [sic] vital but also to formulate resolutions for their eventual promulgation. The composition of its steering committee reflected the dominance of the role of the political and bureaucratic elites in the entire process of effecting the development of economic modernity among the Malays.. . .

'In connection with the problem of capital accumulation and formulation, the government was asked to provide adequate financial facilities to ameliorate the late entry of Malays in trade and commerce' (Tham, 1973: 46-7).

In an important footnote, Tham also points out that:

'The Steering Committee consisted of 6 Malay cabinet ministers; 1 Chinese cabinet minister; 1 Indian cabinet minister; 3 Malay Members of Parliament; 3 Malay Parliamentary Secretaries; the governor of Bank Negara; the Chairman of Rural and Industrial Development Authority and the Manager of the Centre for Small Industries in the Rural and Industrial Development Authority. There were, however, no members from the various Malay Chambers of Commerce' (Tham, 1973: 46).

The frustrations of the Malay bourgeoisie and its resulting aggressiveness is captured by the following statement emerging from the Congress:

'If the bumiputra (indigenous people) do not have a stake in the economy of the country then there is no assurance that in time to come non-bumiputras will be able to carry out their economic activities in peace and security' (quoted in Tham, 1973: 49).

The Second Bumiputra Economic Congress was held in September 1968, a third in 1973 and a fourth in 1981. For a report on the second congress, see Konggeres Ekonomi Bumiputera Kedua and also Tham (1973: 52-3). All the subsequent congresses reiterated and increased economic demands favouring the advancement of Malay capitalism.

24. Though not the first-ever Malay-owned bank, with heavy government backing, it emerged as the largest locally incorporated bank in the country before slipping embarrassingly in 1984 due to the Hong Kong property saga.

25. An increase in the rate of exploitation—which was suggested earlier to have occurred in the manufacturing sector—probably played an important part in contributing to this trend. However, it would be hazardous with the limited information available to attempt here to fully explain this apparent trend (see Lim Lin Lean, 1971; Anand, 1973; Eddy Lee, 1975; Tan Tat Wai, 1977). While the broad patterns of income distribution are related to class relationships, it would be foolhardy to suggest any simple deterministic relationship between the two. Explanation is further complicated by the uneven development of Malaya which has limited the extent of capitalist relations of production on the one hand, and contributed to the heterogeneous character of the capitalist sector itself on the other. It has been suggested that 'the promotion of the manufacturing sector behind tariff walls, accompanied as it has been by a relative neglect of the rural economy, has led to a worsening in income differentials between the urban and rural sectors' (Edwards, 1975: 339). It is probable that uneven inter-regional, as well as urban-rural, spread of industrial growth has also contributed to the trends in income distribution.

26. This report was based primarily on data from the 1957/58 Household Budget Survey and the 1970 Post-Enumeration Survey, both prepared by the government. Strictly speaking, the different bases and methods of the two surveys render them statistically incomparable (Anand, 1973). Nevertheless, in the absence of alternative sources of data, income distribution studies which have relied mainly on these sources provide useful indications of major trends.

27. The Gini Coefficient is a popular measure of the degree of inequality. It is the ratio of income

received under conditions of inequality compared to that received under conditions of perfect equality and can have a value ranging from 0 to 1. The higher the ratio, the greater the degree of inequality.

28. 'Inequality between races contributed to only a relatively small proportion of the *total* inequality of incomes in the country and does not provide a sufficient explanation for the total inequality in the levels of living in Malaysia. Most of the total inequality is apparently due to inequalities within sectors and within each race due to occupational differences, as opposed to inequality between sectors and between races' (Treasury, 1974: 84).

Distribution of Income in Malaya by Race, 1957-1970

Percentage of Households	1957/8			1970				All Races	
	M	C	I	M	C	I	O	1957/8	1970
Bottom 10%	2.8	2.6	2.9	1.4	1.8	1.9	0.3	2.2	1.2
20%	7.0	6.7	7.5	4.8	4.9	5.6	0.7	5.7	4.0
30%	12.8	11.7	12.9	9.1	9.2	9.6	1.5	10.3	7.2
40%	19.1	17.6	19.2	13.4	14.7	15.0	2.8	15.7	11.7
50%	26.6	24.3	26.5	20.2	20.9	20.6	5.5	22.2	17.2
60%	34.9	32.4	34.8	27.3	27.9	28.3	11.5	29.9	24.0
70%	44.7	42.0	44.2	36.8	36.6	36.3	22.2	39.1	33.1
80%	56.5	53.6	55.2	49.0	47.4	46.3	36.8	50.2	43.8
90%	71.5	69.0	69.5	64.8	63.2	60.6	63.5	65.2	58.9
Top 5%[1]	18.0	20.0	20.0	25.0	25.0	28.0	n.a.	22.0	28.0
10%	28.5	31.0	30.5	35.2	36.8	39.4	36.5	34.8	41.1
20%	43.5	46.4	44.8	51.0	52.6	53.7	63.2	49.8	56.2
Gini Ratio	0.361	0.383	0.356	0.451	0.449	0.453	0.611	0.421	0.499

Key: M: Malays, C: Chinese, I: Indians, O: Others.
Sources: 1957/8: Household Budget Survey 1957/8.
1970: Post-Enumeration Survey 1970.
From Lim Lin Lean (1974) and Snodgrass (1975).
[1]Figures for top 5 per cent share of income are from Snodgrass, whose methodology differs slightly from Lim's. The figures have therefore been rounded. These methodological differences also account for the differences in the data presented in this table compared to Table 10.1.

29. Between 1956 and 1970, Federal Land Development Authority (FELDA) schemes had settled a total of 20,700 families (Malaysia, 1971: 125). This is in contrast to the estimate of 10,000 families becoming landless every year, according to the then Deputy Director of FELDA, Aladdin Hashim (*New Straits Times*, 22 June 1974). See also Husin Ali (1976).

30. The viability of this ideology was ensured by the 'corporatist' nature of UMNO politics and its success in conducting the anti-colonial effort on the basis of a coalition of urban (primarily from the ranks of the 'administocrats') and rural (mainly drawn from among rural landlords, rich and middle peasants) Malay petty bourgeoisie.

31. 'In theory Malay special rights apply only to recruitment, and not to promotion within the public service. In practice, however, Malays have been promoted because of race to assure that the highest policy-making positions will be filled by Malays regardless of objective performance standards. Thus, the administrative positions formerly filled by British expatriate officers are today filled almost exclusively by Malays who were promoted at a rapid rate to fill the gap created by "Malayanization"' (Means, 1972: 47).

The percentages of expatriates, Malays, and non-Malays (i.e. Chinese and Indians) among Division I government officers changed from 61.0 per cent, 14.1 per cent, and 20.2 per cent in 1957 to 0 per cent, 36.3 per cent, and 57.6 per cent in 1968 respectively. Over the period, the total number of officers rose from 2,761 to 4,308, while the higher administrative officials in the Malayan Civil Service rose from 360 to 597 over the same period. The corresponding ethnic proportions for the latter sub-group changed from 61.1 per cent expatriates, 35.5 per cent Malays, and 3.3 per cent non-Malays in 1957 to 0.2 per cent, 85.1 per cent, and 13.8 per cent respectively in 1968 (Means, 1972: 47, Tables 2 and 3). Of course, such figures ignore the considerable number of foreign advisers to the government, usually brought in on a contract basis, after independence.

32. 'Power and property may be separated for a time by force or fraud—but divorced never. For so soon as the pang of separation is felt ... property will be purchased by power, or power will take over property. And either way there must be an end to free government' (by Leigh, a nineteenth-century Virginia (USA) stateman, quoted by Shivji, 1976).

33. 'The businessman involved in the sphere of circulation is, no doubt, an essential link in the chain of exploitation. He fully participates in the exploitation. But to identify a link with the chain is absolute obscurantism. In so far as it does not control the state, it is not even a *decisive* link. To confine attention to circulation without even touching production is a political gimmick of the petty bourgeoisie. For to expose the chain of exploitation would mean exposing the ruling classes—both internal and external. Objectively, therefore, this obscurantism does not arise from mere ignorance but from basic class interests. It is class obscurantism!' (Shivji, 1976: 72).

34. The idiomatic local term to characterize such arrangements is 'Ali-Baba' business, where 'Baba' refers to the Chinese capitalist and 'Ali' to the Malay partner.

35. The very nature of some of these activities (e.g. corruption) make them very difficult to document. Some examples of collaboration in the pioneer industry programme can be found in Lindenberg (1973).

36. See J. A. Nagata (1972: 1140). Malay business activity in the colonial period developed mainly in small retail trade. In the early post-colonial period before the NEP, Malay capitalists made the most advances in the public transport industry largely due to government protection, e.g. by route allocation. 'In the manufacturing sector in 1970 only 7% of the professional and managerial group were Malays, compared to 68% Chinese, 4% Indians and 18% foreigners...' (Milne, 1976: 241).

37. 'Malay interests', which accounted for a third of this percentage, refer to government-owned institutions established to advance Malay business where property ownership has not yet been transferred to individual Malays.

38. The most well-known personalities identified with this faction were Mahathir Mohamad, a medical doctor, and Musa Hitam, a political scientist. The former is the author of *The Malay Dilemma*, published in 1970. (For a critique, see Alatas, 1972: 1977.) This book was banned in Malaysia until 1981, after Mahathir became Prime Minister. Among other things—such as a scientifically unacceptable 'genetic explanation' of Malay 'economic inferiority'—the book is an appeal for the development of a Malay bourgeoisie.

39. The literature on the causes, course and consequences of these riots is quite extensive, e.g. see Slimming (1969); Goh (1971); Gagliano (1970); Rahman (1969); National Operations Council (1969); Von Vorys (1975). On the 1969 general election, see Vasil (1969). It has been suggested that the outbreak of violence was premeditated, although there are at least two contrasting views of this. Rahman (1969) views the riots as a result of a communist-inspired conspiracy, while Hoerr (1969), among others, has suggested that the violence was provoked by elements within the ruling party who used the outbreak as an opportunity to mount a 'palace coup'. A third, more common view has been to see the riots as being largely spontaneous, though this should not be interpreted to mean that there was no premeditation at all. However, the alleged premeditation is not generally considered to have been made long in advance, but, rather, in response to fast-moving developments in the highly volatile period around the general election of 10 May 1969. The details of the matter here do not, however, have a major bearing on the following discussion on the significance of the May 1969 events as a historical watershed (see also Von Vorys, 1975). The following quote provides an interesting perspective on the significance of the riots:

'Prime Minister Tunku Abdul Rahman blamed the rioting on Communists and subversives supposedly working in the opposition parties. Yet the real issue at stake was not Communism, but Malay special rights. The instigators of the actual rioting were militant Malays inflamed by the "victory celebrations" of the opposition parties and the fear that the strengthened position of the opposition parties threatened the "loss of their country" to the "aliens". That the greatest atrocities were committed by its own supporters made it difficult for the government to respond with firmness and impartiality in time of crisis, and even more difficult for it to give a full and frank accounting of the riots after the event. . . .

'If its recent public statements are an accurate indication of its analysis, the government has concluded that the 1969 riots were a product of economic conditions; and the main cause was the relative economic deprivation of Malays compared to non-Malays' (Means, 1972: 55, 59).

40. After the riots of May 1969 and continued criticism of the Tunku's leadership of UMNO and the government, Dr Mahathir was expelled from UMNO by the then party leader, Tunku Abdul Rahman. Musa Hitam was sent to do a post-graduate course abroad. Later, Tunku's successor, Razak, accepted Mahathir back into the UMNO fold in 1972 and gave both Mahathir and Musa responsible positions. After the 1974 general election, both were appointed to senior ministerial positions and after Razak's death in early 1976, Mahathir became Deputy Prime Minister to Razak's brother-in-law, Hussein Onn, before succeeding him in mid-1981, with Musa as his deputy in both party and government.

41. 'An important political aspect of the NEP consists in the fact that many of the Malays who play key roles in directing it are also leading politicians in UMNO. It is no coincidence that since 1969, the Minister of Trade and Industry, previously a Chinese, has been a Malay, or that after the resignation of Tun Tan Siew Sin as Finance Minister because of ill-health in early 1974, he was succeeded by a Malay. These events were a translation in terms of Cabinet appointments of Malay determination to direct the economy. The strength of the connection between UMNO leadership and prominence in implementing the NEP is illustrated by the elections for the three Vice-Presidential posts in UMNO, which ranked only below the then President (Tun Razak) and the current Deputy President (Datuk Hussein Onn), held in June, 1975. The highest vote was won by Ghafar bin Baba, Secretary-General of the National Front, Minister for Agriculture and Rural Development, a previous head of MARA, and currently the Chairman of a MARA subsidiary, the Kompleks Kewangan. The second highest vote was won by Tan Sri Tengku Razaleigh [sic], the Treasurer of UMNO. The reason why Tengku Razaleigh was accorded the honorary title of "Bapa Ekonomi Malaysia" (Father of the Malaysian Economy) will be apparent from the wide range of jobs he has held, any one of which would qualify him as a leading figure in the economic sphere. He was the original chairman of PERNAS, and left it only to become Chairman of the state oil company PETRONAS, 1974-76. When Tun Razak appointed him to this post, he stated publicly that it was equivalent in rank to an appointment as cabinet minister. He remained chairman of PERNAS Securities, in which capacity he negotiated the abortive Haw Par deal. He was also Chairman of Bank Bumiputra, as well as being Chairman of the Malay Chamber of Commerce and Industry and Chairman of the National Chamber of Commerce and Industry of Malaysia. The third winning candidate (and since March 1976 Deputy Prime Minister), Dr. Mahathir bin Mohamad, owed his success mainly to his record as a fighter for Malay rights and to support deriving from his cabinet job as Education Minister. But he was also Chairman of FIMA (Food Industries of Malaysia, a government corporation)' (Milne, 1976: 255-6).

42. It may also be suggested that the shifts in Malaysian development planning embodied in the Plan also reflect a more acute awareness of participation in a world economy dominated by US capital and no longer by the British Empire. However, it can also be argued that such a shift in orientation by the government dates from much earlier (Witton, 1971). For some discussion of certain aspects of US involvement in Malaysia in the post-colonial period, especially in the 1970s since the NEP, see Siegel and Ngun (1976).

43. It has been suggested that the interests of small and politically uninfluential non-Malay capitalists have been upset to some extent. For example, government provision of alternative marketing and credit facilities to peasant producers has cut somewhat into the previously exclusive domain of many small commercial and usurious capitalists. However, there are few reliable indications of the significance of such measures and there is little to suggest that these businessmen have been eliminated by the government's measures. The effects of statist capitalist development for the other fractions of capital are not systematically examined in this book.

44. The Third Malaysia Plan (Malaysia, 1976: 5) has defined the poverty line 'to cover minimum food requirements and minimum needs with respect to clothing, housing, consumer durable goods and transport services to sustain a decent standard of living'. No specific figure or a more detailed elaboration of the bases for such measurement are provided.

45. The unemployment rate for the entire labour force was 8.0 per cent in 1970, 6.7 per cent in 1975, 5.6 per cent in 1980, and 5.8 per cent in 1983, whereas the rate for Malays declined from 8.1 per cent in 1970 to 6.1 per cent in 1975 and then rose to 6.5 per cent in 1980 and 7.0 per cent in 1983. Among the other ethnic communities, the Chinese have been relatively more successful in finding

employment, perhaps because of the relatively strong Chinese capitalist presence in the growing 'modern' sector and the relatively higher levels of education in the Chinese community.

46. 'Although schools are "free" in Malaysia, HH [household] out-of-pocket expenditures (OPEC) to keep children in school is substantial . . . for many HHs burdens of this magnitude preclude putting children through secondary school. . . .

'Clearly, those in the "Bottom Forty" of the income distribution can ill afford the OPEC of maintaining even two students in school, particularly if one is in the secondary. No doubt this factor is a major reason for the rapid decrease in enrollment rates as incomes fall irrespective of level' (Meerman, 1977: 8, 10).

There is government assistance of various kinds to reduce the OPEC burden. However, 55 per cent of this assistance is for post-secondary students, of whom very few are from poor backgrounds; 37 per cent of the total goes to secondary school students; and only 8 per cent to others. Meerman concludes his analysis by pointing out that 'most of the Malays supported are from the higher income groups' (Meerman, 1977: 17), thus underscoring the class-biased nature of current educational policy.

'There are more and more Malays in universities. In 1970 there were 3,237 Malays studying for university degrees. In 1975 there were 8,153. The number of Chinese students increased from 4,009 to only 5,217 during the same period. Malay enrollment in technical schools went from 2,865 to 11,579 over the same period while the number of Chinese increased from 537 to 1,810' (Grace, 1976).

The significance of increased Malay enrolment in tertiary institutions should be viewed in light of the earlier comments on the class-biased economic factors affecting success in the schooling system: 'In evaluating the effects of special rights, we should note that the system of quotas for admission to the public service and to higher educational institutions primarily affects the most advantaged segments of Malay society—the traditional elites and urbanized Malays who have already become quite modernized in their styles of life and have access to better secondary educational facilities which enable them to take advantage of Malay special privileges' (Means, 1972: 48).

47. 'Tun Razak has talked of the desire to create not an elite but a "middle-class group" ' (Milne, 1976: 259).

48. 'Current patterns of Malay borrowing give an impression of the recent expansion of the middle class. At the end of 1973, 6.1 per cent of the value of all outstanding loans and advances from commercial banks went to Malays. This increased to 12.2 per cent by 1975, a value of $323 million, $160 million of this went to finance Malay business (e.g. construction, manufacturing, trade), $42 million financed agriculture, while $50 million was loaned for such private purposes as homes and automobiles. Finance company loans to Malays at the end of 1975 was only $82 million (about 25 per cent of that of commercial banks); but $34 million were for personal loans (mostly for financing automobiles) and $22 million for buying or building homes. The next largest category of lending was to agriculture—only about $10 million. . . .

'The urban, business-oriented Malay appears to have benefited more from credit than poorer rural Malays. . . .

'The impression that one gains is a middle class of about 50,000 Malays in the bureaucracy, business, professionals, and the military. These are the Malays who contract the bulk of the loans to start businesses, buy cars, and build homes' (Grace, 1976).

49. Public enterprises include public corporations established by statute by either the federal or state governments, as well as government-owned companies and subsidiaries of either of the foregoing.

50. 'The use of large organizations was based on the belief that the Malay would-be businessman was so disadvantaged in competition with non-Malays that he would be lost without institutional help. This point was made at the Second Bumiputra Economic Congress by Tan Sri Jaffar Albar when he attacked free enterprise as obstructing Malay participation in business. The Congress reaffirmed its belief in free enterprise, but Tun Razak himself said that in implementing The Plan " . . . the Government itself will participate effectively and directly in order to promote a large number of entrepreneurs among the Malays," and stressed the role of large organizations such as MARA. Later, this policy was praised by Tengku Tan Sri Razaleigh (who in turn has headed two of these major organizations) when he claimed that without the use of such organizations the programme to get *bumiputras* into business would be a non-starter.

'The change did not consist in the actual setting up of such institutions after May 1969.... What was different about these bodies was not their existence, but their newly-acquired legitimacy...' (Milne, 1976: 244–5, 248).

The use of public enterprises to develop Malay capitalism was not without its critics. For example, it has been argued that to transfer to a group of Malay capitalists '...a business which is thriving and which they did not create, is the height of absurdity which has never entered the imagination of even the most fanatical capitalist in the entire history of mankind. Why should a small handful of greedy and unenterprising Malays get the benefit of the transfer as opposed to the Malay community represented by the workers of the enterprise and the Government's interest in it?' (S. H. Alatas, 1972b). It has also been argued that even if 30 per cent of the wealth in the corporate sector is owned by Malays in 1990, as projected by the NEP, it will almost certainly be concentrated in the hands of a few Malays (Thillainathan, 1975: 10).

51. E. W. Wheelwright, a consultant to the Malaysian government, has argued: 'There is no possibility of the target being achieved, short of expropriation, or buying into the modern sector....

'The quickest way for the MCIC [Malay Commercial and Industrial Community] target to be achieved would be for the government, through state agencies ... to buy into this foreign sector, on behalf of the Malaysian people' (Wheelwright, 1972: 68–68a).

52. 'Of the $4 billion share capital in the country in 1975, Malays owned $95 million and the trusts owned $220 million. By 1990 Malays are to own $2.4 billion and the trusts to own $7.4 billion out of a total of $32.6 billion. Obviously the key to this restructuring is growth. But it also involves substantial government interest in corporate-ownership—22 per cent of share capital.

'In addition, incentives have been given to corporations to sell shares to Malays and to Malay trusts. Again, the government under the Industrial Coordination Act can coerce corporations to sell. Furthermore, the government can require percentages of new issues to be held unsold until Malay buyers are found and then sold at par rather than current market value' (Grace, 1976). While growth is sometimes seen as a key condition for the restructuring process, it has been suggested that there is also 'a fear among Malays that growth was bound to benefit non-Malays more' (Milne, 1976: 253).

53. 'A government policy to encourage private Malay equity ownership would require raising the income and wealth of the few rich Malays who would be willing to accumulate equities, and in the process increasing the degree of inequality in the distribution of Malay incomes, and of total personal income in Malaysia. The government's commitment to increase Malay share ownership, if it is approached through traditional private ownership, is thus inconsistent with its overriding objective of reducing the degree of income inequality' (Moore, 1975: 44).

54. It is not the author's intention here to document the extent and nature of the development of public enterprise in Malaysia. This has been attempted elsewhere, e.g. see Robinson (1973); Thillainathan (1976); M. Puthucheary (1976); Shamsul Amri (1977).

55. 'The distinction between (private and public enterprises) is particularly significant in Malaysia, where so many public corporations have been established to carry out the objectives of the New Economic Policy.... Foremost among 'the organizations established to achieve this objective is the Perbadanan Nasional Berhad (PERNAS).... Although PERNAS is "motivated by profits ... (and) ... will undertake only those projects which are economically viable," the real test of its achievement will not be whether it makes profits but whether it contributes substantially to the restructing [sic] of Malaysian society and to the much greater participation by Malays in the modern commercial and industrial sectors' (Robinson, 1973: 17).

56. For example, public corporations can sometimes be caught between the expectation that they serve the immediate interests of private Malay capitalists, and the rationale of being profitable and financially solvent before ownership is transferred to private Malay hands, as is stated to be the long-term goal. Of course, such contradictions do not always arise, as, for example, when certain enterprises are set up explicitly to serve only the former goal and others only to achieve the latter.

57. One may disagree with the feasibility of the procedure for eventually turning these enterprises over into the hands of individual Malay businessmen, but this in itself casts little doubt on the interests being served by these public enterprises.

58. Tan Tat Wai has charted the subsidiary and associate companies of three of the largest and most prominent public enterprises set up to advance 'Malay economic interests', namely PERNAS

(*Perbadanan Nasional* or National Corporation), MARA, and UDA or the Urban Development Authority (Tan Tat Wai, 1977: 312, Chart 5.28; 313, Chart 5.29, 314, Chart 5.30).

59. 'It is very important to appreciate these links which considerably minimise the "internal" contradictions, especially between those running the state and those running the economy. It also gives–besides the sharing of common cultural and social values, educational backgrounds, etc.–to the different sections of the "bureaucratic bourgeoisie" a close identity of interests, and self identification with the system itself' (Shivji, 1973: 84).

60. For example, Von der Mehden (1973: 5) found from a survey in Penang in 1972/3 that 'several respondents volunteered that while they had MPs or other politicians on their board of directors they were of little use in solving problems of related government. However, there is no doubt that there has been an increase in the number of politicians who have been brought on the boards of major companies in Malaysia.'

61. '... the "bureaucratic bourgeoisie" only does the consumption! This may be one of the factors, among others, responsible for the conspicuous lack of thrift and zeal of saving, etc. among the members of the "bureaucratic bourgeoisie"!' (Shivji, 1976: 95).

62. Non-Malay capitalists–both foreign and local–have generally accommodated themselves to the new realities of political power. Larger businesses have tended to be more successful in this respect, and it is in this context that the growing phenomena of 'political contributions' and corruption need to be understood. For the statist capitalists, the latter constitutes an important source of income involving the sale of political influence at a price.

63. 'The very wealthy have acquired their wealth from opportunities afforded by their domination of the bureaucracy and politics. Almost all rich Malays have been either senior civil servants or political leaders. Few, if any, are wealthy purely as a result of personal economic enterprise' (Grace, 1976).

See Tan Tat Wai (1977: 458, Table 8.1) for backgrounds and company affiliations of leading Malay directors.

In his study of Malaysia's top 100 corporations, Lim Mah Hui (1980) found that 13 of the 67 Malay directors (i.e. about a fifth) were members of royal families. More than half of the Malay directors had titles bestowed by the state. More than a quarter held political positions, of which 9 were federal or State ministers, 5 were members of parliament, 3 were senators and 1 a State legislator. Lim Mah Hui also classified the 67 by occupation: 24 businessmen, 14 civil servants, 7 politicians, 6 'politician-civil servant' types, 4 'politician-professional' types, 2 military officers, 4 lawyers, 4 accountants or company secretaries, 1 engineer, and 1 doctor.

It may be noted here that of the remaining 512 directors, 121 were identified as non-Malay Malaysians, 74 as Singaporeans, and 317 as 'other foreigners and "don't know"'.

For a glimpse of the holdings of one of the more prominent individual Malay capitalists, Tengku Ariff Bendahara or TAB, see Tan Tat Wai (1977: 315, Chart 5.31). Tengku Ariff Bendahara, a brother of the Sultan of Pahang, was strongly identified with several local non-Malay, including Indian, business interests.

64. As noted earlier, however, many such ostensibly Malay families are actually of Arab, Indian, and Indonesian descent, since indigenous Malay participation in business was very low during the colonial period.

65. For example, especially since the 1970s, the Malaysian government has been active in efforts to stabilize and raise commodity prices of raw materials. Similarly, it supports proposals for a New International Economic Order as well as many other 'Third Worldist' positions, e.g. on the Law of the Sea.

66. 'Foreign interests argue that 55 per cent is not all that much because the corporate sector represents only a small proportion of the GDP. Since only 31 per cent of the GDP comes from the corporate sector, they assert, foreign ownership of the "economy as a whole" is much less (amounting to only 18.8 per cent in 1970)' (Grace, 1976).

The above argument regarding ownership of the capitalist sector is undeniable. However, it ignores the significance of control which does not correspond to ownership. Generally speaking, it is the corporate sector which dominates the capitalist sector in the Malaysian economy. Businesses outside the corporate sector, with some notable exceptions, belong to small capitalists and to petty bourgeois running enterprises primarily with family labour and usually enjoying relatively lower profit rates owing to greater competition.

67. 'The Petroleum Production [*sic*] Act Amendment is of even deeper concern to foreign investors. Many companies are already trying to cooperate with the government on equity participation by Malays. Some are holding off, hoping eventually to negotiate with the government and have the view accepted that their particular company should not submit to government requirements—particularly when it means selling shares at par values. But the Amendment smells of nationalization, and this cannot be acceptable to any foreign interests. As a result, foreign investment in Malaysia has come to a complete standstill and will probably remain so until the foreigners feel that these policies are not going to affect them' (Grace, 1976).

There were negative responses by foreign business-oriented media to the 1975 Act giving Petronas (the government oil company) powers to buy 'management shares' in foreign oil company subsidiaries that would carry disproportionately large voting rights. See *Far Eastern Economic Review*, 16 May 1975, and *The Wall Street Journal*, 22 September 1975.

By the end of 1975, government politicians began relenting and started reassuring foreign investors. Tengku Razaleigh, closely associated with the promulgation of the 1975 Act, stepped down as head of Petronas. The Prime Minister then, Dato' Hussein Onn, personally intervened and speeded up negotiations with the foreign oil companies. In 1977, both he and the then Deputy Prime Minister, Dr Mahathir Mohamad, also head of the Cabinet Investment Committee, went on foreign tours (including visits to the United States) to woo foreign investors.

68. The relatively gentle nature of such encroachments on the terrain of foreign capital may still be resisted. For example, after the enactment of legislation in 1975 to control more of the petroleum industry as well as the manufacturing sector, strong protestations and an 'investment strike' by established capitalist interests forced the government to amend the relevant legislation. Similarly, attempts by public enterprises to gain control of certain foreign-controlled companies were resisted by raising the alarm of 'nationalization'.

69. 'Chinese complaints about the NEP have followed well-defined patterns. One is, without querying the policy itself, to say that the second prong (restructuring the economy to help the Malays) is being given too much attention compared with the first, the eradication of poverty regardless of race. Another line is to complain about implementation. Such complaints may really in some cases relate to disagreements with policy, which the complainer [*sic*] might hesitate to criticize directly.... Other criticisms of implementation accept that government policy is fair, but allege that it is liable to be distorted by officials....

'There were also Indian reactions to the NEP, which paralleled the Chinese ones and were led by the Indian component in the government, the Malaysian Indian Congress' (Milne, 1976: 251, 253).

70. 'The Malaysian Manufacturers Association—made up of smaller Chinese manufacturers—is now bitterly contesting the Act. Some accommodation will probably be found, but if it is not, the economic power of these Chinese is such that some kind of boycotting could occur' (Grace, 1976).

71. The Act has received much adverse publicity in the foreign business press and even in the usually restrained local press (e.g. see *Far Eastern Economic Review*, 6 May 1977: 38–9; *Business Times*, 20 May 1977).

72. It has been suggested that the students who supported the 'Young Turks' in 1969 subsequently became disenchanted by the government's measures to curb students, including stringent legislation to this effect in 1971 and 1975. The December 1974 Muslim youth-led student demonstrations in support of protesting Malay rubber-growing peasants and the development in the 1970s of an 'Islamic fundamentalist' evangelical youth movement espousing an 'anti-materialistic' ideology (*dakwah*) may well be symptomatic of this trend. However, some recent developments suggest the possibility of compromise between at least some of these elements and the state in return for certain limited and largely cosmetic reforms considered consistent with Islam.

73. 'Given the highly ambiguous position of the middle and lower levels of the petty bourgeoisie, such contradictions, if not channelled into a progressive direction by revolutionary forces, can easily be utilised by the reactionary forces' (Shivji, 1973: 85).

74. As with some other aspects of the state's 'racial' policies, this has sometimes antagonized non-Malays, especially those unemployed, who are also seeking jobs. Between 1970 and 1975, Malay unemployment fell from 8.1 per cent to 6.9 per cent, while Chinese unemployment stayed more or less constant at about 7 per cent and Indian unemployment rose from 11.0 per cent to 12.2 per cent (Malaysia, 1976). Unemployment rates have since generally declined in the late 1970s, before rising again in the early 1980s.

75. With non-Malay workers feeling relatively more intimidated by government, and given the widespread suspicion of complicity by much of the established trade union leadership, it is commonly observed that Malay workers have become increasingly prominent in 'grassroot' worker militancy of recent years, though there have also been various efforts to divide and weaken the labour movement along ethnic, religious, gender and other lines. Also, the state's antagonism to even 'yellow' (collaborative) and social-democratic labour organizations and leaders, and various efforts to impose tight state control over the development of industrial relations in Malaysia may lead to new expressions of labour unrest in the future.

CONCLUSION

THE preceding study of class formation in colonial and post-colonial Malaya has sought to identify class contention as the main motive force of history. The history of modern Malaya, like that of other class societies, has ultimately been the history of class contention. The existence of class contention does not always involve collective self-consciousness, nor does it necessarily entail organized activity. Rather, underlying class contradictions are often manifested in phenomena which do not necessarily best express or advance the class interests involved. Class contention, after all, takes place in and through historically given social circumstances which define the range of possible outcomes. For colonial and post-colonial Malaya, these circumstances not only include the world market and the ongoing accumulation of capital, but also the outcome of preceding class contention. Furthermore, specificity and sequence have been shown to be better incorporated into social analysis through the use of a historical case approach rather than by employing an ideal-type model of societal transition.

As defined in this study, classes are constituted by the social relations of production. In the process of production, class relations are necessarily contradictory, and these contradictions constitute, and are manifested in, class contention, both among classes as well as among class fractions. It is important to consider class contradictions, and the class contention which emerges therefrom, in understanding the formation of social classes. As class relations are constantly subject to the outcome of previous contention, classes do not have an existence outside of class contention, and hence history.

Classes are not only defined economically, but also politically and ideologically. Hence, class contention occurs at the political and ideological planes as well as at the economic plane. In this regard, the nature and role of state were related to our perspective of class contention. The state is viewed as an object, as an outcome and as a determinant of ongoing class contention. While class contention is at the core of the unfolding of history, it does not occur in a vacuum of infinite possibilities but in concrete historical conditions which limit the range of possible outcomes. Hence, contention between classes makes history in specific conditions, which are actually the outcome of previous class contention.

What has all this meant for class formation in colonial Malaya and post-colonial Malaysia? In Appendix 1, it is proposed that to study class formation in Malaya, it is necessary to look at the relations of production which arose as a consequence of colonialism, from Malaya's integration into the world economy. Subsequent capital expansion in the sphere of circulation is distinguished from accumulation in the production sphere; the former only gives rise to non-capitalist relations of production dominated by circulation capital, while the latter may give rise to non-capitalist as well as capitalist relations of production, depending on the specific conditions in which production is organized by capital. Figure 11.1 attempts to schematize roughly this general argument as it applies to the Malayan case.

With its integration into the world economy under the auspices of British colonialism, the pre-capitalist class relations of pre-colonial Malaya were radically transformed. The main historical outcome of this has been new non-capitalist relations of production—under the domination of circulation capital—which have continued to change in the colonial as well as post-colonial periods. Capital in the sphere of production initially organized on non-capitalist lines (i.e. utilizing involuntary labour) in circumstances of relative labour shortage which were overcome by labour immigration. However, in the new phase of development born out of the crisis of the early 1930s, capitalist relations became generalized. Recent changes associated with the Green Revolution and the official encouragement of mini-estates have further advanced the development of capitalist relations of production among the padi-growing peasantry.

Part I (Chapter 1) suggested that three main classes existed in pre-colonial Malay society. The ruling class and the state were one. The peasantry were exploited in several ways—by the exaction of corvée labour, commercial tribute and, in some areas, taxes on land, persons, and other items. In addition, the dominant class also appropriated the fruits of the labour of the third group, their slaves and debt-bondsmen. Other than trade and credit related to these forms of surplus appropriation (e.g. usurious relations in connection with debt-bondage), capital did not play a major role in pre-colonial Malay society, especially in production. The transformation of peasant social relations with integration into the world economy is crudely summarized in Figure 11.2.

The integration of Malaya into the world market and the accompanying expansion of capital in the sphere of circulation preceded actual colonial intervention. Under colonial rule, new conditions accelerated these processes (see Chapter 5). Colonial expansion entailed other important implications, initially involving a struggle between the interests of British capital on the one hand, and those of the pre-colonial ruling class on the other. With the imposition of colonial rule, state power favoured the former over the latter, and the pre-colonial forms of pre-capitalist exploitation mentioned above were eliminated. Soon thereafter, the pre-colonial Malay ruling class was reconciled to colonial domination with lucrative intermediate positions subordinate to British officials in the colonial administrative apparatus and other privileges such as large concessions of land. Thus, although the sanctions and class relations through which they previously obtained a surplus were undermined by colonial rule, the members of this class were successfully co-opted as intermediaries in the colonial state apparatus, which was a crucial determinant of access to opportunities for accumulation.

With colonialism, the peasantry was freed from the various forms of pre-capitalist exploitation mentioned earlier, and was instead subject, as a whole, to circulation capital on the one hand, and the dictates of the colonial state on the

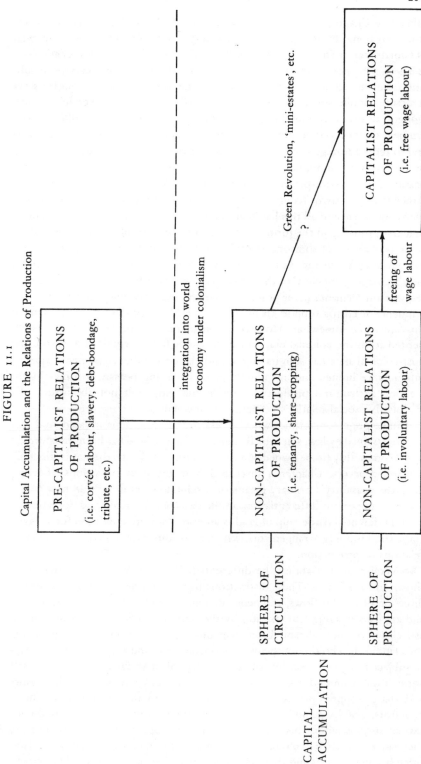

FIGURE 11.1

Capital Accumulation and the Relations of Production

other (see Chapters 2 and 3). Merchant capital obtained commercial profits from engaging in the peasant commodity economy, while usury capital obtained interest from extending credit to the peasantry. Besides legally consolidating the new colonial framework to which peasant interests were subordinated, the colonial state influenced the peasant economy through its tax structure, public spending, policy, and legislation. While generally encouraging agricultural commodity (i.e. 'cash crop') production, the colonial government discouraged peasant rubber planting in favour of plantation interests and to reduce foreign exchange outflows for rice imports, mainly necessitated by the growing immigrant labour force. These colonial efforts to influence peasant development primarily involved the stick (e.g. legislation, penalties), rather than the carrot (conceivably, in the form of incentives and subsidies). One consequence of all this has been the heavy tax incidence on rubber smallholders (primarily in the form of export duty) comparable to the personal income tax liability of someone earning many times as much, i.e. about $60,000 per annum (Augustine Tan, 1967; Khoo Kay Jin, 1978). Whereas Ungku Aziz's charge of 'neglect' of the peasantry is very apt for the colonial era, subsequent interventions in the peasant sector, motivated by the post-colonial government's need for support from among the Malay peasantry, have changed this situation somewhat. However, constrained by the class relations inherited from the colonial era, which it cannot fundamentally transform, the post-colonial state has seen its increasingly lavish rural development expenditure achieve limited and inequitable gains in raising peasant incomes by increasing agricultural productivity while changing, but not abolishing, the exploitative social relations perpetuating inequality.

Unlike pre-colonial times when access to the use of uncultivated land was not constrained by law, since the British colonial era, land has been transformed into a commodity (to be owned and transacted), over which the state ultimately controlled access. Chapter 4 discussed how the new conditions affecting land—the peasantry's primary means of production—set in motion new forces resulting in peasant differentiation on the basis of ownership and operation of land. Differential ownership of land is an important pre-condition for tenancy and share-cropping arrangements, which constitute exploitative non-capitalist relations of production.

Several related strata can be differentiated by the criterion of tenancy as shown in Figure 11.2. These distinctions have important implications for the direction of surplus flows, and hence income distribution. All peasants can be and are usually subject to taxation by the state. However, circulation capital, especially commercial capital, only obtains a surplus from farming peasants; thus landlords who do not themselves operate any land are usually not directly subject to exploitation by commercial capital in so far as they do not sell agricultural commodities (unless obtained as rent payments). All tenants and share-croppers pay rent to those whose land they cultivate. Owners-operators, who by definition own only the land they operate, therefore do not extract surplus labour because their land is not operated by others: nor are they subject to such exploitation. While peasants who own little or no land often become tenants and share-croppers, many become rural wage labourers.

FIGURE 11.2

Changing Social Relations among the Malay Peasantry

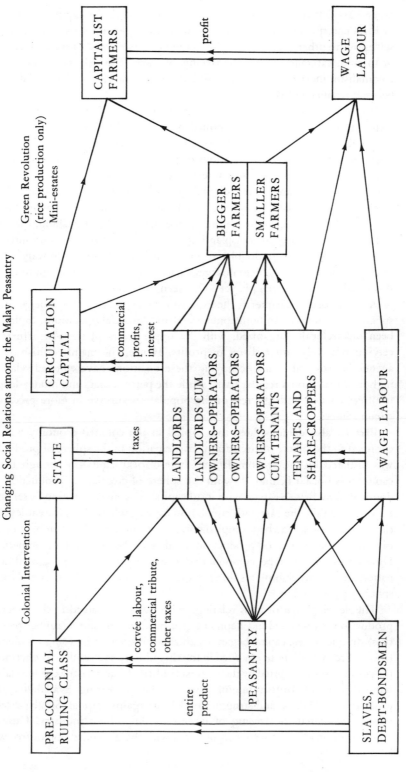

Some have left the peasant sector altogether to work for capitalists in urban or rural enterprises, while others stay within the peasant sector, hiring themselves out to other peasants—usually to big farmers in need of seasonal labour—or to rural capitalists. After the freeing of slaves and debt-bondsmen under colonialism, most had little recourse but to join the ranks of wage labour or become tenants and share-croppers.

While tenancy (and share-cropping) relations still pervade the peasant sector, recent social changes identified with the technological changes of the Green Revolution have started a small but nonetheless significant tendency towards spreading capitalist relations of padi production. Large land-owners, and others with sufficient financial resources, are adopting the newly available, highly profitable, and more 'capital-intensive' farming techniques. While mechanization has reduced some of the labour requirements in farm production (for ploughing and, more recently, for harvesting, threshing, packing, transportation, and even transplanting), the net effect of the more intensive schedule associated with double-cropping has been the spread of wage labour relations and the emergence of larger farms. The longer-term significance of this relatively recent trend is yet to be seen, however.

As described in Chapter 5, the expansion of capital in Malaya began in the sphere of circulation. In both commercial and financial operations, capital has been hierarchically organized, with the upper strata of these structures receiving relatively larger shares of profits. Hence, the mainly British-owned agency houses and banks occupying these positions have enjoyed relatively high profit rates on a regular basis, while the petty traders and money-lenders in direct contact with the rest of the population survive in more precarious circumstances.

Part III also demonstrated that capital in the colonial economy was not confined to the sphere of circulation. Participation in the sphere of production was initiated by the predominantly Chinese local capitalists though British capital was not far behind. As with the sphere of circulation, production was dominated by British capital with local capitalists generally taking lesser roles. However, unlike the case with circulation capital, where the different levels of the hierarchies somewhat complemented one another, the various strata of capital in the sphere of production tended to be in greater competition. Differences of this type compounded other differences (e.g. according to nationality of ownership), resulting in greater contention among capitals in the sphere of production.

The development of class relations with capital involved in the sphere of production is discussed in Chapters 6 (tin production) and 7 (rubber production). In both cases, capital began organizing production by using involuntary labour. Free wage labour emerged in the tin industry as a result of the actions of the colonial state (inspired by the interests of British capital), the reduced labour requirements of British mining capital, the increasing availability of a proletariat in Malaya, and struggles by labour against capital. Similar circumstances facilitated the freeing of labour in the rubber industry. Capitalist relations of production were consolidated with the generalization of free wage labour.

Part IV outlined the emergence and contemporary significance of capitalist fractions. The relationships of particular local capitals to the international commodity circuits and to foreign capital were discussed as criteria for assessing their interests in the development of the national economy, as well as for assessing their relationship to foreign capital. It was clarified in Chapter 8 that these two criteria do not always coincide: development of the national commodity circuits may not involve conflict with foreign capital, while competition with foreign capital does not necessarily entail an interest in the growth of the national economy as a whole. These contradictions suggest that only small proportions of local capital are either unambiguously opposed to imperialism because they are in conflict with or oppressed by foreign capital and disengaged from the international commodity circuits, or completely allied with foreign capital and tied into the world economy. This locates the bulk of predominantly Chinese local capital in more ambiguous positions in relation to these two poles.

Capital in the colonial economy was not wholly inimical to industrialization although, as seen in Chapter 9, domination by British commercial capital (which in turn has been subordinate to British production capital) and the colonial state did undoubtedly stifle the development of industrial capital. Formal independence from colonialism involved some important changes in the class character of the state. Significant changes in the post-war world economy (e.g. the expansion of transnationals), as well as the rise of the dominant local classes, together produced new conditions favouring the development of industrial capital. Nevertheless, continued participation in the world economy and subordination to international monopoly capital still impose limits on the potential for post-colonial industrialization. Having exhausted most import-substitution possibilities by the end of the first post-independence decade, the subsequent emphasis on export-oriented industrialization is also not without its problems, given the growing protectionism in foreign markets.

Some elements of continuity and change in the governing classes of the pre-colonial, colonial, and post-colonial states can be observed. After colonial intervention, members of the pre-colonial ruling class were largely integrated into the colonial state machinery in positions subordinate to British administrators. With the demise of the colonial order in 1957, these Malay 'administocrats' took over the running of the state apparatus. With the Malayan economy dominated by foreign capital, and given the weakness of the (predominantly Chinese) domestic bourgeoisie, a section of this statist petty bourgeoisie successfully manipulated ethnic sentiments to consolidate state power for capital accumulation on its own behalf. The New Economic Policy—announced not long after the general election and racial riots of May 1969—marked the culmination of the ascendance of this fraction within the governing class, which had been waiting and growing in the 'wings' during the 1960s. The rise of this fraction established the necessary political conditions for the transformation of the statist petty bourgeoisie into a statist capitalist class accumulating on the basis of control of state power.

Dominance by this statist capitalist class has unfolded new contradictions—

including ethnic ones—which are redefining the conditions and issues of class contention in contemporary Malaysia. Essentially a product of particular historical circumstances, this class has risen to assert its own class (fractional) interests supposedly by championing policies ostensibly in the interests of the Malay community and also national unity. However, the power and legitimacy of this new social class is, as discussed in the preceding chapter, inextricably linked to developments in the economy. As implied in the study, all classes develop and subsist only within the range of historical possibility offered by previous class contention.

Trends in Class Relations

Not surprisingly, there have been neither empirical studies nor surveys in Malaysia which have tried to analyse the population as a whole in terms of class relations. Studies of income distribution (e.g. Anand, 1982; Tan Tat Wai, 1982), wealth distribution (e.g. J. J. Puthucheary, 1960; Lim Mah Hui, 1980; Sieh, 1982) and social stratification (e.g. Hirschman, 1975) nevertheless provide useful indicators of trends and phenomena linked to underlying class relations. These can be usefully complemented by examination of trends in the labour force, especially over longer periods.

Tables 11.1 and 11.2—based on Appendix 2—sum up the percentage break-down of the working population in 1947, 1957, 1970, and 1980 by ethnicity and gender percentage. The percentage of employers increased from 1.3 per cent in 1947 to 4.0 per cent in 1980. Meanwhile, the percentage of employees grew from 48.1 per cent in 1947 to 61.4 per cent in 1980.

In 1947, 56 per cent of Malays were self-employed, comprising 62 per cent of this category, most of whom were peasants. By 1980, though the Malay proportion of the self-employed had increased slightly to 65 per cent, the self-employed accounted for only 33 per cent of Malays. Conversely, 27 per cent of Malays were employees in 1947 compared to 55 per cent in 1980. The percentage of employees who were Malay rose correspondingly from 25 per cent in 1947 to 48 per cent in 1980. In other words, by 1980, more than half of working Malays were employees, while Malays comprised almost half of all employees. Though Malays comprised 36 per cent of all employers in 1980 compared to 17 per cent in 1947, yet employers remained a very small minority (less than 3 per cent) of Malays even in 1980.

While Chinese comprised 69 per cent of employers in 1947 and 52 per cent in 1980, yet only 2 per cent of Chinese were employers in 1947, rising to 6 per cent in 1980. Hence, though the Chinese still are a slight majority among employers, employers still only make up a small minority of the Chinese population. Meanwhile, the percentage of employees among Chinese has also increased from 56 per cent in 1947 to 64 per cent in 1980, while the proportion of the self-employed fell from 37 per cent in 1947 to 25 per cent in 1980, suggesting the shrinking of the old Chinese petty bourgeoisie (in both town and country), in the context of an increasingly modern capitalistic economy.

The predominantly working-class character of the Indian community has eroded slightly in the post-war period as the percentage of wage-earners has

TABLE 11.1

Percentage Distribution of Employment Status by Gender, 1947, 1957, 1970 and 1980

Employment Status	1947			1957			1970			1980		
	Males	Females	Total	Males	Females	Total	Males	Females	Total	Males	Females	Total
Employer	1.5	0.4	1.3	⎧ 38.4	24.6	35.0	⎧ 37.6	25.0	33.9	4.4	3.0	4.0
(Percentage of total in category)	(93.1)	(6.9)	(100.0)	(82.7)	(17.2)	(100.0)	(77.6)	(22.4)	(100.0)	(75.5)	(24.5)	(100.0)
Own account worker	45.0	28.5	41.2	⎨			⎨			28.9	24.4	27.4
(Percentage of total in category)	(83.9)	(16.1)	(100.0)							(71.2)	(28.8)	(100.0)
Unpaid family worker	5.2	23.5	9.4	4.8	19.1	8.3	11.2	30.6	17.0	4.9	12.1	7.2
(Percentage of total in category)	(42.1)	(57.9)	(100.0)	(43.7)	(56.3)	(100.0)	(45.8)	(54.2)	(100.0)	(45.8)	(54.2)	(100.0)
Employee	48.3	47.6	48.1	56.8	56.3	56.7	51.2	44.4	49.1	61.8	60.5	61.4
(Percentage of total in category)	(77.0)	(23.0)	(100.0)	(75.5)	(24.5)	(100.0)	(72.7)	(27.3)	(100.0)	(68.1)	(31.9)	(100.0)
In employment	100.0	100.0	100.0	100.0	100.0	100.0	100.0	100.0	100.0	100.0	100.0	100.0
(Percentage of total in category)	(76.8)	(23.2)	(100.0)	(75.4)	(24.6)	(100.0)	(69.8)	(30.2)	(100.0)	(67.6)	(32.4)	(100.0)

Sources: Department of Statistics, *Population Census of Malaya* (1947); *Population Census of Federation of Malaya* (1957); *Population Census of Malaysia* (1970, 1980).

TABLE 11.2

Peninsular Malaysia: Employment Status by Ethnicity, 1947, 1957, 1970, and 1980 (per cent)

Employment Status	Malays	Chinese	Indians	Others	All Races
1947					
Employer	0.5	2.3	1.0	1.5	1.3
(Percentage of total in category)	(16.9)	(69.0)	(12.5)	(1.6)	(100.0)
Own account worker	56.1	37.2	8.9	27.3	41.2
(Percentage of total in category)	(61.8)	(34.0)	(3.3)	(0.9)	(100.0)
Unpaid family worker	16.5	4.7	0.4	12.2	9.4
(Percentage of total in category)	(79.0)	(18.6)	(0.7)	(1.7)	(100.0)
Employee	26.9	55.8	89.7	59.0	48.1
(Percentage of total in category)	(25.4)	(43.6)	(29.4)	(1.6)	(100.0)
In employment	100.0	100.0	100.0	100.0	100.0
(Percentage of total in category)	(45.3)	(37.6)	(15.8)	(1.3)	(100.0)
1957					
Employer	48.9	28.2	9.8	14.5	35.0
(Percentage of total in category)	(66.1)	(28.8)	(4.0)	(1.1)	(100.0)
Own account worker					
(Percentage of total in catergory)					
Unpaid family worker	14.1	4.2	0.6	4.1	8.3
(Percentage of total in category)	(80.0)	(17.8)	(0.9)	(1.3)	(100.0)
Employee	37.0	67.6	89.6	81.4	56.7
(Percentage of total in category)	(30.8)	(42.5)	(22.9)	(3.8)	(100.0)
In employment	100.0	100.0	100.0	100.0	100.0
(Percentage of total in category)	(47.2)	(35.7)	(14.5)	(2.6)	(100.0)

1970

Category					
Employer	42.2	26.7	15.0	28.6	3.9
(Percentage of total in category)	(66.7)	(28.0)	(4.5)	(0.8)	(100.0)
Own account worker	22.0	13.1	4.6	20.4	17.0
(Percentage of total in category)	(69.0)	(27.2)	(2.7)	(1.1)	(100.0)
Unpaid family worker	35.8	60.2	80.4	51.0	49.1
(Percentage of total in category)	(39.0)	(43.3)	(16.7)	(1.0)	(100.0)
Employee					
(Percentage of total in category)					
In employment	100.0	100.0	100.0	100.0	100.0
(Percentage of total in category)	(53.5)	(35.4)	(10.2)	(0.9)	(100.0)

1980

Category					
Employer	2.6	5.8	4.6	4.1	4.0
(Percentage of total in category)	(35.5)	(51.5)	(12.3)	(0.7)	(100.0)
Own account worker	32.9	24.7	8.3	32.1	27.4
(Percentage of total in category)	(64.5)	(31.5)	(3.2)	(0.8)	(100.0)
Unpaid family worker	9.2	5.4	3.3	10.0	7.2
(Percentage of total in category)	(67.9)	(26.2)	(4.9)	(1.0)	(100.0)
Employee	55.3	64.1	83.8	53.8	61.4
(Percentage of total in category)	(48.3)	(36.5)	(14.6)	(0.6)	(100.0)
In employment	100.0	100.0	100.0	100.0	100.0
(Percentage of total in category)	(53.6)	(35.0)	(10.7)	(0.7)	(100.0)

Sources: Department of Statistics, *Population Census of Malaya* (1947), *Population Census of Federation of Malaya* (1957), *Population Census of Malaysia* (1970, 1980).

TABLE 11.3

Peninsular Malaysia: Labour Force by Primary Ethnic Group and Activity, 1957, 1970, and 1976

| Activity | 1957[1] | | | | | | | | 1970[2] | |
| | Malays | | Chinese | | Indians | | Total | | Malays | |
	'000	%	'000	%	'000	%	'000	%	'000	%
1. Agriculture, forestry, livestock and fishing	459.8	45.8	100.9	13.3	4.5	1.5	572.8	26.9	495.2	34.5
2. Agricultural products*	289.5	28.8	209.5	27.6	170.0	55.3	672.0	31.6	427.1	29.8
3. Mining and quarry	10.3	1.0	40.0	5.3	6.8	2.2	58.5	2.8	13.3	0.9
4. Manufacturing	26.6	2.6	97.5	12.8	10.1	3.3	135.7	6.4	73.1	5.1
5. Construction	21.8	2.2	32.6	4.3	12.3	4.0	67.8	3.2	13.0	0.9
6. Services†	3.8	0.4	3.0	0.4	4.2	1.4	11.6	0.5	9.5	0.7
7. Commerce	32.0	3.2	127.1	16.7	32.8	10.7	195.2	9.2	64.3	4.5
8. Transport and communications	26.9	2.7	29.2	3.8	16.1	5.2	74.8	3.5	41.5	2.9
9. Services	127.6	12.7	110.0	14.5	48.1	15.7	319.8	15.0	223.9	15.6
10. Miscellaneous Activities	5.9	0.6	9.4	1.2	2.4	0.8	18.1	0.9	74.1	5.
Total	1,004.3	100.0	759.2	100.0	307.2	100.0	2,126.3	100.0	1,435.0	100.0

Sources: 1. Department of Statistics (1960), *1957 Population Census of the Federation of Malaya*, Report No. 14, Kuala Lumpur.
2. Department of Statistics, *1970 Population Census of Malaysia*.
3. Department of Statistics (1980), *Report on the Labour Force, 1976*, Kuala Lumpur, August.

declined from 90 per cent in 1947 to 84 per cent in 1980. As a percentage of all workers, their share has dropped from 29 per cent in 1947 to 15 per cent in 1980.

The data on unpaid family workers appear to suggest inconsistent survey methods. Data collection on this category probably improved significantly in 1970, thus accounting for the unexpected and otherwise unexplainable increase in the share of unpaid family workers in that year. Unpaid family labour among Malay women rose from 35 per cent in 1957 to 41 per cent in 1970, probably due to better survey coverage, before dropping to 16 per cent a decade later, probably because of the female labour absorptive capacity of the export-oriented industries (such as electronics, textiles and garments) which grew rapidly in the 1970s.

Table 11.3 shows that the percentage of the labour force in the agricultural sector fell from 58.5 per cent (1,244,800) in 1957 to 49.6 per cent (1,359,100) in 1970 and 40.2 per cent (968,700) in 1976. The percentage of workers in the manufacturing sector rose from 6.4 per cent (135,700) in 1957 to 9.2 per cent

TABLE 11.3 (*continued*)

| 1970[2] | | | | | | 1976[3] | | | | | | | |
| Chinese | | Indians | | Total | | Malays | | Chinese | | Indians | | Total | |
'000	%	'000	%	'000	%	'000	%	'000	%	'000	%	'000	%
100.0	10.2	6.0	2.1	611.3	22.3	471.3	25.1	92.2	6.8	8.9	2.3	588.2	6.1
92.9	19.5	125.7	43.9	747.8	27.3	522.1	27.8	201.9	14.9	154.8	40.0	380.5	24.1
37.1	3.8	4.6	1.6	55.3	2.0	11.3	0.6	20.9	1.5	3.1	0.8	36.6	1.0
64.5	16.6	13.3	4.6	251.9	9.2	10.3	11.2	327.9	24.2	41.1	10.0	584.5	16.0
43.1	4.4	3.6	1.3	59.9	2.2	62.0	3.3	101.7	7.5	16.6	4.3	179.0	4.9
3.6	0.4	6.4	2.2	19.8	0.7	26.3	1.4	4.1	0.3	14.3	3.7	43.8	1.2
79.8	18.2	29.1	10.2	274.6	10.0	157.7	8.4	323.8	23.9	42.5	11.0	526.1	14.4
39.1	3.9	16.7	5.3	98.0	3.6	71.4	3.8	55.5	4.1	21.7	5.6	149.8	4.1
73.5	17.5	66.3	23.2	472.6	17.3	345.5	13.4	227.6	16.8	84.3	21.8	664.9	18.2
55.6	5.6	14.3	5.1	145.2	5.3	0.0	0.0	0.0	0.0	0.0	0.0	0.0	0.0
90.0	100.0	286.1	100.0	2,736.4	100.0	1,887.9	100.0	1,355.4	100.0	387.3	100.0	3,653.4	100.0

*Requiring substantial processing (e.g. rubber, coconut, oil palm, etc.).
†Including electricity, gas, water and sanitation.

(251,900) in 1970 and 16.0 per cent (584,500) in 1976; the rapid expansion in manufacturing employment during 1970-6 and thereafter reflects the switch from import-substitution to more labour-intensive export-oriented industrialization. The percentage and number of workers in the construction industry also fell from 3.2 per cent (67,800) in 1957 to 2.2 per cent (59,900) in 1970, but grew rapidly to 4.9 per cent (179,000) in 1976, while the percentage of commercial and service (i.e. unproductive) workers rose from 24.2 per cent (515,000) in 1957 to 27.3 per cent (747,200) in 1970 and 32.6 per cent (1,191,000) in 1976.

Taken together with other evidence on the Malaysian economy (e.g. see Table 11.4), it appears that capitalism—including modern industries—has developed considerably since independence. This does not at all imply that the Malaysian economy is on its way, through the various 'stages of growth' supposedly experienced by the 'developed' economies of today, to establishing an integrated advanced industrial economy, as argued by Warren (1980) and

TABLE 11.4

Peninsular Malaysia: Employment by Sector and Race, 1970, 1975, 1980, and 1983

('000)

Sector	Malays	Chinese	Indians	Others	Total
		1970			
Primary	902.3	265.4	154.0	12.9	1,334.6
(Percentage of total in sector)	(57.6)	(19.9)	(11.5)	(1.0)	(100.0)
Secondary	215.6	394.3	57.1	4.7	671.7
(Percentage of total in sector)	(32.1)	(58.7)	(8.5)	(0.7)	(100.0)
Tertiary	359.7	383.9	90.3	10.1	844.0
(Percentage of total in sector)	(42.6)	(45.5)	(10.7)	(1.2)	(100.0)
Total employed	1,477.6	1,043.6	301.4	27.7	2,850.3
(Percentage)	(51.8)	(36.6)	(10.6)	(1.0)	(100.0)
Labour force	1,608.3	1,122.4	338.7	28.6	3,098.0
(Percentage)	(51.9)	(36.2)	(10.9)	(0.9)	(100.0)
Unemployment	130.7	78.8	37.3	0.9	247.7
(Percentage)	(8.1)	(7.0)	(11.0)	(3.1)	(8.0)

1975

Primary	1,009.2	287.3	167.3	12.7	1,476.5
(Percentage of total in sector)	(68.4)	(19.5)	(11.3)	(0.9)	(100.0)
Secondary	336.7	500.0	88.6	7.5	932.8
(Percentage of total in sector)	(36.1)	(53.6)	(9.5)	(0.8)	(100.0)
Tertiary	509.5	515.3	121.6	11.5	1,157.9
(Percentage of total in sector)	(44.0)	(44.5)	(10.5)	(1.0)	(100.0)
Total employed	1,855.4	1,302.6	377.5	31.7	3,567.2
(Percentage)	(52.0)	(36.5)	(10.6)	(0.9)	(100.0)
Labour force	1,975.7	1,390.7	421.8	34.9	3,823.1
(Percentage)	(51.7)	(36.4)	(11.0)	(0.9)	(100.0)
Unemployment	120.3	88.1	44.3	3.2	255.9
(Percentage)	(6.1)	(6.3)	(10.5)	(9.2)	(6.7)

1980

Primary	977.3	260.2	181.4	13.1	1,432.0
(Percentage of total in sector)	(68.2)	(18.2)	(12.7)	(0.9)	(100.0)
Secondary	464.0	589.2	108.2	6.0	1,167.4
(Percentage of total in sector)	(39.7)	(50.5)	(9.3)	(0.5)	(100.0)
Tertiary	692.6	570.4	150.4	10.2	1,423.6
(Percentage of total in sector)	(48.6)	(40.1)	(10.6)	(0.7)	(100.0)
Total employed	2,133.9	1,419.8	440.0	29.3	4,023.0
(Percentage)	(53.0)	(35.3)	(10.9)	(0.7)	(100.0)
Labour force	2,283.2	1,476.7	469.5	30.4	4,259.8
(Percentage)	(53.6)	(34.7)	(11.0)	(6.7)	(100.0)
Unemployment	149.3	56.9	29.5	1.1	236.8
(Percentage)	(6.5)	(3.9)	(6.3)	(3.6)	(5.6)

(continued)

TABLE 11.4 (continued)

1983

Sector	Malays	Chinese	Indians	Others	Total
Primary	958.3	268.1	194.3	14.4	1,435.1
(Percentage of total in sector)	(66.8)	(18.7)	(13.5)	(1.0)	(100.0)
Secondary	521.8	642.0	122.0	6.3	1,292.1
(Percentage of total in sector)	(40.4)	(49.7)	(9.4)	(0.5)	(100.0)
Tertiary	819.6	634.7	172.5	9.8	1,636.6
(Percentage of total in sector)	(50.1)	(38.8)	(10.5)	(0.6)	(100.0)
Total employed	2,299.7	1,544.8	488.8	30.5	4,363.8
(Percentage)	(52.7)	(35.4)	(11.2)	(0.7)	(100.0)
Labour force	2,472.0	1,609.0	522.2	31.7	4,634.9
(Percentage)	(53.3)	(34.7)	(11.3)	(0.7)	(100.0)
Unemployment	172.3	64.2	33.4	1.2	271.1
(Percentage)	(7.0)	(4.0)	(6.4)	(3.8)	(5.8)

Sources: Malaysia (1981: Table 3.10); Malaysia (1984).

Notes: Primary: Agriculture.
Secondary: Mining, manufacturing, construction and transport.
Tertiary: Wholesale and retail trade, public administration, education, health, defence, and utilities.

others. This is reflected, for instance, by the sizeable expansion of labour involved in the (largely unproductive) tertiary sector; a significant portion of this involves 'marginalized' people eking out a living in the so-called 'informal sector', i.e. outside the modern capitalist sector. On the other hand, the prophets of 'underdevelopment' (e.g. Frank, 1969)—who imply that integration into world capitalism necessarily brings about unchanging economic backwardness and stagnation—have been disproved by Malaysia's impressive record of sustained growth.

Table 11.5 shows that the percentage of the labour force holding 'administrative and managerial' positions stood at 1.2 per cent in 1957 and remained at that level in 1980. Professional and technical personnel may be identified as members of the new petty bourgeoisie, or 'middle class', while 'clerical and related', or white-collar workers are often socially identified as part of the 'lower middle class', i.e. also as part of the petty bourgeoisie. Hence, it is clear that this new petty bourgeoisie or middle class has expanded from 5.7 per cent in 1957 to 9.8 per cent in 1970 and 12.8 per cent in 1980, with professional and technical personnel increasing from 2.8 per cent in 1957 to 4.8 per cent in 1970 and 5.6 per cent in 1980 while the clerical group grew from 2.9 per cent in 1957 to 5.0 per cent in 1970 and 7.2 per cent in 1980. Meanwhile, the percentage of the labour force in the agricultural sector fell from 56.4 per cent (1957) to 44.8 per cent (1970) and 34.6 per cent (1980); of these, about 11.7 per cent worked (for wages) on estates (Malaysia, 1981: 163), while some of the others working on agricultural smallholdings (of less than 100 acres) and in fishing also earned wage incomes. Meanwhile, the percentage of 'production workers'—defined as those 'engaged in or directly associated with the extraction of minerals, petroleum and natural gas from the earth and their treatment; processing, assembly and shaping various substances to manufacture articles or produce goods; the construction, maintenance and repair of various types of roads, structures, machines and other products, manufacturing glass and clay products, handling materials, operating transport and other equipment; and performing other labouring tasks requiring primary physical efforts'—rose from 18.9 per cent (1957) to 27.3 per cent (1970) and 33.1 per cent (1980). Hence, those engaged in productive labour—including agriculture—have declined from 75.3 per cent (1957) to 72.1 per cent (1970) and 67.7 per cent (1980).

It appears then that since the country gained independence, the percentage of peasants has fallen, while productive workers, as well as 'unproductive' wage-earners and the salaried middle class or petty bourgeoisie have all increased both absolutely and relatively. These important changes reflect the capitalist development path of an increasingly diversified, but no less 'open' or 'dependent' economy. The exports share of the Gross Domestic Product changed from 47.1 per cent in 1957 to 44.5 per cent in 1970 and 51.8 per cent in 1980, while the ratio of imports rose from 37.5 per cent in 1957 to 39.3 per cent in 1970 and 53.8 per cent in 1980 (Rao, 1976; Treasury, 1982). Although the growth and diversification of the economy has been rapid since independence, changes in economic structure have been consistent with those in the so-called 'dependent capitalist' economies.

One unusual feature of Malaysian economic development strategy, of

TABLE 11.5

Peninsular Malaysia: Labour Force by Ethnic Group and Work Category[1],
1957, 1970, 1976, 1980, and 1983 ('000)

Category	1957[2]				1970[3]				1976[3]
	Malays	Chinese	Indians	Total (%)	Malays	Chinese	Indians	Total (%)	Malays
Professional and technical workers[4]	2.7 (41.0)	3.3 (38.0)	2.3 (11.0)	2.8	4.3 (47.1)	5.2 (39.5)	4.9 (10.8)	4.8	5.3 (50.0)
Administrative and managerial workers[5]	0.4 (17.6)	2.0 (62.4)	1.0 (12.2)	1.2	0.5 (24.1)	1.9 (62.9)	0.8 (7.8)	1.1	0.7 (31.6)
Clerical and related workers[6]	1.7 (27.1)	3.7 (46.2)	4.0 (19.9)	2.9	3.4 (35.4)	6.3 (45.9)	8.1 (17.2)	5.0	7.7 (55.3)
Sales and related workers[7]	2.9 (15.9)	15.9 (66.1)	10.0 (16.8)	8.6	4.7 (26.7)	15.3 (61.7)	9.5 (11.1)	9.1	4.5 (23.1)
Service workers[8]	7.3 (39.7)	8.0 (33.3)	7.6 (12.8)	8.6	6.8 (44.3)	8.6 (17.3)	10.9 (14.6)	7.9	7.6 (47.9)
Agricultural workers[9]	74.2 (62.1)	38.3 (24.3)	50.2 (12.8)	56.4	62.3 (72.0)	21.2 (55.9)	41.0 (9.7)	44.8	45.2 (67.7)
Production, transport and other workers[10]	10.6 (26.5)	28.3 (53.5)	24.6 (18.9)	18.9	18.0 (34.2)	41.6 (55.9)	24.7 (9.6)	27.3	29.0 (45.4)
Total workers	1,004.3 (48.2)	759.0 (36.3)	307.2 (14.7)	2,126.2	1,477.6 (51.8)	1,043.6 (36.6)	301.4 (10.6)	2,850.3	2,211.5 (51.9)

Sources: Ishak Shari and Jomo K. S. (1984: 329-55); Malaysia (1984: 98, Table 3.10).

[1] Classification of the occupations had been based on the Ministry of Labour and Manpower, Dictionary of Occupational Classification, 1980.
[2] Value in brackets shows percentage by ethnic group.
[3] Includes workers who cannot be classified.
[4] Includes professions such as architects, accountants, auditors, engineers, teachers, nurses, doctors, dentists, veterinary surgeons, surveyors and lawyers. For the Malays, a substantial proportion of those employed in this occupational group are made up of teachers and nurses. These two groups are estimated to account for about 76,000 or 53 per cent of their total in 1980.
[5] Includes legislative officials, government administrators, and managers.

course, is its pronounced aim—since 1970—to 'restructure society' (ostensibly to abolish the identification of ethnicity with economic function), especially the effort to create, expand and consolidate a Malay bourgeoisie and petty bourgeoisie by using public funds and the state machinery on a massive scale. In practice, restructuring efforts have largely been aimed at increasing the share of Bumiputra capital as well as the number of Bumiputra businessmen and professionals within the context of the pattern of capitalist development discussed earlier. 'Restructuring'—as officially interpreted—is not intended to change the socio-economic relations between classes or strata; in practice, it only aims to increase Bumiputra ownership and personnel shares in certain more attractive occupations.

TABLE 11.5 (continued)

1976[3]			1980					1983				
Chinese	Indians	Total (%)	Malays	Chinese	Indians	Others	Total (%)	Malays	Chinese	Indians	Others	Total (%)
5.6 (36.9)	5.8 (11.4)	5.6	6.7 (53.7)	6.2 (32.6)	7.2 (11.9)	16.0 (1.8)	6.65	7.5 (54.8)	6.3 (31.1)	8.0 (12.5)	16.1 (1.6)	7.2
1.9 (57.0)	0.7 (6.1)	1.2	0.6 (28.7)	1.9 (62.5)	0.6 (6.1)	3.8 (2.7)	1.05	0.6 (27.4)	2.0 (66.0)	0.5 (5.3)	2.0 (1.3)	1.1
7.1 (36.2)	4.6 (6.9)	7.2	7.2 (52.4)	7.6 (36.6)	6.9 (10.4)	5.8 (0.6)	7.3	7.7 (53.9)	7.7 (36.1)	6.5 (9.6)	3.9 (0.4)	7.5
19.2 (69.2)	7.1 (7.6)	10.1	5.4 (32.1)	15.2 (60.1)	6.2 (7.6)	2.4 (0.2)	8.9	5.9 (35.4)	14.4 (57.7)	5.4 (6.8)	1.0 (0.1)	8.8
9.0 (39.9)	8.8 (11.6)	8.2	9.4 (54.0)	8.8 (33.7)	9.7 (11.5)	9.9 (0.8)	9.2	10.6 (56.2)	9.0 (32.2)	9.5 (10.8)	11.1 (0.8)	6.6
18.6 (19.7)	38.1 (11.9)	34.6	42.0 (69.5)	16.4 (18.1)	33.4 (11.4)	44.0 (1.0)	32.1	37.8 (67.4)	16.3 (19.5)	31.6 (12.0)	45.9 (1.1)	29.6
38.6 (42.6)	34.9 (11.4)	33.1	28.7 (43.7)	44.0 (44.6)	36.0 (11.3)	18.1 (0.4)	34.8	30.0 (44.0)	44.3 (43.6)	38.5 (12.0)	20.0 (0.4)	36.0
58.0 (36.5)	160.7 (10.8)	4,264.4	2,133.9 (53.0)	1,419.8 (35.3)	440.0 (10.9)	29.3 (0.7)	4,023.0	2,299.7 (52.7)	1,544.8 (35.4)	488.8 (11.2)	30.5 (0.7)	4,363.8

[6]Includes clerical supervisors, government executive officials, typists, book-keepers, cashiers, telephone operators, and telegraph operators.

[7]Includes managers (wholesale and retail trade), sales supervisors and buyers, technical salesmen, commercial travellers and manufacturers' agents.

[8]Includes managers of catering and lodging services, working proprietors, housekeeping and related service supervisors, cooks and related workers.

[9]Includes plantation managers and supervisors, planters and farmers, agricultural and animal husbandry workers, forestry workers, fishermen, hunters and related workers.

[10]Includes production supervisors and general foremen, miners, quarrymen, well drillers, motor-vehicle drivers and related workers.

It should be clear from Table 11.5 that employment 'restructuring' is not really an issue anymore—if it ever was—among production workers; management is not overly concerned with workers' ethnicity as long as they work hard and do not threaten management interests. In the agricultural sector, there do not appear to be significant efforts at restructuring among ethnic groups since Bumiputra comprise a large majority in this sector and the state is reluctant to intervene to resolve the land question in a fundamental way. The ethnic percentages in professional and technical occupations on the whole also generally reflect ethnic proportions in the Peninsular Malaysian population, though Bumiputra percentages in specific professions have received considerable attention. By 1980, Bumiputra were significantly under-represented in only two major occupational categories, namely at the 'administrative and managerial' level and in sales-related occupations. Nevertheless, Malay representation has greatly increased since independence in these occupations, though the Chinese proportion still significantly exceeds its share of the population.

In short, restructuring of the occupational distribution pattern has been largely achieved, especially at lower levels of employment. Of course, the sales-related occupations coveted by some Bumiputra are actually trading businesses. Hence, it is clear that the source of tension as far as employment restructuring is concerned is really over businesses—especially questions of ownership and control—and access to professional occupations, which largely concern the petty bourgeoisie. In short, educational, employment, business and promotion opportunities and facilities are the primary sources of inter-ethnic rivalry, and hence conflict, especially among the so-called 'middle-class'. Invoking slogans of historically justified and socially desirable 'affirmative action' on the one hand, and 'meritocracy' on the other, and having few common interests and grounds for cooperation and collaboration (unlike the bourgeoisie), the Malay and non-Malay middle classes experience inter-ethnic conflict most acutely. Hence, it is not surprising to find significant middle-class leadership and support for communal or 'narrow nationalist' movements and activities. Relatively uninhibited by the class considerations and interests of the bourgeoisie, the middle-class leaders make aggressive demands on behalf of their particular ethnic communities, but often inadvertently serve bourgeois interests (of whom they may even be contemptuous). Public polemics are often most aggressively articulated by Malay and Chinese politicians with no direct stake in the matter, predictably in the name of their respective communal interests. Perhaps more significant is that the very nature of 'middle-class' concerns (education, jobs, promotions, etc.) has broader popular appeal than the narrower concerns of the bourgeoisie (e.g. the 30 per cent target of the NEP or the Industrial Coordination Act). This does not, of course, imply that these middle-class elements are conscious servants of their respective bourgeoisies, but only that by using slogans of communal interests and unity, they advance particular class interests as the interests of the entire ethnic community.

Finally, most ominously, these rival communal trends actually justify each other's existence, by claiming to defend and protect the communal interests they purport to represent, against allegedly aggressive encroachments and threats by other ethnic communities, and thus willy-nilly serve each other's interests. This, of course, can ultimately only lead to greater ethnic conflict since the interests involved are fundamentally irreconcilable. Racial war or even a conflagration of the 13 May variety is not inevitable, though present trends do not give much promise of the contrary. It is quite conceivable that ethnic tensions and conflict will remain of the 'cold war' type, that is, without actually erupting, and thus become part and parcel of the Malaysian 'way of life', even more so than it is now. But it is obvious that in such a tense situation, a single spark can be enough to set off an explosion.

Nor are the country's leaders necessarily consciously contributing to this situation. Some may sincerely believe they are caught in a situation not of their own doing, and some may honestly desire an amicable solution acceptable to most parties. Most, however, also genuinely believe that the ethnic interests they advocate are legitimate—which they may well be—and irreconcilable, and therefore need to be acted upon.

The choices available at this stage of Malaysia's history are very limited, and there appears to be no place for a mass and genuinely national (hence multi-ethnic) popular movement to provide an alternative. Nevertheless, the alternatives for the 1980s are ultimately very simple: racial barbarism or justice through liberation.

The NEP: An Alternative Interpretation

Since there is general agreement that the two prongs of the NEP respond—in a particular fashion—to some of the major sources of socio-economic conflict in contemporary Malaysian society, an alternative interpretation of the NEP goals can provide a useful starting point for working towards a more adequate and substantial alternative national economic order.

First, poverty eradication measures should address the roots of income inequality, rather than be guided by some arbitrarily defined poverty line. A more equitable distributive principle would be one based on work effort, rather than property ownership. Existing gaps in the wage structure should be reduced considerably as well, while income derived from title, position, privilege, corruption and property (including capital and land) should be minimized (reference here is to income-generating wealth or property rather than personal property 'for consumption'). Those with property worked by others should not enjoy handsome incomes from the effort of others, while industrious people without much property should enjoy better incomes for their work. Such changes would favour the hard-working and would necessarily threaten the interests of rentiers who live well due to the efforts of others. However, public facilities should be made available to those less capable of being productive, such as children, the aged, the sick, the handicapped, and other destitutes of society.

It should be emphasized that absolute equality of incomes is not feasible in the short run and should not be the immediate goal of redistributive measures. Income differentials will exist and cannot be completely eliminated quickly in view of continuing differentials in the social value of individual work and the continued need for material work incentives, whether of an individual or collective nature. Nevertheless, existing income inequalities are neither necessary for economic development nor socially just by any ethical criteria, including religious principles that favour justice.

For the peasantry, land continues to be the primary means of production and in the Malaysian situation, two measures are important in this regard. Development of new agricultural land—on terms less economically burdensome to settlers than currently offered by FELDA—for land-hungry peasants is greatly needed. Contemporary land hunger is actually the outcome of colonial land law and policies pertaining to land-ownership. In addition, new arrangements affecting cultivated land are needed to overcome problems stemming from and related to land tenancy which persist due to the lack of commitment to fundamental agrarian institutional reform—exemplified for instance, by the virtual non-implementation of the various laws affecting tenancy on padi land. 'Restructuring' in this area should recognize long-term considerations, including land distribution and peasant productivity. Measures which can be considered include, for instance, collective or cooperative agriculture on relatively larger farms which are as productive and efficient as estates and big farms.

Large enterprises, especially foreign-controlled ones, should be run by workers on a cooperative basis, perhaps along lines of 'economic democracy'. With such measures, nationalization will not merely benefit the new managers and others in charge, as under 'state capitalism'. Also, if absolute equalization of wage scales is undertaken immediately, it is likely that many technicians, professionals and skilled workers would no longer earnestly contribute to the enterprise's progress; nevertheless, existing differentials in a particular enterprise can be reduced considerably as part of a series of similar measures undertaken on an economy-wide basis. New enterprises organized on a genuinely cooperative basis should be encouraged; in this regard, the reasons for the fiascos in the contemporary cooperative movement—including the difficulties of developing such enterprises in a capitalist economy, which encourage individual greed while discouraging group cooperation for collective need—should be understood.

A great many other initiatives will, of course, be necessary to develop a more just and self-reliant economy. These measures should be coordinated through a comprehensive and decentralized planning process, i.e. planning will have to be undertaken at all levels of the economy and must involve all parties (especially the productive classes), and not merely be the exclusive responsibility and prerogative of a clique of planners. Efforts to develop a self-reliant economy should take into account the country's economic heritage, including the strengths and weaknesses of uneven development processes under colonialism. In this connection, it must be recognized that the path to self-reliance is a difficult one, especially in an open and dependent economy. Hence, the planning task becomes especially difficult and crucial. However, by identifying and understanding the main weaknesses of the economy (e.g. the weak links between agriculture and industry, or the disparities between padi and export-oriented agriculture, or those between the West and East Coasts), the measures necessary to overcome them can be found.

In conclusion, it needs to be emphasized that while the road to economic and social liberation and justice is fraught with difficulty, the alternative is continued inequality, and, perhaps more ominously, heightened and irresolvable ethnic conflict. While this alternative, the elements of which are outlined above, necessarily threatens certain privileged interests, it offers a means for the resolution of the most pressing and fundamental economic, social and political problems currently facing the country through genuine restructuring, and hence liberation of Malaysian society by establishing a just and self-reliant new national economic order acceptable to the vast majority of the population, especially its productive members.

APPENDICES

Appendix 1
CAPITAL ACCUMULATION, UNEVEN DEVELOPMENT, AND CLASS FORMATION

THE analysis in this book has been inspired by a perspective summarized in this appendix.

Before proceeding to outline the analytical framework used in this book, a brief critical discussion of some of the major existing approaches to the study of development and class formation is provided. Particular attention is given to the 'world systems' approach and to the 'mode of production' framework. The perspective here suggests that several related areas of analysis need to be incorporated in the study of development and class formation; it implies that while historical options are limited by social, and especially economic, conditions, history is ultimately the outcome of class contention in these conditions. Hence, historical specificity and sequence are considered important, and it is deemed necessary to go beyond the evolutionist paradigms, whether of the 'tradition to modernity' type or the 'feudalism to capitalism' variety. The discussion will also suggest how this framework informed the historical analysis of Malaya presented in this book.

Some Limitations of Existing Theoretical Approaches

MODERNIZATION

Most of the existing sociological literature on development and stratification is inspired by the functionalist method (see Frank, 1966; Rhodes, 1968), much of which simply ignores the existence of class relations. One important functionalist tendency, usually associated with Durkheim, does recognize class differences. In this, class divisions are viewed as being necessary and natural for societal evolution and progress. The Durkheimian view sees classes as comprising an interrelated organic whole involving complementarity but not conflict.

The imprecise and surrogate character of many of the basic categories in the modernization literature has been severely criticized by several reviewers (e.g. Bendix, 1967; Gusfield, 1967; Rhodes, 1968; Tipps, 1973). Studies inspired by the modernization approach generally do not incorporate theoretical analysis of class conflict. This is neither accidental nor is it without consequence. Modernization theory, largely inspired by structural functionalism, is methodologically blocked from analysing contradictory class relations. When elements or hints of class analysis are found in such literature, these usually occur despite, rather than because of, the methodology used. Consequently, it is often implicit rather than explicit. This should not be surprising since the functionalist method precludes a theoretical recognition of class divisions based on contradictory, and possibly antagonistic, interests united in a particular social division of labour. Hence, modernization studies do not address themselves to contradictory class relations. It is therefore not useful to turn to the modernization approach for theoretical elucidation to inform class analysis.

DEPENDENCY

There are several major approaches to development studies besides those identifiable with the modernization literature. One of these is the 'dependency' perspective,[1] which basically maintains that certain countries and regions are 'underdeveloped' by those countries and regions upon which they are dependent. Some versions of this approach introduce an underlying class analysis to explain a geo-economic phenomenon of surplus outflow which is seen as the key aspect of the underdevelopment process. These argue that metropolitan capital, usually abetted by local capitalist collaborators, exploits the producing classes in satellite countries and regions. It is held that this basic structural relationship has been maintained over several centuries (since capitalism's ascendancy in the sixteenth century), though its forms have changed over time. While not in disagreement with many aspects of certain specific analyses inspired by this approach,[2] the viability of the key analytical notion of dependence is questionable.

The dominance/dependence distinction cannot be unambiguously applied only to relations between centre and periphery (or metropolis and satellite). While it is true that the social relations involved are far from being egalitarian, symmetrical, mutually beneficial or devoid of exploitative aspects, Lall (1975) has shown that it is ultimately impossible to distinguish between dependence and non-dependence without first equating dependency with specific relations between classes, and then between nations in which these classes are geographically located. Therefore, while 'dependence' may be a useful descriptive term in referring to certain aspects and implications of international class relations, its analytical efficacy is suspect.

WORLD SYSTEMS

In recent years, there have been several important efforts to relate dependency theory to the emerging 'world systems' school of analysis (e.g. Amin, 1974; 1976; Wallerstein, 1974a, 1974b, 1974c). The 'world systems' school does purport to offer a theoretical framework for the analysis of development. It would therefore be useful to examine this perspective, particularly for the insights it may shed on the role of class relations in development. Rather than discuss this in general terms, which cannot be usefully accomplished in a few pages, this exposition will focus on the work of Immanuel Wallerstein, who is considered to be at least a major proponent, if not the dean of this school, in North American social science circles.[3]

First, a brief outline of Wallerstein's view of world systems to enable one to focus on the significance he attributes to class relations. For Wallerstein, a theory of development must be located in a 'social system' in which the elements contributing to social change are internally obtained rather than externally derived. In his view, since the sixteenth century, a single global social system has emerged. This is the capitalist world economy, which is based upon a geographical division of production for the world market involving three zones, namely 'core', 'semi-periphery' and 'periphery'. Each zone is broadly distinguished by the technical basis of its productive activities, as well as by the different modes of 'labour control' adopted by the dominant class concerned. The capitalist world economy is characterized by multiple sovereignties, with core states strongest and those in the periphery weakest. Since the states serve only the interests of the dominant classes, the different strengths of the states will therefore correspond to the different strengths of the dominant classes. State power is used in the world market to distribute products among the different zones, with the core gaining most and the periphery losing out because of the differing strengths of the competing states.

Various aspects of Wallerstein's framework are controversial,[4] but the discussion here will be confined only to certain general aspects involving class relations. As Skocpol

(1977) points out, Wallerstein's model involves two important determinisms. First, socio-economic structure is determined by the technical production options in the world market chosen by the dominant class, i.e. the dominant class chooses among the options determined by the market. The second determinism, related to the first, reduces state structures and policies to determination by dominant-class interests. For Wallerstein then, the form of labour control is a 'market-optimizing strategy of the dominant class alone' chosen from among various options determined by the market (Skocpol, 1977: 1079). While he does not ignore the social relations of production, his emphasis on market determination, i.e. exchange relations, causes Wallerstein to view class relations in an undialectical and a-historical manner. Hence, class relations are not viewed as a historical development from preceding class contradictions conditioned by prevailing market circumstances. Instead, in Wallerstein's framework, class relations are selected by the dominant class from among various market-determined options for the control of labour. The relations of production thus have little significance, being essentially determined by the market. The dominated classes become passive objects for dominant class manipulation in this scheme of things. This presumes that the dominant class makes history in circumstances which are totally beyond the influence of the dominated classes. Similarly, the state becomes a mere tool of the dominant class. That the state is an outcome of class relations and of previous class contention is not recognized in Wallerstein's analysis.

As Murray (1977) argues, Wallerstein's determinism causes him to ignore important differences between various kinds of class relations in the sphere of production. For instance, the significance of the emergence of the exploitation of free wage labour is lost in such an approach. Capitalist relations of production, involving the exploitation of free wage labour, are the only class relations which do not inherently involve extra-economic coercion. They are also the only social relations of production which do not present inherent limits to the expansion of capital. The potential for class contention is always specific to the class relations involved and therefore this cannot be appreciated except by recognizing the particular class contradictions involved. Class conflict, in turn, also affects the development of class relations. All this, and more, is removed from analytical attention by Wallerstein's one-sided emphasis on the sphere of circulation, particularly on the exchange relations of the market. (See also Dupuy and Fitzgerald, 1977; Gerstein, 1977.)

Wallerstein's insistence on recognizing the world market as the setting for capital expansion and class relations is well taken (see Skocpol, 1973). The development of commodity exchange and capital accumulation on a global scale undoubtedly has profound implications for the course of development. The dualist argument by Laclau (1971) that Latin America remains part feudal and part capitalist does not acknowledge these key features of the contemporary world economy. However, Laclau's insistence that some relations of production under the domination of capital do not involve free wage labour, and hence are non-capitalist, should not be ignored. In so far as the 'world systems' analytical framework fails to incorporate the dialectics of class relations, at least in Wallerstein's formulation, it is methodologically unable to adequately incorporate the point made by Laclau.

MODES OF PRODUCTION

The theoretical approach involving the analysis of modes of production and social formations offers the prospect of transcending the problems identified with Wallerstein's 'world systems' model, especially since it gives great attention to class analysis. In contrast to the 'world systems' perspective and, even more so, with the 'dependency' school, this approach has been the subject of very rigorous efforts—especially by the

'Althusserian school'—to define its key theoretical concepts and to formulate its theoretical framework and methods. However, or perhaps precisely for this reason, theoretical conceptualization in this direction has been very controversial and is the subject of considerable debate.[5] The effort by Balibar (in Althusser and Balibar, 1970) to provide a general theory of modes of production is widely viewed as central to discussions of this approach. It is therefore the starting point of the present brief review of the viability of this approach.

Balibar has defined a mode of production as involving a combination of three elements: the labourer, the non-labourer, and the means of production. In his view, these elements are joined by the 'property'[6] connection and the 'real appropriation' connection. ('Relations of production' and 'forces of production' respectively appear to correspond with Balibar's terms.) Balibar's concept of mode of production involves determination—'in the last instance'—by the economic, and also generation of ideological and political structures as 'structures in dominance' (superstructure?) necessary for a mode's viable existence and reproduction. (See also Poulantzas, 1973a, 1975.)

Balibar conceives two types of modes of production. In one type, the coherent internal correspondence between the 'property' connection and the 'real appropriation' connection in a particular mode ensures the indefinite reproduction of the conditions for the mode's continued existence. One suspects that he may want to imply that the survival of the mode is threatened when the relations of production constrain and thus come into contradiction with the development of the forces of production. However, Balibar then explains transition from one mode to another by resorting to a notion of a 'transitional mode of production'. According to Balibar, this mode is characterized by the lack of coherent internal correspondence between the two connections. Apparently, he means that the relations of production are characteristically in contradiction with the forces of production in the transitional modes. Hence, a functionalist-like correspondence between the two connections is an implied feature of the non-transitional modes. The lack of correspondence between the two connections is invoked to explain the necessarily transitory character of the transitional modes. Transition is completed when correspondence is regained in a new non-transitional mode. However, such a formulation begs the issue of transition to the transitional mode itself.[7] Balibar's non-transitional modes of production are apparently devoid of internal contradiction, and hence emerge as static structures of the functionalist type. This may in turn be related to the status of the concept of mode of production, not as an 'object in history', but rather as an 'object in thought'—a suspiciously idealist notion.

Hindess and Hirst (1975) reject Balibar's project of developing 'the general theory of modes of production' as being theoretically impossible. Instead, they attempt to offer 'the general concept of mode of production'. A mode of production is 'an articulated combination of relations and forces of production structured by the dominance of the relations of production. The relations of production define a specific mode of appropriation of surplus labour and the specific form of social distribution of the means of production corresponding to that mode of appropriation of surplus labour' (Hindess and Hirst, 1975: 9-10). They argue that it is the centrality of class struggle which dictates the primacy of the relations of production for analysis. After the publication of their 1975 book, Hindess and Hirst (1977a, 1977b) have since claimed that the logic of their earlier (1975) argument has led them to reject the pertinence of the mode of production concept. They argue that focusing on this concept limits analysis to a very restricted range of economic class relations and neglects the difficulties of conceptualizing more complex forms of class relations. Instead, they argue, it is necessary to directly elaborate concepts of economic class relations and the conditions of their existence in definite social formations.

If the appropriate unit for analysis is the social formation, one has to query how the boundaries of the social formation are to be defined. If the unity to a social formation is provided at the economic level however, then it can be maintained that the only existing social formation today is the global one, with a division of labour involving a variety of commodity production and unified by the world market, which is also the 'space' for the circulation of expanding capital. Alternatively, if the social formation is defined territorially by the domain of a particular state, it renders the unit of analysis subject to political and legal (and therefore undoubtedly ideological) definitional variation.[8]

The concept of social formation poses other difficulties as well. If, as in Balibar's view, the concept of social formation is that of an articulated combination of modes of production, several problems arise. One is the problem already alluded to above, i.e. that of the very viability of the concept of mode of production. Second, it is still unclear to this author, what is actually meant by the articulation of modes of production, and especially by the notion of domination of a specific social formation by a particular mode of production. For example, how does domination by a particular mode affect the forms and relative contributions of surplus (or surplus labour)? Or, how does such domination relate to the forms and relative demographic sizes (and proportions) of various social classes? There is, after all, no necessary correspondence between the demographic size of a surplus-producing class and the proportion it contributes to the total surplus. Therefore, for instance, the largest class in terms of population numbers may not be the class contributing most to the total surplus in a particular social formation.

The difficulties with the 'mode of production' approach then are primarily with some of its theoretical and methodological implications. The basic concept of mode of production for the analysis of social formations is problematic and controversial. What the boundaries of a social formation are, and what precise analytical implications the domination of a social formation by a particular mode of production has, are both important issues not yet elucidated by the 'mode of production–social formation' approach. This is not to deny the various valuable insights offered by this perspective, as was the case with the 'world systems' approach discussed earlier. However, the considerable and important difficulties they involve necessitate the formulation of a fresh theoretical framework, which can draw upon the many valuable theoretical insights offered by the approaches critically reviewed above. In so far as the theoretical and methodological impasses encountered with the perspectives discussed here cannot be transcended, it becomes imperative that an attempt be made to formulate an alternative perspective more adequate for the formidable task of providing an integrated and comprehensive framework for the analysis of development.

Alternative Analytical Framework

The modest theoretical framework presented here is necessarily limited in so far as it has been developed primarily to situate and inform the historical analysis of certain aspects of class formation in Malaya, primarily over the course of the past century. It is greatly influenced by some existing approaches, especially the two perspectives reviewed earlier, which, for reasons already discussed, cannot be accepted unequivocally. This is not to claim methodological originality nor to endorse theoretical eclecticism. Rather, it is a reminder of, as well as a response to, the current state of theoretical work relating to the subject matter of this book.

This section first introduces certain key concepts and then suggests a frame of reference for analysing the changes in class relations that occur with the integration of an area, such as Malaya, into the world economy. The central concepts of social class, capital and the state, as well as related concepts, are discussed. A hypothetical picture of the social relations of production which emerge from the expansion of capital on a global scale is then formulated and some of the implications for the study of development and class formation discussed.

CLASS

We begin with the concept of social class. Class relations are basically defined with reference to the social relations of production.[9] The social relations of production and the forces of production always exist in a contradictory relationship. (The social relations of production include the relations among members of the producing class to one another as well as to their means of production, and their owners, in the immediate process of production, this also being known as the labour process.) While class relations are constituted by the relations of production, the two are not identical. Each social class has not merely an economic aspect, but political and ideological aspects as well (Poulantzas, 1973a). However, in so far as the economic criterion is determinant, attention will be focused on this in the discussion of class formation in this book.

Classes exist when non-producers appropriate a share of the product of the producers. The extraction of this share—known as the 'social surplus', or 'surplus labour', or 'the surplus' for short—is always ensured, directly or indirectly, by coercion exercised by the appropriating class. Social relations of production therefore involve exploitation of the producers by the non-producing appropriators. Since exploitation is ultimately guaranteed by coercion, the relations of production also involve domination of the exploited class by the exploiting class. Hence, these may also be termed the 'dominated class' and the 'dominant class' respectively. Therefore the class interests of the producers and the non-producing appropriators in the direct process of production are necessarily opposed.

After identifying class relations with reference to the social relations of production, it is important to deepen the analytical framework by distinguishing class fractions. 'Fractions are distinct from simple strata since they coincide with important economic differentiations and, as such, can even take on an important role as social forces, a role relatively distinct from that of other fractions of their class' (Poulantzas, 1973a: 38). A class fraction therefore shares common interests which put it in relative contradiction with other fractions of the same class. Such contradictions often have great significance for social change. However, it is always important to be aware that there are also class commonalities which unite the fractions of a single class.[10]

Class contention is not viewed here only in terms of overt struggle waged along clear-cut class lines.[11] Rather, it refers to the always extant contradictory relations between, as well as among, classes and class fractions. Therefore, class contention may also be conceived of as the existing interaction of contradictory class and fractional interests. In other words: contradictory class as well as class fractional interests give rise to class contention and hence to social change. Class contention does not only result from the tussle between the producing class or classes and the class or classes which appropriate the surplus produced. Dominant-class interests are neither homogeneous nor identical. Thus, Parts III and IV of this book were both premised on the recognition that capital is not homogeneous and that conflict exists among groups of particular capitals which form capitalist class fractions. The same is true of the dominated class or classes. In other words, class relations in general are contradictory and where there is class contradiction there is class conflict. This provides an important perspective for the book. Social change and development demand explanation and class dialectics are crucial in this regard. It is in this broad sense then that the history of class society is that of class contention. However, it is only at specific historical conjunctures, usually when common class location coincides with organized movements as well as collective consciousness, that conflict becomes very apparent. Such historical conjunctures may give rise to radically new class configurations, especially when the protagonist class or classes are sufficiently organized and effectively guided by an ideology capable of leading the transcendence of the old social order to a new one. However, it should be remembered that the class structure of society is constantly, though usually less dramatically, subject to historical transformation. Class relations are never reproduced without change. In discussing the reproduction of social relations of production, one is also talking of the reproduction—i.e. growth (or expansion), replication (or conservation), and dissolution—of specific social classes, or in other words, of class formation. Class formation not only defines the contradictions generating class contention, but is also subject to the outcome of conflict among classes and class fractions.

COMMODITY

Before turning to the concept of capital, it is necessary to introduce the concept of a commodity (see Sweezy, 1942). This is important because the existence of capital to some extent presupposes the existence of commodities. Further, as will be shown, production organized by capital is necessarily commodity production and capitalist relations of production require the existence of labour power as a commodity. Every commodity embodies two aspects—use value and exchange value. Objects of human use in all societies possess use value. However, use values per se do not directly involve social relations. What distinguishes commodities from other use values is their exchange values relative to one another. The existence of commodities implies the existence of things produced for exchange rather than for direct use by their own producer, hence necessarily entailing exchange relations. Quantitative exchange relations involving commodities are, in reality then, only a manifestation of social relations among owners of commodities. When commodity production has been generalized, the purpose of social production is realized only through exchange. Simple or petty commodity production by definition then, involves individual producers, producing with their own individual means of production, and satisfying needs through exchange with other similar producers.

CAPITAL

The concept of capital used in this book has two key aspects—as self-expanding value, and as involving particular social relations.[12] The first aspect implies an inherent tendency for capital to accumulate, while the second indicates that this expansion necessarily entails certain social relations. In other words, the expansion of capital involves certain social relations. The total social capital is the aggregate of particular capitals, and in the process of accumulation, capital enters different circuits and acquires various forms, as will be elaborated below.

Capital exists in the sphere of circulation as well as in the sphere of production. A capitalist is therefore one accumulating capital in either sphere of economic activity. In the sphere of circulation, capital appears in two main forms—commercial capital and usury capital. Commercial or merchant capital is involved in commercial transactions, i.e. the realm of commodity exchange. Usury, finance or interest-bearing capital generally entails the loan of cash funds or other forms of credit in order to recoup a higher sum later, the difference usually being called 'interest'. In the sphere of production, constant capital and variable capital may be distinguished. The former refers to capital in the form of means of production, while the latter refers to the costs of reproducing the labour force.

Capital in the sphere of circulation, or 'circulation capital' for short, is not directly involved in the sphere of production. Hence, it does not directly organize production. The expansion of circulation capital generally accompanies the spread of commodity relations, i.e. commodity production and exchange. Therefore, the expansion of circulation capital may also involve the reorientation, and possibly even the reorganiz-ation, of production. However, it is important to note that the reorganization of pro-duction is ultimately undertaken by those directly in control of the labour process, even though circulation capital may indirectly contribute to such changes, e.g. by the indirect investment in production by usury capital via the peasant producer.

Capital in production has direct control over the labour process which it may reorganize to suit changing conditions. When capitalists invest in production, they may accumulate on the basis of capitalist as well as non-capitalist relations of production. Capitalist relations of production involve the exploitation of free wage labour while non-capitalist relations entail exploiting involuntary labour, which may be either unfree wage labour (e.g. indentured labour) or non-wage labour (e.g. slavery). Hence, capital in the sphere of production does not necessarily involve capitalist relations of production.

CAPITALIST RELATIONS OF PRODUCTION

What really distinguishes capitalist relations of production from other relations of production therefore is the sale of the free wage labourer's ability to work, known as 'labour power', for the payment of a wage. It is this feature, i.e. labour power as a com-modity, which distinguishes capitalist relations of production from non-capitalist production relations. In this connection, it is important to emphasize that, unlike non-capitalist relations of production, the commodity form of labour power does not pose immanent barriers to the accumulation of capital.

Free wage labour, then, is characteristic of capitalist relations of production. Labour is free in capitalist relations of production in at least a double sense. First, the producers do not own and are hence free of the means of production, i.e. they are a proletariat. Second, labour power is free to be sold as a commodity on the market, i.e. it is not tied as serfs or slaves are, for example. Freedom for the proletariat then does not imply more than these juridico-economic freedoms. It must be recognized that the first aspect of the worker's freedom is essentially (economically) coercive, in so far as it compels the pro-ducer to find means for survival, usually by trying to sell his or her labour power. However, proletarianization of the producer alone does not necessarily result in capitalist relations of production. Here, proletarianization refers only to the separation of producers from the means of production. It does *not* refer to wage employment. Hence, while wage labourers are proletarians, not all proletarians are wage workers. As is shown in Chapter 5 of this book, impoverishment of the peasantry has also led to land tenancy, a non-capitalist relationship. The significance of the free status of the proletariat should not be overlooked. When capital is involved in production before a free wage labour force is available, it usually organizes production on the basis of non-capitalist relations, i.e. it uses involuntary labour rather than free wage labour.

Unlike the overtly coercive non-capitalist relations of production involving in-voluntary labour, capitalist relations of exploitation are obscured by the apparently equivalent exchange between capitalist and wage labourer. However, the wage paid to the worker is merely payment for the producer's ability to work (labour power) and not for the actual labour rendered. The value of labour actually obtained from workers by the capitalist class exceeds that of the wage, i.e. the value of labour power. Hence, only by exposing the distinction between the value of labour and the value of labour power can the essence of capitalist exploitation be revealed. The share of the social product appropriated by non-producers can be termed the 'social surplus'. The surplus (or surplus labour) obtained from capitalist exploitation is termed 'surplus value'. Unlike the case with non-commodity (i.e. use-value) production, the surplus in capitalism takes on the value form. This is because capitalism is characterized by generalized commodity exchanges, involving the production of values, i.e. exchange values. The sale of commodities is therefore essential for capital to realize surplus value and hence for the accumulation of capital.

THE STATE

One other important category discussed in the book should now be introduced. While it is not possible to enter here into an extensive discussion of the nature of the capitalist state[13] (see Miliband, 1961; Poulantzas, 1973b; Espsing-Anderson et al., 1976), or even more specifically of the colonial state and the post-colonial state (see Alavi, 1972; Bamat, 1977; Hein and Stenzel, 1974; Kalecki, 1967; Leys, 1975; Mamdani, 1976; Meillasoux, 1970; Pompermayer, 1973; Quijano, 1971; Saul, 1975), it is important to outline how the state is viewed in this study.

To begin with, it is useful to locate one's perspective in contradistinction with other extant views on the state particularly in relation to class relations, since it is this that is of most interest here. The liberal political science view of the state as a neutral, 'pluralist' body whose activities are seen as responses to the demands of varied and often competing interests in a classless society is rejected. Another more interesting, but nonetheless one-dimensional and reductionist view sees the state as a mere 'instrument' of the ruling class. A third view sees state structure as determined by the structural imperatives of the socio-economic system. The 'structuralist' perspective is in turn different from a fourth approach which recognizes and distinguishes three aspects of the state, i.e. as object, as product (or outcome), and also as determinant of class conflict.

The fourth (multi-dimensional) view mentioned above was employed in this book. It is only a perspective on the state and certainly does not amount to being a theory of the state. The state is hence viewed here in relation to class conflict, and not as being somehow beyond it. This approach integrates many insights of both the 'instrumentalist' and the 'structuralist' perspectives without being subject to their difficulties, especially in so far as these are due to limitations of a uni-dimensional perspective. In other words, the role of the state as a determinant of class contention, in the author's view, accommodates many 'instrumentalist' propositions about the nature of the state. Similarly, 'structuralist' arguments are also partially acceptable, since another aspect of the perspective recognizes that the state is also a product or outcome of continuing class conflict. In a sense, then, this view suggests that the existing debate between 'structuralist' and 'instrumentalist' proponents is, to some extent, a false one, in so far as they may be addressing different dimensions of the state. These different perspectives may actually shed light on particular dimensions of the state which may add up in a complementary fashion to offer a more complete (multidimensional) view of the state.

Hence, the view of the state that is adopted here sees: (i) state structure as a *product* of class contention (also, state power is not a given, unchanging monolithic object, but is always subject to class conflict); (ii) state actions and the operations of the state apparatus as a *determinant* of class contention; (iii) political power and control of the state as an *object* of class contention. Different aspects of the state attain a different significance not only in relation to the analyst's particular interest, but also at different moments in the conflict between classes. Hence, the activity of the colonial and post-colonial state apparatus will always embody all three aspects, but these may be of differing interest at various times. (In Chapters 3, 5, and 10 of this book, there is some discussion of the state as a product of class conflict. In Chapter 10, state power is clearly the object of class conflict, and in Chapters 3, 4, 5, 6, 7, 9 and 10, the aspect of the state as a determinant of class conflict is highlighted.)

In Chapter 10 it is argued that in the 1970s, the governing statist capitalist class fraction has advanced its interests through the development and use of state power. This is interpreted as an outcome of inter-fractional class conflict, especially over the first dozen years after independence. The governing statist petty bourgeoisie, comprising mainly powerful politicians and senior civil servants, successfully enhanced its political dominance over the other local capitalist fractions (discussed in Chapter 8). By expanding state power, and hence its own power as a capitalist class fraction, it has been able to pursue capital accumulation in its own interests. (Thus, the discussion of this in Chapter 10 exemplifies the three-dimensional perspective of the state proposed here.)

WORLD MARKET AND CAPITAL ACCUMULATION

The transformations associated with integration into the world economy may also be schematized. For the purposes of this discussion, it may be noted that the world economy has two important aspects. One is the existence of a world market, this being the arena for all commodity exchange. The second aspect is the ongoing accumulation of capital. At this point, three aspects of the accumulation of capital may be noted: the development of tendencies identified with monopoly; the different phases of capital expansion; and the social division of labour which corresponds to the different phases of the accumulation of capital. All three aspects of capital accumulation have important implications for the analysis of uneven and combined development and of the associated processes of class formation.

There is little reason to maintain that capital expansion is inimical to development unless one introduces moral or ethical criteria to define development, as Seers (1973) does. The phenomena often associated with terms such as 'underdevelopment', 'peripheral development', 'economic backwardness', and 'dependency' should instead be viewed as historical outcomes of ongoing uneven development. Ongoing capital accumulation dominated by capitalist interests at the 'centre' of the system is not eternally opposed to industrialization in the 'periphery', as the expansion of industrial capital in Malaya demonstrates (see Chapter 9). The potential for such development is recognized by the view that the different phases of capital accumulation relate to a changing social division of labour on a global scale.

In the expansion of capital, two distinct components of uneven and combined development are significant. The first is ongoing capital accumulation, involving both capitalist as well as non-capitalist relations of production. In other words, capitalist (capital) accumulation as well as non-capitalist (capital) accumulation proceed simultaneously. The second component occurs within the capitalist sector (which comprises those productive enterprises characterized by capitalist relations of production) and involves the development of monopoly capital (Sweezy, 1942). (Two often simultaneous tendencies contribute to the latter: the 'concentration' of capital involving the normal expansion of particular capitals through accumulation; and the 'centralization' of capital which entails the combination of existing capitals.) The two components of uneven development interact with each other in concrete historical conditions to give rise to specific changing forms and conditions of uneven development. For example, one important element of uneven development is the different 'organic compositions of capital' ('capital-labour ratio' in neoclassical economic terms) which characterize particular capitals in production. Another element is the relatively higher level of development of the forces of production in the capitalist sector compared to the non-capitalist sector.

It was noted earlier that capital accumulation proceeds in two related, but distinct, spheres, i.e. circulation and production. On the one hand, the spread of commodity production has generally kept ahead of capitalist relations in production. On the other hand, circulation capital has preceded capital in the sphere of production. The development of commodity production and exchange has generally contributed to the expansion of commercial capital. The extension of commodity production and exchange has not only been generally accompanied by the expansion of commercial capital, but is also, in fact, a precondition for the latter process. In other words, the precondition for the operation of commercial capital is the existence of a market. While circulation capital is subordinate to capital in production, commercial capital may dominate non-capitalist commodity-producing relations of production. In the former case, the interests of capital are unified, though contention exists over the division of surplus value. In the latter case, however, production and circulation are dominated by different classes—the non-capitalist exploiting class and the commercial capitalist class. Although the exploiting class in the production process is subordinated to circulation capital, it remains a non-capitalist exploiting class.

By promoting commodity production, merchant capital can stimulate the development of the social forces of production and open up the possibility of reorganizing production along different lines. However, commercial capital is incapable of transforming non-capitalist relations of production into capitalist relations of production (Kay, 1975). Merchant capital's basic reliance on the non-capitalist exploiting class involved in production prevents it from reconstituting the social relations of production along capitalist lines despite its own undermining of the pre-capitalist relations of production. As far as the Malayan experience is concerned, for example, the transformation of the peasantry under the colonial impact—the subject of detailed discussion in Part II of this book—exemplifies the impasse that the penetration of circulation capital has led to thus far. Circulation capital's contact with the peasantry did not consolidate the pre-colonial relations of production even at the formal level, but instead resulted in new motions of class formation and thus in new social relations of production. However, while the distinction between capital in the sphere of production and capital in the sphere of circulation is important, it does not imply that capital is incapable of extending from one sphere to another in the process of capital expansion (as is shown in Chapters 5 and 9).

The implications of the expansion of circulation capital for the social relations of production must be seen in the context of the world economy in which circulation capital is subordinate to production capital. While it is still the most prevalent form of capital in much of the 'periphery', when viewed in the context of the world economy circulation capital is subordinate to production capital in the 'centre'. The procurement of cheap means of production for the 'centre' and realization of surplus value by the sale of manufactured commodities have been among the primary tasks of circulation capital in the 'periphery' in its service to production (industrial) capital at the 'centre'.

RELATIONS OF PRODUCTION, CAPITAL ACCUMULATION,
AND CAPITALISTS

The social relations of production in the world economy may be classified under one of two categories according to the extent and nature of capital expansion. Some production has been directly organized by capitalists, e.g. modern industry and plantation agriculture, while other production, though subordinate to capital, has not been under direct capitalist organization, e.g. peasant agriculture. With its integration into the world economy, however, the latter too is subject to the expansion of capital. Thus, all production in the world economy is subject to the ongoing accumulation of capital in the world market. Hence, all production, whether or not directly organized by capital, is ultimately dominated by capital. However, the implications of being subject to the accumulation of capital vary with the specific relations to capital involved. Hence, whether, to what extent, and in what manner capital is involved in the spheres of circulation and production become significant.

The two categories of production mentioned above therefore involve, on the one hand, relations of production not directly organized by capital, and on the other hand, those directly organized by capital. The distinction to be made therefore hinges on whether capital is confined to the sphere of circulation or is directly involved in production.

The first category includes production organized by a non-capitalist class which has come into contact with capital in the sphere of circulation. The resulting relations of production are integrated into the world economy dominated by capital and, in this sense, are no longer pre-capitalist relations of production. However, in so far as the expansion of capital is confined to the sphere of circulation, capitalist relations of production cannot emerge. Instead, the outcome is one of non-capitalist relations of production under the domination of capital in the sphere of circulation. These may or may not resemble the pre-capitalist relations of production in form. In Parts I and II of this book, it is argued that the transformation of the indigenous peasantry under British colonialism primarily gave rise to the emergence of non-capitalist relations of production which did not resemble the pre-colonial relations of production even in form.

The second category refers to production directly organized by capital. When a proletariat has not already emerged from preceding developments, as has been the usual case in the early phase of integration into the world economy, obtaining a labour force becomes imperative.[14] This has typically been achieved either by reorganizing the existing social relations of production or by relying on an immigrant labour supply. Since pre-capitalist developments have usually not created a local pool of free wage labour, capital has little choice but to organize production on non-capitalist lines. In Part III, this is shown to have been the case in nineteenth-century and early twentieth-century Malaya. However, the subsequent creation of a proletariat is common, usually being attributable to the new tendencies which emerge as a consequence of integration into the world economy. The emergence of such a proletariat is often a result of developments generated by the integrative process under capital's domination. However, this by no means implies that capitalists must consciously or actively set such a process in motion. While they well may, often enough such a process is the unplanned outcome of certain phases of capital accumulation. This result may or may not coincide with the intentions or the interests of the capitalist class.[15] The creation of this proletariat establishes a crucial condition facilitating the emergence and generalization of capitalist relations of production.

What is being suggested here is that capital expansion did not typically develop capitalist relations of production either in the course of reorganizing pre-capitalist production relations, or when new enterprises for production were first being established during the early phase of the integration of the 'periphery' into the world economy. Instead, capital accumulation based on non-capitalist relations of production tends to be the initial consequence of capital expansion whether in the sphere of circulation only or in the sphere of production as well. It must be emphasized that not only the pre-capitalist relations of production, but also the conditions and manner of integration, are important in influencing the class configurations which emerge in the world economy (Cliffe,

1977). Thus, while the present discussion of Malaya began with an investigation into pre-colonial class relations in Part I, considerable attention was given in both Parts II and III to world and local economic conditions as well as to the role of the colonial state in influencing social and economic transformation. One might add that subsequent developments, especially class conflict, have had an important bearing on the development of class relations.

It is proposed that social relations of production of the first category (i.e. pre-capitalist production which has been subjected to domination by capital) are less likely than those of the second category (i.e. production which has been organized by capital from the outset) to evolve into capitalist relations of production. In the former case, domination by capital involves only capital in the sphere of circulation. Hence, capital expansion is taking place primarily outside the sphere of production and hence does not directly contribute to reconstituting the social relations of production along capitalist lines (though such a transformation may occur as an indirect consequence of the expansion of circulation capital). In the latter case, capital accumulation occurs in the production sphere itself and hence can directly encourage and facilitate the development of capitalist relations of production. (The former case was illustrated by Part II's examination of the transformation of the peasantry under colonialism which has not (yet) resulted in the generalization of capitalist relations of production, while Part III's treatment of the expansion of capital and the emergence of free wage labour illustrates the latter case.)

Capitalist relations tend to become general in production organized by capital. In retrospect then, non-capitalist relations of production organized by capital may be considered 'proto-capitalist' since they tend to be of a transitional nature, eventually tending to give way to capitalist relations of production. Capitalist relations of production are far from having been generalized, however, especially for economic activities not directly organized by capital. And in so far as such non-capitalist relations are already subject to capital's domination, the potential for further transformation into capitalist relations may be limited (as was the case—see Part II—for the Malay peasantry). (The varying circumstances of capital expansion mean that this is not an eternal situation but one which may well change.)

Yet, after noting that pre-capitalist relations reconstituted on non-capitalist lines by circulation capital tend to be more resistant to being further transformed into capitalist relations in comparison with non-capitalist relations initially constituted by production capital, it must be emphasized that no necessary evolution of relations of production under the domination of capital is being posited here.[16] This is not to imply that social relations of production develop in a completely arbitrary or random fashion. Integration into the world economy defines the context and hence the limited possibilities for development. The development of class relations also necessarily involves class contention in concrete historical circumstances,[17] since classes do not exist outside of class conflict.

Summary

The 'intellectual dead-end of ahistorical model-building' (Wallerstein, 1974a: 388) is a problem which appears especially to plague ideal-type perspectives on development, whether of the 'tradition to modernity' evolutionary mould or of the 'feudalism to capitalism' transition kind. This difficulty may stem from a failure to recognize 'that to be historically specific is not to fail to be analytically universal' (Wallerstein, 1974a: 391). Such an appreciation for historical specificity should not be misconstrued to mean that there is no place for generalization in the scientific study of society. To quote from Giovanni Arrighi's critique of Andre Gunder Frank: 'It is always possible, indeed necessary to analyse what different socio-economic formations, or different historical phases of the same socio-economic formation have in common—but a theoretical framework such as that used by Frank, that systematically prevents the identification of the particularity of contradictions can hardly be expected to clarify their general aspects' (Arrighi, 1971). Hence, it was argued, it is only meaningful to identify the general through recognizing the particular. Likewise, the particular is not to be analysed alone but in conjunction with the general.

A commitment to historical analysis alone is not sufficient to avoid the pitfalls of determinism in social analysis, e.g. in the view that classes are determined by exchange relations—a problem common to both Frank and Wallerstein. To quote again from Arrighi's critique: 'It is by focusing on relations of production and the degree of development of productive forces, that we can show the *differentia specifica* of different epochs, whereas if we focus our attention on exchange relations, we tend to see everything immutable' (Arrighi, 1971). Sharing this view, a theoretical framework to consider the kinds of relations of production which are produced by integration into the world economy was proposed.

The preceding discussion of the theoretical premises and perspectives that have influenced this study consists essentially of two parts. In the first part, several key analytical concepts were introduced. In elaborating these, several distinctions were drawn which relate to subsequent propositions made, and also inform the present historical case study of Malaya. Social class was defined with reference to the social relations of production. The concept of class fraction was then suggested to enhance analysis of class contradictions and class contention. The concept of the commodity introduced the subsequent discussion of the concept of capital, and some implications of the distinction between the sphere of production and the sphere of circulation were then considered for the analysis of the consequences of capital expansion. Then, we discussed our perspective on the state in relation to class dialectics—i.e. as object, outcome and determinant of class contention.

The latter part of this section proposed some consequences of integration into the world economy. It began with two aspects emphasized by world systems theorists— existence of a single world market and of capital accumulation on a global scale. The significance of capital accumulation for class relations was hypothesized depending on whether capital expansion occurs in the sphere of circulation alone or also in the sphere of production. While capital in the sphere of circulation can only involve non-capitalist relations of production, production capital may involve either non-capitalist or capitalist relations of production. (Unlike non-capitalist relations of production, capitalist relations of production do not pose inherent constraints on the capital accumulation process.) Study of the transformation of the social relations of production constitutes the main aspect of the treatment of class formation in this book.

One aspect of the approach adopted should be emphasized. In contrast to the assumption of world market determinism mediated by dominant class choice found in at least some versions of the 'world systems' approach, the present framework attributes primacy to class conflict in the unfolding of history (Brenner, 1976). Class relations are located in society, and are therefore related to world market conditions and the ongoing expansion of capital. By focusing on class contradictions situated in concrete social conditions, social change can be understood dialectically, rather than as a mere outcome of mechanical determination by the market. Class relations are viewed in the context of the world economy as entailing complex articulations between the sphere of production and the sphere of circulation, and involving different relations of production, rather than as the outcome of the mode of labour control chosen by the dominant class from among options determined by the world market.

In a sense, it is also being insisted here that the study of development and class formation should be inter-disciplinary, i.e. with reference to how contemporary social science discussion and investigation is currently established. To isolate the economic study of the market, capital accumulation and uneven development, from the sociological treatment of social class and class conflict and from political science's attention to the state, is to restrict artificially the depth and scope of social investigation and analysis. But such compartmentalization is not merely accidental. Rather, it is an outcome of the relationship of the social sciences to the rest of society. While it may be wishful thinking to expect a fundamental change in the nature of the social sciences divorced from concomitant changes in society itself, this should not deter one from initiating the endeavour to transform the very character of social science in conjunction with the broader tasks in anticipation of such social transformations.

The preceding discussion attempted to specify the key concepts and frame of reference which inspired the present discussion of certain aspects of class formation in Malaya. This general theoretical framework makes only limited efforts at the kind of generalization which characterizes much of the existing literature on development (of all shades). By identifying a variety of related factors which comprise the process of development, the significance of societal specificity and historical sequence in social change is also being underscored. Hence, what is being conducted here is a historical case approach rather than elaborate abstract ideal-type patterns of transition, whether of the modernization theory kind (i.e. involving transition from traditional to modern patterns of stratification) or of the linear evolutionary structuralist type (i.e. involving different stages of societal evolution including a necessary transition from feudalism to capitalism). Such an approach does not deny the existence and significance of general aspects of the issues with which this discussion is concerned. However, appreciation of these general aspects is only socially and historically meaningful in conjunction with a consideration of the particular aspects as well. It is not the general that determines the particular, but rather the general that is manifest in the particular. Hence, this study attempts to analyse how general concepts—such as world market, capital accumulation, relations of production, class contradictions, class contention, and the state—take on concrete social and historical meaning.

1. Although there have been some efforts to elevate this approach to the status of a theory of dependency, this trend has been resisted by at least one of its foremost elaborators (e.g. Cardoso, 1977).

2. Many efforts to outline the general structures of dependency have produced undialectical, and therefore unchanging (ahistorical), characterizations of historical development. See the critical and self-critical reviews by Arrighi (1971); Cardoso (1977); Frank (1977); Lall (1975); Leys (1975, 1976); and O'Brien (1975).

3. This is not the place for an overview of the scope and depth of his contribution. Instead, see Hechter (1975) and Murray (1977).

4. See Murray (1977) and Skocpol (1977). Some other problems associated with Wallerstein's work include his three-tier perspective incorporating an intermediate category (e.g. semi-periphery) which generally serves to play a residual explanatory role. Also, despite the historical content of his study, Wallerstein fails to develop a historically informed theory. Instead, his framework is marked by the existence of certain seemingly unchanging relations. Arrighi's (1971) criticisms of A. G. Frank are very relevant in this regard. This difficulty also contributes to

Wallerstein's difficulties with the analysis of transition (see Brenner, 1976).

5. See Althusser and Balibar (1970); Amin (1976); Asad and Wolpe (1976); Balibar (1973); Hindess and Hirst (1975, 1977a, 1977b); Rodinson (1973); Taylor (1975, 1976); and Zubaida (1976).

6. In this regard, it seems to us that Bettelheim (1975) has a far less formalist/legalist view of this category.

7. John Taylor (1976) suggests this problem can be resolved. In the course of social reproduction, the elements for sustaining an existing mode must necessarily be regenerated since a mode must, by definition, be capable of reproducing itself. However, elements which undermine it can emerge in the course of reproduction as well, i.e. a mode of production can bring about its own negation. There is no reason why the process 'must necessarily be confined to reproducing only the mechanisms ensuring its own existence' (Taylor, 1976: 67). Fair enough, but then why bring in the concept of transitional mode if all modes are potentially transitional? Taylor (1976: 58) also points out that other analyses based on Balibar's formulations see both transitional and non-transitional modes as characterized by non-correspondence between the two connections. While this deals with the problem of transition in Balibar, it does not explain the need for a distinction between transitional and non-transitional modes.

The author's rejection of Balibar's notion of transitional mode should not be read to mean a rejection of the analysis of transition itself. On the contrary, the very significance of such analysis has required the rejection of Balibar's approach as being inadequate.

8. Unable to resolve this difficulty, several considerations which influenced the choice of the unit of analysis employed in this study, were offered earlier.

9. This is not the place to review alternative views of social class although these undoubtedly exist. Some other useful work on the concept of social class include C. Anderson (1974); Dos Santos (1970); Poulantzas (1973, 1975). Poulantzas has emphasized that class relations and hence class positions should not be confused with the actual occupants of such positions.

10. 'But it should not be forgotten that we are still basically concerned with a single class and that our attitude towards these fractions and strata, whether we are discussing alliances with them or predicting their political behaviour (especially their instability), should be framed accordingly' (Poulantzas, 1973a: 38).

11. This broad view of class conflict as involving more than just class-conscious or organized activity is shared by others. The term 'class contention' is preferred here as it does not bear certain connotations associated with other terms.

'Lest it be misunderstood, let me hasten to add that the vulgarised notion of class struggle as bloody, violent civil war is not scientifically accurate. Violent class struggles are a feature of revolutionary situations undergoing rapid changes with the old social order having exhausted all its potentialities, crumbling and the new social order taking over. But in a class society, class struggles continue in a hundred and one ways which may not always be recognizable as such' (Shivji, 1973: 61).

'While class struggle constitutes the motive force in history, it is not always clear and pure as class struggle and may take varied forms under different concrete conditions. In non-revolutionary situations much of the class struggle is latent and even unidentifiable as such at any particular moment.... In fact, classes hardly become fully class conscious except in situations of intense political struggle' (Shivji, 1976: 8).

12. This view is obviously different from the common neoclassical view of capital, including the Cambridge school variant, and also from most formulations identified with classical political economy. For elaboration, see Sweezy (1942).

13. It should be noted that the state is far from being an unchanging monolithic object. Rather, it is created, and its fate is tied to social reproduction. Likewise with the notion of 'state power'. In this regard, it is important to be aware of the subtle distinction between the juridical 'right to rule', which is necessarily ideologically grounded, and the political 'power to rule'.

14. Capital is not usually directly involved in reorganizing pre-capitalist relations of production. Even when pre-capitalist relations need to be reorganized to supply labour, it is the state which usually undertakes this task on behalf of capital, e.g. by stimulating the forces of proletarianization.

15. The contemporary alarm over 'overpopulation' and the 'threat from the marginals' can be seen in this light as an unintended outcome of systematic proletarianization without the corre-

sponding generation by capital of sufficient wage employment opportunities.

16. This is, of course, a different point from the one suggesting a linear evolutionary sequence of modes of production in the history of human societies.

17. This formulation transcends the traditional historians' interpretation which reduces such transformations to a mechanical and agentless view of historical advance.

Appendix 2

EMPLOYMENT STATUS OF PERSONS BY ETHNIC GROUP AND GENDER, 1947, 1957, 1970, and 1980

Employment Status	Malays			Chinese		
	Males	Females	Total	Males	Females	Total
1947						
Employer	3,334	752	4,086	15,858	860	16,718
Own account worker	396,737	85,397	482,134	227,109	38,013	265,122
Unpaid family worker	54,684	86,613	141,297	18,618	14,531	33,149
Employee	186,714	44,701	231,415	314,410	83,446	397,856
In employment	641,469	217,463	858,932	575,995	136,850	712,845
1957						
Employer } Own account worker	395,488	94,307	489,795	181,475	32,130	213,605
Unpaid family worker	55,492	85,944	141,436	19,278	12,222	31,500
Employee	301,366	68,965	370,331	369,526	141,264	510,790
In employment	752,346	249,216	1,001,562	570,279	185,616	755,895
1970						
Employer } Own account worker	476,490	154,918	631,408	215,138	49,565	264,703
Unpaid family worker	136,608	192,035	328,643	71,865	57,824	129,689
Employee	418,425	117,869	536,294	408,815	186,537	595,352
In employment	1,031,523	464,822	1,496,345	695,818	293,926	989,744
1980						
Employer	36,993	16,423	53,416	62,734	14,725	77,459
Own account worker	459,879	210,222	670,101	247,119	80,131	327,250
Unpaid family worker	82,602	104,307	186,909	35,362	36,690	72,052
Employee	792,688	331,322	1,124,010	560,106	289,796	849,902
In employment	1,372,162	662,274	2,034,436	905,321	421,342	1,326,663

Sources: Department of Statistics, *Population Census of Malaya* (1947), *Population Census of Federation of Malaya* (1957), *Population Census of Malaysia* (1970, 1980).

Note: The 1957 and 1970 Censuses do not distinguish between 'employer' or 'own account worker'. Instead both 'employer' and 'own account worker' are categorized together as 'self-employed'.

Appendix 2 (continued)

	Indians			Others			Total		
	Males	Females	Total	Males	Females	Total	Males	Females	Total
					1947					
	3,006	33	3,039	355	22	377	22,553	1,667	24,220
	25,471	1,162	26,633	5,900	833	6,783	655,217	125,455	780,672
	985	294	1,279	998	2,039	3,037	75,285	103,477	178,762
	188,813	79,702	268,515	12,835	1,851	14,686	702,772	209,700	912,472
	218,275	81,191	299,466	20,088	4,795	24,883	1,455,827	440,299	1,896,126
					1957					
	29,095	986	30,081	6,976	1,024	8,000	613,034	128,447	741,481
	1,427	234	1,661	1,007	1,260	2,267	77,204	99,660	176,864
	194,854	79,873	274,727	41,340	3,693	45,033	907,086	293,795	1,200,881
	225,376	81,093	306,469	49,323	5,977	55,300	1,597,324	521,902	2,119,226
					1970					
	37,678	5,243	42,921	5,352	1,955	7,307	734,658	211,681	946,339
	7,616	5,478	13,094	1,976	3,222	5,198	218,065	258,559	476,624
	161,441	68,081	229,522	10,544	2,452	12,996	999,225	374,939	1,374,164
	206,735	78,802	285,537	17,872	7,629	25,501	1,951,948	845,179	2,797,127
					1980					
	12,954	5,588	18,542	918	191	1,109	113,599	36,927	150,526
	27,938	5,638	33,576	5,248	3,363	8,611	740,184	299,354	1,039,538
	6,917	6,643	13,560	1,198	1,482	2,680	126,079	149,122	275,201
	221,483	118,018	339,501	10,523	3,901	14,424	1,584,800	743,037	2,327,837
	269,292	135,887	405,179	17,887	8,937	26,824	2,564,662	1,228,440	3,793,102

Appendix 3
PENINSULAR MALAYSIA: POPULATION
BY ETHNIC GROUP
('000)

Area and Year	Malays	Chinese	Indians	Others	Total
Straits Settlements					
1891	211	227	54	17	509
1901	214	282	55	18	569
1911	232	370	81	23	708
1921	249	501	102	28	879
1931	274	659	129	36	1,098
Federated Malay States					
1891	235	165	20	2	422
1901	315	302	58	5	683
1911	427	436	174	11	1,046
1921	516	498	309	14	1,337
1931	601	719	385	28	1,733
Unfederated Malay States					
1911	758	112	13	17	900
1921	862	181	62	21	1,125
1931	1,056	331	111	29	1,527
Peninsular Malaysia					
1911	1,373	695	240	35	2,342
1921	1,569	857	440	43	2,910
1931	1,863	1,285	573	67	3,789
1947	2,427	1,885	535	76	4,923
1957	3,126	2,334	696	123	6,279
1970	4,672	3,131	936	70	8,810
1980	6,316	3,865	1,171	75	11,427

Sources: Population census (various years).

Note: 'Malays' include immigrants of Malay stock and all indigenous peoples of the Malay Peninsula and Archipelago.

Appendix 4
PENINSULAR MALAYSIA: ETHNIC STRUCTURE
OF POPULATION, 1911–1957
(Percentage of Total Population)

Race	Census Year						
	1911	*1921*	*1931*	*1947*	*1957*	*1970*	*1980*
Bumiputras	59	54	49	50	50	53	55
Chinese	30	29	34	38	37	36	34
Indians	10	15	15	11	11	11	10
Total	99	98	98	99	98	99	99

Sources: Lim Chong-Yah (1967: Table 7.5); Department of Statistics, *1980 Population Census of Malaysia*.

Appendix 5

PENINSULAR MALAYSIA: POPULATION GROWTH
BY ETHNIC GROUP, 1911–1980

Ethnic Group	Population ('000)							Population Increase ('000)					
	1911	1921	1931	1947	1957	1970	1980	1911–21	1921–31	1931–47	1947–57	1957–70	1970–80
Bumiputras[*]	1,370	1,569	1,864	2,428	3,125	4,672	6,316	199	295	564	697	1,547	1,644
Chinese	693	856	1,285	1,885	2,334	3,131	3,865	163	429	600	449	797	734
Indians[1]	239	439	571	531	707	936	1,171	200	132	-40	176	229	235
Others	27	42	68	65	112	70	75	16	25	-3	47	-42	5
Total	2,339	2,907	3,788	4,908	6,279	8,809	11,427	568	881	1,120	1,371	2,530	2,618

Sources: H. Fell, *1957 Population Census of the Federation of Malaya*, Report No. 14, 3; J. E. Nathan, *The Census of British Malaya*, 29; *1980 Population Census of Malaysia*.

[1]Bumiputras—then known as Malaysians (before the formation of Malaysia)—include Indonesians and Aborigines, while Indians include Pakistanis.

Appendix 6

PENINSULAR MALAYSIA: POPULATION BY STATE, 1891–1980

('000)

State	1891	1901	1911	1921	1931	1947	1957	1970	1980
Penang	231	248	271	292	340	446	572	776	955
Malacca	92	95	124	154	187	239	291	404	465
Perak	214	330	502	611	786	954	1,221	1,569	1,805
Selangor	82	169	294	401	533	711	1,013	982	1,516
Negri Sembilan	65	96	130	179	234	268	365	482	574
Pahang	57	84	119	146	180	250	313	505	799
Johore	n.a.	n.a.	180	282	505	738	927	1,277	1,638
Kedah	n.a.	n.a.	246	339	430	554	702	955	1,116
Kelantan	n.a.	n.a.	287	309	362	449	506	685	894
Perlis	n.a.	n.a.	33	40	49	70	91	121	148
Trengganu	n.a.	n.a.	154	154	180	226	278	405	541
Federal Territory	–	–	–	–	–	–	–	648	977
Total Peninsular Malaysia	–	–	2,339	2,907	3,788	4,908	6,279	8,810	11,427
Sabah	–	–	–	–	–	–	–	654	1,011
Sarawak	–	–	–	–	–	–	–	976	1,308
Malaysia	–	–	–	–	–	–	–	10,439	13,747

Sources: H. Fell, *1957 Population Census of the Federation of Malaya*, Report No. 14, 3; Department of Statistics, *Population Census of Malaysia 1980*.

Notes: 1. The State figures for 1931 and 1947 include 'unlocated population'.
2. The 1947 figures include nomadic aborigines.
3. The areas of the various States in 1957 in square miles were: Johore (7,330), Kedah (3,660), Kelantan (5,750), Malacca (640), Negri Sembilan (2,565), Pahang (13,873), Penang (397.8), Perak (7,980), Perlis (310), Selangor (3,166.5), and Trengganu (5,027.5). Total area for Peninsular Malaysia was 50,700 sq. miles.

Appendix 7
POST-WAR NATURAL RATES OF
POPULATION INCREASE, 1947-1980

	Crude Rate: Per 1,000 of Estimated Mid-year Population			
Year	Malays	Chinese	Indians	Peninsular Malaysia
1947	17.0	29.6	33.3	23.5
1948	17.4	31.0	32.1	24.1
1949	26.6	31.8	36.6	29.6
1950	23.2	29.9	31.3	26.2
1951	27.6	28.5	32.2	28.3
1952	30.6	30.9	32.2	30.8
1953	30.6	31.9	32.3	31.3
1954	31.4	31.5	33.8	31.6
1955	31.1	31.6	34.4	31.6
1956	35.1	32.7	36.5	34.3
1957	33.2	33.5	38.5	33.7
1958	32.6	31.3	36.4	32.4
1959	32.9	31.1	37.3	32.7
1960	32.0	30.4	35.6	31.8
1961	33.8	31.3	36.5	33.1
1962	31.8	30.7	34.1	31.6
1963	31.7	29.7	33.5	31.1
1964	33.3	29.5	33.2	31.9
1965	30.1	28.6	31.4	29.6
1966	32.6	28.2	30.6	30.7
1967	29.8	27.6	29.4	28.9
1968	30.9	26.6	27.2	28.9
1969	28.9	24.9	25.6	27.1
1970	27.8	25.4	24.8	26.6
1971	28.8	26.0	23.4	27.2
1972	28.5	24.5	23.1	26.4
1973	27.1	23.1	21.5	25.0
1974	28.0	22.8	22.9	25.5
1975	27.8	21.4	22.5	24.9
1976	27.0	24.2	22.9	25.5
1977	27.5	20.5	21.9	24.4
1978	26.8	20.8	22.2	24.2
1979	28.0	20.3	22.9	24.7
1980	29.1	20.9	24.3	25.8

Sources: Lim Chong-Yah (1967: 192, Table 7.4); Department of Statistics, Monthly Statistical Bulletin (various issues).

GLOSSARY

adat	custom
asing	foreign
bahar	measure of weight approximately equivalent to 375 lb.
Bumiputra	literally, 'Sons of the Soil'; indigenous people
chettiar	Indian money-lender
Chetti	Indian money-lender (colloquial)
dagang	foreign
dakwah	Islamic mission
dulang	pan (for mining tin or for food)
dusun	orchard (usually fruit)
fomes lignosus	major root disease affecting rubber trees
gadai	pawn
gantang	measure of volume approximately equivalent to 5 lb. of un-husked rice and 8 lb. of dehusked rice
hartal	general strike
Imperata cylindrica	lalang (type of long grass weed)
jual janji	conditional sale
kampung	village
kangany	foreman (Tamil)
Kangchu	Chinese holder of documented rights awarded by the Sultan of Johore which authorized the holder to cultivate a specific area with his own capital and labour, and gave him the monopoly over gambling, pawnbroking, spirits and opium there. The holder was also able to take a certain collection on the export of pepper and the import of rice. In return, he paid rent, licence fees, and other duties.
Kerah	corvée labour
konfrontasi	confrontation
Konggres Ekonomi Bumiputra	Bumiputra Economic Congress
kuala	river confluence
ladang cultivation	shifting cultivation
laksamana	admiral
mentri besar	chief minister
mukim	parish-like land unit, less than district
negeri	country or Malay State (province)
Nusantara	Malay Archipelago
orang asli	aborigine
orang tebusan	indentured labourer
orlong	measure of distance
padi	paddy rice
pikul	measure of weight equal to $133\frac{1}{3}$ lb.
pulang belanja	return of expenses

raja	king
rakyat	commoner, people or subjects
relong	measure of area equivalent to 0.711 acre in Kedah
sawah/bendang	wet rice field
sewa	rent
sewa hidup	negotiable rent
sewa mati	fixed rent
sewa tunai	cash rent
sinkheh	new immigrant
Sultan	Muslim ruler
tanah mati	land no longer being worked
Temenggong	high-ranking Malay minister; viceroy
tolong menolong	mutual help

BIBLIOGRAPHY

Abdul Aziz, Ungku (1957), 'Economic Survey of 5 Villages in Nyalas, Malacca' (Universiti Malaya, Department of Economics).

—— (1958), 'Land Disintegration and Land Policy in Malaya', *Malayan Economic Review*, 3, 1: 22-9.

—— (1962), 'Facts and Fallacies about the Malay Economy, In Retrospect, with New Footnotes', *Ekonomi*, 3, 1 (December).

—— (1963), *Subdivision of Estates in Malaya, 1951-60* (3 volumes) (Kuala Lumpur: Universiti Malaya, Department of Economics).

—— (1964), 'Poverty and Rural Development in Malaya', *Kajian Ekonomi Malaysia*, 1, 1 (June): 70-105.

Abdul Kadir b. Wan Yusoff (1975), 'Kajian Sosio-Ekonomi Komuniti Nelayan dan Petani', MA thesis, Universiti Malaya.

Abdul Rahman, Tunku (1969), *May 13, Before and After* (Kuala Lumpur: Penerbit Utusan Melayu).

Abdullah b. A. Kadir (1970), *The Hikayat Abdullah* (An Annotated Translation by A. H. Hill) (Kuala Lumpur and Singapore: Oxford University Press).

Afifuddin Hj. Omar (1972), 'Social Implications of Farm Mechanization in the Muda Scheme' (Alor Setar: MADA, mimeo.).

—— (1973a), 'The Social, Political and Economic Framework of Muda Rice Farmers: A Historical Perspective' (Alor Setar: MADA, mimeo.).

—— (1973b), 'Some Aspects of the Socio-economic Value System of the Muda Rice Farmers in Developmental Perspective' (Alor Setar: MADA, mimeo.).

—— (1978), 'Peasants, Institutions and Development in Malaysia: The Political Economy of Development in the Muda Region', Ph.D. thesis, Cornell University.

Agarwal, M. C. (1965), 'Rural Cooperative Credit—A Malaysian Case Study', *Kajian Ekonomi Malaysia*, 2, 2 (December).

Agoes Salim (1967), 'The Marketing of Smallfarm Rubber in Malaysia', Ph.D. thesis, University of Wisconsin.

Ahmad Sa'adi (1960), 'The Development of Malaya's Rice Industry, 1896-1921', BA (Hons.) graduation exercise, Universiti Malaya, Singapore.

Aiyer, Neelakandha (1938), *Indian Problems in Malaya. A Brief Survey in Relation to Emigration* (Kuala Lumpur: The 'Indian' Office).

Alatas, Syed Hussein (1971), *Thomas Stamford Raffles: Schemer or Reformer?* (Sydney: Angus & Robertson).

—— (1972a), *Siapa Yang Salah?* (Singapore: Pustaka Nasional).

—— (1972b), *The Second Malaysia Plan 1971-1975: A Critique* (Singapore: Institute of Southeast Asian Studies, Occasional Paper).

—— (1977a), *Intellectuals in Developing Societies* (London: Frank Cass).

—— (1977b), *The Myth of the Lazy Native* (London: Frank Cass).

Alavi, Hamza (1972), 'The State in Postcolonial Societies: Pakistan and Bangladesh', *New Left Review*, 74.

—— (1975), 'India and the Colonial Mode of Production', *Economic and Political Weekly*, August 1975 (Special Number).

Allen, G. C. and Donnithorne, A. G. (1954), *Western Enterprise in Indonesia and Malaya* (London: Allen & Unwin).

Allen, J. de V. (1968), 'The Kelantan Rising of 1915: Some Thoughts on the Concept of Resistance in British Malayan History', *Journal of Southeast Asian History*, 9, 1 (September): 241-58.

―――― (1970), 'Malayan Civil Service, 1871-1941: Colonial Bureaucracy/Malayan Elite', *Comparative Studies in Society and History*, 12 (April): 149-78.

Althusser, Louis and Balibar, Etiene (1970), *Reading Capital* (London: New Left Books).

Amin, Samir (1972), 'Underdevelopment and Dependence in Black Africa', *Journal of Modern African Studies*, 10, 4: 503-24.

―――― (1974a), *Accumulation on a World Scale* (2 volumes) (New York: Monthly Review Press).

―――― (1974b), *Migrations in Africa* (London: Oxford University Press).

―――― (1976), *Unequal Development* (New York: Monthly Review Press).

Aminuddin Baki (1966), 'Debt-Slavery in Perak', *Peninjau Sejarah*, 1.

Anand, Sudhir (1973), *The Size Distribution of Income in Malaysia* (World Bank working paper); a revised version was published for the World Bank in 1983 as *Inequality and Poverty in Malaysia: Measurement and Decomposition* (New York: Oxford University Press).

Anderson, Charles (1974), *The Political Economy of Social Class* (Englewood Cliffs: Prentice-Hall).

Anderson, Kent P. (1968), 'Peasant and Capitalist Agriculture in a Developing Country', Ph.D. thesis, Massachusetts Institute of Technology.

Anderson, Perry (1974), *Lineages of the Absolutist State* (London: New Left Books).

Arasaratnam, Sinnappah (1970), *Indians in Malaysia and Singapore*, 1st edition (Kuala Lumpur: Oxford University Press).

Arrighi, Giovanni (1971), 'The Relationship between the Colonial and the Class Structures: A Critique of A. G. Frank's Theory of the Development of Underdevelopment' (Dakar, Senegal: UN African Institute for Economic Development and Planning, mimeo.).

Arrighi, Giovanni and Saul, John (1973), *Essays on the Political Economy of Africa* (New York: Monthly Review Press).

Arudsothy, P. (1968), 'The Labour Force in a Dual Economy', Ph.D. thesis, Glasgow University.

Asad, Talal and Wolpe, Harold (1976), 'Concepts of Modes of Production', *Economy and Society*, 5, 4.

Bach, Robert L. (1976), 'Historical Patterns of Capitalist Penetration in Malaysia', *Journal of Contemporary Asia*, 6, 4: 458-76.

Balibar, Etiene (1973), 'Self Criticism: An Answer to Questions from "Theoretical Practice"', *Theoretical Practice*, 7/8 (January).

Bamat, Tomas (1977), 'Relative State Autonomy and Capitalism in Brazil and Peru', *Insurgent Sociologist*, 7, 2 (Spring).

Banaji, Jairus (1976), 'Kautsky's "The Agrarian Question"', *Economy and Society*, 5, 1 (February): 1-49.

Baran, Paul and Hobsbawn, Eric (1961), 'The Stages of Economic Growth', *Kyklos*, 14, 2.

Barlow, Colin (1978), *The Natural Rubber Industry* (Kuala Lumpur: Oxford University Press).

Barlow, Colin and Chan Chee Keong (1968), 'Towards an Optimum Size of Rubber Holding', *Natural Rubber Conference 1968*.

Barnard, Rosemary (1970), 'Organization of Production in a Kedah Rice Farming Village', Ph.D. thesis, Australian National University.

_____ (1973), 'Role of Capital and Credit in a Malay Rice Producing Village', *Pacific Viewpoint*, 14, 2 (May): 113-36.

_____ (1979), 'The Modernization of Agriculture in a Kedah Village 1967-1978', *Review of Indonesian and Malaysian Affairs*, 13, 2 (December).

Bass, Jerome R. (1971), 'The New Malaysian Government', *Asian Survey*, 11, 10 (October): 970-83.

Bastin, John (1968), 'Britain as an Imperial Power in Southeast Asia in the Nineteenth Century', in J. S. Bromley and E. H. Kossman (eds.), *Britain and the Netherlands in Europe and Asia*: 174-89.

Bauer, P. T. (1948a), *The Rubber Industry: a Study in Competition and Monopoly* (London: Longmans).

_____ (1948b), *Report on a Visit to the Rubber Growing Smallholdings of Malaya, July-September 1946* (London, HMSO).

_____ (1961a), 'Some Aspects of the Malayan Rubber Slump', in T. H. Silcock (ed.), *Readings in Malayan Economics* (Singapore: Eastern Universities Press): 185-200.

_____ (1961b), 'The Economics of Planting Density in Rubber Growing', in T. H. Silcock (ed.), *Readings in Malayan Economics* (Singapore: Eastern Universities Press): 236-41.

_____ (1961c), 'The Working of Rubber Regulation', in T. H. Silcock (ed.), *Readings in Malayan Economics* (Singapore: Eastern Universities Press): 242-67.

_____ (1961d), 'A Rejoinder', in T. H. Silcock (ed.), *Readings in Malayan Economics* (Singapore: Eastern Universities Press): 276-83.

_____ (1961e), 'Malayan Rubber Policy', in T. H. Silcock (ed.), *Readings in Malayan Economics* (Singapore: Eastern Universities Press): 300-16.

Beaglehole, J. H. (1969), 'Malay Participation in Commerce and Industry: The Role of RIDA and MARA', *Journal of Commonwealth Political Studies*, 7, 3: 216-45.

Beckford, George (1972), *Persistent Poverty* (New York: Oxford University Press).

Benham, F. C. (1961), 'The Rubber Industry', in T. H. Silcock (ed.), *Readings in Malayan Economics* (Singapore: Eastern Universities Press): 284-99.

Bernstein, Henry (1976), 'Underdevelopment and the Law of Value: A Critique of Kay', *Review of African Political Economy*, 6 (May-August).

Berube, Louis (1968), *Report of an Economic Survey of the Fishing Marketing Problem in Malaya* (Kuala Lumpur: Ministry of Agriculture and Cooperatives).

Bettelheim, Charles (1975), *Economic Calculation and Forms of Poverty* (New York: Monthly Review Press).

Bhati, U. N. (1971), 'Economic Determinants of Income on Irrigated Paddy Farms in Tanjong Karang, West Malaysia', Ph.D. thesis, Australian National University.

_____ (1973), 'Farmers' Technical Knowledge and Income—A Case Study of Padi Farmers in West Malaysia', *Malayan Economic Review*, 18, 1 (April).

_____ (1976), *Some Social and Economic Aspects of the Introduction of New Varieties of Paddy in Malaysia* (Geneva: UN Research Institute of Social Development).

Blake, Donald J. (1976), 'Foreign Investment in Malaysia', in N. K. Sarkar (ed.), *Foreign Investment and Economic Development in Asia* (Bombay: Orient Longman Ltd.).

Blythe, W. J. (1947), 'Historical Sketch of Chinese Labour in Malaya', *Journal of the Malayan Branch, Royal Asiatic Society*, 20, 1: 64-114.

_____ (1969), *The Impact of Chinese Secret Societies in Malaya* (London: Oxford University Press).

Bodenheimer, Susanne (1971), 'Dependency and Imperialism in Latin America', in K. T. Fann and D. C. Hodges, *Readings in U.S. Imperialism* (Boston: Porter Sargent).

Bonilla, Frank and Girling, Robert (eds.) (1973), *Structures of Dependency* (Palo Alto: Stanford University, Institute of Political Studies).

Bonney, R. (1971), *Kedah 1771-1821* (Kuala Lumpur: Oxford University Press).

Boulding, Kenneth and Mukherjee, Tapan (eds.) (1972), *Economic Imperialism* (Ann Arbor: University of Michigan Press).

Bowring, Philip (1976), 'No Time for Socialism', *Far Eastern Economic Review* (6 August).

Bray, F. A. and Robertson, A. F. (1980), 'Sharecropping in Kelantan, Malaysia', *Research in Economic Anthropology*: 209-44.

Brenner, Robert (1976), 'Agrarian Class Structure and Economic Development in Pre-Industrial Europe', *Past and Present*, 70 (February): 30-75.

Buchanan, Keith (1967), *The Southeast Asian World* (London: George Bell).

Burawoy, M. (1976), 'The Functions and Reproduction of Migrant Labour: Comparative Material from Southern Africa and the United States', *American Journal of Sociology*, Vol. 81, No. 5.

Cairncross, A. K. (1953), *Home and Foreign Investment 1870-1913* (Cambridge: Cambridge University Press).

Caldwell, Malcolm (1977a), 'The British "Forward Movement", 1874-1914', in Mohamed Amin and M. Caldwell (eds.), *Malaya: The Making of a Neo-colony* (London: Spokesman Books): 13-37.

—— (1977b), 'War, Boom and Depression', in Mohamed Amin and M. Caldwell (eds.), *Malaya: The Making of a Neo-colony* (London: Spokesman Books): 38-63.

—— (1977c), 'From "Emergency" to "Independence", 1948-57', in Mohamed Amin and M. Caldwell (eds.), *Malaya: The Making of a Neo-colony* (London: Spokesman Books): 216-65.

Callis, H. G. (1942), *Foreign Capital in Southeast Asia* (New York: Ams Press).

Cardoso, C. F. S. (1975), 'Colonial Modes of Production', *Critique of Anthropology*, 4 & 5 (Autumn).

Cardoso, Fernando Henrique (1972), 'Dependency and Development in Latin America', *New Left Review*, 74.

—— (1977), 'The Consumption of Dependency Theory in the United States', *Latin American Research Review*, 12, 3 (Summer): 7-24.

Castles, S. and Kosack, G. (1973), *Immigrant Workers and Class Structure in Western Europe* (London: Oxford University Press).

Chai Hon Chan (1967), *The Development of British Malaya; 1896-1909*, 2nd edition (Kuala Lumpur: Oxford University Press).

Chamhuri Siwar (1976), *Kehendak dan Bentuk Reformasi Tanah di Malaysia* (Kuala Lumpur: Dewan Bahasa dan Pustaka).

Chandra Muzaffar (1977), 'Some Political Perspectives on the New Economic Policy' (Paper for the Fourth Malaysian Economic Convention, Kuala Lumpur, May).

Chandrasekaran Pillay (1974), 'UMNO: Protection of the Malay Community', M. Soc. Sc. thesis, Universiti Sains Malaysia.

Chee Peng Lim (1975), 'The Role of Small Industry in the Malaysian Economy', Ph.D. thesis, Universiti Malaya.

Chen Ta (1923), *Chinese Migrations, With Special Reference to Labor Conditions* (Washington, D. C.: Government Printing Office).

Cheng Siok Hwa (1969), 'The Rice Industry of Malaya: A Historical Survey', *Journal of the Malayan Branch, Royal Asiatic Society*, 42, 2: 130-44.

—— (1970), 'Estate Labour, Management and Ownership in Malaya, 1960', *Kajian Ekonomi Malaysia*, 7, 1 (June).

Chew, Ernest (1965), 'British Intervention in Malaya: A Reconsideration', *Journal of Southeast Asian Studies*, 6, 1 (March): 81-93.

Chou, K. R. (1966), *Studies on Saving and Investment in Malaya* (Hong Kong: Academic Publications).

Chung Kek Win (1962), 'The Effect of Capital Availability and Credit on the Use of

Resources in Padi Farming', M. Agr. Sc. thesis, Universiti Malaya.

Clairmonte, Frederick (1960), *Economic Liberalism and Underdevelopment* (London: Asia Publishing House).

Clarke, J. (1977), 'Some Problems in the Conceptualization of Non-capitalist Relations of Production', *Critique of Anthropology*, 2, 8 (Spring).

Cliffe, Lionel (1977), 'Rural Class Formation in East Africa', *Journal of Peasant Studies*, 4, 2 (January).

Cohen, Robin (1972), 'Class in Africa: Analytical Problems and Perspectives', in R. Miliband and J. Saville (eds.), *The Socialist Register 1972* (London: Merlin): 231-55.

Colletta, Nat J. (1975), 'Malaysia's Forgotten People: Education, Cultural Identity and Socio-economic Mobility among South Indian Workers', *Contributions to Asian Studies*, 7: 87-112.

Comber, Leon (1959), *Chinese Secret Societies in Malaya, A Survey of the Triad Society, 1800 to 1900* (Locust Valley, New York: Association for Asian Studies).

Coquery-Vidrovitch, Catherine (1976), 'The Political Economy of the African Peasantry and Modes of Production', in P. C. W. Gutkind and I. Wallerstein (eds.), *The Political Economy of Contemporary Africa*.

Courtenay, P. P. (1972), *A Geography of Trade and Development in Malaya* (London: George Bell).

Cowan, C. D. (1961), *Nineteenth Century Malaya* (London: Oxford University Press).

Cowgill, J. V. (1928), 'System of Land Tenure in the Federated Malay States', *Malayan Agricultural Journal*, 16 (May): 181-93.

Cunyngham-Brown, J. S. H. (1971), *The Traders: A Story of Britain's South-East Asian Commercial Adventure* (London: N. Neame).

Cutler, A. (1975), 'Ground Rent and Capitalism', *Critique of Anthropology*, 4 & 5 (Autumn).

M. Dahlan Hj. Aman (1973), 'Theories and Policies of Modernization: An Application of A. G. Frank's Critique with Particular Reference to Malaysia (West Malaysia)', MA thesis, Monash University.

Das, S. K. (1963), *The Torrens Systems in Malaya* (Singapore: Malayan Law Journal).

De Silva, S. B. D. (1983), *The Political Economy of Underdevelopment* (London: Routledge & Kegan Paul for Institute of Southeast Asian Studies, Singapore).

De Koninck, Rodolphe (1981), 'Of Rice, Men, Women and Machines', in H. Osman-Rani, Jomo K. S., and Ishak Shari (eds.), *Development in the Eighties, with Special Emphasis on Malaysia*, Special Double Issue of *Jurnal Ekonomi Malaysia* (Bangi: Universiti Kebangsaan Malaysia, Faculty of Economics).

Disney, Nigel (1977), 'Accumulation on a World Scale', *Insurgent Sociologist*, 7, 2 (Spring).

Dobb, Maurice (1947), *Studies in the Development of Capitalism* (New York: International Publishers); reissued in 1963.

Dobby, E. H. G. (1955), 'Padi Landscapes of Malaya', *Malayan Journal of Tropical Geography*, 6.

――― (1957), 'Padi Landscapes of Malaya', *Malayan Journal of Tropical Geography*, 10.

Doering, Otto (1973), 'Malaysian Rice Policy and the Muda River Irrigation Project', Ph.D. thesis, Cornell University.

Dos Santos, Teotonio (1970a), 'The Concept of Social Classes', *Science and Society*, 34; 2 (Summer).

――― (1970b), 'The Structure of Dependence', *American Economic Review*, 60, 2 (May): 231-6.

Drabble, John H. (1973), *Rubber in Malaya, 1876-1922: The Genesis of the Industry* (Kuala Lumpur: Oxford University Press).

――― (1974), 'Some Thoughts on the Economic Development of Malaya under British Administration', *Journal of Southeast Asian Studies*, 5, 2 (September): 199-208.

Drake, P. J. (1969), *Financial Development in Malaysia and Singapore* (Canberra: Australian National University Press).

Drummond, S. and Hawkins, D. (1970), 'The Malaysian Elections of 1969: An Analysis of the Campaign and the Results', *Asian Survey*, 10 (April): 320-35.

Duewell, J. and Hj. Osman Mohd. Noor (n.d.), 'Socioeconomic Survey of Tenancy Patterns in Trengganu Padi Production' (mimeo.).

Dunn, F. L. (1971), *Rain-Forest Collectors and Traders: A Study of Resource Utilization in Modern and Ancient Malaya* (Kuala Lumpur: Malayan Branch of the Royal Asiatic Society).

Dupuy, A. and Fitzgerald, P. (1977), 'A Contribution to the Critique of the World System Perspective', *Insurgent Sociologist*, 7, 2 (Spring).

Edwards, C. B. (1975), 'Protection, Profits and Policy: An Analysis of Industrialisation in Malaysia', Ph.D. thesis, University of East Anglia.

―――― (1976), 'Rubber in the World Economy—History and Development' (Institute of Development Studies, University of Sussex, Brighton conference paper, June).

Elliston, G. R. (1967), 'The Role of Middlemen in the Fishing Industry of West Malaysia', *Review of Agricultural Economics Malaysia*, 1, 2 (December).

Emerson, Rupert (1936), 'The Chinese in Malaya', *Pacific Affairs*, 7, 3 (September).

―――― (1937), *Malaysia, A Study in Direct and Indirect Rule* (New York: Macmillan); reprinted in 1964.

Emmanuel, Arghin (1972), 'White Settler Colonialism and the Myth of Investment Imperialism', *New Left Review*, 74.

Enloe, Cynthia (1968), 'Issues and Integration in Malaysia', *Pacific Affairs*, 41, 3 (Fall): 372-85.

Esman, Milton (1972), *Administration and Development in Malaysia* (Ithaca: Cornell University Press).

Esping-Andersen, G., Friedland, R. and Wright, E. O. (1976), 'Modes of Class Struggle and the Capitalist State', *Kapitalistate*, 4/5.

Evers, Hans-Dieter (1978), 'Chettiar Moneylenders in Southeast Asia', *Asie Du Sud*, No. 582.

Fann, K. T. and Hodges, D. C. (eds.) (1971), *Readings in U.S. Imperialism* (Boston: Porter Sargent).

Federal Agricultural Marketing Authority (FAMA) (1968), *National Agricultural Marketing Seminar Proceedings*, 13-18 November, Kuala Lumpur.

Federal Industrial Development Authority (FIDA) (1975), 'Labour and Wage Rates', in *An Invitation for Investment in Malaysia* (Kuala Lumpur: Federal Industrial Development Authority).

Fermor, L. L. (1939), *Report upon the Tin Mining Industry of Malaya* (Kuala Lumpur).

Fieldhouse, D. K. (1961), 'Imperialism: An Historiographical Revision', *The Economic History Review* (Second Series), 14, 2: 187-209.

―――― (1965), *The Colonial Empires* (London: Weidenfeld & Nicolson).

Firth, Raymond (1966), *Malay Fishermen: Their Peasant Economy*, 2nd edition (London: Routledge & Kegan Paul).

Fisher, C. (1964), *Southeast Asia* (London: Methuen).

Fisk, E. K. (1961), 'Productivity and Income from Rubber in an Established Malay Reservation', *Malayan Economic Review*, 6, 1 (April): 13-21.

―――― (1963a), 'Features of the Rural Economy', in T. H. Silcock and E. K. Fisk (eds.), *The Political Economy of Independent Malaya* (Berkeley: University of California Press).

―――― (1963b), 'Rural Development Policy', in T. H. Silcock and E. K. Fisk (eds.), *The Political Economy of Independent Malaya* (Berkeley: University of California Press).

―――― (1964), *Studies in the Rural Economy of South East Asia* (Singapore: Eastern Universities Press).

Foster-Carter, A. (1976), 'From Rostow to Gunder Frank', *World Development*, 4, 3.

Frank, Andre Gunder (1966a), 'Sociology of Development and Underdevelopment of Sociology', in James D. Cockcroft *et al.* (eds.), *Dependence and Underdevelopment* (New York: Anchor Books).

——— (1966b), 'The Development of Underdevelopment', in A. G. Frank (1969), *Latin America: Underdevelopment or Revolution* (Monthly Review Press).

——— (1977), 'Dependence is Dead, Long Live Dependence and the Class Struggle: An Answer to Critics', *World Development*, 5, 4 (April): 355-70.

Freedman, Maurice (1960), 'The Growth of a Plural Society in Malaya', *Pacific Affairs*, 33, 2 (June): 158-68.

——— (1961), 'The Handling of Money: A Note on the Background of the Economic Sophistication of Overseas Chinese', in T. H. Silcock (ed.), *Readings in Malayan Economics* (Singapore: Eastern Universities Press).

Fujimoto, Akimi (1975), 'Farm Management Case Study of Peasant Rice Farming in Kelantan', M. Agri. Sc. thesis, Universiti Malaya.

Furnivall, J. S. (1939), *Netherlands India* (Cambridge: Cambridge University Press).

——— (1956), *Colonial Policy and Practice* (New York: New York University Press).

Gagliano, Felix V. (1970), 'Communal Violence in Malaysia 1969: The Political Aftermath' (Athens, Ohio: Ohio Centre for International Studies, Papers in International Studies, Southeast Asia Series No. 13).

Gamba, Charles (1959), 'Poverty and Some Socioeconomic Aspects of Hoarding, Saving and Borrowing in Malaya', *Malayan Economic Review*, 4, 2 (October).

——— (1962), *The Origins of Trade Unionism in Malaya* (Singapore: Eastern Universities Press).

Gandy, Ross (1976), 'More on the Nature of Soviet Society III', *Monthly Review*, 27, 10 (March).

Geertz, Clifford (1963), *Agricultural Involution* (Berkeley: University of California Press).

Geohegan, J. (1873), *Note on Emigration from India*.

Gerstein, Ira (1977), 'Theories of the World Economy and Imperialism', *Insurgent Sociologist*, 7, 2 (Spring).

Gibbons, D. S. (ed.) (1983), *Daftaran Pekebun Kecil Getah Semenanjung Malaysia, 1977; Laporan Sementara* (Kuala Lumpur: Rubber Industry Smallholders Development Authority).

Gibbons, David, De Koninck, Rodolphe, and Ibrahim Hassan (1980), *Agricultural Modernization, Poverty and Inequality: The Distributional Impact of the Green Revolution in the Regions of Malaysia and Indonesia* (London: Saxon House).

Gibbons, D. S., Lim Teck Ghee, Elliston, G. R., and Shukur Kassim (1981), *Land Tenure in the Muda Irrigation Area: Final Report Part 2: Findings* (Penang: Universiti Sains Malaysia, Centre for Policy Research).

Gibbons, D. S. and Zakaria Ahmad (1971), 'Politics and Selection for the Higher Civil Service in New States: The Malaysian Example', *Journal of Comparative Administration*, 3, 3.

Goh Cheng Teik (1971), *The May Thirteenth Incident and Democracy in Malaysia* (Kuala Lumpur: Oxford University Press).

Golay, Frank (1969), 'Malaysia', in F. Golay *et al.*, *Underdevelopment and Economic Nationalism in Southeast Asia* (Ithaca: Cornell University Press).

Goldman, Richard H. (1974), 'The Evolution of Malaysia's Rice Policy in the Context of Economic and Political Development' (Universiti Sains Malaysia, mimeo.).

——— (1975), 'Staple Food Self-sufficiency and the Distributive Impact of Malaysian Rice Policy', *Food Research Institute Studies*, 14, 3: 251-93.

Gordon, Shirle (n.d.), 'Contradictions in the Malay Economic Structure', *Intisari*, 1, 2: 30-40.

Gosling, L. A. P. (1959), *The Relationship of Land Rental Systems to Land Use in Malaya*

(Ann Arbor: University of Michigan Press).

Grace, Brewster (1976), 'The Politics of Distribution in Malaysia', *American Universities Field Staff Report*, 24, 9.

Griffin, Keith (1969), *Underdevelopment in Spanish America* (London: Allen & Unwin).

Gullick, J. M. (1958), *Indigenous Political Systems of Western Malaya* (London: Athlone Press).

Guyot, Dorothy (1971), 'The Politics of Land: Comparative Development in Two States of Malaysia', *Pacific Affairs*, 44, 3 (Fall): 368–89.

Hairi Abdullah (1965), 'Kemiskinan di Kawasan Kampung', *Ekonomi*, 6, 1 (December).

A. Halim bin Hj. Ismail (1970), 'Some Economic Aspects of Peasant Agriculture in West Malaysia', Ph.D. thesis, Oxford University.

Hanrahan, Gene (1954), *The Communist Struggle in Malaya* (New York: Institute for Pacific Studies).

Harrisons and Crosfield (1943), *One Hundred as East India Merchants: Harrisons and Crosfield 1844–1943* (London: Portsoken Press).

Hassan Hj. Ali (1973), 'Masaalah Petani Di Kampung Kawah', *Jernal Antropoloji dan Sosioloji*, 2.

Hechter, M. (1975), 'Review Essay on the Modern World System', *Contemporary Sociology*, 4 (May): 219–22.

Hein, W. and Stenzel, H. (1974), 'The Capitalist State and Underdevelopment in Latin America—the Case of Venezuela', *Kapitalistate*, 1, 1.

Hensman, Rohini (1976), 'Capitalist Development and Underdevelopment', *Economic and Political Weekly*, XI, 15 (17 April).

Hill, R. D. (1967), 'Agricultural Land Tenure in West Malaysia', *Malayan Economic Review*, 12, 1: 99–116.

Hilton, Rodney (ed.) (1976), *The Transition from Feudalism to Capitalism* (London: New Left Books).

Hindess, Barry and Hirst, Paul (1975), *Pre-Capitalist Modes of Production* (London: Routledge & Kegan Paul).

———— (1977a), *Mode of Production and Social Formation* (London: Macmillan).

———— (1977b), 'Mode of Production and Social Formation in *Pre-Capitalist Modes of Production*. A Reply to John Taylor', *Critique of Anthropology*, 8, 2 (Spring).

Hirschman, Albert O. (1968), 'The Political Economy of Import-substituting Industrialization in Latin America', *The Quarterly Journal of Economics*, 82, 1 (February).

Hirschman, Charles (1971), 'Ownership and Control in the Manufacturing Sector of West Malaysia', *UMBC Economic Review*, 7, 1.

Ho, Robert (1967), *Farmers of Central Malaya* (Canberra: Australian National University Press).

———— (1968), 'The Evolution of Agriculture and Land Ownership in Saiong Mukim', *Malayan Economic Review*, 13, 2.

———— (1969), 'Rice Production in Malaya: A Review of Problems and Prospects', *Malayan Journal of Tropical Geography*, 29: 21–32.

———— (1970), 'Economic Prospects of Malayan Peasants', *Modern Asian Studies*, 4, 1: 83–92.

Hobson, John (1902), *Imperialism: A Study* (London: Allen & Unwin).

Hoerr, O. D. (1969), ('Report on Malaysia' Harvard Development Advisory Service Memorandum).

Hoffmann, Lutz (1973), 'Import Substitution, Export Expansion and Growth in an Open Developing Economy: The Case of West Malaysia', *Welt-wirtschaftliches Archiv*, 109.

Hoffmann, Lutz, and Tan Tew Nee (1975), 'Pattern of Growth and Structural Change in West Malaysia's Manufacturing Industry 1959–68', in David Lim (ed.), *Readings on*

Malaysian Economic Development (Kuala Lumpur: Oxford University Press).

Horii, Kenzo (1972), 'The Land Tenure System of Malay Padi Farmers: A Case Study of Kampong Sungei Bujor in the State of Kedah', *The Developing Economies*, 10, 1 (March): 45-73.

_____ (1981), *Rice Economy and Land Tenure in Malaysia: A Comparative Study of Eight Villages* (Tokyo: Institute of Developing Economies).

Horii, Kenzo *et al.* (1975), 'An Economic Study of Padi Farming in West Malaysia' (mimeo.).

Huang Chih Lien (黃枝連)(1971), 馬華社會史導論 *Ma-hua she-hui tao-lun (A Social Analysis of Sino-Malayan Society)*.

Huang, Yukon (1971), 'The Economics of Padi Production in Malaysia', Ph.D. thesis, Princeton University.

_____ (1975a), 'Some Reflection on Padi Double-cropping in West Malaysia', in David Lim (ed.), *Readings in Malaysian Economic Development* (Kuala Lumpur: Oxford University Press).

_____ (1975b), 'Tenancy Patterns, Productivity and Rentals in Malaysia', *Economic Development and Cultural Change*, 23, 4 (July): 703-18.

Hui Lai Fing, J. (1968), 'Slavery in Nineteenth Century Perak Malay Society', BA graduation exercise, Universiti Malaya.

Husin Ali, S. (1964), *Social Stratification in Kampong Bagan* (Singapore: Malayan Branch of the Royal Asiatic Society).

_____ (1966), 'A Note on Malay Society and Culture', in T. Alishahbana (ed.), *The Cultural Problems of Malaysia in the Context of Southeast Asia* (Kuala Lumpur: University of Malaya Press): 65-74.

_____ (1972), 'Land Concentration and Poverty among Rural Malays', *Nusantara*, 1.

_____ (1975), *Malay Peasant Society and Leadership* (Kuala Lumpur: Oxford University Press).

_____ (1976a), *Apa Erti Pembangunan?* (Kuala Lumpur: Dewan Bahasa dan Pustaka).

_____ (1976b), 'Social and Political Constraints on Economic Growth and Development in Malaysia', in Lim Teck Ghee and V. Lowe (eds.), *Modernization of Asia* (Kuala Lumpur: Heinemann).

Hyman, Gerald (1975), 'Economics in Krian', Ph.D. thesis, University of Chicago.

Hymer, Stephen H. (1970), 'Economic Forms in Pre-colonial Ghana', *Journal of Economic History*, 30.

Indorf, Hans H. (1969), 'Party System Adaptation to Political Development in Malaysia during the First Decade of Independence, 1957-1967', Ph.D. thesis, New York University.

International Bank for Reconstruction and Development (IBRD) (1955), *The Economic Development of Malaya* (Baltimore: Johns Hopkins University Press).

_____ (1963), *Report on the Economic Aspects of Malaysia* (Washington: International Bank for Reconstruction and Development).

International Labour Office (ILO) (1962), *The Trade Union Situation in the Federation of Malaya (Report of a Mission from the International Labour Office)* (Geneva: International Labour Office).

Ishak Shari (1977), 'Some Comments on the Eradication of Poverty under the Third Malaysia Plan', *Southeast Asian Affairs 1977* (Singapore: Institute of Southeast Asian Studies).

Ishak Shari and Jomo Kwame Sundaram (1981), 'Income Redistribution and the State in Peninsular Malaysia', in H. Osman-Rani, Jomo K. S., and Ishak Shari (eds.), *Development in the Eighties, with Special Emphasis on Malaysia*, Special Double Issue of the *Jurnal Ekonomi Malaysia*, Nos. 3 & 4 (Bangi: Universiti Kebangsaan Malaysia, Faculty of Economics).

———— (1982), 'Malaysia's Green Revolution in Rice Farming: Capital Accumulation and Technological Change in a Peasant Society', in Geoffrey Hainsworth (ed.), *Village-level Modernization in Southeast Asia: The Political Economy of Rice and Water* (Vancouver: University of British Columbia Press).

———— (1984), 'The New Economic Policy and "National Unity": Development and Inequality 25 Years after Independence', in S. Husin Ali (ed.), *Ethnicity, Class and Development in Malaysia* (Kuala Lumpur: Malaysian Social Science Association): 329-55.

Ishak Shari and Rogayah M. Zain (1978), 'Some Aspects of Income Inequality in Peninsular Malaysia 1957-70', in H. T. Oshima and T. Mizoguchi (eds.), *Income Distribution by Sector and over Time in East and Southeast Asian Countries* (Manila: Council of Asian Manpower Studies).

Ishak Tadin (1960), 'Dato Onn and Malay Nationalism, 1946-1957', *Journal of Southeast Asian History*, 1, 1 (March): 56-88.

Jackson, James C. (1964), 'Smallholding Cultivation of Cash Crops', in Wang Gungwu (ed.), *Malaysia: A Survey* (New York: Praeger).

———— (1965), 'Smallholder Rubber Cultivation in Malaya, 1952-62', *Oriental Geographer*, 9, 1.

———— (1968), *Planters and Speculators, Chinese and European Agricultural Enterprise in Malaya, 1786-1921* (Kuala Lumpur: University of Malaya Press).

———— (1972), 'Rice Cultivation in West Malaysia', *Journal of the Malayan Branch, Royal Asiatic Society*, 45, ii.

Jackson, R. N. (1961), *Immigrant Labour and the Development of Malaya, 1786-1920* (Kuala Lumpur: Government Printers).

Jago, E. (1940), 'Malaya and the Economic War', *The Asiatic Review*, 36 (January–October).

Jain, R. K. (1970), *South Indians on the Plantation Frontier in Malaya* (Sydney: University of New England Press).

Jang Aisjah Muttalib (1972), *Pemberontakan Pahang 1891-1895* (Kota Baru: Dian).

Jegatheesan, S. (1976), *Land Tenure in the Muda Irrigation Scheme*, MADA Monograph No. 29 (Telok Chengai, Alor Setar: MADA).

———— (1977), *The Green Revolution and the Muda Irrigation Scheme*, MADA Monograph No. 30 (Telok Chengai, Alor Setar: MADA).

———— (1980), 'Progress and Problems of Rice Mechanization in Peninsular Malaysia', National Padi Conference, Kuala Lumpur, 26-28 February.

Johns, B. L. (1975), 'Import-substitution and Export Potentials—The Case of Manufacturing Industry in West Malaysia', in David Lim (ed.), *Readings in Malaysian Economic Development* (Kuala Lumpur: Oxford University Press).

Johnson, T. J. (1977), 'What Is to be Known? The Structural Determination of Social Class', *Economy and Society*, 6, 2 (May): 194-233.

Jomo Kwame Sundaram (1978), 'Rural-Urban Dimensions of Socioeconomic Relations in Northern Peninsular Malaysia. A Report from Three Villages', in Kamal Salih et al., *Rural-Urban Transformation and Regional Underdevelopment: The Case of Malaysia* (Nagoya: United Nations Center for Regional Development).

———— (1980a), 'Capital, Colonialism and Contradiction in the Making of the Sino-Singaporean Bourgeoisie', *Southeast Asian Studies*, 18, 1.

———— (1980b), 'Consequences of Adopting an Export-oriented Industrial Strategy in Malaysia', *ASEAN Business Quarterly*, 4, 3.

———— (1980c), 'How Malaysian Unions Were Shaped by State Policies', *ASEAN Business Quarterly*, 4, 3.

———— (1981a), 'Spontaneity and Planning in Class Formation', in Ulf Himmelstrand (ed.), *Spontaneity and Planning in Development* (Sage Press).

_____ (1981b), 'Schooling for Disunity: Education in Colonial Malaya', *Jurnal Pendidikan*, VIII.

_____ (1981c), 'The Ascendance of Bureaucrat Capitalists in Malaysia', *Alternatives, A Journal of World Policy*, VII, 4 (December): 467-90.

_____ (1981d), 'Recent Trends in Malaysian Income Distribution', *Pacific Viewpoint*, 22, 2.

_____ (1983a), 'Problems and Prospects of the New Economic Policy in Light of the Fourth Malaysia Plan', in Jomo K. S. and R. J. G. Wells (eds.), *The Fourth Malaysia Plan, Economic Perspectives* (Kuala Lumpur: Malaysian Economic Association).

_____ (1983b), *Development and Population: Critiques of Existing Theories* (Kuala Lumpur: Population Studies Unit, Universiti Malaya).

_____ (1983c), 'Malaysia's New Economic Policy and National Unity: Development and Inequality Twenty-five Years after Independence', *South East Asian Economic Review*, Vol. 4, No. 2 (August): 71-104; reprinted in Sritua Arief and Jomo K. S. (eds.) (1983), *The Malaysian Economy and Finance* (East Balmain, New South Wales: Research Organization of South East Asian Economies).

_____ (1984), 'Malaysia's New Economic Policy: A Class Perspective', *Pacific Viewpoint*, 25, 2: 153-72.

Joseph, K. T. (1964), 'Problems of Agriculture', in Wang Gungwu (ed.), *Malaysia: A Survey* (New York: Praeger).

Junid Abu Saham (1975), 'The Role of British Industrial Investments in the Development of the Malaysian Economy', Ph.D. thesis, University of Hull; published in 1980 as *British Industrial Investment in Malaysia 1963-1971* (Kuala Lumpur: Oxford University Press).

Kahin, G. M. (1964), 'Malaysia and Indonesia', *Pacific Affairs*, 37, 3 (Fall): 253-70.

Kalecki, Michal (1967), 'Observations on Social and Economic Aspects of Intermediate Regimes', *Coexistence*, 4.

Kanapathy, V. (1970), *The Malaysian Economy, Problems and Prospects* (Singapore: Asia Pacific Press).

Kasper, Wolfgang (1974), *Malaysia: A Study in Successful Economic Development* (Washington, DC: American Enterprise Institute).

Kay, Geoffrey (1975), *Development and Underdevelopment* (London: Macmillan).

Kemp, Tom (1967), *Theories of Imperialism* (London: Dobson).

Kessler, Clive (1974), 'Islam and Politics in Malay Society: Kelantan 1886-1969', Ph.D. thesis, University of London; published in 1977 (Ithaca: Cornell University Press).

Khatijah Ahmad (1967), 'A Comment on Government Policies on Padi and Rice Marketing', *Review of Agricultural Economics Malaysia*, 1, 2: 32-47.

Khoo Kay Jin (1978), 'The Marketing of Smallholders' Rubber', in Kamal Salih *et al.*, *Rural-Urban Transformation and Regional Underdevelopment: The Case of Malaysia* (Nagoya: United Nations Center for Regional Development).

Khoo Kay Kim (1966), 'The Origins of British Administration in Malaya', *Journal of the Malayan Branch, Royal Asiatic Society*, 39, 1.

_____ (1972), *The Western Malay States 1850-1873. The Effects of Commercial Development on Malay Politics* (Kuala Lumpur: Oxford University Press).

Khoo, Philip (1977), 'Industrialization—Issues and Policies' (Fourth Malaysian Economic Convention, Kuala Lumpur, May).

Khor Kok Peng, Martin (1979), 'Dependence and the Malaysian Economy', M. Soc. Sc. thesis, Universiti Sains Malaysia.

_____ (1983a), *Recession and the Malaysian Economy* (Penang: Institut Masyarakat).

_____ (1983b), *The Malaysian Economy: Structures and Dependence* (Kuala Lumpur: Marican).

Kinney, William P. (1975), 'Aspects of Malayan Economic Development, 1900-1940',

Ph.D. thesis, London School of Oriental and African Studies.

Knorr, K. (1945), *World Rubber and its Regulation* (Palo Alto: Stanford University Press).

Knowles, M. I. (1936), 'The Expansion of British Influence in the Malay Peninsula, 1867-1885: A Study in Nineteenth Century Imperialism', Ph.D. thesis, University of Wisconsin.

Kondapi, C. (1951), *Indians Overseas: 1838-1949* (New Delhi: Indian Council of World Affairs).

Kratoska, Paul H. (1975a), *The Chettiar and the Yeoman: British Cultural Categories and Rural Indebtedness in Malaya* (Singapore: Institute of Southeast Asian Studies, Occasional Paper No. 32).

—————— (1975b), 'Peasants, Yeomen and Rice Farmers. Cultural Categories in British Malaya', Ph.D. thesis, University of Chicago.

Kuchiba, M. and Tsubouchi, Y. (1967), 'Paddy Farming and Social Structure in a Malay Village', *The Developing Economies*, 5, 3: 463-85.

—————— (1968), 'Cooperation Patterns in a Malay Village', *Asian Survey*, 8.

Kuchiba, M., Tsubouchi, Y. and Maeda, N. (1965), 'A Padi Farming Village in the Northwestern Part of Malaya, Interim Report: The Fragmentation of Land-holding', *Southeast Asian Studies*, 3, 1 (June): 22-51.

—————— (1979), *Three Malay Villages: A Sociology of Paddy Growers in West Malaysia* (Kyoto: Kyoto University, Center for Southeast Asian Studies).

Labour Research Department (1926), *British Imperialism in Malaya* (London: Labour Research Department).

Laclau, Ernesto (1971), 'Feudalism and Capitalism in Latin America', *New Left Review*, 67.

Ladejinsky, Wolf (1977), 'Agricultural Policies of British Malaya', in Louis J. Walinsky (ed.), *Agrarian Reform as Unfinished Business* (Oxford University Press).

Lai Kok Chew (1978), 'Income Distribution among Farm Households in the Muda Irrigation Scheme: A Developmental Perspective', *Kajian Ekonomi Malaysia*, 15, 1 (June).

Lai Kok Chew and Ani Arope (1971), 'Towards Optimal Size of Rice Farms', *MARDI Agricultural Economic Bulletin*, 1, 2 (April).

Lall, Sanjaya (1975), 'Is "Dependence" a Useful Concept in Analyzing Underdevelopment?', *World Development*, 3, 11/12: 799-810.

Lasker, Bruno (1950), *Human Bondage in Southeast Asia* (Chapel Hill: University of North Carolina Press).

Leaver, R. (1977), 'The Debate on Underdevelopment: On Situating Gunder Frank', *Journal of Contemporary Asia*, 7, 1.

Lee, Eddy (1975), 'Income Distribution in a Developing Economy: A Case Study of West Malaysia', D.Phil. thesis, Oxford University.

—————— (1976), *Rural Poverty in West Malaysia, 1957-70* (Geneva: International Labour Office, World Employment Programme Working Paper).

—————— (1977), 'Development and Income Distribution: A Case Study of Sri Lanka and Malaysia', *World Development*, 5, 4 (April): 279-90.

Lee, George (1973), 'Commodity Production and Reproduction amongst the Malayan Peasantry', *Journal of Contemporary Asia*, 3, 4: 441-56.

Lee Kok Huat (1967), 'The 1960 Agricultural Census', *Kajian Ekonomi Malaysia*, 4, 2: 1-21.

Lee Poh Ping (1974), 'Chinese Society in Nineteenth and Early Twentieth Century Singapore: A Socio-economic Analysis', Ph.D. thesis, Cornell University; published in 1978 as *Chinese Society in Nineteenth Century Singapore* (Kuala Lumpur: Oxford University Press).

Lee Sheng Yi (1966), 'The Development of Commercial Banking in Singapore and the

States of Malaya', *Malayan Economic Review*, 11, 1 (April).

―――― (1974), *Monetary and Banking Development in Malaysia and Singapore* (Singapore: University of Singapore Press).

Levine, David (1975), 'The Theory of the Growth of the Capitalist Economy', *Economic Development and Cultural Change*, 24, 1 (October).

Lewis, W. Arthur (1954), 'Economic Development with Unlimited Supplies of Labour', *Manchester School*, 22, 2 (May).

Leys, Colin (1975), *Underdevelopment in Kenya. The Political Economy of Neo-colonialism* (London: Macmillan).

―――― (1976), 'The "Overdeveloped" Post-colonial State: A Re-evaluation', *Review of African Political Economy*, 5.

―――― (1977), 'Underdevelopment and Dependency: Critical Notes', *Journal of Contemporary Asia*, 7, 1.

Li Dun Jen (1982), *British Malaya: An Economic Analysis*, 2nd edition (Petaling Jaya: Institute for Social Analysis); 1st edition published in 1955 (New York: American Press).

Lim Chong-Yah (1967), *Economic Development of Modern Malaya* (Kuala Lumpur: Oxford University Press).

Lim, David (1973), *Economic Growth and Development in West Malaysia 1947-1970* (Kuala Lumpur: Oxford University Press).

―――― (1975), 'Industrialization and Unemployment in West Malaysia', in David Lim (ed.), *Readings on Malaysian Economic Development* (Kuala Lumpur: Oxford University Press).

Lim Lin Lean (1971), *Some Aspects of Income Differentials in West Malaysia* (Kuala Lumpur: University of Malaya, Faculty of Economics and Administration, Monograph Series on Malaysian Economic Affairs).

―――― (1974), 'Pattern of Income Distribution in West Malaysia, 1957-1970' (Geneva: ILO, Income Distribution and Employment Program).

Lim Mah Hui (1978), 'Ownership and Control in a Dependent Economy: The Case of Malaysia's 100 Largest Corporations', Ph.D. thesis, University of Pittsburgh; published in 1980 as *Ownership and Control of the One Hundred Largest Corporations in Malaysia* (Kuala Lumpur: Oxford University Press).

Lim Sow Ching (1968), 'A Study of the Marketing of Smallholders' Rubber at the First Trade Level in Selangor' (Kuala Lumpur: Rubber Research Institute).

Lim Teck Ghee (1971), 'Peasant Agriculture in Colonial Malaya: Its Development in Perak, Selangor, Negri Sembilan and Pahang, 1874-1941', Ph.D. thesis, Australian National University; published in 1977 as *Peasants and Their Agricultural Economy in Colonial Malaya, 1874-1941* (Kuala Lumpur: Oxford University Press).

―――― (1974), 'Malayan Peasant Smallholdings and the Stevenson Restriction Scheme, 1922-28', *Journal of the Malayan Branch, Royal Asiatic Society*, 47, ii: 105-22.

―――― (1976), *Origins of a Colonial Economy: Land and Agriculture in Perak 1874-1897* (Penang: Penerbit Universiti Sains Malaysia).

Lim Teck Ghee et al. (1974), *Land Tenure Survey, Farm Locality DII Muda Irrigation Scheme* (Penang: Universiti Sains Malaysia, Centre for Policy Research).

Lim Teck Ghee, Gibbons, David, and Shukor Kassim (1980), 'Accumulation of Padi Land in the Muda Region: Some Findings and Thoughts on their Implications for the Peasantry and Development', Conference on 'The Peasantry and Development in the ASEAN Region', 26-29 May.

Lindenberg, Marc (1973), 'Foreign and Domestic Investment in the Pioneer Industry Program, Malaysia 1965-70. Political, Economic and Social Impacts', Ph.D. thesis, University of Southern California.

―――― (1975), 'Multinational Corporations and Reinvestment Rates: The Case of the

Socio-cultural Considerations', *Asia Research Bulletin*, 2, 2.

Nanjundan, S. (1950), *Indians in the Malayan Economy* (New Delhi).

Narifumi, M. (1974), 'The Changing Peasant World in a Melaka Village', Ph.D. thesis, University of Chicago.

Narkswasdi, Udhis (1968), *A Report to the Government of Malaysia on the Rice Economy of West Malaysia* (Rome: Food and Agricultural Organization).

Narkswasdi, U. and Selvadurai, S. (1967a), *Economic Survey of Padi Production in West Malaysia, Report No. 1—Selangor* (Kuala Lumpur: Ministry of Agriculture and Cooperatives).

———— (1967b), *Economic Survey of Padi Production in West Malaysia, Report No. 3—Malacca* (Kuala Lumpur: Ministry of Agriculture and Cooperatives).

National Operations Council (1969), *The May 13 Tragedy: A Report* (Kuala Lumpur: Government Printers).

Ness, Gayl D. (1965), 'Modernization and Indigenous Control of the Bureaucracy in Malaysia', *Asian Survey*, 5, 9 (September): 465–73.

———— (1967), *Bureaucracy and Rural Development in Malaysia* (Berkeley and Los Angeles: University of California Press).

Neuman, S. G. (1971), 'The Malay Political Elite: An Analysis of 134 Malay Legislators, Their Social Background and Attitudes', Ph.D. thesis, New York University.

Newbold, T. J. (1971), *Political and Statistical Account of the British Settlements in the Straits of Malacca, with a History of the Malayan States* (2 volumes) (Kuala Lumpur: Oxford University Press); first published in 1839.

Ngun, B. A. and Siegel, L. (1976), 'The U.S. in Malaysia', *Pacific Research*, 7, 4 (May–June): 8–12.

Nordin Selat (1976), *Kelas Menengah Pentadbir* (Kuala Lumpur: Penerbit Utusan Melayu).

Nove, Alec G. (1974), 'On Reading A. G. Frank', *Journal of Development Studies*, 10, 3 & 4 (April/July).

Nyce, R. (1962), 'The "New Villages" of Malaya: A Community Study', Ph.D. thesis, Hartford Seminary Foundation.

O'Brien, Donal Cruise (1972), 'Modernization, Order and the Erosion of a Democratic Ideal: American Political Science 1960–70', *Journal of Development Studies*, 8, 4 (July): 351–78.

Ocampo, J. F. and Johnson, D. L. (1972), 'The Concept of Political Development', in James D. Cockcroft *et al.* (eds.), *Dependence and Underdevelopment* (New York: Anchor Books).

O'Connor, James (1975), 'Productive and Unproductive Labor', *Politics and Society*, 5, 3: 297–336.

Ooi Jin Bee (1959), 'Rural Development in Tropical Areas with Special Reference to Malaya', *Malayan Journal of Tropical Geography*, 12.

Ouchi, T., Saeki, N., Takahashi, A., and Tanaka, M. (1977), *Farmer and Village in West Malaysia* (Tokyo: University of Tokyo, Faculty of Economics).

Owen, Roger and Sutcliffe, Bob (eds.) (1972), *Studies in the Theory of Imperialism* (London: Longman).

Paige, J. M. (1975), *Agrarian Revolution: Social Movements and Export Agriculture in the Underdeveloped World* (New York: Free Press).

Palmer, Ingrid (1976), *The New Rice in Asia. Conclusions from Four Country Studies* (Geneva: U.N. Research Institute for Social Development, Report No. 76.6).

Parkinson, Brian K. (1975), 'Non Economic Factors in the Economic Retardation of the Rural Malays', in David Lim (ed.), *Readings on Malaysian Economic Development* (Kuala Lumpur: Oxford University Press).

Parkinson, C. Northcote (1960), *British Intervention in Malaya, 1867–1877* (Singapore: University of Malaya Press).

Parmer, J. Norman (1960), *Colonial Labor Policy and Administration. A History of Labor in the Rubber Plantation Industry in Malaya, c.1910–1940* (Locust Valley: Association for Asian Studies).

—— (1962), 'Attempts at Labour Organization by Chinese Workers in Certain Industries in Singapore in the 1930s', in K. G. Tregonning (ed.), *Papers on Malayan History* (Singapore: Journal of Southeast Asian History).

—— (1964), 'Chinese Estate Workers' Strikes in Malaya in March 1937', in C. D. Cowan (ed.), *The Economic Development of Southeast Asia* (London: George Allen & Unwin).

—— (1966), 'Malaysia 1965: Challenging the Terms of 1957', *Asian Survey*, 6, 2 (February): 111–18.

Patterson, Orlando (1977), 'Slavery', *Annual Review of Sociology*, 3: 407–49.

Pluvier, Jan M. (1965), *Confrontations: A Study in Indonesian Politics* (Kuala Lumpur: Oxford University Press).

Pompemayer, M. (1973), 'The State in Dependent Societies', in Frank Bonilla and Robert Girling (eds.), *Structures of Dependency* (Palo Alto: Stanford University, Institute of Political Studies).

Popenoe, Oliver (1970), 'Malay Entrepreneurs: An Analysis of the Social Backgrounds, Careers and Attitudes of the Leading Malay Businessmen in West Malaysia', Ph.D. thesis, London School of Economics.

Poulantzas, Nicos (1973a), 'On Social Classes', *New Left Review*, 78 (March/April).

—— (1973b), *Political Power and Social Classes* (London: New Left Books).

—— (1975), *Classes in Contemporary Capitalism* (London: New Left Books).

Power, J. H. (1971), 'The Structure of Protection in West Malaysia', in B. Balassa *et al.*, *The Structure of Protection in Developing Countries* (Baltimore, Maryland: Johns Hopkins University Press).

Prasad, P. H. (1974), 'Reactionary Role of Usurers' Capital in Rural India', *Economic and Political Weekly*, IX, 1305–8 (August), Special Number.

Purcal, John (1971), *Rice Economy* (Kuala Lumpur: University of Malaya Press).

Purcell, Victor (1948), *The Chinese in Malaya* (London: Oxford University Press).

—— (1951), *The Chinese in South-East Asia* (London: Oxford University Press).

Puthucheary, J. J. (1960), *Ownership and Control in the Malayan Economy* (Singapore: Eastern Universities Press).

Puthucheary, M. C. (1977), 'Public Enterprise and the Creation of a Bumiputra Entrepreneurial Community' (Paper for the Fourth Malaysian Economic Convention, Kuala Lumpur, May).

Pye, Lucian W. (1965), *Guerilla Communism in Malaya* (Princeton: Princeton University Press).

Quijano, Anibal (1971), *Nationalism and Capitalism in Peru* (New York: Monthly Review Press).

A. Rahim Said (1974), 'Developing Indigenous Entrepreneurship in West Malaysia', MA thesis, Cornell University.

Raja Mohar b. Raja Badiozaman (1963?), 'Malay Land Reservation and Alienation', *Intisari*, 1, 2: 20–2.

—— (1976), 'Foreign Investment—The Malaysian Experience' (Annual Lecture of the Malaysian Economic Association).

Rao, S. K. (1972), 'Planning in Malaysia', *Ekonomi*, 12, 2.

Ratnam, K. J. and Milne, R. S. (1970), 'The Parliamentary Election in West Malaysia', *Pacific Affairs*, 43, 2.

Raza, M. Ali (1969), 'Legislative and Public Policy Developments in Malaya's Industrial Relations', *Journal of Developing Areas*, 3 (April): 355–72.

Razak Yahya (1974), 'Reform from Above with Reference to Rural Development in

Malayan Economy (Singapore: Longmans).

_____ (1961), 'A Note on the Working of Rubber Regulation', in T. H. Silcock (ed.), *Readings in Malayan Economics* (Singapore: Eastern Universities Press).

Sim, V. (n.d.), *Biographies of Prominent Chinese in Singapore* (Singapore: Nan Kok Publications).

Simoniya, N. A. (1961), *Overseas Chinese in Southeast Asia—A Russian Study* (Ithaca: Cornell University, Southeast Asian Studies Program Department).

Sinclair, Keith (1967), 'Hobson and Lenin in Johore: Colonial Office Policy towards British Concessionaires and Investors, 1878–1907', *Modern Asian Studies*, 1, 4: 335–52.

Skinner, G. W. (1957), *Chinese Society in Thailand. An Analytical History* (Ithaca: Cornell University Press).

Skocpol, Theda (1973), 'A Critical Review of Barrington Moore's "Social Origins of Dictatorship and Democracy"', *Politics and Society* (Fall).

_____ (1977), 'Wallerstein's World Capitalist System: A Theoretical and Historical Critique', *American Journal of Sociology*, 82, 5 (March): 1075–90.

Slimming, John (1969), *Malaysia: Death of Democracy* (London: J. Murray).

Smith, E. and Goethals, P. (1965), *Tenancy among Padi Cultivators in Malaysia: A Study of Tenancy Conditions and Laws affecting Landlord-Tenant Relations* (Kuala Lumpur: Ford Foundation; mimeo.).

Smith, T. E. (1964), 'Immigration and Permanent Settlement of Chinese and Indians and the Future Growth of the Malay and Chinese Communities', in C. D. Cowan (ed.), *The Economic Development of Southeast Asia* (London: Allen & Unwin).

Snider, Nancy (1970), 'Race: Leitmotiv of the Malaysian Election Drama', *Asian Survey*, 10, 12 (December): 1070–80.

Soernarno, Radin (1960), 'Malay Nationalism 1900–1945', *Journal of Southeast Asian History*, 1, 1 (March): 9–15.

Song Ong Siang (1902), *One Hundred Years' History of the Chinese in Singapore* (London: J. Murray); reprinted in 1967 (Kuala Lumpur: University of Malaya Press) and 1984 (Singapore: Oxford University Press).

Snodgrass, Donald R. (1975), 'Trends and Patterns in Malaysian Income Distribution, 1957–70', in David Lim (ed.), *Readings on Malaysian Economic Development* (Kuala Lumpur: Oxford University Press).

Stahl, K. M. (1951), *The Metropolitan Organization of British Colonial Trade* (London: Faber & Faber).

Stavenhagen, Rodolfo (1975), *Social Classes in Agrarian Societies* (Garden City: Anchor Books).

Stenson, Michael (1970), *Industrial Conflict in Malaya* (Kuala Lumpur: Oxford University Press).

_____ (1980), *Class, Race and Colonialism in West Malaysia: The Indian Case* (St. Lucia: University of Queensland Press).

Stubbs, R. S. (1974), *Counter-insurgency and the Economic Factor. The Impact of the Korean War Prices Boom on the Malayan Emergency* (Singapore: Institute of Southeast Asian Studies, Occasional Paper No. 19).

Sumitro Djojohadikusumo (1968), *Trade and Aid in Southeast Asia. Volume I: Malaysia and Singapore* (Melbourne: Cheshire Publishing).

Sutcliffe, R. B. (1971), *Industry and Underdevelopment* (London: Addison-Wesley).

_____ (1972), 'Industrialization in the Third World', in R. Owen and B. Sutcliffe (eds.), *Studies in the Theory of Imperialism* (London: Longman).

Suyama, T. (1962), 'Pang Society: The Economy of Chinese Immigrants', in K. G. Tregonning (ed.), *Papers on Malayan History* (Singapore: Journal of Southeast Asian History).

Swettenham, Frank (1948), *British Malaya. An Account of the Origin and Progress of British*

Influence in Malaya (London: Allen & Unwin).

Swift, Michael G. (1957), 'The Accumulation of Capital in a Peasant Economy', reprinted in T. H. Silcock (ed.), *Readings in Malayan Economics* (Singapore: Eastern Universities Press).

_____ (1963), 'Malay Peasants', in R. D. Lambert and B. F. Hoselitz (eds.), *The Role of Savings and Wealth in Southern Asia and the West* (Paris: UNESCO): 219-44.

_____ (1964), 'Capital, Saving and Credit in a Malay Peasant Economy', in R. Firth and B. S. Yamey (eds.), *Capital Saving and Credit in Peasant Societies* (London: Allen & Unwin): 133-56.

_____ (1965), *Malay Peasant Society in Jelebu* (London: Athlone Press).

_____ (1967), 'Economic Concentration and Malay Peasant Society', in M. Freedman (ed.), *Social Organization*: 241-69 (London: Frank Cass).

Szentes, Tamas (1971), *The Political Economy of Underdevelopment* (Budapest: Akademi Kiados).

Tan, Augustine H. H. (1967), 'The Incidence of Export Taxes on Small Producers', *Malayan Economic Review*, 12, 2.

Tan Soo Hai, D. E. (1963), *The Rice Industry in Malaya, 1920-1940* (Singapore: Malaya Publishing House).

Tan Tat Wai (1977), 'Income Distribution and Determination in West Malaysia', Ph.D. thesis, Harvard University; published in 1982 (Kuala Lumpur: Oxford University Press).

Tan Tew Nee (1973), 'Import Substitution and Structural Change in the West Malaysian Manufacturing Sector', M. Ec. thesis, Universiti Malaya.

Tay Gaik Yeong (1969), 'British Economic Policy towards the Malays in the Federated Malay States, 1921-1934', MA thesis, Universiti Malaya.

Taylor, John (1975), 'Review of Pre-capitalist Modes of Production, Part 1', *Critique of Anthropology*, 4, 5.

_____ (1976), 'Review of Pre-capitalist Modes of Production, Part 2', *Critique of Anthropology*, 2, 6.

Tham Seong Chee (1973), 'Ideology, Politics and Economic Modernization: The Case of the Malays in Malaysia', *Southeast Asian Journal of Social Science*, 1, 1.

Therborn, Goran (1976), *Science, Class and Society* (London: New Left Books).

Thio, Eunice (1957), 'The Turning Point in Britain's Malayan Policy', *The Historical Journal* (Singapore: University of Malaya), 3.

Thoburn, John T. (1970), 'Ownership of Shares in U.K.-incorporated Public Rubber Planting and Tin Dredging Companies in Malaysia', *Kajian Ekonomi Malaysia*, 7, 2.

_____ (1971), 'Exports in the Economic Development of West Malaysia', Ph.D. thesis, University of Alberta; published in 1977 as *Primary Commodity Exports and Economic Development: Theory, Evidence and a Study of Malaysia* (London: John Wiley & Sons).

_____ (1975a), 'Exports and Economic Growth in West Malaysia', in David Lim (ed.), *Readings on Malaysian Economic Development* (Kuala Lumpur: Oxford University Press).

_____ (1975b), 'Exports and the Malaysian Engineering Industry: A Case Study of Backward Linkage', in David Lim (ed.), *Readings on Malaysian Economic Development* (Kuala Lumpur: Oxford University Press).

Thompson, Virginia (1943), *Post-Mortem on Malaya* (New York: Macmillan).

_____ (1947), *Labour Problems in South-east Asia* (New Haven: Yale University Press).

Tilman, Robert O. (1961), 'The Public Services of the Federation of Malaya', Ph.D. thesis, Duke University.

_____ (1964), *Bureaucratic Transition in Malaya* (Durham: Duke University Press).

_____ (1969), 'Education and Political Development in Malaysia', in R. O. Tilman,

Wolff, Richard O. (1974), *The Economics of Colonialism. Britain and Kenya, 1870–1930* (New Haven: Yale University Press).

Wolters, O. W. (1970), *The Fall of Srivijaya in Malay History* (Kuala Lumpur: Oxford University Press).

Wong, C. S. (1963), *A Gallery of Chinese Kapitans* (Singapore: Dewan Bahasa dan Kebudayaan Kebangsaan, Ministry of Culture).

Wong, David (1975), *Tenure and Land Dealings in the Malay States* (Singapore: Singapore University Press).

Wong Lin Ken (1960), 'The Trade of Singapore, 1819–69', *Journal of the Malayan Branch, Royal Asiatic Society*, 33, iv (December).

–––––– (1964), 'Western Enterprise and the Development of the Malayan Tin Industry to 1914', in C. D. Cowan (ed.), *The Economic Development of Southeast Asia* (London: Allen & Unwin).

–––––– (1965), *The Malayan Tin Industry to 1914* (Tucson: University of Arizona Press for the Association of Asian Studies).

Wong Lin Ken and Wang, C. S. (1960), 'Secret Societies in Malaya', *Journal of Southeast Asian History*, 1, 1 (March).

Wright, Eric Olin (1976), 'Class Boundaries in Advanced Capitalist Societies', *New Left Review*, 98 (July/August).

Yeo Kim Wah (1971), 'British Policy toward the Malays in the Federated Malay States, 1920–1940', Ph.D. thesis, Australian National University; published in 1982 as *The Politics of Decentralization: Colonial Controversy in Malaya 1920–1929* (Kuala Lumpur: Oxford University Press).

–––––– (1976), 'The Communist Challenge in the Malayan Labour Scene, September 1936–March 1937', *Journal of the Malayan Branch, Royal Asiatic Society*, 49, ii: 36–79.

Yip Yat Hoong (1968), 'Recent Changes in the Ownership and Control of Locally Incorporated Tin Dredging Companies in Malaya', *Malayan Economic Review*, 13, 1 (April): 70–88.

–––––– (1969), *The Development of the Tin Mining Industry of Malaya* (Kuala Lumpur: University of Malaya Press).

Yong Chin Fatt (1967), 'Chinese Leadership in Nineteenth Century Singapore', *Journal of the Island Society*, 8: 1–18.

–––––– (1968), 'A Preliminary Study of Chinese Leadership in Singapore 1900–1941', *Journal of Southeast Asian History*, 9, 2 (September).

Yusof, B. N. (1967), 'Malay Nationalism, 1945–1957', MA thesis, University of Otago.

Zahara Mahmud (1969), 'The Pioneering of Wet Rice Growing Traditions in West Malaysia—a Restudy with Special Reference to the State of Kedah', *Geographica*, 5.

–––––– (1970), 'The Period and Nature of "Traditional" Settlement in the Malay Peninsula', *Journal of the Malayan Branch, Royal Asiatic Society*, 43, ii.

Zainal Abidin b. Abdul Wahid (ed.) (1970), *Glimpses of Malaysian History* (Kuala Lumpur: Dewan Bahasa dan Pustaka).

Zubaida, Sami (1976), 'Islam and Capitalism', *Sociological Review*, 24, 1.

INDEX

Numbers in italics refer to Tables and Figures.